Rising above Sweatshops

Rising above Sweatshops

Innovative Approaches to Global Labor Challenges

EDITED BY LAURA P. HARTMAN,
DENIS G. ARNOLD, AND
RICHARD E. WOKUTCH

Forewords by Ken Block, Frank Vogl, and
Norman E. Bowie

Research funded through a grant from the
Ethics Resource Center Fellows Program

Westport, Connecticut
London

Library of Congress Cataloging-in-Publication Data

Rising above Sweatshops : innovative approaches to global labor challenges
/ edited by Laura P. Hartman, Denis G. Arnold, and Richard E. Wokutch ; forewords by
Ken Block, Frank Vogl, and Norman E. Bowie.
    p. cm.
    Includes bibliographical references and index.
    ISBN 1–56720–618–2 (alk. paper)
    1. International business enterprises—Personnel management. 2. International business
enterprises—Developing countries—Moral and ethical aspects. 3. Employee rights—
Developing countries. 4. Social responsibility of business—Developing countries. 5.
Sweatshops—Developing countries. 6. Globalization. I. Hartman, Laura Pincus. II. Arnold,
Denis Gordon. III. Wokutch, Richard E.
HF5549.5.E45R57   2003
658.3'009172'4—dc21   2003052901

British Library Cataloguing in Publication Data is available.

Library of Congress Catalog Card Number: 2003052901
ISBN: 1–56720–618–2

First published in 2003

Praeger Publishers, 88 Post Road West, Westport, CT 06881
An imprint of Greenwood Publishing Group, Inc.
www.praeger.com

Printed in the United States of America

The paper used in this book complies with the
Permanent Paper Standard issued by the National
Information Standards Organization (Z39.48–1984).

10 9 8 7 6 5 4 3 2 1

To the workers whose daily labors ground the supply chain; to the morally innovative managers who are helping to create workplaces in which workers are both productive and treated with dignity; to the nongovernmental organizations who strive to ensure a just workplace for all; and to the government officials who strive to protect all of these efforts.

Contents

Illustrations

FIGURES

PHOTOGRAPHS

Acknowledgments

The editors and authors wish to express sincere gratitude to all of the individuals who shared with us their experiences and ideas in connection with the research that supports this book, including the workers, managers, representatives of nongovernmental organizations, and other individuals who were willing to be interviewed in furtherance of this work. In addition, earlier versions of many chapters were reviewed by colleagues at the Society for Business Ethics as well as the Ethics Resource Center Fellows Program. This book would have sorely suffered without their valuable input. We wish to thank Gary Weaver for drafting an overview of an earlier rendition of the research, as well as each of the authors for their insights, patience, and commitment to this important venture. Finally, the researchers are grateful to the Ethics Resource Center's Fellows Program for recognizing the value that this work holds for those who are involved in these efforts on a daily basis and for supporting the underlying research through its grant process.

Foreword

When the editors first asked me what I thought about the findings described in this book, all I could think of was the old adage "It's like arguing against clean water!" Coming up with reasons why a major corporation conducting its business internationally wouldn't want to do "good" things for all its workers and for the communities in which they work is like arguing against clean water. "Who wouldn't want clean water?" I queried. "In fact," I remember saying, "what business leader, knowing the water *isn't* clean (and who doesn't have the resources to make it so), would buy it—at any price?" In other words, doing good is a pretty obvious objective and why would a business leader be involved in something that wasn't?

Since then, I've been thinking.

Globalization has shattered the traditional corporate governance paradigm that American companies used during the post–World War II period to organize themselves for growth and prosperity. Gone are the days when companies could point solely to their share price and P/E ratio as the primary measure or bases for success. The bar that defines corporate reputation has been fundamentally raised. Corporate integrity is no longer about simply obeying the law or meeting legal minimums. A company's obligations now extend beyond mere compliance with regulation or not running afoul of enforcement agencies. Measuring "reputational capital" in the United States and abroad has become an extraordinarily complex exercise involving numerous transnational and other interests over which global companies have little or no direct control.

The global corporate governance movement is beginning to coalesce around a new paradigm that describes how companies must organize for long-term growth, viability, and sustained competitive advantage. The centerpiece of this paradigm is a seamless commitment to an enterprise-wide core purpose or vision that serves as the basis for strategic visioning and planning and a set of core business values and ethical principles that determine business practices, policies, and processes. In other words, a global firm's reputation for integrity is, in part, determined by the degree to which the firm honors its core purpose and does not permit exigencies, crises of the moment, or marketplace differences to supplant long-standing core business values and ethical principles in driving company decision making. Fundamentally, this is a leadership responsibility and imperative at all levels of a global firm.

As an ethics officer in a major American corporation, I often hear from my colleagues at other companies that they find it difficult to "gain a place at the table" when strategic business discussions are taking place and action plans are being formulated. They complain that short-term financial considerations often seem to trump other issues when day-to-day management decisions are being made. And why, they ask, does management tend to overlook the serious business of building reputational capital when long-term strategic plans are being made and to favor more tangible financial capital?

In 1992 a dozen or so ethics officers (largely from the U.S. defense industry) came together and founded the Ethics Officer Association (EOA). Today, the EOA has nearly 800 members including ethics officers from more than half of the *Fortune* 100. Unfortunately, despite this rapid growth, strategic integrity planning remains all-too-often absent from executive decision making. Even as the focus on globalization and corporate social responsibility has increased the amount of attention being paid to international standards of corporate conduct, the bottom line often dominates the planning process. The deliberate, diligent, and thorough assessment of ethical considerations pertinent to a business initiative is often overlooked or short-shrifted when the final reviews are conducted regarding a major new activity. It is only after trouble brews that management recognizes its failure to have foreseen the outcome.

It is not that management acts devoid of personal or organizational integrity, but rather that ethical neutrality is displayed through inattention and lack of focus. It is most often not an intentional act to cut corners, ignore best practices, or implement poor policy that results in scandal, humiliation, and shareholder scorn, but rather the simple inertia of trading operational efficacy for executing difficult decisions based on sound personal values and attention to the core values of the organization. Leaders bring their personal integrity to their work, but it is often easier to take ethical values for granted than it is to be diligent about deploying them.

We all know that doing business in developing countries can reduce costs since there is freedom to act without the restraints of laws and regulations usually present in more developed countries. This is especially true with respect to the environment, safety, health, compensation, child labor, and other concerns for working people. We have all observed that companies that engage in actions on foreign soil that are regarded as ethically unacceptable at home frequently suffer a negative impact on their corporate reputations. If we believe that laws and regulations serve as the floor on which to base our fundamental decision making in the global marketplace, then the shifting sands of culturally diverse rules and practices provide a weak basis for the exercise of corporate ethics. Good and fair business activity must instead be rooted in a core philosophy based on consistent adherence to principles of integrity, respect, quality, excellence, trust, and citizenship.

The marketplace has changed fundamentally in the past 50 years. Wise business leaders understand that, to be successful in the twenty-first century, they must fundamentally change the mental algorithms on which they predicate the conduct of their business. Reputational capital is from inception built on the core ideology, vision and goals of the enterprise, and on principles that do not change as a function of locale, but rather guide the people who make up the corporate entity through the tough choices poised in the gap between short-term interests and long-term objectives. This book challenges those of us in corporate management positions to truly and purposefully think about making investments in the intangible realm of reputation building, even when the cost calculus can be exercised only through faith that reputational capital is imputed to the asset side of the balance sheet.

The authors of the cases in this book present us with new research that does not seek to defend all of the actions of the companies they studied, but instead provides insight into several model activities that might be replicable in the domain of "doing the right thing"—even when the cost of doing so may be high in the short run. This research explores initiatives in developing countries in which the decision makers set out to establish programs intentionally based on respect for human dignity, safety, and cultural sensitivity. We now know that it is possible for companies to operate or contract with factories in developing countries that are accountable to their communities and workers—and still be profitable.

This book does not address the question of how profitable an enterprise must be to maintain consistency in guiding its strategic decisions through an overarching core philosophy. Rather it presents success in the face of the intangible—the commitment to build reputational capital at the expense of short-term profit objectives. Although the researchers have focused on activities that are measurable and objective in terms of financial statements, this study leaves unanswered the question of "how much is enough of a good thing." Faith that reputational capital can be used to offset occasional failure, inadvertent breaches of public trust, rogue conduct, and cultural misjudgments translates to a willingness to forgo immediate and short-term gain for longer-time, strategic success interests. As an added benefit, this research suggests that the resultant boosts in morale, productivity, community relations, lower attrition, stability, worker commitment, and reduced risk will truly enhance the balance sheet over the long haul.

Although the traditional business model is predicated, in part, on the production of high-quality products in a reliable manner and at a very low price, corporations are now driven to think (and feel) more broadly about how these objectives are met. Stakeholders—the customers, shareholders, employees, suppliers, and the communities in which they live—now demand more corporate attention regarding transparency, fairness, and respect for human rights and dignity. Havoc is wreaked on those business entities that transgress the confidence of their stakeholders. The impact of negative press that accompanies a trade of ethically suspect short-term gain for long-term interests is most often not overcome.

The programs presented here demonstrate that at least some executives are changing their approach to the global marketplace. Borne perhaps of necessity, fed by competition, and nurtured by successful new ventures, arguing against clean water seems less likely in the new millennium. I am not sufficiently naïve to think that we will see an end to those who ignore the necessity of keeping the water clean, but fewer will persist in the argument out loud. It's in poor taste, and nobody wants to hear it.

Ken Block
Director, Business Ethics and Compliance
Raytheon Company

Foreword

This important book will contribute to the opening of a new chapter in the controversial debate about globalization. It does not vindicate the included firms of charges of exploitative labor practices in poor countries; instead, it shows that even these companies are striving to put in place operational systems that are humane and socially responsible and that yield benefits to people in developing countries, while strengthening the corporate bottom line.

The globalization debate has become bitter, and the forces on both sides have become entrenched. Spokesmen for major corporations and business organizations issue statements replete with reams of statistics, showing that globalization is key to economic growth in dozens of countries. They highlight studies by the World Bank and others to show that globalization is reducing global poverty. Yet, they rarely listen to those who criticize globalization or engage in dialogue with them.

Meanwhile, the antiglobalization protesters demonstrate great skill in securing the media's attention and promoting a negative image of the actions of multinational enterprises. As a result, for example, consumers today in Western Europe and North America have a popular picture of tens of thousands of Asians making shoes and clothing in sweatshops, which according to the watchdog group *Sweatshop Watch* are workplaces where workers are subjected to "extreme exploitation, including the absence of a living wage or benefits, poor working conditions, such as health and safety hazards, and arbitrary discipline."[1]

The globalization debate urgently needs to move to a more pragmatic and productive level. This demands, however, that solid evidence come to the fore that demonstrates that business is finding effective approaches to even the most complex globalization problems. The solutions cannot be just one-of-kind; they need to be replicable. The approaches of corporations need to be framed within broad management strategies that are embraced by chief executive officers and that drive the policies of globalizing enterprises. This book provides rich material in these areas.

Professor Laura P. Hartman and her coauthors have combined insights into the practice and the theory of model labor relations in factories controlled by Nike, adidas, and others in a variety of countries, including Vietnam, Thailand, and Brazil. This site research is accompanied by an articulation of total responsibility management that, as Sandra Waddock and Charles Bodwell state later in this volume, enables "companies to define the responsibility goals and to develop appropriate management, measurement, and integration processes to help them to meet these goals."

The globalization debate needs this book's heavy dose of reality and common sense. Over the past 15 years the world has witnessed an explosion in business involving corporations headquartered in the world's leading industrial nations and the economies of the developing world and those of Central and Eastern Europe. Multinational enterprises have purchased foreign productive assets on an unprecedented scale; they have contracted massive orders from thousands of locally owned factories across Asia and Latin America; and, they have extracted vast quantities of oil, gas, and metals from Africa, Central Asia, the Middle East, and other emerging economies.

The benefits of the global business expansion, however, have not been evenly spread across the world's poorer nations. Many of the very poorest countries have been bypassed. In many other countries, there is a perception that only domestic elites, rather than the mass of the people, have gained. Moreover, there has been no shortage of allegations of environmental damage and human rights abuse against multinational firms. And, few of the charges have been as sharp as those related to the exploitation of people in sweatshops in very poor nations.

The overwhelming majority of multinational corporations involved in supplying the world's most affluent markets with relatively low-cost footwear, apparel, sporting goods, toys, and many other consumer products did not assign priority to social responsibility issues when they first expanded their purchases from Third World factories. For the most part they selected foreign contractors on the basis of the competitive prices they offered to produce quality products and on their record as reliable suppliers of goods. Rarely did the contracting multinational firms focus on labor conditions in those distant factories. Rarely did they determine whether the foreign factory owners employed children, accepted the rights of workers to organize, or maintained decent workplace health and safety standards. Rarely did the multinational companies develop corporate ethics codes that covered these kinds of social conditions, let alone management systems to see that there was compliance with such codes.

Moreover, few CEOs of major multinational corporations publicly demonstrated concern about social conditions in poor countries in general, and about the treatment of young people in these countries in particular. As Professor Hartman points out, the International Labour Organization estimates that there are some 250 million children between the ages of 5 and 14 who are employed in economic activity in developing countries, with almost half working on a full-time basis. There are many times as many youths between the ages of 14 and 18 in full-time employment in the poorer countries, and there are upward of 125 million young people who have never had the opportunity to attend school at all.

The antiglobalization protesters have demanded, at a minimum, for example, that multinational companies treat all of their workers, including those in subcontracted plants, with respect and that they pay special attention to the conditions under which youths are employed, including educational opportunities that can be provided to young people. Frequently, these protesters portray all multinational companies as being negligent.

The authors represented in this book, however, understand that the popular Asian sweatshop image masks important realities. The truth is that there has been little attention paid to firms that are striving to work constructively with Third World workforces to build conditions in which workers can have a meaningful sense of dignity. This book seeks to redress the distorted popular picture by providing well-researched examples of good labor practices.

Professor Hartman and her colleagues are not interested in the multinational companies that set about window dressing and that just pay lip service to doing the right thing as a result of public pressure. Nor is she interested in companies that adopt minimum acceptable standards to ensure that they avoid the spotlight of public protest. The author stresses that her aim is not to "find a middle ground between all of the competing interests, but to find the highest ground in terms of the return on investment for the organizations, the moral imperatives of labor advocates and the emotion-laden, though profit-maximizing tendencies of consumers."

This book has found such examples at factories owned by footwear manufacturers whose social responsibility reputations were dragged through the mud in the 1990s. Both Nike and adidas contract hundreds of Third World factories, and the researchers of this book were in no position to undertake comprehensive corporate-wide visits, or to fully examine the firms' claims that all of their factories complied with high corporate standards. But, the detailed models of good corporate practice that are explained here serve the vital purpose of showing what is possible and how a North American or West European company can have a positive influence on the lives of poor peoples in impoverished parts of the globe.

The field research in this study supports the contention that socially responsible labor practices strengthen multinational firms. Professor Hartman's work shows that ensuring that suppliers to multinational corporations operate in line with decent health, safety, and labor standards yields multiple benefits. These include heightened productivity, stronger morale, decreased attrition, enhanced worker commitment and loyalty, better relations with local communities, improved social cohesion and civil stability, lower training costs, strengthened corporate reputation, reduced corporate risk management, greater corporate shareholder trust, and more positive consumer perceptions.

The case studies are an important starting point, but they are not sufficient. It is just too easy for large companies, especially when they are in the eye of the antiglobalization storm, to showcase a few model factories. Skepticism among consumers, the media, and many civil society organizations is just too great these days for examples of a few such factories to carry much weight.

However, far more credibility is secured when it is seen that these companies have detailed, complex, and effective compliance programs in place, including systems to set workable standards, train workers, provide incentives for managers, and monitor performance. The authors provide outstanding descriptions of the systems that these organizations have put in place and the research of international organizations to verify these systems.

In addition, this book underscores a vital message about globalization: *Success depends above all on the approaches taken by the leaders of multinational corporations. CEOs of multinational corporations have nowhere to hide today.* Increasingly they are going to be judged by their performance on global social responsibility. They will find that they need the wisdom and examples contained in this book to guide their actions. Companies can have excellent compliance officers and fine-sounding ethics codes supported by detailed social responsibility policies, but they all will be rendered meaningless over time if, when Wall Street is pressing and the balance sheet is suffering, the CEO puts profits above principles.

Frank Vogl
President, Vogl Communications, Inc.

NOTE

1. See http://www.sweatshopwatch.org/swatch/questions.html#sweatshops.

Foreword

The nature and extent of the obligations that multinational corporations have to workers in factories throughout the developing world is one of the most controversial issues of our time. We academics bemoan the specialization that has overtaken academic life. When looking for a single-volume treatment of a complex and controversial issue, we seek one that brings multiple perspectives to bear on the problem. *Rising above Sweatshops: Innovative Approaches to Global Labor Challenges* is just such a book. The editors of this volume have commissioned a series of theoretical essays that, when read together, provide a sophisticated overview of the complex moral, political, economic, and managerial issues of the global labor market. By itself, this would be an important accomplishment. However, the editors have also commissioned a collection of new case studies that provide examples of corporations that have responded in innovative ways to difficult issues concerning global labor practices. This outstanding collection of theoretical perspectives and case studies deserves a wide audience.

The economic case for free trade is overwhelming in the utilitarian sense that it most efficiently maximizes the production of goods and services. However, as protestors of globalization have pointed out, there are externalities that cause pain and suffering and there are real issues of justice. How do we achieve the benefits of international business while mitigating some of the harmful effects? This volume helps to answer that question via a multidisciplinary collection of theoretical articles and a rich array of case studies that demonstrate how managers of global companies can reap the rewards of offshore production while dealing humanely and justly with their workers.

Ethical concerns about the treatment of workers by multinationals first arose with exposés about sweatshops. Many North Americans felt guilty that the athletic shoes and university sweatshirts they owned were made by people receiving less than a dollar an hour working in conditions that—at least by American standards—were deplorable. North Americans also expressed grave concern that many of the workers in these factories were children (often under the age of 14). Claims by economists that these workers are better off working in factories than being unemployed or working on farms in rural areas did not eliminate our unease. Under pressure from critics some multinational firms responded by creating industry-wide codes of conduct (standards of good practice) and by having their suppliers audited to make sure that those suppliers were following the standards of good practice. Critics responded with calls for a more aggressive pace of change and independent auditors. However, there are important issues concerning the treatment and compensation of workers that go beyond that debate.

To get at these broader issues, let us begin with the case that can be made for globalization. The economic case is well known, but there is a philosophical case as well. The philosophical case for globalization may be traced to the Enlightenment, a period of modern European history that, regrettably, is out of favor in many parts of academe. Enlightenment thinkers looked back in horror at the religious strife and nationalistic zeal that caused so many deaths and so much suffering throughout Europe in the 1600s. The notion that we all share a common humanity meant that differences in religion and in national background were unimportant and were, from the moral point of view, irrelevant. A cosmopolitan philosophy that celebrated the extensive family of human beings was endorsed and defended. But the limited level of economic development made the implementation of the cosmopolitan ideal impossible. However, by the end of the twentieth century economic possibility had caught up with the Enlightenment philosophy. As Francis Fukuyama argued in *The End of History and the Last Man,* the entire world had adopted or was on the brink of adopting democracy and capitalism. Thus, "the end of history" as the struggle of how political and economic institutions should look.

This period of euphoria lasted about a decade and was followed by massive protests against globalization. And what were the criticisms of the protesters? First, they argued that traditional theories of economic development had ignored the cost of "monetary discipline" on the least advantaged of society. Second, they contended that development itself was harmful to traditional industries and destructive of indigenous culture. Third, they argued that the benefits of development were unfairly distributed across the population. The fourth argument was that multinationals, in a desperate race to reduce costs, would move from country to country as they cut costs. The result was a "race to the bottom" in which multinationals sought suppliers or products in countries with the lowest wages and the weakest environmental standards. Fifth was the claim that multinationals violated the basic human rights of workers. Finally, on a macro level, some critics argued that globalization benefited the rich developed countries at the expense of poor undeveloped ones. These charges are discussed in this volume by authors from diverse academic disciplines. But this volume is not limited to a theoretical discussion of these issues. There are country-by-country analyses of how these issues are being addressed by major international corporations. The study shows that criticism, especially from powerful nongovernmental organizations (NGOs), can promote change. Many American academics will be surprised to discover the role that European-based NGOs play in helping to shape corporate conduct. Significantly, the study explains how some companies have responded in creative and practical ways to criticism of their labor practices by substantially improving the conditions in which their employees work. And we are reminded that some companies have always treated their employees on the global assembly line with dignity and respect. We are thus given hope that exemplary corporations will prevail rather than that the bad will drive out the good.

This volume should be of great interest to academics in a number of areas. For business schools, the volume presents alternative models of economic development as well as case studies of companies that are attempting to act justly in the global marketplace. The volume has much to offer political scientists about the behavior, power, and moral fervor of NGOs. It presents a challenge to economists to consider the distributive impact of policy recommendations and to address the so-called negative externalities of international business transactions. It provides an opportunity for philosophers to test their abstract ethical theories against the reality of international business transactions.

But this study can contribute even more than that to academe. The ethical practice of international business involves a balancing act. We need to understand and respect the distinct moral features of cultures other than our own. Since the cases in this volume focus on cultures that are not economically well-developed capitalist democracies, persons in area studies will have a rich set of cases with which to teach understanding and respect. But ultimately representatives of different cultures must come together to work out a set of operating principles that respect basic human rights and apply universally in international business. Case studies showing how companies can respect such rights should be of interest to those involved in international programs of all types and to those who teach in peace studies programs. When representatives of companies, workers, and NGOs can agree on a common set of principles for governing interactions among them, peace is possible. In facilitating that process, this volume makes its own contribution to the Enlightenment dream.

Norman E. Bowie
Elmer L. Andersen Chair in Corporate Responsibility,
Carlson School of Management and Department of Philosophy,
University of Minnesota, Twin Cities

CHAPTER 1

Rising above Sweatshops: An Introduction to the Text and to the Issues

Laura P. Hartman, Denis G. Arnold, and Sandra Waddock

Business Leaders don't have to wait—indeed, increasingly they can't afford to wait—for governments to pass and enforce legislation before they pursue "good practices" in support of international human rights, labor and environmental standards within their own operations and in the societies of which they are a part.

—Mary Robinson, United Nations High Commissioner for Human Rights[1]

RESEARCH IMPETUS

We are all parties to the conflicts incited by globalization; we don't have to leave our dens to see images of protest on television screens. Unfortunately, further investigation often only clouds the controversies for those not intimately involved. Frequently multinational enterprises (MNEs) are left with little direction or guidance regarding a recommended response to these disputes.

Attention usually focuses on multinationals' real or alleged "sweatshop" treatment of workers in developing economies. However, many firms have been spurred on by this attention toward ameliorating workplace conditions, had begun the process at the time the media uproar began, or have always maintained superior standards for the workplace. Insufficient attention has been paid to firms that engage in truly good and beneficial activities with regard to their workforces, where the result is not a "sweatshop" environment, but is rather a healthy workplace where laborers are respected and are treated with dignity.

The purpose of this book is twofold: First, we strive to provide a practical and theoretical overview of the global labor challenges confronting MNEs. Second, we showcase creative management approaches to resolving global labor challenges. It is our expectation and hope that the discussion of these programs will serve to stimulate the moral imaginations of corporate decision makers worldwide toward innovative proactive solutions to what seem to be the most difficult global labor conflicts and challenges. Our hope is that working conditions will thereby improve and workers' rights will be respected. Workers have basic rights that should not be violated, notwithstanding the geographical locale of their work. But those rights often appear to conflict with the economic and commercial exigencies of both developing countries and MNEs. Thus, creative approaches are critical if workers' rights are to be respected within the constraints faced by developing countries and MNEs.

The aim of this analysis is to spur creative thought rather than to conduct systematic investigations of the complete effectiveness of existing programs. The latter is beyond the scope of this study. Nonetheless, we are sufficiently confident in the design and purpose of these programs to suggest that they merit consideration by other multinationals as potential models for addressing labor problems associated with globalization.

CONVENTIONAL ARGUMENTS REGARDING WORKING CONDITIONS

The Conventional Case for Poor Working Conditions

The exploitation of a national resource—labor—allows developing countries to expand export activities and to improve their economies. Economic growth brings more jobs, which will cause the labor market to tighten, which in turn will force companies to improve conditions to attract workers.[2] Though it is an unpopular sentiment with the general consuming public, economist Paul Krugman claims that the maintenance of substandard labor conditions is clearly supported by economic theory— "[t]he overwhelming mainstream view among economists is that growth of this kind of employment is tremendous good news for the world's poor."[3] In fact, when asked whether there were too many sweatshops in poor nations, economist Jeffrey D. Sachs replied that his concern was "not that there are too many sweatshops, but that there are too few."[4]

These conclusions are based on the contention that free trade without labor restrictions generates future prosperity and better working conditions for the host country by providing that developing country with access to cheaper goods and, in turn, opportunities to exploit cost advantages in export markets.[5] Theoretical and empirical research suggest that one of the most effective ways to increase the competitiveness of a developing economy and to improve job prospects is to create a better-trained workforce through work experience and training.[6] In short, jobs—even terrible jobs—provide some "positive externalities" for a society—benefits that accrue to others who are not parties to the transaction between a laborer and employer. Job-related skills, and the general ability of individuals to function as elements of the global economy, provide benefits to the host country society at large that are not specifically part of the contractual agreement between laborer and employer. Overall, in this view, the best hope for workers in substandard conditions lies in the sustainable improved economic and social conditions that economic growth brings—a durable economic growth that will occur only if developing countries can capitalize on their low-cost advantage to attract development.[7]

In addition, free market theory suggests that people work in sweatshop conditions because it is the most rational means available to them for furthering their own ends. Moreover, these choices prove optimal for a developing country's economy, as they represent agreements among many producers and consumers of labor regarding desirable exchanges of labor (from the labor producers) and wages or other benefits (from the consumers of labor, in this case, MNEs and the purchasers of their goods and services). In short, however much we may not like some of what we see in the labor conditions of developing nations, this is the market at work, and the market works to generate overall improvements in economic welfare for a society.

The Conventional Case against Poor Working Conditions

Free markets—in labor or in products—generate many benefits, but their ability to generate those benefits presumes that certain boundary conditions hold. For example, transactions among buyers and sellers optimally satisfy the interests of each, provided that there is a free flow of information (e.g., buyers get an accurate description of what they are buying), the transaction is truly voluntary (e.g., sellers are not forced to sell via coercion), people are able to make rational decisions about their self-interest (and so, for example, small children cannot be held to the terms of any "contract" they enter into), and there are many buyers and sellers (e.g., no potential for exploitative monopoly exists). Criticism of MNE practices in developing countries often stems from the fact that one or more of the conditions for efficient free markets does not hold, or is in some way circumvented by the multinational. In that case, the normally expected benefits of a free market are not guaranteed; there is a market failure. For example, the seemingly interminable international debate about infant formula sales in developing countries revolves around allegations that Western formula manufacturers and their distributors cannot hide behind a free market defense of their actions because their actions violate the preconditions of efficient market transactions. Such violations occur, according to the critics, when end-user illiteracy prevents proper use of the product or appropriately skeptical responses to Western-style marketing campaigns (i.e., people aren't making fully rational decisions about their self-interest, and buyers are not getting an accurate description of what they are getting into).

One kind of argument for not tolerating poor working conditions in developing countries is premised on the claim that the preconditions for efficient markets are not met. For example, workers may agree to labor under poor conditions, but only because they have no other choice. Alternatively, when they have a choice (e.g., leave a poor rural area for factory work in a far-away industrial center), they may not be able to make a fully informed choice because of lack of information about just what they are becoming involved in. Furthermore, such labor choices, once made, can be difficult to undo once additional information is learned "on the job" (e.g., it can become practically difficult to get out of a labor agreement and return to one's rural home). Thus, critics argue, the fact that workers agree to labor under poor conditions does not necessarily mean that this is the kind of agreement that constitutes the normal workings of a well-functioning free market in jobs and labor.

A second kind of argument offered by critics challenges the benefits, or "positive externalities," that even poor employment allegedly brings to a society. For example, critics argue that the kinds of skills developed in much routine factory work hold no promises of great economic and social development, either for the individual employee or the entire society. Moreover, the transition from agricultural and cottage industries to factory-based work is argued to have numerous negative externalities, that is, social costs that are not covered by the wages paid by a multinational to its employees. The social disruption caused by urban migration is one such negative consequence, as people move from lives characterized by the informal social support networks of family and village to lives characterized by urban anonymity and dependence on overstressed public social services.

Overall, then, the global market may not be an effective arbiter of the trade-offs between improved working conditions and levels of economic development, production cost, and product price. A nonindustrialized developing country may tolerate various substandard practices if the result is a growing economy. Producers may tolerate some degree of labor practice constraint if the result does not raise the cost of production significantly. Consumers will tolerate modest price increases if they are assured that the worst labor practices have been eliminated. But markets are a poor mechanism for establishing appropriate boundaries. Many economists claim that, over time, markets will correct even the most substandard practices, but some economists and many noneconomists remain unconvinced.

Moreover, critics argue that regardless of what kinds of benefits do or do not accrue from the practice of substandard labor conditions, it simply is not right to subject individuals to extended periods of back-breaking or mind-numbing labor in conditions that put their own health and welfare at risk. In short, any person deserves better conditions than those. Thus, in addition to the various pro and con arguments as to the real or illusory benefits and costs of poor working conditions for multinationals and developing countries, there remain fundamental objections to certain labor practices, the cogency of which does not depend on cost and benefit calculations. Basic concerns of human dignity and morality simply rule some practices "out of bounds."

A Third Alternative: Looking Beyond the "Dark Side"

A common response to the foregoing criticisms, of course, is to note that no matter how well-meaning and accurate the criticisms, there is simply no viable alternative for people in the labor markets of many developing countries. In fact, a recent article titled "What Can Businesses Do to Appease Anti-Globalization Protestors?" concluded "not very much."[8] But is that so?

Two facts seem unavoidable, but point us toward an alternative stance on these issues. First, attempts to redress substandard labor conditions must take into account the pressures of globalization and the poor economic conditions of developing nations. As long as the extreme global disparity in wages and living conditions exists among countries, working conditions that are unacceptable in one area may well be sought after in others (sometimes referred to as the "race to the bottom"). Second, regardless of the economic conditions of developing nations, it remains true that companies that profit from egregious working conditions often are subject to onslaughts of media and consumer criticism, and that substandard working conditions may sometimes result in damaged workers, damaged societies, and long-term economic problems.

Consequently, it is important for MNEs to find some way to (1) work within the constraints of developing nation economies and social conditions, while (2) respecting the worldwide concern about the ways in which workers are treated. It probably will do workers and MNEs little good if MNEs simply abandon them and retreat to Western labor markets. But neither will it do workers and MNEs any good if concerns about labor conditions are simply ignored. As ethicist Thomas Donaldson observes, finding proper solutions for these problems requires walking the line between cultural relativism and moral absolutism if we are to allow for necessary differences in conditions while discouraging truly exploitative practices.[9]

What, then, is to be done? Too much media attention has focused on the dark side of global labor decisions. When people read newspapers or students study the behavior of multinationals in developing economies, they read or learn only about the sweatshop treatment of workers. However, many firms now maintain high standards in their global factories. In sum, insufficient attention has been paid to firms that engage in morally praiseworthy activities with regard to their workforces, resulting in not a sweatshop environment but rather an economically viable enterprise in which laborers are respected and treated with dignity. Those positive examples are the focus of this study. Focusing on such positive examples provides the best opportunity for moving debate beyond the entrenched, polarized political narrative of economic efficiency versus workers' rights.

Furthermore, companies may find that there is a positive benefit to dealing proactively with questions of global labor practices. To take a simple aspect of this issue, consider just how committed employees are likely to be to an organization that treats them abusively? If in fact the predictions of the free market defense of poor labor conditions come true, and developing countries enjoy ever greater levels of economic growth and welfare, it seems unlikely that employees will show much long-term commitment to organizations that treated them poorly. Nor are employees likely to function as good organizational citizens while working at such organizations; why should someone "go the extra mile" to help an abusive employer?

Arguments for taking a proactive stance toward global labor issues also arise from the global marketplace. Consumers in industrialized countries increasingly show concern for the labor reputations of the companies from whom they purchase goods and services. Similarly, some evidence suggests that potential employees increasingly care about the ethical reputations of the companies for whom they work, such that it costs more for low-reputation companies to hire high-quality employees. Even corporations show signs of taking increasing care to avoid becoming a business partner of firms whose questionable practices might taint the company.

BEYOND CONVENTIONS: ALTERNATIVES TO SWEATSHOPS

At the Core: Human Rights

Clearly, the proliferation of guiding principles, systemic approaches to implementing standards, and reporting initiatives creates a situation of complexity and even conflicting requirements for managers. Thus, some consolidation or rationalization is likely to emerge as the millennium progresses and companies continue to try to evolve their codes and their labor practices. Despite the proliferation of standards, however, there is in fact basic agreement among many regarding the fundamental rights that should be accorded to all workers.

In the eighteenth century the philosopher Immanuel Kant argued that other persons should always be treated as an end unto themselves, and never as a means only. Persons are free and rational creatures and as such, argued Kant, they have intrinsic value that must be respected. This means that the desires, goals, and aspirations of other persons must be given due consideration. This Enlightenment idea serves as a basis for the principle that constitutes Article 1 of the United Nations Universal Declaration of Human Rights. This principle holds that "All human beings are born free and equal in dignity and rights. They are endowed with reason and conscience and should act towards one another in a spirit of brotherhood."[10]

The Universal Declaration of Human Rights has engendered controversy insofar as its 30 articles identify both negative and positive rights. Negative rights constitute shields against the unjust violation of individual freedoms. If humans possess negative rights, then other persons retain correlative duties that require that they refrain from actions that interfere with those individual freedoms. Positive rights, on the other hand, constitute entitlements to things that are necessary for the exercise of individual freedom. If humans possess positive rights, then other persons retain correlative duties that require that they provide individuals with those things that are necessary for the exercise of individual freedoms.

Critics have argued that these rights are simply too expansive, and that positive rights are unjustifiable in the absence of contractual agreements that stipulate the existence of other rights.[11] In reply, philosophers such as Alan Gewirth and Henry Shue have developed rigorous and persuasive arguments in defense of the most fundamental or basic human rights.[12] As a result of their work, as well as that of others, it is possible to identify *freedom* and *well-being* as the most basic human rights. Freedom is here understood as a person's ability to control his or her behavior without undue external pressure and with knowledge of the relevant circumstances. Possessing well-being entails having the general abilities and conditions required for a person to be able to act in a manner consistent with his or her considered preferences. These rights are both negative and positive. Furthermore, they transcend national, cultural, and legal boundaries insofar as they apply to humans by virtue of the fact that humans enjoy reason and conscience.

In reply to a philosophical defense of human rights, it might be asserted that human rights are merely Western values with little applicability to non-Western societies. There are at least two strategies for replying to such an assertion. First, this claim might be challenged on conceptual grounds by asking whether or not the arguments deployed in defense of human rights apply only in the context of Western societies. Arguments of precisely this variety have been deployed to demonstrate that on conceptual grounds the assertion is mistaken.[13] Second, this assertion might be challenged on empirical grounds by pointing to a convergence of beliefs from Western and non-Western societies regarding human rights. Donaldson and Thomas Dunfee look to the convergence of religious, cultural, and philosophical beliefs to identify "hypernorms," or basic precepts so fundamental they serve as foundations on which all other norms or activities are to be judged.[14] One recent analysis specifically reviewed global labor standards to determine whether in this array of emerging standards there existed any such hypernorms with respect to labor standards.[15] The following basic labor rights were determined to be relatively universally acknowledged in the range of codes and documents reviewed for that study:

- Just and favorable working conditions, including a healthy working environment and a limit to the number of hours a human should have to work each day
- Minimum age and working conditions for child labor
- Nondiscrimination requirements regarding the *relative* amount that a worker should be paid and the right to equal pay for equal work
- Freedom from forced labor
- Free association, including the right to organize and to bargain collectively in contract negotiations

Thus, analysis of existing labor standards suggests that, at least in theory, there is considerable agreement about what rights *ought* to be respected. The five labor rights described above are specific examples of the instantiation of freedom and well-being. Indeed, the general rights of freedom and well-being described above would require even more expansive labor rights. Nonetheless, the results of this study provide ample evidence that human rights are not merely a Western idea.

As a result of the significant power that they wield in the formal sector of developing economies, MNE mangers who wish to ensure that the rights of their workers are protected are well positioned to do so. The program studies in Part II of this book illustrate some of the initiatives undertaken in this regard by morally innovative managers.

Positive Deviancy

In 2001 the Ashridge Centre for Business and Society conducted an extensive survey of the world's 500 largest companies to determine the most significant strategies in connection with global human rights. Its research concluded that there were four key factors that were critical in determining a firm's success when dealing with these issues. In keeping with our earlier observations regarding the role of codes and management processes, the Ashridge Centre survey indicated the importance of a well-rounded approach covering both formal policies and formal and informal actions by management to foster commitment to those polices. The four specific strategies identified in the Ashridge Centre study included (1) keeping up with the debate through monitoring and analyzing media coverage and other information sources, (2) evidencing company commitment to these issues through senior management responsibility and accountability as well as communication throughout the firm, (3) generating change by setting examples throughout the supply chain, and (4) managing risk by implementing proactive and progressive policies and procedures.[16]

More generally speaking, at the core of the emergence of labor standards and the search for best practice companies is the notion that human beings, wherever they are and whatever work they are doing, should be treated with dignity and respect. Principles, standards, and reporting systems are emerging in large measure because markets left to their own devices are a questionable mechanism for ensuring that high standards are met. While it is clear that some degree of consolidation in the proliferation of standards and reporting practices discussed above is likely to take place in the future, it is equally clear that the issue of labor standards is here to stay. One manner in which to consider possible solutions, and the one that serves as the backbone of this research, is to evaluate the occurrences of "positive deviancy" in connection with global labor challenges.

Positive deviancy refers to the anomaly that *some* firms have actually managed to respect the human rights and dignity of their workers while still managing to reap a profit, thus continuing to justify the globalization of the firms' labor force. If some firms can manage this effort, then why can't others? And what are these firms doing that others might not? What have they learned through their positive (or negative) experiences, from which other firms can learn? Scholars Jerry Sternin and Robert Choo, in coining the phrase,[17] contend that exploration of these positive deviants can lead to progressive responses from those who did not previously succeed. Adapting the idea to our particular area of study, firms should look for positive deviants in their industries—those firms that are exhibiting the desired levels of performance—and try to understand what is different about their behavior. They suggest that by doing so firms are likely to find the "keys to creating real change—change that . . . brings immediate and sustainable benefits."[18]

Therefore, companies that hope to stay on the cutting edge of competitive practice must increasingly understand this reality of the global marketplace and follow the lessons learned that are evidenced in the programs in this series, and must put that understanding into practice in the reality of their own facilities as well as those in their supply chain.

Strategic Considerations

The motivation for the corporate engagement that serves as the basis for the programs described in this book stems from a variety of catalysts, including the recognition that the implementation of labor-related standards can have a positive impact on numerous strategic considerations such as the following:

- Productivity
- Morale
- Decreased attrition
- Lower training costs
- Corporate reputation
- Risk management
- Trust among stakeholders
- Worker commitment and loyalty
- Relationships with the community
- Social cohesion and civil stability
- Consumer perceptions[19]

Furthermore, as firms globalize, they are realizing the tremendous benefits of implementing some of the management learning that has emerged in the United States and Europe in the past few decades. These benefits include the following:

- *Increased leverage* earned by exclusive contracts with suppliers to encourage or even require suppliers to put into practice workplace-enhancing projects such as education programs and minimum wages, resulting in some cases in higher productivity and improved performance, as well as enhancements in the workplace standards in supplier factories;
- *Greater awareness of human/employee rights issues* and enhanced and enlightened compliance with local and international laws that results in a reduction in litigation or other costs of liability for omissions, alleviating the concerns of shareholders and potentially even enhancing the firm's brand image. A related benefit in some cases may also arise through the domino effect of encouraging respect for the rule of law in countries in which such respect may be a new concept;
- *Improved relationships with key stakeholders,* including customers and investors, as a consequence of respecting human rights and the dignity of workers, thus

ensuring that profits continue to be generated and providing further justification of the globalization of the firms' labor force.

Additional benefits inure to those firms that take these voluntary steps toward a greater awareness of human and employee rights issues. They also improve their reputation among media organizations, policy activists, and many consumers. This helps to reduce the concerns of shareholder groups that their investments will suffer losses either through actual legal liability or through negative media attention and resulting consumer concerns that can undermine a company's brand image.

Moreover, social or ethical investors and the research services that support them now regularly pressure companies to improve not only their internal working conditions but also those of their suppliers. Recent research evidences significant concern, for example, with regard to human rights violations, substandard working conditions, low environmental standards, and child labor.[20] When survey respondents were asked whether they would support restrictions on the import of goods into the United States if the goods had been made in countries in which these circumstances prevailed, respondents strongly supported the restrictions, in particular in situations involving the use of child labor.[21]

Negative publicity associated with discovery of sweatshop conditions or child labor practices has hurt the reputation of major companies such as Nike, Wal-Mart, and Liz Claiborne, just to name a few. Shell Oil and British Petroleum both gained worldwide attention for their failure to enact appropriate policies and procedures to protect the human rights of their and their suppliers' workers, moving them from the financial pages to the front page. Yet now, Shell's annual triple-bottom-line report, "People, Planet and Profits," garners positive media attention, which could result in a positive impact on its financial bottom line.[22] In fact, recently the International Finance Corporation, Instituto Ethos and SustainAbility released a report of the first large-scale study that evidences that companies in emerging markets gain financially from sustainability efforts.[23] The report concludes that "it does pay for businesses in emerging markets to pursue a wider role on environmental and social issues,"[24] citing cost reductions, productivity, revenue growth, and market access as areas of greatest return for MNEs.[25]

Other firms have also decided to bring these issues into the light of day through social and environmental reports that are generally issued at the same time annually as their more traditional annual reports. "Clearer," adidas-Salomon's[26] social and environmental report covering 2001, for example, explores case studies of various suppliers whose practices they have been able to improve substantially and also offers an overview of the supplier factories that still need improvement[27] and the areas in which adidas has not yet reached its social goals.[28]

Increased public awareness about working conditions in developing nations in particular, puts tremendous pressure on companies and countries to establish and implement basic labor, human rights, and environmental standards. For this reason, some of the most innovative or creative responses to some of these workplace challenges may be found coming from the very firms that are subject to the public or media criticism.

Companies who take voluntary steps toward improved handling of human and employee rights issues also may find that they improve the labor markets and social capital of the developing countries in which they operate. First, they may become the employer of choice among those people best positioned in local labor markets. In addition, the respect for human rights and for the rule of law may encourage others to behave similarly even in countries that historically have been characterized by abuse, self-dealing, and cronyism, especially if other organizations in those countries see that they are now on the losing end of the competition for the best workers.

Moreover, there is an increased connection between traditionally northern perspectives of social responsibility and global operations. At a recent presentation at Harvard University, British Petroleum CEO John Browne asserted that MNEs have an increasing responsibility as they venture into less developed parts of the globe.[29] "There is a powerful case for the view that it is through cooperation and interdependence that any society advances from one level of development to the next. Trust is the basis for globalization which gives us the chance to take the next step, and that is an opportunity we mustn't waste."[30] The critical factor, he claims, in restoring trust is to demonstrate that the presence of a corporation in emerging markets is a source of human progress, not decline. In fact, he argues, a firm's failure to globalize and to bring these opportunities to the emerging nations of the world is equivalent to denying the world's poor the chance to improve their standard of living and to share in the prosperity that others enjoy. There is a responsibility to participate in the world's markets—the challenge is to do so in a manner that respects basic human rights.

Thus, by emulating positive deviants, we see a way for MNEs to avoid being included in the endless parade of negative stories about poor working conditions, terrible treatment of workers, and egregious flouting of internationally accepted labor and working standards.

ORGANIZATIONAL STRUCTURE

This book is organized into two distinct sections. Part I of the book provides a common context for the cases that are presented in Part II. In Part I the reader is introduced to the variety of lenses through which the current global labor challenges might be critically analyzed—the perspec-

tives of economics, law, philosophy, public policy, and strategic management are each represented.

To ensure that we share a common understanding of the current global
labor context, we begin in chapter 2 with an overview of that context. In
her essay "The Global Context: Multinational Enterprises, Labor Standards, and Regulation," Jill Murray provides an extraordinary window
into the facts, contentions, and legal regulations of the "new sweatshop"
discourse. The chapter paints a broad picture of the kinds of labor abuses
that exist in the world today and then charts the rise of interest in the new
sweatshop, particularly the potentially controversial case in which powerful MNEs from the developed world manufacture consumer goods
through a globalized subcontracting chain. The relationship between these
two issues—labor abuses and certain MNEs—is then considered. Powerful and sometimes conflicting views are held in many academic disciplines
about what this relationship is and should be. In an attempt to clarify the
obligations of MNEs, the scope and meaning of international labor law
are discussed. Finally, the chapter suggests the kinds of steps firms should
take if they wish to act in accordance with the articulated norms of "decent
work."

In chapter 3, "The Economic Context: Grounding Discussions of Economic Change and Labor in Developing Countries," Jonathan D. London
provides an overview of economic issues regarding global labor practices.
Once the exclusive domain of workers, managers, and state agencies, decisions regarding the management, social development, and human rights
of workers in developing countries are subject to wider and more intense
scrutiny. Although work and employment in developing countries have
long held the interest of scholars, today these issues are at the center of
much wider discussions concerning the functioning, regulation, and future development of the world economy. Remarkably, however, many
discussions of global labor challenges still exhibit the lack of a basic awareness of the complex dynamics of industrial relations in developing countries. London grounds his discussion of work and employment practices
in globalized industries in an examination of the changing context of industrial relations in developing nations. In the context of global economic
change, the chapter clarifies the meaning and significance of *industrialization* and *industrial* and highlights the actors and institutions that govern
the use of labor in developing nations.

Chapter 4 represents the fundamental philosophical grounding of our
research. Ethical concerns are at the core of the dispute concerning global
labor practices. Both critics and defenders of MNEs deploy explicitly
moral arguments concerning the welfare of workers worldwide in defending their conclusions. In his essay "Philosophical Foundations: Moral
Reasoning, Human Rights, and Global Labor Practices," Denis G. Arnold
explains how moral reasoning, together with an understanding of basic

human rights, can help the moral manager to produce morally innovative solutions to global labor challenges. The chapter draws from the work of Alan Gewirth, Amartya Sen, and Martha Nussbaum to provide both a justification of the rights to freedom and well-being and an application of those rights to the circumstances of MNE workers. In so doing the chapter provides a moral basis both for the applications of human rights discussed in the remaining two chapters of Part I, and for the programs and initiatives described in Part II of the book.

In chapter 5, "Philosophy Applied I: How Nongovernmental Organizations and Multinational Enterprises Can Work Together to Protect Global Labor Rights," Michael A. Santoro identifies the unique roles that nongovernmental organizations (NGOs) play in the debate over global labor practices. The movement to hold MNEs responsible for human rights has largely been channeled through NGOs. Many NGOs are cooperating with MNEs to improve human rights conditions in Third World factories. However, many human rights NGOs remain ambivalent about whether the better course is to confront or to cooperate with MNEs. Using interviews with managers of MNEs and NGO leaders, this chapter examines the strategic choices behind cooperative labor rights efforts as well as the reasons why many NGOs choose instead to pursue confrontational tactics.

Finally, as the concluding chapter in Part I, chapter 6 explains how the philosophy articulated in chapter 4 may be applied by MNE managers. In "Philosophy Applied II: Total Responsibility Management," Sandra Waddock and Charles Bodwell discuss strategic management through the lens of the total responsibility management (TRM) approach that is emerging among MNEs. TRM approaches are, like quality management systems, systemic, holistic, and process oriented. The TRM approach provides a framework consisting of three core elements or processes that can be used by managers to guide the implementation of codes of conduct. These general processes are (1) inspiration or vision setting; (2) integration of the vision and values established into strategy, human resource, and operating practices; and (3) innovation, which involves establishing indicators that measure responsibility performance and provides a basis for improvements, remediation where necessary, and learning. Transparency and accountability for impacts and outcomes are also essential elements of TRM approaches, particularly with respect to labor.

Part II of the book contains MNE and NGO program analyses that were produced according to the research process outlined below. The programs examined in this study provide examples of innovative responses to difficult issues concerning global labor practices that many companies increasingly face. The experiences of the studied companies can be helpful in providing others with alternatives to the perceived unhappy dilemma of either enduring a public relations backlash or terminating operations in various countries.

In chapter 7, "Nike, Inc.: Corporate Social Responsibility and Workplace Standard Initiatives in Vietnam," Laura P. Hartman and Richard E. Wokutch provide an in-depth overview of Nike's code of conduct and the steps Nike has taken toward greater accountability for the actions of its suppliers. In 1998, Nike CEO Phil Knight delivered a speech at the National Press Club that became a turning point in Nike's approach to the issues facing its suppliers. In that speech, Knight accepted responsibility at the corporate level for the labor activities of its suppliers by establishing six initiatives for the firm, including among others, the expansion of worker education programs and an increase in the firm's support of its microenterprise loan program. Nike had discovered that investments in the personal and professional development of its workers (through the After-hours Education Program) and investment in the communities surrounding its suppliers' factories (through its Jobs and Microenterprise Loan Program) represented investments in Nike's future, as well. These and other programs are discussed.

In chapter 8, "adidas-Salomon: Child Labor and Health and Safety Initiatives in Vietnam and Brazil," Laura P. Hartman, Richard E. Wokutch, and J. Lawrence French describe adidas-Salomon's published Standards of Engagement (SoE), the stated aim of which is to ensure that all of its suppliers' factories are safe, fair places to work. They go on to describe in detail the implementation of the SoE program in Thailand and Brazil, as well as a partnership between private-sector competitors and the Vietnamese government that seeks to encourage higher health and safety standards in suppliers that are not currently subject to MNE codes of conduct. An additional program analysis highlights a creative response to child labor in the factory of an adidas-Salomon supplier.

Additional program analyses that demonstrate creative responses to globalization challenges can be found in other chapters of Part II.

In chapter 9,"Levi Strauss & Co.: Implementation of Global Sourcing and Operating Guidelines in Latin America," Tara J. Radin describes the operation of Levi Strauss's global sourcing and operating guidelines, its "Terms of Engagement," in several Latin America countries. The case explains how the guidelines help sourcing partners to create continuous improvements to working conditions in Mexico; cultivate value-based management from the ground up in El Salvador; and promote worker rights in Guatemala.

In chapter 10, "Dow Chemical Corporation: Responsible Care Program in Thailand," Richard E. Wokutch describes a voluntary international chemical industry initiative, Responsible Care,[31] and focuses on its implementation by Dow Chemical Company in its operations in Thailand. This program promotes the responsible development, use, and disposal of chemicals and chemical byproducts.

In chapter 11, "Pro-Child Institute: Combating Child Labor through Collaborative Partnerships in the Brazilian Shoe Industry," J. Lawrence French and Richard E. Wokutch describe valuable returns from a collaborative partnership between NGOs, the Brazilian government, and the private sector concerning child labor in the Brazilian shoe industry. A trisector partnership such as this can reduce social and local environmental risks and can create new business opportunities if incorporated into key business activities.[32]

In chapter 12, "International Labour Organization: Factory Improvement Programme," Ivanka Mamic and Charles Bodwell describe the ILO's Local Manager Development Program focusing on responsibility management and factory-level improvements. Participation in the training program should increase the capacity of managers to respond to the competing demands being placed on them, facilitate the sharing of best practices, and result in changes being implemented at the factory level.

In chapter 13, "Chiquita Brands International, Inc.: Value-Based Management and Corporate Responsibility in Latin America," Tara J. Radin describes the corporate responsibility program of Chiquita Brands International, Inc. The case illustrates how Chiquita has operationalized corporate responsibility to promote respect for workers and ecosystem conservation on its farms in Latin America.

Each program analysis verifies the existence of the particular described program and the validity of its claims regarding basic factual matters, and it determines the ascertainable impact of the program on its participants. The primary value in reviewing MNE responses to these challenges lies in the exploration of creative solutions to global labor challenges.

RESEARCH PROCESS

As discussed above, there is evidence that investing in human resources has a significant positive impact on the bottom line in terms of lower costs, as well as greater productivity, lower attrition and, as a result, lower training costs. The program analyses produced for this book illustrate MNEs' programs that are designed to provide a value to the worker while still allowing the firm to maintain a profit and do more than just survive. We seek to focus attention on that which should be *replicated* in the global workplace, rather than that which should be chastised; that is, on the initiatives that represent real, although not perfect, attempts to manage responsibility.

Areas of Exploration

Given the particular differences among firms, and our goal of identifying and exploring a variety of alternative management approaches to this challenge, there was no one set of questions that existed as a guide to this exploration. In an effort to provide other firms with a foundation for replication, the program investigators sought to conduct a review of each program to include, where appropriate, information relating to the program's establishment, approval process, implementation process, training, continued assessment, and exit strategy. Researchers used a general interview protocol to better understand the nature of those stages that provided for discretion depending on the project or program explored. This interview protocol was satisfied both through discussions with key decision makers at a firm's global headquarters, decision makers on site in country, other workers who may have been involved in any of the stages noted above, as well as external stakeholders, where possible. The protocol included the following question areas:

- What does this firm do that should be showcased as a model of labor conditions?
- Why did this firm choose to implement this activity, program, protection, response? What served as a catalyst for the establishment of this program? What is the incentive for establishing this particular labor-friendly program?
- What was the process by which this program, and so on, was established or implemented?
- Through what approval process did this idea need to travel to receive final approval to move forward?
- What was the involvement or response of the workforce (or other community or stakeholders) to the establishment of this program?
- What type of training program was necessary to begin implementation of this program?
- How was the program put into place? Were there any barriers to implementation of the program?
- How do you see this program's evolution in the future, if at all?
- What is the involvement of the workforce (or other community or stakeholder) in the implementation of this program?
- Is there any provision for external review or assessment of the program on a one-time or continuing basis?
- What is the process by which the program will be reviewed or assessed internally? To whom is this information reported?
- On what basis is this program or will this program be measured and what is considered to be a "success"? On what basis will the firm decide to continue or discontinue this program?
- What is the probability of the firm's labor-friendly program continuing after a key decision maker or supporter leaves the firm (where relevant)?
- What impact does the firm expect this program to have on the firm or its stakeholders, in the short or long term?

- How does this program affect the firm's bottom line?
- Does the firm yet have in place or plan to develop an exit strategy once it has determined to discontinue the program?

Generally, our meetings with labor representatives involved an exploration of their particular fundamental needs and the trade-offs that they have been willing to make to have those needs met. Meetings with management representatives sought to determine whether alternative economic approaches to meeting these needs have been successful and, if not, why not (i.e., what are the economic or cultural barriers to doing so?). The outgrowth of these discussions is a balance of the competing interests, with sensitivity to the needs of all parties involved.

Country Reports

Attempts to redress substandard labor conditions must account for the pressures of globalization and the poor economic conditions of developing nations. In an effort to ensure the greatest, most effective application of the program analyses included in this series to other global workplaces, a dedicated Web site includes an overview of host country demographics for the countries represented by the program analyses, as well as an overview of their economic, social, religious, legal, and natural environments. In this way, replication in other countries of the programs described in these studies may be modified accordingly based on relevant variations in that particular environment. For instance, if a program exists in a country in which unemployment is comparatively high, that particular program might not be as effective or even possible in another country in which unemployment is comparatively lower. Moreover, a program that is extraordinarily effective today might later prove to be less effective as a result of a change in the country's socioeconomic environment. By reviewing the environment in which these programs were implemented, other firms will be better able to gauge the potential effect of the program in their own firm's operations. In addition to a basic factual review, the socioeconomic overview for each country addresses the following questions, as appropriate:

- What impact does this country's legal environment have on labor decisions (including whether there are protections of human rights embedded in this country's political system or documents)?
- How are unions organized in this country? How does a person become a member? What issues are considered the most critical by the unions, and what is the current focus of their efforts? Who runs the unions?
- What impact does this country's cultural or religious environment have on labor decisions?

- What impact does this country's physical or natural environment have on labor decisions?
- What impact does this country's economic and political environments have on labor decisions?
- What is the general response in this country to unions or other forms of employee association?

Information relating to each country in which a program is located is provided in this vein at this book's website located at http://pres.depaul.edu/hartman/beyondsweatshops/countryreports.

Study Limitations

This project seeks not to find a *middle ground* between all of the apparently competing interests, but instead to find the *highest ground for all* in terms of respect for the rights of workers, return on investment for the owners of enterprises, and consideration for the preferences of consumers. The project strives to evaluate the economic implications of substandard conditions, and to search for ways to balance those considerations with ethical imperatives. We hope to have documented a set of realistic solutions to the challenge of global labor conditions that will enable organizations to conduct business profitably, ethically, and with accountability in developing economies.

Limitation regarding Scope of Study Topics

This study does *not* purport to suggest that any one solution is the best solution to a particular labor challenge posed by contemporary corporate globalization. In fact, by virtue of its research process, in some instances the study does not have the capacity to evaluate the ultimate efficacy of the particular program in alleviating concerns regarding wage levels or maximum hours worked—some of the most challenging issues facing MNEs. This is a substantial shortcoming of this study; however, it is due to the fact that few systematic corporate programs regarding this issue are available for study. On the other hand, ameliorating living conditions through better working conditions goes far beyond wages and hours, alone.[33] It is arguable that, in fact, providing value such as educational opportunities and health benefits are *more* critical to personal development than are wages since the former two benefits can help to break the cycle that constrains these individuals in their current environments.

Limitation regarding Organizations That Were Included

The specific programs chosen for inclusion in this research were identified through a combination of investigation and access. Believing that intense media scrutiny might force subject firms to be creative in their responses to common globalization challenges, the series investigators, through independent research, identified several firms whose labor practices were subject to media scrutiny over the past several years. From this group, the investigators sought to learn how these firms responded to exposure and what they were doing currently in this area. From the subgroup of those firms that were actively engaged in alternative management solutions, the investigators sought access to workplaces and management for further research.

This process of inclusion necessarily has limitations. For instance, if a firm denied the investigators full access to all workplaces chosen by the investigators, that organization could not be included in the study. Similarly, if the laudable activities of a firm in this regard have not been made public, the investigators of course would not have included it in the original group. Moreover, it cannot be stated clearly enough that inclusion of a program in this text should not serve as a blanket certification that all programs initiated by this firm should serve as model programs, nor that this particular firm has always and will always engage in ethical conduct.

Critics of MNEs abound; critics of the firms represented in this book abound. Firms were not excluded from this volume simply because some NGOs or other stakeholders were unhappy with some of the activities of the subject firms. We sought activities that evidenced moral imagination and that were replicable by MNE managers and others who might seek similar solutions. Though it is important to address the valid concerns of NGOs or other critics of MNEs (and, in fact, this is precisely the subject of some of the contributors' previous work), providing a systematic response to these NGO or other critics with regard to any activities that did not fit into this category is outside the scope of this book.

Limitations regarding Third-Party Verification

The objective served by this study was to identify possible alternative practices for consideration by management when faced with labor challenges. Funding for the study from the Ethics Resource Center supported the identification and description of these programs or activities. Our aim was to document and to explain the *operation* of programs designed to address labor problems associated with globalization; our aim was not to conduct systematic investigations of the effectiveness of these programs. To do the latter would have required a level of investigation into technical aspects of working conditions in factories that is beyond the scope of this study. We have, of course, been able to make some assessments regarding the actual impact these programs have had and these do appear to be positive. Moreover, we are sufficiently confident in the design and purpose of these programs to suggest that they merit consideration by other

MNEs as potential models for addressing labor, health, safety, and environmental problems in a developing country context.

Each program analysis therefore verifies the existence of the particular program, the validity of its claims regarding basic factual matters, and the ascertainable impact of the program on its participants. While the series investigators did interview program participants and others affected whenever possible, and sought objective perspectives on each program, the research would benefit from future third-party verification of the long-term impact of each program. As such, the editors and contributors to this text strongly encourage follow-up studies of the programs included herein for the purpose of providing additional details, information, and assessment.

NOTES

1. Mary Robinson, "Beyond Good Intentions: Corporate Citizenship for a New Century," World Leaders Lecture to the Royal Society for the Encouragement of Arts, Manufacturers and Commerce, London (7 May 2002) http://www.bsr.org/BSRResources/Magazine/Columnists.cfm?DocumentID = 842&DocumentType ID = 23.

2. There is little doubt, at least, that the trend has been toward globalization. Between 1990 and 1998, global foreign direct investment inflows increased 291 percent; world merchandise exports increased 212 percent; and the average daily currency turnover increased 283 percent. William Halal and Kenneth Taylor, "21st Century Economics: A Synthesis of Progressive Economic Thought," *Business and Society Review* 107, no. 2 (Summer 2002): 255–74, p. 260.

3. National Center for Policy Analysis, "Sweatshops Offer Ways to Survive," citing Alan R. Myerson, "In Principle, a Case For More 'Sweatshops,'" *New York Times*, 22 June 1997, online version: http://www.ncpa.org/pd/pdint152.html.

4. Ibid.

5. Steven Chapman, "How Americans Can Stop Child Labor Abroad," *Chicago Tribune*, 4 December 1994, p. 3.

6. International Labour Organization, *World Employment Report 1998–1999* (Geneva: International Labour Organization, 1999) p. v.

7. Development can also take place for reasons other than a pure cost advantage. As we have seen in Asia, the investment climate is equally important, where FDI decisions reflect real as well as perceived risks, for example, political stability, the rule of law, exchange rate stability, market intervention, or monopoly structures.

8. Joel Oestreich, "What Can Businesses Do to Appease Anti-Globalization Protestors?" *Business and Society Review* 107, no. 2 (Summer 2002): 207–20, p. 207.

9. Thomas Donaldson, "Values in Tension: Ethics Away from Home," *Harvard Business Review* (September 1996): pp. 48, 58.

10. United Nations Department of Public Information, "Universal Declaration of Human Rights," http://www.unhchr.ch/udhr/lang/eng.htm (accessed 31 July 2002).

11. Perhaps the most well known criticism of positive right may be found in the early work of Robert Nozick. See Robert Nozick, *Anarchy, State, and Utopia* (New York: Basic Books, 1974).

12. Alan Gewirth, *Reason and Morality* (Chicago, Ill.: University of Chicago Press, 1978); and Henry Shue, *Basic Rights* (Princeton, N.J.: Princeton University Press, 1980). A more detailed discussion of these perspectives can be found in chapter 4.

13. See Amartya Sen, "Human Rights and Asian Values," in *Business Ethics in the Global Marketplace*, ed. Tibor R. Machan (Stanford, Calif.: Hoover Institution Press, 1999), pp. 37–62. See also chapter 4 of the present volume.

14. Thomas Donaldson and Thomas W. Dunfee, *Ties that Bind: A Social Contracts Approach to Business Ethics* (Cambridge, Mass.: Harvard Business School Press, 1999).

15. Laura P. Hartman, Bill Shaw, and Rodney Stevenson, "Exploring the Ethics and Economics of Global Labor Standards: A Challenge to Integrated Social Contract Theory," *Business Ethics Quarterly* 13, no. 2 (2003): 193–220.

16. Andrew Wilson, "Special Report: Business and Human Rights," *Corporate Social Responsibility Magazine, Special Report* 2, no. 1 (2001): p. 7.

17. Jerry Sternin and Robert Choo, "The Power of Positive Deviancy," *Harvard Business Review* (January/February 2000), reprint F00101.

18. Sternin and Choo, "Power of Positive Deviancy," p. 3.

19. Illustrations are drawn from an ongoing research program by the Management and Corporate Citizenship Programme, International Labour Office, Geneva, Switzerland, in cooperation with the Center for Corporate Citizenship. Researchers from this program have interviewed over 100 managers, workers, and union representatives in visits to corporate headquarters of numerous multinationals and their purchasing offices and factories in China, Vietnam, and Thailand, where products are actually manufactured. See also Corporate Social Responsibility—Europe, "Business and Human Rights Programme," (2001), http://www.csreurope.org/csr_europe/activities/Programmes/humanrights/humanrights.htm. In addition, strong case support for these contentions can be found in International Finance Corporation, Instituto Ethos and SustainAbility, "Developing Value: The Business Case for Sustainability in Emerging Markets," (July 2002), available at http://www.ifc.org/sustainability/docs/Developing_Value_Final.pdf.

20. Turgut Guvenli and Rajib Sanyal, "Ethical Concerns in International Business: Are Some Issues More Important than Others?" *Business and Society Review* 107, no. 2 (Summer 2002): pp. 195–206.

21. Guvenli and Sanyal, "Ethical Concerns in International Business," p. 201.

22. In addition, Shell publishes a report titled "Business and Child Labor: A Management Primer," which outlines the challenges of child labor facing management in a variety of countries. Of particular interest is the fact that Shell admits in the primer that there is no easy answer. The primer notes that terminating the children might have an enormous and unintended financial impact on the families of those workers; yet it also acknowledges the fact that Shell does not allow children working at its or its suppliers' sites—a dilemma addressed in greater detail in the later adidas case found in this volume.

23. International Finance Corporation, "Developing Value."

24. Ibid.

25. See matrix in International Finance Corporation, "Developing Value."

26. adidas-Salomon customarily uses a lower-case "a" to begin its name.

27. adidas-Salomon, "Clearer: Social and Environmental Report 2001" (Herzogenaurach, Germany: adidas-Salomon, 2000).

28. John Browne, "The Role of Multinational Corporations in Economic and Social Development of Poor Countries," presentation at Harvard University, 3 April 2002 (http://www.ethicalcorp.com/printtemplate.asp?idnum = 206).

29. Browne, "Role of Multinational Corporations."

30. "Responsible Care" is a registered trademark.

31. Business Partners for Development, "Results and Recommendations for Businesses" (2002) http://www.bpdweb.org/docs/biz4of5.pdf (accessed 1 August 2002), p. 9.

32. See, for example, Oestreich, "What Can Businesses Do?" Oestreich contends that, while the antiglobalization contingent argues for higher wages and conditions, those contentions are based on a uniquely Western idea of how to combine efficiency with justice and shaped by the nineteenth- and twentieth-century American and European experience. He suggests, in the alternative, that "what is being demanded focuses on cultural and structural issues far more sweeping than traditional union demands." Ibid.

33. See, for example, Hartman, Shaw, and Stevenson, "Exploring the Ethics and Economics of Global Labor Standards"; and Denis G. Arnold and Norman E. Bowie, "Sweatshops and Respect for Persons," Business Ethics Quarterly, v. 13, no. 2 (April 2003): 221–42.

PART I

Perspectives on Global Labor Practices and Challenges

## CHAPTER 2

The Global Context: Multinational Enterprises, Labor Standards, and Regulation

Jill Murray[1]

INTRODUCTION

The aim of this chapter is to place into context the role of multinational enterprises (MNEs) and their efforts to implement global labor standards. It provides a broad picture of the kinds of labor abuses that exist in the world today and then charts the rise of interest in the "new sweatshop," particularly the potentially controversial case in which powerful MNEs from the developed world manufacture consumer goods through a globalized subcontracting chain. The relationship between these two issues—labor abuses and certain MNEs—is then considered. Many academic disciplines, including economics, international trade theory, business ethics, moral philosophy, labor law, and development policy, hold powerful and sometimes conflicting views about what this relationship is and should be in. In an attempt to clarify the obligations of MNEs, the scope and meaning of international labor law are discussed. Finally, the chapter suggests the kinds of steps firms should take if they wish to act in accordance with the articulated norms of "decent work."[2] The focus of the chapter will be on labor standards per se, including the fundamental principles and rights identified by the International Labour Organization. These instruments are, of course, grounded in the human rights regime, which is discussed in more detail in chapter 4.

SCOPE OF THE PROBLEM

Unfortunately, it is easy to paint a picture of labor suffering in the contemporary world.[3] This picture exists both at the level of aggregate statistics, and in the detail of labor violations by individual states and firms as experienced by individual workers, their families, and communities. There are some evident regional and subregional patterns here (for example, the poorest nations in the world continue to suffer from a general lack of economic development), yet many commentators stress that the "decent work deficit" exists in all states, developed and developing alike.[4]

According to the International Labour Organization (ILO), some 250 million children working throughout the world are "deprived of adequate education, good health and basic freedoms."[5] Neil Kearney, General Secretary of the International Textile, Garment and Leather-Workers' Federation, writes of children in the Philippines who "from the age of four work 11 hours a day stitching dresses for the dolls of children of the same age in industrialized countries. These youngsters have barely enough to enable them to eat. They suffer from back pains and hand cramps. They are stopped from going to the toilet. They are beaten when they make mistakes."[6]

Failure to provide a healthy and safe working environment continues to ruin and even claim lives. The ILO reports that "every year about 250 million workers suffer accidents in the course of their work, and over 300,000 are killed. Taking account of those who succumb to occupational disease, the death toll is over 1 million people a year."[7]

Many workers in developing countries receive extremely low pay and are subject to poor working conditions, in both relative and absolute terms. There is a growing literature on the conditions of workers in the factories producing for developed world MNEs, including assessments by activist nongovernmental organizations (NGOs) such as the groups NikeWatch, Sweatshop Watch, National Labor Committee, and others. Though refuted by the organizations NikeWatch challenges, the group's most recent report in relation to wages in an Indonesian factory producing for Nike and adidas found that although minimum wage laws were met, rates of pay were so low that unreasonable amounts of overtime were necessary to attain a living wage. For example, workweeks of 70 hours and over were common.[8]

In research that the current contributor is undertaking, some Chinese factories that produce for the Australian market were found to require workers to live in extremely spartan and unhealthy conditions. For example, workers were given only a small ration of water with which to serve all their needs (washing, cooking, cleaning). Authoritarian control and arbitrary discipline are also observed problems in some of these Chinese factories, as they are in others throughout the world. In such circumstances, it is impossible for workers to attain the freedom and dignity that the international human rights regime ensures them.[9]

In some countries, workers who try to band together in trade unions to collectively bargain for better conditions are often punished for their efforts. Every year, the ILO deals with reports of countries in which these fundamental human rights are breached. In some cases, we see that freedom of association is simply not possible because of the legal regime established in a particular country as a whole. Indeed, most trade union movements have grown in the face of initial state opposition (including, for example, in Chile and South Korea).[10] China is an important example because it is now the highest recipient of foreign direct investment (FDI) in the developing world.[11] In China, the All China Federation of Trade Unions has a state-sanctioned monopoly on union activity, and Zhu and Campbell conclude that "safeguarding the legitimate interests of employees is strictly a subsidiary role" to other functions, including ensuring worker discipline and output.[12] In other cases, abuses can occur at the level of the firm either despite government policy or with its implicit collusion. It is claimed that workers in an Indonesian factory supplying Nike and adidas are "afraid that involvement in union activities could endanger their lives."[13] Kearney describes an instance of such abuse at that factory:

Carmen Rosario is a small, frail teenager working in the Dominican Republic's garment industry. She started work at 13 and endured some horrendous conditions, until, together with colleagues, she . . . began to organize a union. Her employers embarked on a campaign of intimidation and harassment, culminating in late 1997 in an attack by hired thugs using baseball bats with nails driven through them. Carmen suffered multiple injuries, including a broken arm. Her co-worker, Ingrid Bastardo, who was seven months pregnant, was beaten and punched and kicked in the stomach.[14]

Even in instances in which firms have committed themselves to upholding the principle of freedom of association (for example, in a corporate code of conduct), there may be many obstacles to achieving practical implementation on the ground.[15]

The right of workers to work free from discrimination is also often violated in both developing and developed countries. Labor markets continue to be segregated along gender lines, with women performing the most precarious and least well paid work.[16] The issues of discrimination with which firms must deal can arise in a range of circumstances. One MNE studied by the present author had investigated the opening of a mine in the Philippines. MNE representatives negotiated with local leaders in the remote region and agreed to take on a workforce. Because of existing gender roles in the local culture, the firm was offered an exclusively male workforce. Ensuring equality of opportunity in such circumstances is a difficult challenge for a corporation.[17] Moreover, Kearney describes instances of assault on the reproductive rights of workers: "In Mexico, young women workers were subjected to compulsory pregnancy tests monthly. . . . In a Guatemala City plant, a supervisor routinely punched young women workers in the stomach each fortnight to seek out those who might be pregnant."[18] Sexual harassment and violence at work is also a continuing problem. For example, Connor reports that "workers who want to claim legally-mandated menstrual leave must still go through the humiliating process of proving they are menstruating by pulling down their pants in front of female factory doctors."[19]

Forced labor (including bonded labor and slavery) still exists. Some countries are accused of systemic use of unfree labor, including China[20] and Burma (Myanmar).[21] In June 2002 ILO's Committee of Experts cited Sudan as failing to abide by the core labor convention on forced labor, and noted the existence of "practices of abduction, trafficking and forced labor affecting thousands of women and children."[22] In the developed world, the use of involuntary prison labor in privately run prisons is a re-emerging problem.[23] Concern is not limited to state violations of workers' rights. Claims that amount to "an allegation of participation in slave trading" have also been made, for example, claims of collusion between an American MNE and the ruling junta in Burma.[24]

To attract FDI, some states create areas known as export processing zones (EPZs), in which some domestic labor regulations may not apply.[25] In some countries, such as Bangladesh, the EPZs are completely excluded from the operation of domestic labor law. A report from the Organization for Economic Co-operation and Development (OECD) states that there are over one thousand EPZs in the world, employing 27 million people.[26]

At the same time as these alleged abuses are occurring, many suffer from poverty and all of the associated disadvantages that come from the lack of work. Some 150 million people in the world are fully unemployed, and many millions more suffer from underemployment.[27] Women are more likely to be in marginal low-paid jobs, and are more likely to be out of work.[28] About half a billion workers "cannot earn enough to raise their families above the $1(U.S.)-a-day poverty line."[29] The poorest region in the world, Sub-Saharan Africa, made little economic progress during the 1990s.[30] That is, although we can identify a policy concern with the suffering of workers, we can also identify an interest in ensuring that the opportunities that work can bring are more evenly distributed over the globe. In economic and development theory there are highly developed debates about mechanisms of job creation, and whether or not the *quality* of employment should be compromised to achieve a greater *quantity* of jobs. Some suggest a trade-off between the two. This chapter is written from the perspective adopted by ILO, which is that a minimum floor of protection is an end in itself, and is also likely to contribute to levels of productivity to support economic growth.

LINKING LABOR ABUSES WITH THE MNE

"New Sweatshop" Discourse

When the role of the MNE is considered in relation to the statistics and vignettes related above, several things must be borne in mind. First, labor abuses may occur in domestic enterprises that produce solely for the home market of a particular country, and therefore the link between globalized economic forces and domestic labor exploitation may be indirect or irrelevant. Indeed, it is most likely that the law of the economic jungle operates with least restraint in the dark corners of the unregulated "informal" sector producing goods and services for the home market. In some of the poorest countries in the world, this sector is the largest source of jobs.

Second, the MNE is not the single, monolithic entity it is sometimes portrayed as being. Transnational business relations exist in many different forms, each of which may present a different mode of interaction between actors in different countries. Not all MNEs are large; some MNEs are small or medium-sized enterprises (for example, importing firms that operate small purchasing and contract compliance operations in a number of countries). Not all MNEs are engaged (directly or indirectly) in manufacturing; indeed, a rising proportion operate in the services sector.[31] Not all MNEs engage staff through direct employment or subcontracting; other modes, such as the use of franchise or locally run joint venture, may be used. The level of foreign ownership and control of any particular transnational enterprise will vary across a wide spectrum, as will the culture instigated through these arrangements at the enterprise level. Despite the upsurge in information about the MNE and globalization, little is known about the employment practices of many internationalizing firms.[32]

Despite the probability that a great deal of suffering arises in domestic business and in areas with little or no employment, and despite the complexity and breadth of MNE structure and activity, public and academic attention is often focused on one particular issue: MNE's treatment of workers in factories in the developing world who produce goods for sale (mostly in the developed world). Within this narrow category, special attention is focused on the sector involving textile, clothing, and footwear manufacture. Within *this* group, the high-profile companies who are producing famous brand-name commodities sold in the developed world have found themselves in the eye of the storm over the globalization of labor and its exploitation by MNEs. This book is itself a product of this highly specialized interest. It is claimed by some that transnational production is achieving high profits at the expense of worker welfare in the same way that early capitalism exploited the vulnerable more than a hundred years ago. The new sweatshops are now seen as "part and parcel of the globalized expansion of the bottom of the industrial pyramid."[33]

The reasons for the reversion to the language of the sweatshop are clear. First, there has been a significant shift in the modes of production for goods in the clothing, textile, and footwear sectors; with lowering barriers to international flows of goods, services, and capital, some corporations have chosen to shift production from their home country to host states in which production costs (especially labor costs) are lower.[34] Thus, the claim of "factory-less" production is one of the key symbols of globalization for many: the multinational company that directly employs no manufacturing workers yet relies on the labor of such workers who are employed in factories in the developing world.[35] Second, the power imbalance between extremely large, profitable developed-world firms and the producing factory workers in developing countries is stark. Third, the problems of regulation and accountability arising from the subcontracting production chain have added to the public attention on such firms, particularly in light of claims that the MNE actually employs no one to produce its goods. The idea that responsibility can be outsourced along with production has proved untenable. Nike's experience with this issue evidenced this conclusion. Fourth, there remain conflicting interests in local and national governments that are not necessarily aligned with the interests of the workers themselves. Finally, the MNE producers of high-profile branded goods have been the subject of spectacular revelations about the unacceptable conditions in some of their supplying factories.[36]

As commentators have noted of the nineteenth-century discourse on sweated labor, this revived concern about sweatshops involves the *selection* and *construction* of particular issues from the enormous range of available evidence. Now, as then, the workers studied through the sweated labor lens—usually women producing textiles, clothing, and footwear—are a small minority of vulnerable workers.[37] The focus on manufacturing factories may tend to obscure other modes of labor exploitation, for example, the trading of women's labor in the domestic service, sex work, and "entertainment" industries.[38] Indeed, the manufacturing sector "covers only a minority of employees in most countries and its wages are often unrepresentative of the overall labor market."[39]

Issues Raised by the Sweatshop Charge

The sweated labor discourse has retained its power as a rallying point for social activism.[40] We are familiar with tracts, such as the following, which point out the disjunction between the wages earned by the producing workers and the final cost to developed-world consumers of the products made:

In a Chinese factory producing Disney toys, a seventeen year old girl earns just over £1a day. She works on average eleven hours a day, seven days a week. When she finishes her day's work she sleeps in a ten by twelve foot room with eleven colleagues. There is no private toilet.... A Chinese toy worker would have to work three months to earn as much as we spend on toys for one child at Christmas.[41]

While such statements paint a vivid picture that strongly suggests undesirable labor practices, closer attention reveals that the conclusions we can reasonably draw from these facts are more complex. What if, for example, the local minimum wage was less than £1 a day? In this case, the employing company may be providing a higher standard than required by domestic law. Some empirical work including the cases discussed in this text show that, in general, "multinational enterprises have higher wages and better benefits than domestic firms."[42]

We are not told what the local cost of living is, and therefore have no basis on which to assess the adequacy of the wage in terms of worker need. Even if we found that £1 per day was insufficient to support a decent life, what conclusions flow? Some have argued that even sweatshop employment is preferable to no employment at all, and may be ultimately productive of positive economic change.[43] The issue of hours of work is also difficult to assess without more information; for example, one week's work involving these hours would not necessarily breach minimum standards in the developed world, including the European Union's Working Time Directive.[44] It is not always a common practice to assess the adequacy of workers' wages with reference to the value of the product they make; automobile workers in countries like the United States and Australia would also have to work for several months before their pay is the equivalent of the cost of one of the cars they make. Moreover, it may be years before such workers could accrue the *disposable* income to make such a purchase.

Finally, we do not know what the worker described above thought about her work. Was her job a crushing burden undertaken out of sheer necessity? Was it a better alternative than other available work or unemployment? Was it a pathway to a better job, or a dead end? What did *she* want from her working life in general and from that job in particular? If, for example, the firm proposed a trade-off between hours and pay, which would she choose?

To all these questions can be added others of greater moral depth and complexity for the corporation. For example, even if the local laws sanctioned the apparently low wage and long hours, were the worker's conditions *morally right*, given the corporation's capacity to pay and its obligations under international law (discussed below)? Even if this job was a better (and perhaps chosen) alternative for the worker, should a firm exploit such local low standards and life choices when it is able to do more? How much more is enough? And across what range of issues should the firm consider such questions—just the central issues of pay and hours? What about maternity leave, training and development, job security, health and safety, sickness and unemployment insurance, worker participation and industrial democracy, the right to work free from harassment and arbitrary discipline, the right to join a trade union? What about general assistance to the community at large beyond the workplace, as was proposed by codes such as the Sullivan Principles for firms operating in South Africa under the apartheid regime?[45] What happens when the local regulatory environment actively prevents the corporation from doing what it thinks is right in one of these areas?

These questions raise issues that cut across many academic and public policy disciplines (economics, philosophy, development theory, international trade theory, and so on). Within these disciplines there is a range of views about the benefits of transnational business activity for workers.[46]

However, it would be wrong to see the MNE as reaching decisions about its corporate responsibilities in a regulatory vacuum, or simply selecting from among the various competing theories when deciding what its role should be. MNEs do not have to construct their responsibilities to labor in a vacuum. It is necessary to recognize that a legitimate and widely accepted regime of international labor law, recently bolstered, provides a framework in which firms should make their decisions. It is to this regime that we now turn.

INTERNATIONAL LABOR LAW AND THE ROLE OF MNES

The Nature of International Labor Standards

Before the nature of MNEs' legal obligations is outlined, it is necessary to set out some of the background on the nature of the regime of international labor law and the principles on which it is based. A thorough understanding of both the letter and spirit of these laws and principles is critical, given the complex regulatory environment in which firms operate.

As states began to move into a modern regulatory mode following the industrial revolution, the arena of labor regulation was predominately national. That is, over time in developed countries, it came to be agreed that the state should intervene to ensure a floor of labor standards below which no one should fall, either directly through legislation or indirectly through state support of collective bargaining.[47] Over the course of the nineteenth century, however, concerns about the impact of competition *between* states grew. It was feared that without some way of coordinating state actions, no state could afford to institute higher labor standards for fear that it would be at a competitive disadvantage in relation to states that maintained lower standards.[48] Thus, current concerns about a regulatory "race to the bottom" have a long history.

The ILO was created in 1919, in part, in response to that concern. The ILO's constitution states that "the failure of any nation to adopt humane conditions of labor is an obstacle in the way of other nations which desire to improve conditions in their own countries."[49] Despite this overt reference, the contradictory desire of the founding nations to protect their national sovereignty in labor matters meant that the ILO was not given the binding powers it would need to guarantee the implementation of international labor law. Rather, the ILO was structured in such a way that its member states retained the choice of whether or not to adopt the instruments (conventions) created by the International Labour Conference, the ILO's rule-making body. The exception to this general rule was that all member states were regarded as being bound to uphold the principle of freedom of association, whether or not the relevant conventions had been adopted by the national authorities, on the grounds that adherence to this principle was inherent in the organization's constitution. There are no binding mechanisms in the ILO supervisory structure to enforce conventions once adopted. Rather the ILO relies on a sophisticated system of monitoring and reporting and on enforcement through national legal systems.[50]

The centrality of the principle of freedom of association to the ILO's philosophy is critical to an understanding of the system of international labor law. In declaring that "labor is not a commodity," the ILO meant that labor market outcomes should be mediated having regard to certain values, including the dignity and independence of labor. The process by which these values are to be given expression in the workplace is that of free collective bargaining, in which workers are entitled to representation by trade unions of their own choosing.[51] As this author has written elsewhere,

The underlying philosophy of the ILO . . . was that, "absent the state," the status quo is an imbalance of power which favored the employer over the employee. If a particular state has not been willing or able to create a legal and social environment in which the right to freedom of association is realizable, then nothing exists to counter the power of the employer. . . . What corporate codes of conduct must do, therefore, is to *effectively self-limit the firm's power* to ensure that a more equalized balance can emerge from the collective representation of workers and those affected by its operations. The likelihood of this occurring voluntarily is, of course, a matter of concern for many activists, and the reason why very few commentators are willing to consign all labor regulation to the sole responsibility of firms.[52]

It is important to recognize, then, that the primary obligations for guaranteeing labor rights and the processes of their collective determination fall on states, not firms. ILO conventions are international labor rules *ad-dressed to states*.[53] (That is not to say that some provisions of some conventions do not specify obligations on employers.[54] This issue is discussed further below.)

The importance of this fact can be seen in a number of instances. First, some of the terms of the conventions specify fundamental human rights; the right is expressed in a form that requires certain limitations on state power for its full achievement.[55] It is not theoretically or practically possible for non-state actors to guarantee such rights. Generally speaking, firms are not able themselves to limit state power in the ways defined by the convention, and the use of such corporate power in the context of democratic government is likely to be problematic. For example, in a state in which the legal regime constrains freedom of association, such as China, even the best-intentioned firm cannot achieve true freedom of association for its workers. It is not possible for a firm to end the criminalization of nonsanctioned union activity in that country, even if the firm were willing to deal with any nonsanctioned union joined by its workers.

Second, some of the core conventions require the creation of national policies that, by their very nature, are beyond the scope of firms to devise and implement. An illustrative example is the requirement that ratifying states "declare and pursue a national policy designed to promote, by methods appropriate to national conditions and practice, equality of opportunity. . . ."[56] In the absence of an effective national policy of that kind, a workplace policy of gender equality may be simply unable to alter the effects of gender discrimination (e.g., in relation to access to education) in that country.

Third, some of the core conventions permit the ratifying state to select from among an array of regulatory options, usually after consulting representatives of workers and employers. It is unlikely that an individual actor (such as a multinational corporation) would have the knowledge or expertise to make such a selection, and in any event the ILO does not recognize the legitimacy of non-state actors in unilaterally making such decisions. The clearest example of regulatory choice in a core convention can be seen in relation to child labor; here, states can select from a range of minima, depending on their view of their level of economic development and general social progress (such as the extent to which the education system has evolved). For example, the core convention states, "A Member [state] whose economy and administrative facilities are insufficiently developed may, after consultation with the organizations of employers and workers concerned, where such exist, initially limit the scope of application of this Convention."[57]

In summary, then, the system of international labor regulation *is* a system; it is not a set of specific rules that itemize good and bad behavior of firms. The system relies on and is a constituent of the national realm of labor law. It also relies on and is constitutive of the development of collective labor relations at the national and transnational level. The aim of such relations is to secure fairness and dignity at work—the goal of decent work as recently restated by the ILO's Director General, Juan Somavia.[58]

The Core Labor Standards Revolution

In 1996 an influential report from the Organisation for Economic Co-operation and Development (OECD) noted, "The debate on trade and labor standards has been made more complex because of a lack of agreement on a list of the labor standards that are relevant to this issue and their definition."[59] A mere four years later the OECD noted, "The international community has made significant progress in developing a consensus with respect to the definition and recognition of a small set of core labor standards."[60] In 1998 the ILO created its Declaration on Fundamental Principles and Rights at Work, which definitively identified those ILO conventions (in the areas of forced labor, child labor, discrimination, and freedom of association) that were "core."[61] This refocusing of the ILO's efforts and organizational structure has achieved a significant increase in state ratification of the core labor standards, and renewed efforts aimed at achieving the full implementation of conventions once ratified. For example, the new Convention on The Worst Forms of Child Labor has been ratified by over 70 countries since its creation in 1999, "the fastest ratification rate of any Convention in ILO history."[62]

There has also been an upsurge of international and intergovernmental support for the ILO's Declaration. In recent years the World Bank has sought to integrate respect for the core labor standards into its policies and has prepared some interesting materials that are designed to explain how the core standards work.[63] The European Commission has released a Communication that confirms the European Union's (EU) support for the universality of the ILO's core labor standards and proposes a range of measures to support their implementation.[64] The link between trade preferences and labor standards in the EU's relations with non-European states is being reviewed to ensure that all elements of the ILO core conventions are equally weighted in the various agreements.[65] The 2001 UN Conference on the Least Developed Countries devised a plan that called for states to "respect, promote and realize" the core labor conventions as set out in the ILO Declaration.[66] The meeting of G8 ministers in 1999 declared that "core labor standards should be respected wherever a person works so as to help share prosperity in a globalized world."[67] The leaders of the states represented at the Third Summit of the Americas held in 2001 declared that they were committed to "promoting compliance with internationally recognized core labor standards" of the ILO Declaration,[68] as did the Organization of American States General Assembly.[69]

A New Focus on Corporate Self-Regulation

This period, which saw the refocusing of the ILO's attention on its core labor standards, also saw a rise in interest in the role private economic actors, especially firms, could play in securing labor (and other) standards.[70] Corporate codes of conduct have been increasingly used by firms, especially those operating from America. Important support for such private initiatives has also been expressed at national,[71] international,[72] and intergovernmental levels (see below). The new significance placed on corporate codes of conduct has been welcomed by some as an opportunity to expand the scope of regulation, particularly into the difficult-to-regulate informal sectors.[73] Others have expressed concern that this process is being touted as an alternative to state regulation, thus hastening the apparent crisis in governance by the state identified in some of the globalization literature.[74] As noted above, it is counterproductive to suggest that firms can be seen as the sole implementers of the core labor standards, so from both theoretical and practical perspectives it is necessary to see corporate efforts as part of a regulatory continuum.

These two trends—the clarification of the identity of core labor standards and the renewed focus on the firm as a significant actor in achieving them—led to the revitalization of instruments designed to guide the decision making of firms in relation to labor practices. The two most significant of these instruments are OECD's Guidelines for Multinational Enterprises[75] (which was revised in 2000 in such a way as to strengthen its links to the ILO core standards) and the ILO's Tripartite Declaration on Multinational Enterprises.[76] The former document takes the form of a recommendation from OECD member states to firms that operate in or from their territory. While it is not binding, it is an authoritative statement of the expectations of OECD governments, and its national supervisory structure has been strengthened of late.[77]

The Role of Firms

Assess the National Environment

To be most effective, both from an internal and an external perspective, and to address some of the labor challenges to which the cases in this book respond, MNEs must start with some knowledge of the labor regimes in the countries in which they seek to operate. In some cases, an MNE will simply move into that system as if it were a domestic enterprise (for example, by engaging local labor experts to draw up contracts, negotiate with labor officials, and so on). When entering a market, the first responsibility of firms will be to obey national laws or to suffer the penalties within national systems of enforcement.[78] This stricture is complicated in two ways. First, in most of the world, there is a "law–practice gap" between the letter of the law and its implementation.[79] We see this gap often in connection with the actual "permissibility" of (though legal prohibition against) child labor in some developing countries. In such cases the firm may have a choice between acting within the sphere of domestic legal regulation or operating outside it in line with existing local norms. In countries in which legal systems are known to be undeveloped and in which the law–practice gap is recognized as being wide, the firm has a heightened responsibility to act in ways that are consistent with its obligations and the dictates of international labor and human rights law.

Second, national laws may conflict with international norms even when they are fully and properly applied in the domestic sphere. It is not uncommon for national minimum wage provisions to set a rate of pay lower than that needed to provide for the level of protection sought in international human rights instruments.[80] This circumstance provides a clear example of the moral obligation on the firm to *do more* by attempting to ensure that the international labor rules are respected, notwithstanding the relevant domestic laws.

Assess the Application of the Core Labor and Human Rights Standards

As we have seen, international labor law coexists with domestic labor law systems. In instances in which there are gross failures in national law and practice, it may be that all that stands between workers and their complete subjugation are the rights and principles enunciated through the international system. Firms have a prima facie obligation to educate themselves about the terms and generally accepted meanings of the relevant provisions of these international instruments. This obligation derives from the interpenetration of international labor law in the domestic realm of the countries in which the firms operate. Just as they should have appropriate regard for domestic legal requirements, they also need to understand the international principles that apply in that state. Further, some international instruments directly address firms, including the OECD Guidelines for Multinational Enterprises. The guidelines require firms to "respect the human rights of those affected by their activities consistent with the host government's international obligations and commitments."[81] Similar appeals to firms are made in the United Nation's Global Compact.[82]

In considering whether to invest in, operate from, or purchase goods and services from a particular state, firms should have regard for the level of abuses of these fundamental labor rules. A threshold decision must be made as to whether or not it is morally possible or legally prudent to engage in economic activity in countries in which systematic, serious fundamental labor violations occur.[83] For example, systemic systems of discrimination such as those that existed in South Africa under the apartheid regime or systems of forced labor that continue in Myanmar (Burma) have led to widespread calls for businesses not to invest and consumers not to purchase goods produced under such conditions. Such decisions need not be taken in isolation, as in most cases there will be a wealth of material and advice on which the firm can draw. The strengthening of institutions at the national level (such as the Ethical Trading Initiative in Britain) and the international level (such as the ILO's Business and Decent Work program) has meant that resources available to firms now have a more practical focus in helping firms and others identify ethical choices.

However, in today's world there are comparatively few countries that are regarded as so completely lacking in respect for human rights that there is broad consensus against the advisability of business investment in them. For example, the use of prison labor in China to produce goods for export has been of concern for some time; but countries such as the United States have chosen a policy of engagement rather than one of mandatory disinvestments (as was ultimately proposed in relation to the former South African regime). Thus China retains its most favored nation status as a trading partner of the United States. MNEs may therefore find themselves operating in countries that permit or even encourage some labor and human rights abuses at work. What, then, is the role of the firm?

It was shown above that firms cannot "uphold" or "adopt" the ILO core labor standards in isolation from states. Their obligation, particularly in the absence of state support, is to actively work to secure the rights, freedoms, principles, and standards implicit in the ILO core to the extent possible in their sphere of influence. They should not commit to the letter of the core labor and human rights standards, but should instead embrace the spirit of these standards in a way that will establish meaningful action in the absence of state compliance. Generally speaking, firms should also consider wider societal action to lobby for changes to state policy in line with the ILO core, or support multilateral or intergovernmental efforts aimed at that end.

The actual micropolicies this will evolve in each firm will depend on the nature of the national and workplace contexts. So, in relation to freedom of association, although it would be appropriate for a state to proclaim that it upheld freedom of association, the obligation for MNEs is not limited to a passive acceptance of the principle. Where there are problems for worker organization and "voice" in a particular national culture, the MNE's responsibility is to ensure that systems and processes are created to provide equivalent rights (so far as is possible). Putting up a notice stating that "freedom of association is respected" is of little use—positive steps must be taken to ensure that workers' genuine collective interests are respected. The OECD Guidelines on MNEs elaborate what the principles of freedom of association and the right to collectively bargain mean for firms; for example, MNEs have a positive obligation to "engage in constructive negotiations . . . with representatives with a view to reaching agreements on employment conditions."[84]

In relation to child labor, the OECD Guidelines also serve to define firm-level actions in line with the principles of the ILO: MNEs have a positive obligation to *"contribute to* the effective abolition of child labor."[85] A similar formulation exists in relation to forced labor and the requirement to avoid discrimination. Just how the firm is to contribute to the effective abolition of these labor abuses is not specified in detail, yet the obligation to make an effective (and therefore real) contribution is clear. How the individual firm adapts to these requirements will depend on all the circumstances of its operations: whether or not children (as defined) are routinely used in the MNEs' supplying factories, the kinds of community programs available to support the replacement of child labor, and state and other support that would promote the kind of multidisciplinary approach favored by the ILO. (See chapters 9 and 10 for additional discussion of MNE responses to conditions of child labor.)

Some of a firm's obligations in relation to other conditions of employment matters have their roots in the core labor and human rights standards. For example, the Universal Declaration of Human Rights states that "everyone who works has the right to just and favorable remuneration ensuring for himself and his family an existence worthy of human dignity."[86] The ILO's Tripartite Declaration interprets this principle in the following terms: MNEs operating in developing countries should provide "the best possible wages, benefits and conditions of work, within the framework of government policies. These should be related to the economic position of the enterprise, but should be at least adequate to satisfy basic needs of the workers and their families."[87]

Assess the Possibilities for Elaboration and Extension of the Core Conditions

It has already been observed that the system of international labor law does not provide a set of clearly defined rules that firms can apply to their individual workplaces in any jurisdiction in the world, nor is it designed to do so for the reasons discussed above. It is also the case that most *national* systems of labor law do not specify the minutiae of work rules for individual firms; most articulate minimum standards above and around which firms can elaborate the conditions of work they offer to employees. Where there are problems with applying national laws or adhering to the core labor and human rights codes or in achieving good labor relations and productivity at work, firms need to consider how these frameworks could be elaborated on and extended to other areas affecting worker–employer relations. Individual MNE elaborations can be found in the corporate overviews included later in this book.

Some of the subject areas in which this process of elaboration could occur are already part of the generalized systems designed to shape MNE behavior, including the OECD guidelines and the ILO's Tripartite Declaration (see above). For example, the OECD instrument requires firms to "take adequate steps to ensure occupational health and safety in their operations,"[88] and "provide the public and employees with adequate and timely information on the potential environment, health and safety impacts of the activities of the enterprise."[89] MNEs should "to the greatest extent practicable, employ local personnel and provide training with a view to improving skill levels . . ."[90] and "provide adequate education and training to employees in environmental health and safety matters."[91] MNEs should also provide "reasonable notice" when contemplating actions "which would have major effects upon the livelihood of their employees."[92] The following chapters in this book provide examples of the various ways that workplace initiatives can be creatively applied to improve the working lives of ordinary people.

CONCLUSION

The MNE's decisions about labor do not exist in a regulatory vacuum. As this chapter has attempted to show, they are enmeshed in systems of national and international labor regulation. While these fundamental principles and rights at work are clearly expressed, complex issues for firm-level decision making can arise, particularly when the states in which firms operate themselves violate (or fail to support) the core labor and human rights codes. One glance at the national labor codes of most countries will show us that most jurisdictions lavish significant regulatory concern on the detail of labor rules, even if these do not in the end specify actual outcomes to be adhered to. We should therefore not be surprised that no simple, "black and white" set of rules has emerged that firms can adopt as a template for ethical business activities around the world. Instead, the national/international system presents a series of fundamental principles with which the firm must use everything in its power to comply and invites firms to elaborate on these minima when shaping the actual working conditions in each workplace. If there is to be a "race to the top" driven by corporate initiatives,[93] it should be grounded in respect for this system and supported by greater transparency so that what is learned by one firm can be spread among others in similar positions. It is hoped that this book will contribute to that process.

NOTES

1. I would like to acknowledge the assistance of the following people in the development of the ideas used in this chapter: Sean Cooney, Colin Fenwick, Serena Lillywhite, and Anthony O'Donnell. Any errors are my sole responsibility.

2. International Labour Organization, *Decent Work, Report of the Director-General to the 87th International Labor Conference* (Geneva: ILO, June 1999).

3. Reports are constantly being produced and updated. Useful sources include the Web sites of the ILO: http://www.ilo.org and of the International Confederation of Free Trade Unions: http://www.icftu.org.

4. See, for example, ILO, *Reducing the Decent Work Deficit—A Global Challenge, Report of the Director-General to the 89th International Labor Conference* (Geneva: ILO, June 2001).

5. ILO, *Decent Work*, p. 17.

6. Neil Kearney, "Corporate Codes of Conduct: The Privatised Application of Labor Standards," in *Regulating International Business*, Sol Picciotto and Mayne Ruth (Houndsmill, Basingstoke: Macmillan/Oxfam, 2000), p. 206.

7. ILO, *Decent Work*, p. 39.

8. Tim Connor, *We Are Not Machines: Despite Some Small Steps Forward, Poverty and Fear Still Dominate the Lives of Nike and Adidas Workers in Indonesia* (Oxfam/Community Aid Abroad, March 2002), http://www.caa.org.au/campaigns/nike/reports/machines/index.html (accessed 1 July 2002), p. 21.

9. I am grateful to my colleagues Sean Cooney, from the University of Melbourne, and Serena Lillywhite, from the Brotherhood of St Laurence Ethical Trading Project, for allowing me to use this material.

10. These cases are discussed in A. V. Jose, ed., *Organized Labour in the Twenty-First Century* (Geneva: International Institute of Labour Studies, 2002).

11. Hilary K. Josephs, "Labor Law in a 'Socialist Market Economy': The Case of China," *Columbia Journal of Transnational Law* 33 (1995): p. 559.

12. Yu Zhu and Iain Campbell, "Economic Reform and the Challenge of Transforming Labor Regulation in China," *Labor and Industry* 7 (1996): p. 42.

13. Connor, *We Are Not Machines*, p. 31. Connor reports Nike's response, that it abhors any form of intimidation that would prevent workers from openly discussing factory conditions, p. 9.

14. Kearney, "Corporate Codes of Conduct," p. 205.

15. See, for example, D. O'Rourke, "Monitoring the Monitors: A Critique of PricewaterhouseCooper's Labor Monitoring," http://web.mit.edu/dorourke/www/ (accessed 1 August 2002).

16. ILO, *Decent Work*.

17. Jill Murray, unpublished case study on corporate codes of conduct, on file with author.

18. Kearney, "Corporate Codes of Conduct," p. 205.

19. Connor, *We Are Not Machines*.

20. Jill Murray, "Corporate Codes of Conduct and Labor Standards," in *Mastering the Challenge of Globalization: Towards a Trade Union Agenda*, ed. Robert Kyloh (Geneva: ILO, 1998), p. 95.

21. See ILO, *Forced Labor in Myanmar (Burma), Report of the Commission of Inquiry,*

http://www.ilo.org/public/english/standards/relm/gb/docs/gb273/myanmar. htm (accessed 1 July 2002).

22. ILO, press release ILO/02/31, "ILO Annual Conference Adopts New Measures to Tackle the Challenges of Globalisation," http://www.ilo.org/public/ english/bureau/inf/pr/2002/31.htm (accessed 1 July 2002).

23. Colin Fenwick, "Slaves of the State: The Implications of Private Prisons for International Regulation of Prison Labor," paper presented at the "Cycles of Labor Regulation" Conference, held by the Regulatory Institutions Network and the History Program of the Research School of Social Sciences at the Australian National University, Canberra, June 2002 (on file with author). See, too, Colin Fenwick, *Private Benefit from Forced Prison Labor: Case Study on the Application of ILO Convention 29, Report to the International Confederation of Free Trade Unions,* July 2001, http://www.icftu.org/displaydocument.asp?Index = 991212919&Language = EN (accessed 1 July 2002).

24. See, for example, Anita Ramasastry, "Corporate Complicity: From Nuremberg to Rangoon: An Examination of Forced Labor Cases and their Impact on the Liability of Multinational Corporations," *Berkeley Journal of International Law* 91 (2002): 91–147, p. 110.

25. ICFTU, *A Trade Union Guide to Globalization,* http://www.icftu.org/ displaydocument.asp?Index = 991209485&Language = EN (accessed 1 July 2002).

26. OECD, *International Trade and Core Labor Standards* (Paris: OECD, 2000), p. 36.

27. ILO, *Decent Work,* p. 22.

28. ILO, *Decent Work,* p. 23.

29. Gordon Betcherman, "An Overview of Labor Markets World-Wide: Key Trends and Major Policy Issues," *World Bank Employment Policy Primer* (Geneva: World Bank, April 2002), p. 2.

30. Betcherman, "Overview of Labor Markets World-Wide," p. 6.

31. See, for example, United Nations Conference on Trade and Development (UNCTAD), *World Investment Report 2001: Promoting Linkages* (Geneva: UN, 2001), p. 66.

32. This is certainly the case in relation to Australian MNE operations.

33. Miriam Ching Yoon Louie, *Sweatshop Warriors: Immigrant Women Workers Take On the Global Factory* (Cambridge, Mass.: South End Press, 2001), p. 34.

34. Sol Picciotto, "What Rules for the World Economy?" in *Regulating International Business,* Sol Picciotto and Ruth Mayne (Houndsmill, Basingstoke: Macmillan/Oxfam, 2000). For example, in the Australian context, an Industry Commission Inquiry found that "firms in the labor intensive textile, clothing and footwear industries have benefited from operating in countries with much lower labor costs. Much Australian foreign direct investment occurs in China, where labor costs are 4 percent of those in Australia." *Industry Commission, Implications for Australian Firms Locating Offshore,* Report No. 53 (Canberra: Australian Government Publishing Service, 1996), p. 54.

35. UNCTAD, "Working for Manufacturers Without Factories," in *World Investment Report 1994: Transnational Corporations, Employment and the Workplace* (New York: United Nations, 1994), p. 193.

36. See, for example, David Hess, "Social Reporting : A Reflexive Law Approach to Corporate Social Responsiveness," *Journal of Corporation Law* 25 (1999): 41–86, n. 22.

37. See, for example, Paul Blythell, "Women in the Workforce," in *The Industrial Revolution and British Society*, P. O'Brien and R. Quinault (Cambridge: Cambridge University Press, 1993).

38. See generally Dong-Sook S. Gills and Nicola Piper, eds., *Women and Work in Globalising Asia* (London and New York: Routledge, 2002).

39. Betcherman, "Overview of Labor Markets World-Wide," p. 10.

40. Jill Murray and Anthony O'Donnell, "'Sweat or Starve': Sweated Labor and the Regulatory Imagination in Australia," paper presented at the "Cycles of Labor Regulation" Conference, held by the Regulatory Institutions Network and the History Program of the Research School of Social Sciences at the Australian National University, Canberra, June 2002 (on file with author).

41. Press release by the World Development Movement (U.K.) (1996), quoted in Murray, "Corporate Codes of Conduct," p. 97.

42. Betcherman, "Overview of Labor Markets World-Wide," p. 20.

43. See, for example, Paul Krugman, "In Praise of Cheap Labor," http:// web.mit.edu/krugman/www/smokey.html (accessed 1 July 2001).

44. I have argued elsewhere that the European law permits a workweek of 78 hours in some cases. In instances in which member states have adopted some or all of the available derogations for particular workers, many have only minimal limitations on their working time established in European law. See Jill Murray, *Transnational Labor Regulation: The ILO and EC Compared* (The Hague: Kluwer Law International, 2001), p. 200.

45. Murray, "Corporate Codes of Conduct."

46. Some argue for more sweatshops. See, for example, Krugman, "In Praise of Cheap Labor." For a useful overview of the economic literature, see Drusilla Brown, "International Trade and Core Labor Standards: A Survey of the Recent Literature," *Labor Market and Social Policy Occasional Papers No. 43* (Paris: OECD, 2000).

47. See, for example, B. A. Hepple, ed., *The Making of Labor Law in Europe* (London: Mansell, 1986).

48. For a detailed discussion, see Murray, *Transnational Labor Regulation*, p. 16.

49. The constitution and labor conventions of the ILO can be found on its Web site, http://www.ilo.org.

50. See, for example, Virginia Leary, "Lessons from the Experience of the ILO," in *The United Nations and Human Rights: A Critical Appraisal*, ed., Philip Alston (Oxford: Clarendon Press, 1992), p. 580.

51. For a useful discussion of the meaning of these concepts, see Paul O'Higgins, "'Labor Is Not a Commodity': An Irish Contribution to International Labor Law," *Industrial Law Journal* 26 (1997): 225–34.

52. Jill Murray, "Labor Rights, Corporate Responsibilities: The Role of ILO Core Standards," in Rhys Jenkins and others, eds., *Corporate Responsibility and Ethical Trade: Codes of Conduct in the Global Economy, Earthscan UK* (forthcoming 2003).

53. Murray, "Labor Rights, Corporate Responsibilities."

54. Steven Ratner, "Corporations and Human Rights: A Theory of Legal Responsibility," *Yale Law Journal* 111 (2001): p. 443.

55. For example, article 2 of convention 87 states, "Workers and employers, without distinction whatsoever, shall have the right to establish and, subject only to the rules of the organization concerned, to join organizations of their own choos-

ing without previous authorization." Firms cannot grant this right, because it can only be fully achieved through the absence of state action contrary to the right. Convention concerning Freedom of Association and Protection of the Right to Organize, 1948.

56. Article 2, convention 111, Convention concerning Discrimination in Respect of Employment and Occupation, 1958.

57. Article 5, convention 138, Convention concerning Minimum Age for Admission to Employment, 1973. See Jill Murray, "The Sound of One Hand Clapping? Regulation Theory and International Labor Law," *Australian Journal of Labor Law* 14 (2001): p. 306.

58. See n. 2, above.

59. OECD, *Trade, Employment and Labor Standards* (Paris: OECD, 1996), p. 10.

60. OECD, *International Trade and Core Labor Standards* (Paris: OECD, 2000), p. 9.

61. ILO Declaration on Fundamental Principles and Rights At Work and Its Follow-Up, adopted by the International Labor Conference at its 86th Session, Geneva, 18 June 1998, http://www.ilo.org/public/english/standards/decl/declaration/text/index.htm (accessed 1 July 2002).

62. ILO, *Reducing the Decent Work Deficit*, p. 3.

63. World Bank, Core Labour Standards Took Kit, http://wbln0018. worldbank.org/HDNet/hddocs.nsf/View + to + Link + WebPages/AE07D22AF8 F2088285256935005BAD6A?OpenDocument (accessed 1 July 2002).

64. Commission of the European Communities, Promoting Core Labor Standards and Improving Social Governance in the Context of Globalization, Communication from the Commission to the Council, the European Parliament and the Economic and Social Committee, Brussels, COM (2001) 416 final.

65. Jill Murray, "The European Union's External Powers and Labor Standards," paper presented at the University of Oxford Institute of European and Comparative Law Colloquium on Constitutionalism and Employment Policy in European Union Law, May 2002.

66. United Nations Third Conference on the Less Developed Countries, Brussels, May 2001, Program of Action for the Least Developed Countries (A/CONF.191/11), p. 11.

67. The G8 Labor Ministers, "Labor Policies in a Rapidly Changing Global Economy" (1999), http://www.g7.utoronto.ca/g7/labour/labourfeb24.htm (accessed 1 July 2002).

68. Summit of the Americas, Final Declaration (22 April 2001), http://www. americascanada.org/eventsummit/declarations/declara-e.asp (accessed 1 July 2002).

69. Organisation of American States, Inter-American Democratic Charter, (2001), article 10, http://www.oas.org/charter/docs/resolution1_en_p4.htm (accessed 1 July 2002).

70. Murray, "Codes of Conduct and Labor Standards"; Janelle Diller, "A Social Conscience in the Global Marketplace? Labor Dimensions of Codes of Conduct, Social Labelling and Investor Initiatives," *International Labor Review* 138 (1999): 99–129.

71. For example, the British government has established the Ethical Trading Initiative, which is "an alliance of companies, NGOs and trade union organizations committed to working together to change business behavior by identifying and

promoting good practice in the implementation of codes of labor practice." Mike Blowfield, Ethical Trading Initiative, "Governance and Supply Chains : An Ethical Approach to Responsibility," http://www.eti.org.uk/pub/publications/2001/12-art-govsupp/index.shtml (accessed 1 July 2002).

72. Commission of the European Communities, *Green Paper on Promoting a European Framework for Corporate Social Responsibility*, July 2001, COM (2001) 366 final.

73. A. Fung, D. O'Rourke, and C. Sabel, "Realizing Labor Standards," *Boston Review* 26 (2001): pp. 1–35. For a commentary on this article, see Jill Murray, "The Sound of One Hand Clapping? The Ratcheting Labour Standards Thesis and International Labour Law," *Australian Journal of Labour Law* 14 (2001): 306–26.

74. See generally Gunther Teubner, ed., *Global Law Without a State* (Dartmouth: Aldershot, 1997).

75. OECD, The OECD Guidelines for Multinational Enterprises, http://www.oecd.org/EN/document/0,,EN-document-187-5-no-27-24467-187,FF.html (accessed 1 July 2002).

76. ILO, Tripartite Declaration on Multinational Enterprises, http://ilolex.ilo.ch:1567/public/50normes/ilolex/pdconv.pl?host = status01&textbase = iloeng&document = 2&chapter = 28&query = %28%23docno%3D28197701%29 + %40ref&highlight = &querytype = bool (accessed 1 July 2002).

77. Jill Murray, "A New Phase in the Regulation of Multinational Enterprises," *Industrial Law Journal* 30 (2001): 255–72.

78. For example, the ILO Tripartite Declaration on MNEs states, "All parties concerned by this Declaration should respect the sovereign rights of States, obey the national laws and regulations, give due consideration to local practices and respect relevant international standards." General Policies, 8.

79. For a number of case studies see, for example, Sean Cooney, Tim Lindsay, Richard Mitchell, and Ying Zhu, eds., *Law and Labour Relations in East Asia* (Sydney: Federation Press, forthcoming 2003).

80. For a very useful discussion of this issue, see David Steele, "The 'Living Wage' Clause in the ETI Base Code: How To Implement It?" http://www.eti.org.uk/pub/publications/2000/06-livwage/index.shtml (accessed 1 July 2002).

81. OECD Guidelines, II, General Policies, 2.

82. United Nations, The Global Compact: Executive Summary of a High Level Meeting to Launch the Global Compact (July 2000), http://www.un.org/partners/business/gcevent/press/summary.htm (accessed 5 October 2000).

83. Ratner, "Corporations and Human Rights."

84. OECD Guidelines, IV, Employment and Industrial Relations, 1(a).

85. OECD Guidelines, IV, Employment and Industrial Relations 1(b), emphasis added.

86. United Nations, Universal Declaration of Human Rights, 1948, General Assembly Resolution 217 A (III), Article 23 (3), http://www.unhchr.ch./html/intlinst.htm.

87. ILO Tripartite Declaration, 34. Similar provisions exist in many of the codes and guidelines. For example, the Ethical Trading Initiative's Basic Code states, "Wages and benefits paid for a standard working week meet, at a minimum, national legal standards or industry benchmark standards, whichever is higher. In any event, wages should always be enough to meet basic needs and to provide

some discretionary income." http://www.eti.org.uk/pub/publications/2000/06-livwage/index.shtml (accessed 1 July 2002).

88. OECD Guidelines, IV Employment and Industrial Relations, 4(b).

89. OECD Guidelines, V Environment, 2(a).

90. OECD Guidelines, IV Employment and Industrial Relations, 5.

91. OECD Guidelines, V Environment, 7.

92. OECD Guidelines, IV Employment and Industrial Relations, 6.

93. This concept is discussed by Bob Hepple, "Labor Regulation in Internationalized Markets," in *Regulating International Business*, Sol Picciotto and Ruth Mayne.

## CHAPTER 3

The Economic Context: Grounding Discussions of Economic Change and Labor in Developing Countries

Jonathan D. London

As industries globalize, the livelihood of workers in developing countries assumes an increasingly global relevance. Once the exclusive domain of workers, managers, and state agencies, decisions regarding the management, social development, and human rights of workers in developing countries are subject to wider and more intense scrutiny, if for diverse and sometimes contradictory reasons. Although work and employment in developing countries have long held the interest of scholars, today these issues are at the center of much wider discussions concerning the functioning, regulation, and future development of the world economy. Indeed, there are now quite lively debates about the practical possibilities of global corporate codes of conduct, even as discussions about the desirability, design, and implementation of such codes reveal fundamental disagreements among various actors and stakeholders.[1] Remarkably however, many discussions of global labor challenges lack even a basic awareness of the dynamics of industrial relations in developing countries. This chapter suggests ways of grounding discussions of work and employment practices in globalized industries through an examination of the changing context of industrial relations in developing countries.

This chapter pursues two aims: The first is to clarify the meaning and significance of industrialization and industrial relations in developing countries and to show how changes in global divisions of production and labor have transformed the calculus of industrial relations in developing country settings. The second is to illustrate why grounding discussions of labor and human resources in developing countries requires an appreciation of local institutions and the diverse, competitive, and frequently conflicting interests of various actors and stakeholders that govern the use of labor in different industries and countries.

The chapter has five sections: Section 1 discusses the meanings and significance of development, developing countries, and industrialization. Section 2 defines industrial relations and discusses their characteristic features in developing countries. Section 3 identifies the significance of globalization to industrial relations in developing countries. Section 4 probes the interests of key stakeholders shaping developing countries' industrial relations systems. The final section examines the various institutional forms governing work and employment practices in developing countries.

Conceiving of industrial relations in developing countries poses major analytic challenges. It requires incorporating the global *and* the local into a unified, historically informed, but constantly changing understanding of complex processes. Hence, to grasp the context of industrial relations in developing countries requires not only an appreciation of large-scale processes of social change within and across different countries and at the level of the world system itself, but also a sensitivity to the varied organizational and operational attributes of global industries, to subtle matters of work organization on the shop floor, and to the historically rooted economic, political, and cultural institutions that govern work, employment, and the social reproduction of labor in different developing-country settings. By clarifying these issues, this chapter seeks to provide a foundation for the program analyses in the chapters that follow and the challenges to which they aim to respond.

DEVELOPMENT, DEVELOPING COUNTRIES, AND INDUSTRIALIZATION

Global labor challenges both shape and are structured by changing work and employment practices in developing countries. Unfortunately, popular discussions of work and employment in globalizing industries commonly ignore the complex and variable contexts in which economic production takes place. For example, many discussions of work and employment in globalizing industries betray little or no reflection on basic concepts such as *development* and *developing countries*. Persistent inattention to the significance and meaning of such basic concepts risks glossing over quite important distinctions and controversies and encourages the embrace of quite problematic assumptions. To ground discussions of global labor challenges in developing countries, it is thus worth specifying our terms and, in particular, gaining due appreciation of the empirical and normative controversies concerning master concepts such as development, developing countries, and "industrialization."

Development and Developing Countries

The term *development* has a contested meaning. While mainstream economists equate development with economic growth (preferably achieved through trade),[2] others view development as enhanced human welfare, expanded human capabilities, and increased individual choice.[3] Still others reject use of the terms *development* and *developing country* altogether. To arrive at a practicable understanding of these two terms it is important to register two principal objections to their uncritical use.

The term development is problematic because its use often carries with it the assumption that economic growth produces linear and ultimately universal improvements in human welfare, an assumption that does not correspond with world historical experience. If, by contrast, we employ the term *economic change* instead of development, we effectively free ourselves from the problematic assumption that economic growth *automatically* begets human progress, improved welfare, and so on. Skepticism of the term development is not to question the importance of economic growth or the desirability of progress, but rather to signal due appreciation of the complex origins of economic growth as well as an awareness of the complex social forces that typically govern the distribution of the costs and benefits of economic growth.

Whereas the term development confuses change with some fuzzy notion of progress, the term developing countries obscures the tremendous diversity of the world's middle- and low-income countries. Should we really lump Taiwan and Angola in the same category? What about Argentina, a developing country that appears to be in decline? The term *global south* may be more preferable than developing countries as a way of describing the world's middle- and low-income countries. Global south implies neither progress nor retreat; it also captures the power differentials and unequal exchange that have historically and undeniably characterized relations between "northern" (i.e., industrialized) countries and the rest of the world.

Objections to the terms development and developing country are too important to ignore. As a practical matter, however, development has come to be closely identified with the processes of economic growth and industrialization, and developing countries refers to countries that are either in the process of industrializing or have yet to begin. Industrialization is significant not only because it expands economic output, but also because it transforms a country's social, economic, and political institutions. For that reason, development theorists have historically been concerned with understanding the determinants and effects of industrialization, including the changing dynamics of work and employment. To begin to understand the contemporary context of work and employment in developing countries, we must appreciate the similarity and diversity of countries' experiences with industrialization.

To be sure, developing countries exhibit broad historical similarities. For example, typically they display large agrarian sectors alongside relatively smaller industrial ones. They also frequently exhibit national and local state authorities that actively intervene in the economy so as to shape and structure industrial growth. Alexander Hamilton, Fredrich List, Park Chung Hee, and Jiang Zemin are all examples of political leaders who pursued interventionist policies to promote industrialization in very different developing country contexts. Yet, appreciating developing countries' similarities also helps us to appreciate their differences. While many low- and middle-income countries remain largely agrarian and exhibit comparatively small industrial sectors, numerous others have experienced decades of industrialization and urbanization. And although countries such as South Korea and Taiwan have registered such improvements in living standards during the past half century that they have shed their developing country label, numerous other developing countries remain deeply mired in poverty, with the worst off seeming to act as mere containers of surplus population, missing out on the benefits of global economic growth while incurring many of its costs.

Industrialization and the Significance of Duality

Despite important differences, most developing countries share a common denominator: Their economies exhibit structural dualism, that is, a comparatively small "modern" industrial sector coexists alongside a larger agrarian and often precapitalist one, with the latter being organized around subsistence agriculture, characterized by low productivity and inefficiency and, hence, economic stagnancy. Duality is in many respects the master concept of development economics.[4] Indeed, any discussion of work and employment in developing countries benefits from an appreciation of duality's historical significance, in theory and in practice.

Appreciation of dualism's significance is hardly new: Among others, Malthus and Marx deeply understood that the pace and character of industrial development in an economy depended crucially on the extent and character of interactions between agrarian and industrial regions. Marx and his latter-day adherents boldly predicted that developing countries could expect to transform into industrial ones in terms broadly similar to one another, famously stating that "the country that is more developed industrially only shows to the less developed the image of its own future."[5] Marx was far from alone in his expectation. In the early 1960s the anti-Marxist W. W. Rostow and other "modernization" theorists were also vitally concerned with dualism. Rostow's influential stage theory of economic growth construed development as a transition from primitive traditionalism to modern industrialism.[6] For Rostow, more a cold-war political strategist than an economist, the transformation of developing countries into industrial ones was as much a counterinsurgency objective as an economic one. By contrast, Marx and his later adherents initially viewed agrarian transformation in developing countries as an inevitable step in the long but inexorable march of developing countries toward industrialization and proletarian revolution. In practice, both Rostow and Marx were wrong. For by the end of the 1960s most developing economies continued to experience both sharp dualism and economic stagnancy.

Theory and Practice of Industrialization

But the 1960s were also the heyday of development economics, the hallmark of which lay not in its focus on dualism per se, but in its attempts to understand and overcome dualism. This involved ongoing efforts to explain the determinants and effects of industrialization as well as the advocacy of policies to overcome dualism, principally through investments in agricultural and (especially) industrial infrastructure. Linking establishment and critical theories of industrialization with the variable experiences of developing countries and contemporary development policies can help to ground discussions of contemporary work and employment practices in developing countries.

In the 1960s many developing countries had just recently gained their national independence, and developing countries' governments (hereafter national states) assumed a preeminent role in structuring national industrial development. Indeed, national states in developing countries seemed uniquely qualified to the task: As repositories of capital and technical expertise, national states appeared uniquely capable of overcoming a number of obstacles to industrial growth, such as the limited availability of capital in poor regions, inferior productive technologies, and the small size of markets in developing countries for manufactured goods—which tended to undermine the incentive to invest in industry.[7] With the focus of development policies increasingly on industry, many development theorists warned against ignoring agriculture and, more specifically, emphasized the importance of intersectoral terms of trade between agriculture and industry.[8] These theorists recognized the potential importance of agriculture to domestic capital accumulation and stressed that a combination of opportunistic agricultural landlords, government action, and domestic and international trade could effectively spur a shift of "surplus labor" from the low-productivity agricultural sector to the higher-productivity industrial sector, thereby enhancing overall productivity, facilitating capital accumulation, and creating conditions for expanding industrial investment.

Critics of mainstream development theory were always dubious of its predictions. As early as the 1950s critical scholars of development in both South and North America recognized that developing countries' continued reliance on raw materials and agricultural exports so structured developing economies as to threaten their long-term prospects for achieving industrialization.[9] Not only did exporting developing economies tend to take on an enclave (and, hence, dualist) character, but declining terms of trade constantly undermined the economic value of developing countries' exports. Cardoso and Faletto further argued that the sharp dualism and economic stagnancy that Latin American developing economies exhibited, far from being original conditions, were themselves the product of the historically exploitative character of ties between industrial and developing economies.[10] Rather than promoting development and integrating rural and industrial sectors, these relations exacerbated dualism by encouraging enclave-like industrial regions and adversely transformed economic and political life in developing countries. To break the cycle of "dependent development," Cardoso and others advocated various policies of import substitution industrialization (ISI), which sought to foster and protect the development of domestic manufacturing industries by imposing protective tariffs against manufactured imports from industrialized countries. At the time, conventional development economists were not unsympathetic, yet the practice of ISI strategies produced widely divergent results.

Importantly, efforts to promote ISI in Latin America often depended heavily on foreign investments and credit. After the 1973 oil crisis, and the subsequent development of Euro-dollar markets, Latin American countries borrowed heavily to promote ISI industrial development. Often, these policies faltered badly, eventually creating massive foreign debt, leading to the so-called lost decade of the 1980s, when Latin American development was strangled by crushing debt loads. Furthermore, investments in ISI did little to alleviate the structural dualism that had already characterized Latin American economies. Indeed, capitalist transformation of agriculture in Latin America tended to produce landlessness and massive migration to urban areas, but few industrial jobs. Indeed, although the "surplus labor" concept remains an important part of development theory, skeptics have charged that models of development depending on surplus labor tended to overestimate the degree of unemployment in agriculture while understating the difficulty of reallocating labor between sectors.[11]

By the 1980s the failure of ISI to trigger industrialization transformed into a widespread cynicism among development economists regarding the capacity of states in developing countries to spur economic growth. Prominent development theorists such as Lal voiced criticism of development policy centered on states, and instead viewed states as anathemas to economic growth.[12] Many such critics compared the poor development performance of Latin America and Africa to a number of East Asian economies that were said to have experienced both rapid economic growth and industrialization by adhering to Ricardian principles of free markets, export-oriented industrialization (EOI) based on natural comparative advantage, and state noninterventionism. Yet further investigation of the sources of economic growth and industrialization sparked a critique of the neoclassical critics, as a number of scholars argued convincingly that economic growth in Japan, South Korea, and Taiwan was the result of massive interventions into the economy.[13] Still others pointed out that East Asian industrialization had exceptional antecedents. Cumings, for example, argued that East Asian industrialization occurred under unique conditions, namely in countries with unusually competent bureaucracies, unusual access to foreign capital and technology, and unusual access to international markets.[14]

The seemingly arcane controversies surrounding development and underdevelopment in East Asia and Latin America have had a powerful influence on contemporary development policy. Historical complexities notwithstanding, the central lessons drawn from both Latin American and East Asian industrialization, at least by establishment economists and the politically and financially influential World Bank, were that macroeconomic stability, fiscal austerity, and export orientation were the keys to rapid economic growth and industrialization. These principles, known collectively as the "Washington Consensus," have dominated development thinking and policy making since the mid-1990s, despite significant evidence that the most successful industrializers deployed strategic combinations of ISI and EOI policies.[15] To be sure, however, Washington Consensus policies have helped to facilitate large expansions in trade from developing countries and have facilitated a shift in industrial employment to the global south.

INDUSTRIAL RELATIONS IN DEVELOPING COUNTRIES

At its broadest level "industrial relations in developing countries" refers to relations among workers, firms, states, international agencies, and various civic organizations and public interest groups concerned with work and employment in developing countries. Industrial relations in developing countries are important precisely because they can strongly influence the scale, scope, pace, and character of industrialization and economic change in a given society, including its occupational structure and its social relations of production, both on a national scale and at the grass roots. Scholars of development have recognized the significance of industrial relations in developing countries for well over a century and yet, until recently, understandings of the subject tended to exhibit the same theoretical and practical shortcomings as modernization theory itself. Namely, the assumption that developing countries' industrial relations systems would gradually progress from a state of primitive cultural traditionalism to more advanced, rational industrial systems and would gradually develop industrial relations similar to already industrialized countries such as the United States. In practice, industrial relations in developing countries exhibit remarkable diversity, as they depend on a constellation of social, political, economic, and cultural forces. While industrial relations in developing countries do display important similarities, the context of industrial relations may vary sharply even within particular industries.

Convergence and Industrial Relations in Developing Countries

In *Industrialism and Industrial Man,* Kerr, Dunlop, Harbison, and Meyers contend that through technological diffusion from the West, developing countries would gradually adopt "a logic of industrialism" that would wipe away culture-bound traditionalism and clear a path for patterns of industrial relations broadly similar to those exhibited in early industrializers such as the United States.[16] Kerr and associates predicted a gradual convergence in developing countries' industrial relations systems around democratic pluralism and voluntarist principles of collective bargaining.[17] In reality, patterns of economic change and industrial relations in developing countries have continued to display quite different developmental features. The basic problem with the convergence model of industrial relations was that it presupposed the existence of a democratic polity and a relative balance of power between employers and workers.[18]

Characteristics of Industrial Relations Systems in Developing Countries

Industrial relations in developing countries are subject to a dizzying array of social forces, as they are constituted through the interplay of both local and extralocal forces that operate on a variety of social scales. Examples of large-scale political and economic influences on industrial relations include colonialism and neocolonialism, development of postcolonial states, national and international economic cycles, changing political orientation of national governments as well as their economic and social policies, emergence and decline of national labor movements, and local influence of multilateral organizations such as the World Bank and the International Monetary Fund (IMF). Of course, industrial relations also depend on the ecological and demographic features of a particular country, such as its geographic location and the socioeconomic status of its population, including its level of educational attainment and the settlement patterns of its labor force. These ecological and demographic features, in turn, both shape and are shaped by the interplay of state industrialization strategies, different industries' and firms' business strategies, the technological sophistication and human resource requirements of various economic activities, and the strategies workers deploy to ensure their own subsistence and welfare and that of their families.

Democratic pluralist politics and balanced power among industrial relations stakeholders have not been the predominant pattern in practice. Until recently (and with only a few exceptions), developing countries' characteristic political feature has been authoritarianism, under which national states seek to dictate most aspects of the industrialization process, including work and employment relations. Authoritarian states do so, not by sponsoring voluntarist bargaining arrangements, but instead by subordinating workers through corporatist industrial relations that either co-opts or excludes workers from vital employment decisions.[19]

Patterns of industrial relations in developing countries are also strongly determined by the structure of economic growth. In many developing countries industrialization is starkly uneven, producing economies displaying only small islands of industry [typically in rural and industrial activities dominated by multinational enterprises (MNEs)] amid a sea of low-productivity simple-commodity production. Hence, analysts who focus exclusively on industrial relations in the relatively small and MNE-dominated sectors are prone to ignore the large proportion of developing countries' populations engaged in other spheres of agricultural and industrial production, particularly those geared toward domestic consumption or those in the informal sector.[20] Indeed, in many developing countries, the vast majority of workers operate outside or on the margins of formal employment relations. These workers often have their own, quite distinctive, industrial relations concerns, such as the governance of informal employment relations with local but globally linked subcontractors.

Economic Context of Industrial Relations

Even within developing countries, there are basic differences in industrial relations across different industries and enterprises. The type, technology, and ownership of production each have wide-ranging implications for the organization of work and the character and conduct of labor relations.[21] Compare, for example, variations in the organization, technologies, and ownership of production across various industries, such as mining, factory production, and plantation agriculture. These variations may determine the size of the workforce, location and duration of production, safety conditions, educational requirements, types of labor monitoring and management, as well as the formation of workers' motivation and political culture.[22] There are, finally, a range of underlying economic factors that constantly impinge on industrial relations across enterprises, industries, and countries. These concern product and factor markets, both of which may cause temporal variation in the scale of production and individual enterprises' budgetary constraints. Whether or not and to what extent these considerations invite the occurrence of sweatshop labor is a question best appreciated through an examination of the nature of changes in the global economy, power differentials among industrial relations actors, and the institutions governing work and employment in diverse developing-country settings.

SIGNIFICANCE OF GLOBALIZATION

Developing countries exist in a world economy that is increasingly integrated through trade and is undergoing fundamental shifts in patterns of industrial production. Popular discussions of labor in developing countries vaguely refer to these processes as *globalization* or *economic globalization*. By globalization I refer to social, political, economic, and cultural processes that regularly transcend national boundaries.[23] In economic terms, globalization centers on the expansion of cross-border trade and capital flows. Economic globalization is, in this respect, quite an old process that traces back at least hundreds of years. There have, on the other hand, been fundamental changes in the character of economic globalization, particularly since the 1960s. These shifts have transformed the context of employment and work in developing countries in three important ways. First, trade in manufactured goods is proportionally more important to developing countries than at any previous juncture. Second, globalizing industries have transformed some segments of developing countries' populations into relatively prized commodities, whereas comparatively larger segments have been rendered superfluous to global cycles of capital accumulation. Third, to pursue industrialization on the basis of labor-intensive manufacturing, developing countries must reconstitute their labor institutions in fairly specific ways.

Capital Mobility and the Changing Geography of Production

Most fundamentally, economic globalization has entailed a reordering of spatial divisions of labor and production in the world economy and remarkable growth in the volume and pace of cross-border trade and capital flows. Before the 1960s, economic processes of production tended to be organized within national bounds and concentrated in the world's industrialized countries.[24] Exports from developing countries consisted mostly of primary goods, such as raw materials and agricultural items. As indicated, these export enclaves were commonly dominated by investors from industrialized countries. Foreign direct investments in developing countries' manufacturing industries initially emerged as a strategy of overcoming trade barriers instituted in developing countries to protect infant manufacturing industries. Yet since the 1960s the world has experienced an unprecedented shift, as a range of manufacturing activities were relocated from the industrialized countries to the lower-wage countries, frequently for export to developed economies as inputs or finished goods. Shifts in production were, in turn, enabled, transformed, and catalyzed by improvements in transport and communications technologies, as well as in the productive capabilities of developing countries. By the 1980s an increasing number of industries were organized transnationally, with the manufacture of a single item depending on flexible, just-in-time production, coordinated across many different locales.

The shift to increasingly transnational and flexible offshore production was motivated by a quest for capital accumulation and profits. These are benefits sought after by MNEs and domestic producers alike. For MNEs, slowing productivity gains and declining profits in industrialized countries produced a dilemma: whether to invest in industrial upgrading (through worker training and equipment upgrades, for example), an option that entailed some risk and most certainly a dip in profits, or to shift their productive activities overseas to take advantage of considerably cheaper factor costs. For states and firms in developing countries, developing the capacity to produce internationally competitive manufactures represented an opportunity to boost foreign export earnings, expand economic growth, and spur increased domestic investment. However, unceasing competitive pressures complicate matters, for the variable cost of labor drives MNEs to continually relocate and restructure production. Footwear production, to take one example, was initially shifted from the United States to Taiwan and Korea, but as wages increased in those countries, production was moved once again, to locations such as Indonesia and Thailand and, later, China and Vietnam. More recently, U.S. provisions doubling the allowable importation of textiles from Africa have occasioned a migration of East Asian capital to African countries. Hence, in many globalized manufacturing industries, the search for cheap labor does indeed appear to encourage a so-called race to the bottom, in which the countries with the most exploited labor "win" investment from increasingly footloose global capital. Such a race to the bottom is only encouraged by the changing organization of globalized manufacturing industries.[25]

The organizational attributes of industries reflect MNE strategies for reducing production costs and lowering risk. Gereffi has classified globalized manufacturing industries into two main types: *Producer driven industries* are those industries whose industrial structure is dominated by original equipment manufacturing firms. Large retailers, on the other hand, govern *buyer-driven industries*.[26] In some industries such as footwear, producer- and buyer-driven chains coexist. Both producer- and buyer-driven commodity chains may rely heavily on subcontractors, which may in turn be from the country in which production is located or from a third country that locates so as to exploit cheap labor. Finally, it is worth noting that although increasing foreign direct investments have changed patterns of employment and work in many developing countries, they have done so unevenly: In 1991 the World Bank noted that only 20 countries, mostly in Asia and Latin America, accounted for 90 percent of the net foreign investment flows between 1981 and 1990.

Feminization and Informalization of Global Manufacturing

International experience contradicts the proletarianization thesis of Marx and the convergence theses of various modernizationists. Rather, the world has developed globalized industries that, while employing increasing quantities of developing countries' labor, nonetheless remain concentrated in urban areas, are highly selective in their use of labor, and render giant swaths of developing countries' populations redundant, obsolete, and otherwise superfluous. Although between 1950 and 1990 the share of Third World labor in agriculture fell by 40 percent, and although we have seen massive urbanization in developing countries, we have not seen equally impressive growth in industrial employment.[27] Indeed, patterns of industrial employment in developing countries exhibit two trends at odds with the predictions of previous development theory: the feminization and informalization of industrial production.

MNEs and other employers in developing countries exhibit a high degree of selectiveness in whom they employ. Whereas industrial employment in developing countries during the 1960s and 1970s centered on male labor, in today's globalized manufacturing industries, such as apparel, footwear, and toys, it is young female labor that is the prized commodity. Globally linked manufacturers prefer young female workers for their comparatively low cost, docility, diligence, and dependence.[28] It is well known that a labor force made up of women, especially when drawn from rural areas and diverse linguistic groups, exhibits a much lower propensity to organize for economic or political reasons than do men, except when the women are faced with the most blatant violations of their humanity, such as physical, verbal, or sexual abuse. Women in globalized industries often are kept in the dark as to their rights and the determination of their pay: workers in MNEs (or their subcontractors) often work according to piece, a rate system that obscures vital information regarding wage calculations among factory managers.[29] The wages that female workers earn through employment in globalized industries are often sufficient only to reproduce their own labor power. Despite the protests of various corporate interests, in many developing countries wages for manufacturing are often sufficiently low that workers (and their families) must supplement their factory wages through engagement in precapitalist (i.e., subsistence) agriculture, or in the urban informal sector.

The informalization of manufacturing activities is a second feature of globalized production. To appreciate its significance, we must appreciate the contemporary relevance of informal employment and duality. Recall that in development theory, the rural and industrial sectors of a country are clearly distinguishable. Yet in practice, the lines between the rural and urban sectors, formal and informal economies, and wage-laborer and subsistence farmers have grown quite hazy indeed. For patterns of economic change in developing countries have transformed rural social structures themselves. In today's industrializing economies, the term *proletarianization* is less instructive than *depeasantization*, a condition in which rural labor is dispossessed of land (and its means of subsistence) through differentiation or displacement, and in which labor subsequently becomes reliant on markets to secure its livelihood, though not necessarily in the form of formal wage relations. Rather, foreign or domestic subcontractors may seek to draw on rural labor through informal contracts, often involving home-based activities that draw rural women and children into production. Because relations between MNEs and subcontractors are characteristically unstable, the conditions under which informal home-based piece-rate work occurs are difficult to monitor or control. For the same reason, informally organized production promises employers substantial cost savings.

Globalized Labor and the Reconfiguration of National States

Most mainstream economists and investors regard expanding international trade as *the* primary engine of economic growth and industrialization in developing countries. Critics of mainstream economics and business as usual charge that, while economic growth and industrialization are robustly associated with improved human welfare, an overemphasis on trade and industrialization often marginalizes other worthy development aims, such as improving human welfare through social development and more broad-based income-generating initiatives. While normative debates rage, trade has indeed become increasingly important to developing countries' economies.[30] For although the value of trade between the world's richest countries accounts for roughly 75 percent of the world's total, the value of developing countries' exports typically constitutes a larger proportion of a particular country's gross national product than it does in rich countries. For that reason, trade-related economic activities in developing countries can be important economically, politically, and socially, even if trade-related activities might engage only a small portion of a developing country's labor force. In that context, developing countries national states' trade-oriented industrialization strategies decisively shape the character of industrialization and the conditions of employment. States in many developing countries are centrally concerned with enhancing the cost-competitiveness of their labor.[31] To do so, they often implement policies that depress real wages, deter labor organizations, and disregard labor laws already on the books. In Mexico, the real value of the minimum wage fell by some 60 percent between 1982 and 1992.[32] Thomas finds EOI strategies of industrialization to be associated with erosion of state's labor protection policies and wages across a range of countries.[33]

INDUSTRIAL RELATIONS STAKEHOLDERS

Industrial relations in developing countries concern a plurality of actors and are by no means limited to those directly engaged in employment and production. By stakeholders I refer to the parties directly engaged in, seeking to regulate, or otherwise affected by work and employment in a particular setting. I draw this distinction not to minimize the importance of broader social concerns, but to highlight the complex calculus of interests that determine work and employment and their outcomes, however broadly their effects may range. I include the following as stakeholders in developing countries: workers and their families; employers of various stripes and the hierarchy of management in their enterprises, state agencies, multilateral institutions, and assorted nongovernmental organizations (NGOs). Remarkably, most accounts of global labor in developing countries describe the interests of workers, firms, states, and other stakeholders in quite general terms. In practice, stakeholders are a diverse lot— they pursue different and frequently contradictory aims and they wield widely differing degrees of power and influence over other actors in the industrial relations system.

Workers and Labor Organizations

An outstanding feature of labor in developing countries is its structural marginalization vis-à-vis firms and state agencies. This truism can be appreciated in terms of workers' bargaining power, their rights, and their limited ability to organize to bolster both bargaining power and rights.

In developing countries the scale of industrialization typically remains restricted and fails to absorb vast quantities of labor. In many developing economies the difference between employment and unemployment may dictate access to basic human needs, not merely reductions in consumption. As labor power is often the only commodity that workers possess, they must sell it in a context of surplus labor (Marx's "reserve army"). Workers are thus often doubly cursed by reduced bargaining power on the one hand and low wages on the other.[34] With reduced bargaining power often comes reduced protection. Workers in many developing countries routinely operate under conditions that violate national labor policies and international labor conventions. Even within countries, workers in export processing zones (EPZs) must sometimes forfeit citizenship rights enjoyed outside the zone walls.[35] Loss of rights is even more pronounced when labor migrates overseas, which can strip workers of formal protections granted at home. More rarely, international migrants gain rights when they labor in a foreign country context, but this is usually contingent on their citizenship. Illegal immigrants are subject to considerable risk, as captured in a number of (in industrialized countries) lightly publicized controversies concerning the condition of workers in places such as Guam, a territory of the United States.

Given this basic structural weakness, it is not at all surprising that mass labor organization in developing countries has been historically limited to small or otherwise strategic sectors in which the labor requirements or strategic importance of work involved limits employers' ability to tap alternate labor supplies. Labor unions in developing countries are as diverse as developing countries themselves, but are normally quite weak. Still, labor organizations, such as unions, do indeed represent a potentially important actor in a developing country's industrial relations system. Because of the typically small size of industrial sectors in developing countries, union density tends to fall well below that in industrialized countries, with the striking exception of the United States. But union density does not determine a union's power. Here it is important to underscore unions' diverse political and economic *orientations*. Although an economically oriented labor union typically focuses its attention on wage concerns, politically oriented unions directly engage in political activities.

This is not to say that unions in developing countries can always, or even frequently, act autonomously. Indeed, an outstanding feature of labor relations in developing countries is the state's subjugation of labor to strict controls. Often, for example, state labor agencies must officially recognize a union before it is allowed to operate, and may closely monitor participation, if not dictate, interfere with, or otherwise influence union practices. Such strict state control is the bread and butter of a *corporatist* industrial relations regime. Siddique has distinguished between *exclusionary* corporatist regimes, which occur under bureaucratic authoritarian states bent on excluding unions from politics, and *inclusive* corporatist regimes, in which states strike bargains with labor and co-opt them for political gain.[36] The preponderance of corporatist industrial relations regimes in developing countries is thus another reason for the weakness of unions. But again, it is dangerous to generalize. For over time, the political power of states waxes and wanes, as does the position of labor vis-à-vis the state and employers. South Africa, South Korea, and Mexico are three important examples of societies in which unions have at times exerted profound influence on government decisions regarding work and employment.

At 57.98 percent of the labor force in 1993, South Africa's labor movement was able to develop into a potent political force. Seidman demonstrated how Black trade unionists in South Africa affected political change through militant practices, even in the context of the apartheid police state.[37] Webster has subsequently shown the ability of South African labor, in coordination with the newly democratic state, to craft one of the few tripartite industrial relations regimes in the developing world.[38] In South Korea, labor unions that were originally quite weak and subject to brutally violent repression, were able to gradually strengthen themselves over the course of an industrialization drive that ultimately lifted Korea to OECD status. In the process, despite modest union density, South Korean labor emerged as a major political force, not only in pressing its economic concerns in the strategic Chaebol but also, with students at its side, becoming a driving force for democratization.[39] Now, in the context of democratized politics, South Korean unions are battling the state once again, this time trying to prevent post–Asian Financial Crisis reforms from ruining the full-time employment regime.

Finally we come to Mexico, which for decades was a classic case of the inclusive corporatism noted above. For years Mexico's ruling PRI tightly controlled labor. Riding the oil boom of the 1970s, the undemocratic state protected its legitimacy through massive jobs program—in return for political support.[40] When the oil bonanza ended, the state had to eliminate those jobs at considerable political cost. The state also began to pursue a deflationary wage regime to improve Mexico's export competitiveness. On the watch of the PRI and now President Vincente Fox, the Mexican unions have faced a government that is frequently hostile to labor demands. At the same time, ebbs and flows in the U.S. economy have left hundreds of thousands of Mexican maquiladoras workers out of work, while Mexican and MNEs have migrated from unionized areas near the U.S. border, to cities such as Puebla, where these firms draw on indigenous migrant labor from neighboring states. With guidance from industrial engineers at Duke University, President Fox and other Latin American leaders are now promoting the Plano de Puebla Panama, which will extend maquiladoras production southward, so that foreign and Mexican firms can take advantage of lower wages. This does not bode well for labor unions in Mexico.

National States and State Agencies

In developing-country contexts, national states assume a particularly important role in structuring industrial relations. Kurvilla and Mundell observe that in many developing countries, industrial legacies of colonialism have deeply influenced industrial relations policies; in the postcolonial order newly formed states were quick to recognize the political advantages of labor subordination.[41] State agencies in developing countries also wield unique powers to craft and implement industrialization strategies and formal labor market institutions. Although the global economy has seen significant shifts in the division of production and labor among and within nations (see below), the increasingly global nature of capitalism has not, as some observers predicted, been accompanied by a shrinkage of the state's economic role but, instead, a reconfiguration of this role. Governments in developing countries increasingly make decisions regarding labor and employment practices with deliberate attention to strategies for interfacing with globalizing production systems. That entails indirect competition with other countries.

Here, industrial development strategies and associated policies in developing countries are of primary importance. In choosing their development strategy, state agencies in developing countries have historically chosen some combination of import substitution industrialization policies (ISI), which aim to protect and develop domestic industries (usually through tariffs and other means), and export-oriented industrialization strategies (EOI), in which countries attempt to earn foreign exchange. Because ISI typically involves greater state intervention and produced spectacular failures in Latin America, international financial institutions have pushed poor countries to adopt EOI policies, even though evidence indicates that the most rapidly industrializing countries, such as Taiwan and Korea, pursued a combination of EOI and ISI, or secondary ISI, whereby these countries gradually moved into the production of higher value added items through industrial upgrading strategies geared to increase international competitiveness.

But industrialization strategies have implications that extend far beyond trade, influencing everything from the regulation and taxation of foreign investors to social policy and wage controls. Moreover, the character of industrial relations systems often depends on the character of the political and economic regimes under which they were devised and institutionalized, with significant changes coming only at moments of regime changes, such as the toppling of a colonial regime, a transition between two economic regimes or, most rarely, the emergence of powerful labor movements. At a broad level then, grounding discussions of work and employment in developing countries requires sensitivity to distributions of economic and political power.

Employers

The most simplistic analyses of labor in developing countries miss crucial differences between employers. The power of employers in developing countries is largely contingent on their size and on their relative strategic importance in the economy and, increasingly, on a firm's specific location in a given globalized industry. Hence, generalizing about the practices of firms inevitably produces problems. Although employers' interests may vary within and across industries, it is possible and worthwhile to draw some basic distinctions among three different classes of employers.

We can start with MNEs themselves, often the most influential firms in a given globalized industry. For if the structural position of workers in an economy renders them weak, the structural position of MNEs in developing countries assigns them special privileges and powers. The power of MNEs is, of course, highly variable and should not be either underestimated or exaggerated. That said, governments in developing countries are characteristically dependent on foreign investors as sources of capital, technology, and employment. Foreign subcontractors represent a second class of employers. Increasingly, MNEs, particularly in buyer-driven industries, rely heavily on foreign subcontractors to organize and undertake production of manufacturing and, in so doing, assume much of the inherent risk. Relations between foreign subcontractors and MNEs are typically unstable. Finally, there are those subcontractors or joint-venture partners that are indigenous to developing countries.

Firms in globalized industries also exhibit quite different orientations, depending on a range of factors. Foreign subcontractors as well as domestic suppliers may flout labor standards that MNEs observe. On the other hand, MNEs are themselves a diverse bunch: Although some may be quite opportunistic or unnecessarily compromising of workers' rights, others (perhaps still a minority) take workers' welfare quite seriously. While many firms in globalized industry are centrally concerned with exploiting cheap labor, many others worry about enhancing and increasing productivity by exploiting innovations in both productive machinery and human organization. Following a global movement, many firms in developing countries are beginning to experiment with flexible specialization and just-in-time production methods, or lean manufacturing, a productive strategy that entails a shift away from Taylorist assembly line production methods and their associated risks.

Multilateral Organizations and International Financial Institutions

Beyond governments lies a set of multilateral institutions, such as the ILO, World Bank, and WTO. These institutions themselves have quite diverse constituencies and value orientations. Briefly, the WTO leadership has been outwardly hostile to the idea of incorporating labor standards into trade agreements, claiming that such proposals encroach on limits of national sovereignty.[42] The World Bank, by comparison, has generally concerned itself with creating investor friendly environments, but encourages developing countries to pursue labor intensive manufacturing industries, precisely those industries in which global labor challenges are most acute. Maskus, for example, concludes that improved labor standards should be pursued through indirect means such as a core labor standards clause in WTO agreements, poverty reduction, education, and transparency, rather than sanctions-based codes of conduct.[43] Finally, the ILO, among the oldest of all multilateral institutions, has historically seen its efforts to promote the welfare of workers marginalized by the economic strategies promoted by WTO and World Bank, not to mention state agencies themselves. Yet the recent upsurge in attention to global labor standards has reinvigorated the organization, and it is receiving more political support and resources to carry out its work.[44] In 1998 the ILO approved a Declaration on Fundamental Principles and Rights at Work, focusing attention on the four internationally recognized core principles: freedom of association and the "effective recognition of the right to collective bargaining," freedom from forced labor, the "effective abolition of child labor," and nondiscrimination in employment. Still, questions about the ILO's capacity to enforce such standards remains, as many developing-country governments have outwardly opposed regular reporting on the observance of such principles, let along any sanctions-based enforcement regime.[45]

Third-Party Monitors

But outside the multilateral institutions are a host of actors that have directly involved themselves in labor standards monitoring. The increasing awareness of global labor challenges is no doubt owed in large part to the increasingly collaborative (though still diffuse) activities of workers' organizations, NGOs, and students from around the world. These groups have sometimes proved formidable in casting attention on morally repugnant labor practices, and have proposed, demanded, and sometimes implemented various monitoring systems to protect workers' interests. While many in corporate circles question the legitimacy of these groups and harbor deep suspicion about their aims,[46] such advocacy groups undeniably play an important role in monitoring labor practices in developing countries. MNEs, in their efforts to bring in their own monitors, whether Big-Five consultancies or Ivy League business schools, however well intended, stand accused of being concerned primarily with burnishing their public image, while badly misrepresenting or misreporting conditions under which their workers labor.[47] Despite considerable normative disjuncture over the role of third-party monitors and their appropriate relations to MNEs, third-party monitors have indeed become important stakeholders and cannot be ignored.

LABOR INSTITUTIONS AND INDUSTRIAL RELATIONS IN DEVELOPING COUNTRIES

Individual actors determine work and employment conditions, but they do so within broader institutional contexts that shape and constrain their actions. North defines institutions as "the humanly devised constraints that structure political, economic, and social interaction."[48] Organizations are one particularly important type of institutional form, as they are individual instruments of collective action. State agencies, employers, and labor unions are undoubtedly the most important organizations in a developing country's industrial relations system. We have already observed the consequence of these actors' differential power. Yet organizations do not act in a vacuum. There is a broader institutional terrain that structures their actions. Rodgers provides a concise and useful description of four other kinds of social institutions that influence industrial relations.[49] He terms these "labor institutions" because they "affect or derive from the incorporation of labor in production, the remuneration and working conditions of labor, and associated social and income guarantees."[50] According to Rodgers, formal labor market institutions and informal labor market institutions directly influence employment relations, whereas underlying formal institutions and underlying informal rules are those institutions that lay beyond the labor market, but nonetheless exert powerful influence over its operation. Although these four institutional forms are in practice inseparable, we can use Rogers's taxonomy to illustrate both the characteristic significance of these different institutional forms and their influence in specific empirical instances.

Formal Labor Market Institutions

Formal labor market institutions are written rules that establish the rights and obligations of parties to an employment relation. States play a central role in a developing country's industrial relations systems precisely because of their unique capacity to craft and impose legally binding formal labor market institutions across an entire territorial domain or across entire industries. They do so through laws, ordinances, and regulations specifically designed to govern employment relations in an economy. For example, many countries have quite strict national laws regarding the formation and sanctioning of labor unions. But formal labor institutions on smaller social scales are equally crucial. As Rogers expresses it, the most basic formal labor market institution "is the employment contract which defines the nature of the jobs, the conditions under which they are done, and the rights and obligations attached to them."[51] Other formal labor market institutions include voluntary collective bargaining agencies, rules for wage determination, as well as job hierarchies and promotion schemes within firms.[52] The globalization of production has introduced at least one notable twist to formal labor market institutions: States, in their attempts to lure investors, are increasingly willing to cede their rule-making capacities to managers of EPZs, whose own formal labor institutions may differ considerably from life beyond the zone's gates. Hence, some charge that globalized production has significantly altered, even undermined, the capacity of national states to influence formal labor market institutions.

Informal Labor Market Institutions

Informal labor market institutions relate to but are not synonymous with the informal economy mentioned above. Rather, they encompass all aspects of employment that are not explicitly determined through formal legislation or contracts. Although carrying no legal status, informal labor market institutions vitally affect labor and employment relations. Rogers cites the informal transmission of skills among workers, and workers' and managers' internalization of informal workplace habits and procedures.[53] But he emphasizes that informal institutions frequently exhibit hierarchies of power and differential access to economic, informational, or other resources. Employer discrimination, physical and mental abuse, and arbitrary rules are routine features of production on any shop floor, especially in developing countries. Informal labor market institutions are, as we might expect, more important when we cross the blurry line between the formal and informal sectors. In industries in which workers operate autonomously from direct management, such as those industries employing sharecropping and extensive home-based subcontracting, informal rules regarding work and compensation determine most facets of the employment relation. In these instances, employers can take advantage of imbalances of access to land, work, and credit.[54] The informal sectors of economies are, by definition, organized around informal labor institutions. Hence, informal labor institutions make up a vital part of any industrial relations systems and range from the innocuous to sweatshop practices, such as mandatory overtime, arbitrary dismissals, or a sign on a workplace wall stating "If you don't come in on Sunday, don't come in on Monday."[55]

Underlying Formal Social Rules

All countries exhibit an array of underlying formal institutional rules, which, according to enforcement, can be strong or weak influences on employment relations. Examples of such rules include a country's system of rights, property laws, and state-defined rights, extending from guarantees of access to certain public goods to political rights concerning expression and association. The characteristic weakness of enforcement in many countries means that both workers and employers can and do disregard these rules.

Underlying Informal Social Rules

Values, norms, culture, and ideology all make up a country's underlying informal social rules. As Rogers notes, culture and ideology affect perceptions of particular social groups in the labor market, such as women and ethnic groups. They also affect work motivation, the social valuation of leisure, and the perceived need for compensation and consumption.[56] Labor supply, in turn, is subject to various household, kinship, and community systems. Among analyses of workers in developing countries, Wolf's *Factory Daughters* is an outstanding example of the tensions that informal rules introduce into employment relations, as culturally defined struggles among workers and families over autonomy figured centrally in workers' attitudes and behaviors.[57] As Rogers succinctly states, "These underlying social rules are the means by which patterns of behavior are internalized, hierarchical relations legitimized, and social divisions of labor determined."[58]

Contrary to popular media accounts, the determinants of work and employment in developing countries are quite complex. However globalized production may be, the social relations of production are both global and local. To understand patterns of work and employment in developing countries thus requires stepping off the global plane; grasping the social, economic, and political context of industrialization; and understanding the various institutions that govern the mobilization, employment, and social reproduction of labor in that given local setting.

CONCLUSION

Long ignored, work and employment conditions in developing countries now have a global political importance. Whether in Ho Chi Minh City, Mexico City, or New York City, decisions about the labor and employment practices in developing countries are subject to a battery of sometimes-conflicting financial, social, and political considerations. Viewed most cynically, sweatshops are now an important public relations consideration for increasing numbers of manufacturers, brand-name merchandisers, and retailers. Yet as this very volume attests, many firms are taking an initiative to address "global labor challenges." How, whether, and to what extent these challenges can be met will depend crucially on our ability to grasp the dynamics of industrial relations in developing countries in a more comprehensive and reliable manner.

Industries globalize, and capital moves across borders with unprecedented ease. Even labor is increasingly mobile, though in markedly small volumes. Given the unprecedented scale and speed of these changes, it is hardly surprising that popular discussion of work and employment in developing countries tends to dwell on globalization, but it often does to such an extent that local dynamics become simply an afterthought, as if grasping changes at the global level were itself sufficient to explain labor relations in *any* developing-country setting. The actual determinants of work and employment in developing countries are, of course, far more complicated than that. For however globalized in organization and scope, all production is profoundly local, and to understand patterns of work and employment in developing countries requires an appreciation of the social, economic, and political context of industrialization and the various institutions that govern the mobilization, employment, and social reproduction of labor for that given local setting.

In this chapter I have sought to provide background to these matters by examining the changing context of industrial relations in developing countries. I have shown that there are indeed a dizzying array of variables that are constitutive of and influenced by work and employment in developing countries and that the global and local dynamics that affect labor and employment in developing countries have experienced a fundamental shift in recent years and are now subject to rapid and continuous change. But I have also sought to demonstrate that production is profoundly local and, as such, is embedded in local institutions and that actors in industrial relations systems pursue diverse and at times contradictory aims, and in any case defy generalization.

Finally, I have argued that although new production systems do not necessarily improve work and employment conditions, there may indeed be scope for harnessing labor standards to productivity-enhancing methods. The problem here lies in incentives to address the tedium and low wages that are the hallmark of much industry in the global south. To the extent that answers are to be found through experiments in actual enterprises, subsequent chapters promise to spark much-needed practical debate.

NOTES

1. Compare, for example, David Henderson, *Misguided Virtue: False Notions of Corporate Social Responsibility* (London: Institute for Economic Affairs, 2001), http://www.iea.org.uk/record.php?type=publication&ID=143; and Archon Fung, Dara O'Rourke, Joshua Cohen, and Charles Sabel, *Can We Put An End To Sweatshops?* (Boston, Mass.: Beacon Press, 2001).

2. See, for example, Dilip K. Das, *Global Trading System at the Crossroads: A Post-Seattle Perspective* (New York and London: Routledge, 2001).

3. A. K. Sen, *Commodities and Capabilities* (Amsterdam: Elsevier Scientific Publishing, 1982).

4. Joseph E. Stiglitz, "Duality and Development: Some Reflections on Economic Policy," in *Development, Duality and the International Economic Regime*, ed. Gary Saxonhouse and T. N. Srinivasan (Ann Arbor, Mich.: University of Michigan Press, 1999).

5. Karl Marx, *Capital: Volume 1* (New York: Vintage Books, 1977).

6. W. W. Rostow, *The Stages of Economic Growth: A Non-communist Manifesto* (Cambridge, England: Cambridge University Press, 1960).

7. Ragnar Nurkse, *Problems of Capital-Formation in Underdeveloped Countries* (New York: Oxford University Press, 1962 edition); P. *Rosenstein-Rodan,* "Notes on the Theory of the Big Push," in *Economic Development for Latin America*, ed. Ellis, proceedings of a conference held by the International Economic Association (London: Macmillan, 1961, 1963).

8. A. Lewis, "The Shifting Fortunes of Agriculture," in *Agriculture and its Terms of Trade* in Proceedings of the Tenth International Conference of Agricultural Economists, LaLitha Mahal, Mysore, India (London: Oxford University Press, 1960); G. Ranis, "Industrial Sector Labor Absorption," *Economic Development and Cultural Change* (April 1973); G. Ranis and J. Fei, *Development of the Labor Surplus Economy: Theory and Policy* (Burr Ridge, Ill.: Irwin, 1964).

9. Raul Prebisch, *The Economic Development of Latin America and its Principal Problems* (New York: United Nations, 1950) and Hans W. Singer, "The Distribution of Gains Between Investing and Borrowing Countries," *American Economic Review* 40 (1950): 473–85.

10. F. H. Cardoso and Enzo Faletto, *Dependecnia e Desenvolvimento (Dependency and Underdevelopment)* (Santiago: ILPES, 1967).

11. Albert Berry and Frances Stewart, "The Evolution of Development Economics and Gustav Ranis's Role," in *Development, Duality and the International Economic Regime* (Ann Arbor, Mich.: University of Michigan Press, 1999).

12. D. Lal, *The Poverty of Development Economics* (London: Institute of Economic Affairs, 1983).

13. Chalmers Johnson, *MITI and the Japanese Miracle* (Berkeley, Calif.: University of California Press, 1984); Alice Amsden, *Asia's Next Giant: South Korea and Late Industrialization* (New York: Oxford University Press, 1989); and Robert. W. Wade, *Governing the Market: Economic Theory and the Role of Government in Taiwan's Industrialization* (Princeton, N.J.: Princeton University Press, 1992).

14. Bruce Cumings, "The Origins and Development of the Northeast Asian Political Economy: Industrial Sectors, Product Cycles, and Political Consequences," *International Organization* 38, no. 1 (winter, 1984): 1–40.

15. John Williamson, "What Washington Means by Policy Reform," in *Latin American Adjustment: How Much Has Happened?* ed. John Williamson (Washington, D.C.: Institute for International Economics, 1990).

16. Charles Kerr, John T. Dunlop, Frederick H. Harbison, and Charles A. Meyers, *Industrialism and Industrial Man* (Middlesex: Penguin, 1964).

17. S. A. Siddique, "Industrial Relations in a Third World Setting: A Possible Model," *The Journal Of Industrial Relations* 31 (September 1989), pp. 385–401.

18. A. K. Ubektu, "An Industrial Relations System for a Developing Country: The Case of Nigeria" (Ph.D. thesis, Sussex, U.K., Sussex University, 1981), cited in Siddique, "Industrial Relations in a Third World Setting."

19. Frederic C. Deyo, "State and Labor: Modes of Political Exclusion in East Asian Development," in *The Political Economy of the New Asian Industrialism*, ed. Frederic C. Deyo (Ithaca, N.Y. and London: Cornell University Press, 1987), pp. 182–222; Siddique, "Industrial Relations in a Third World Setting."

20. Manuel Castells and Alejandro Portes, "The World Underneath: The Origins, Dynamics, and Effects of the Informal Economy," in *The Informal Economy: Studies in Advanced and Less Developed Countries*, ed. Alejandro Portes, Manuel Castells, and Lauren Bentos (Baltimore, Md.: Johns Hopkins University Press, 1989), p. 1137.

21. Ibid. n. 16.

22. Charles Berquist, *Labor in Latin America: Comparative Essays on Chile, Argentina, Venezuela, and Colombia* (Stanford, Calif.: Stanford University Press, 1986).

23. This definition is taken from N. Yeates, *Globalization and Social Policy* (London: Sage, 2001).

24. Gary Gereffi, "Global Production Systems and Third World Development," working paper series on New International Context of Development, no. 4, UW-Madison Global Studies Research Program, 1993.

25. It would be a mistake to view economic globalization and its effects as being limited strictly to manufacturing activities. Recent decades have also seen a steady, if less dramatic, intensification of trade in agricultural and extractive commodities. Increasing trade in agricultural items has included trade in wheat, corn, soy, but more explosively in nontraditional agricultural items, such as coffee, fresh fruit and vegetables, cut flowers, and the like. Expanding trade in extractive commodities has included everything from minerals to seafood. Extractive economies, though tending to be less labor intensive, have expanded thanks to advances in transport technologies. There has also been important growth in services, including the proliferation of financial service "exports" from industrialized to developing countries. Tourism, the world's largest industry in value terms, has proved an important "export" for developing countries.

26. Gary Gereffi, "The Organization of Buyer-Driven Commodity Chains: How U.S. Retailers Shape Overseas Production Networks," in *Commodity Chains and Global Capitalism*, ed. Gary Gereffi and Miguel Korzeniwicz (Westport, Conn.: Praeger, 1994).

27. Farshad Araghi, "The Great Global Enclosure of Our Times: Peasants and the Agrarian Question at the End of the Twentieth Century," in *Hungry for Profit: The Agribusiness Threat to Farmers, Food, and the Environment*, ed. Fred Magdoff, John Bellamy Foster, and Fredrick H. Buttel (New York: Monthly Review Press, 2000), pp. 145–60.

28. Ching Kwan Lee, "Localistic Despotism" and "Familial Hegemony," in *Gender and the South China Miracle: Two Worlds of Factory Women* (Berkeley, Calif.: University of California Press, 1998), pp. 109–36, 137–59.

29. Heather White, "Educating Workers: A Response to "Realizing Labor Standards," (2001), htttp://bostonreview.mit.edu/BR26.1/white.html.

30. The economist Dani Rodrik points out that the developing countries that have fared best in the past decade were those that pursued the most aggressive

trade agendas, such as China. One might argue, on the contrary, that increasing competition between developing countries for limited market shares will reduce the overall benefit to be had from future increases in trade.

31. Henk Thomas, "The Erosion of Trade Unions," in *Globalization and Third World Trade Unions: The Challenge of Rapid Economic Change,* ed. Thomas Henk (London and New Jersey: Zed Books, 1995), pp. 3–27; Sarosh Kuruvilla, "Economic Development Strategies, Industrial Relations Policies and Workplace IR/HR Practices in Southeast Asia," in *The Comparative Political Economy of Industrial Relations,* ed. Kirsten S. Weaver and Lowell Turner (Madison, Wis.: IRRA, 1995), pp. 115–50.

32. Afredo Hualde Alfaro, "Corporatism, Nationalism, and Industrial Relations in Mexico," in *Colonialism, Nationalism, and the Institutionalization of Industrial Relations in the Third World,* ed. Sarosh Kuruvilla and Bryan Mundell (Stamford, Conn.: JAI Press, 1999).

33. Thomas, "Erosion of Trade Unions."

34. Siddique, "Industrial Relations in a Third World Setting."

35. International Confederation of Free Trade Unions, *Behind the Wire: Anti-Union Repression in the Export Processing Zones* (Brussels: ICFTU, 1998).

36. Siddique, "Industrial Relations in a Third World Setting."

37. Gay Seidman, "Social Movement Unionism in Transition: Labor and Democratization in South Africa," in *Research on Democracy and Society: Extremism, Protest, Social Movements, and Democracy,* ed. Frederick Weil (Stamford, Conn.: JAI Press, 1996).

38. Eddie Webster, "Diffusion of the Molotov Cocktail in South African Industrial Relations: The Burden of the Past and the Challenge of the Future" in *Colonialism, Nationalism, and the Institutionalization of Industrial Relations in the Third World,* ed. S. Kuruvilla and B. Mundell (Stamford, Conn.: JAI Press, 1999), pp. 19–58.

39. Hagen Koo, "The Dilemmas of Empowered Labor in Korea: Korean Workers in the Face of Global Capitalism," *Asian Survey* 40 (March/April 2000), pp. 227–50.

40. Alfaro, "Corporatism, Nationalism, and Industrial Relations in Mexico."

41. Sarosh Kuruvilla and Bryan Mundell, "Introduction" and "Conclusion" in *Colonialism, Nationalism, and the Institutionalization of Industrial Relations in the Third World* (Stamford, Conn.: JAI Press, 1999), pp. 1–17, 71–298.

42. Kyle Bagwell and Richard W. Staiger, "The Simple Economics of Labor Standards and the GATT," NBER working paper, no. w6604, 1998.

43. Keith E. Maskus, "Should Core Labor Standards Be Imposed Through International Trade Policy?" *World Bank Working Paper* No. 1817 (August 1997), http://www.worldbank.org/research/trade/wp1817.html.

44. Kimberly Ann Elliott, "The ILO and Enforcement of Core Labor Standards," *International Economics Policy Brief* (Washington, D.C.: Institute for International Economics, July 2000, updated April 2001), http://www.iie.com/policybriefs/news00–6.htm.

45. Elliott, "ILO and Enforcement of Core Labor Standards."

46. Henderson, *Misguided Virtue.*

47. Dara O'Rourke, "Comments on the Vietnam Section of the Tuck School Report: Nike, Inc.: Survey of Vietnamese and Indonesian Domestic Expenditure Levels," http://web.mit.edu/dorourke/www/PDF/tuck.pdf (1998); Dara O'Rourke, *Smoke from a Hired Gun: A Critique of Nike's Labor and Environmental Auditing in*

Vietnam as Performed by Ernst & Young (San Francisco, Calif.: Transnational Resource and Action Center, 2002), http://www.corpwatch.org/trac/nike/ernst/.

48. Douglas North, *Institutions, Institutional Change, and Economic Performance* (New York: Cambridge University Press, 1990).

49. Gerry Rodgers, "Labour, Institutions and Economic Development: Issues and Methods" in *The Institutional Approach to Labour and Development*, ed. G. Rogers, K. Foti, and L. Lauridsen (London: Frank Cass, 1996), pp. 4–25.

50. Rodgers, "Labour, Institutions and Economic Development," p. 6.

51. Rodgers, "Labour, Institutions and Economic Development."

52. Ibid.

53. Ibid.

54. Ibid.

55. This example is taken from the infamous Triangle Shirtwaist Factory in New York.

56. Rodgers, "Labour, Institutions and Economic Development."

57. Diane Wolf, "Linking Women's Labor with the Global Economy: Factory Workers and Their Families in Rural Java," in *Women Workers and Global Restructuring*, ed. Kathryn Ward (Ithaca, N.Y.: ILR Press, 1990), pp. 141–78.

58. Wolf, "Linking Women's Labor with the Global Economy," p. 8.

CHAPTER 4

Philosophical Foundations: Moral Reasoning, Human Rights, and Global Labor Practices

Denis G. Arnold

Ethical concerns are at the core of disputes concerning global labor practices. Critics charge multinational enterprises (MNEs) with the inhumane and unjust treatment of workers in developing nations. Economists retort that satisfying the demands of these critics will result in fewer jobs in developing nations, thereby reducing social welfare.[1] To properly evaluate these claims, and others like them, it is first necessary to provide an analysis of the ethical obligations of MNEs regarding global labor practices.

One set of ethical norms that is a prominent feature of contemporary public discourse, especially as it pertains to international affairs, is that of human rights. The promulgation of the United Nations Universal Declaration of Human Rights, together with the advocacy of organizations such as Amnesty International and Human Rights Watch, has led to the widespread acceptance of human rights as a basic tool of moral evaluation by individuals of widely divergent political and religious beliefs. Increasingly, the language of human rights is a prominent feature of debates regarding globalization and global labor practices.

This chapter explains how moral reasoning, together with an understanding of basic human rights, can help the moral manager to produce morally innovative solutions to global labor challenges. The chapter provides both a justification of the rights to freedom and well-being and an application of those rights to the circumstances of MNE workers. In so doing the chapter provides a moral basis both for the applications of human rights discussed in the remaining two chapters of Part I and for the programs and initiatives described in Part II of the book. Other important human rights issues confronting MNEs, such as the morally appropriate stance to take toward regimes that engage in systematic human rights violations, are necessarily beyond the scope of this essay.[2]

The chapter is organized into five sections. The first section introduces the idea of the moral manager. The second section provides an overview of the moral point of view. In the third section a justification of the rights to freedom and well-being is provided. The fourth section provides guidance concerning what it means to respect the rights to freedom and well-being at work. Finally, guidance for MNE managers who choose to be moral innovators is offered in the last section.

THE MORAL MANAGER

Ethics, or moral philosophy, is concerned with what is right and what is good. At its core, the study of ethics is the study of how we should live. Ethics, as a discipline, is concerned with our reasons for thinking that one course of action is right and that another course of action is wrong. In the Western philosophical tradition, the formal study of ethics extends back in history at least 2,400 years to Plato's academy in ancient Athens. Because they are so basic, ethical questions are an inescapable feature of the human condition. Questions concerning respect, fairness, courage, friendship, and integrity, to name only a few examples, arise with frequency both in our personal lives and in our working lives. However, the obligations of a professional manager differ significantly from those of an individual, a parent, or a citizen. For example, a manager has an obligation to senior executives and ultimately to the owners of the enterprise to ensure that his or her subordinate employees work in a manner consistent with the enterprise's accepted policies and procedures.

The unique moral obligations of managers are grounded in the particular role managers play in organizations. Peter Drucker provides a succinct definition of the role of a modern manager:

When I first began to study management, during and immediately after World War II, a manager was defined as "someone who is responsible for the work of subordinates." A manager in other words was a "boss," and management was rank and power. This is probably still the definition a good many people have in mind when they speak of "managers" and "management."

But by the early 1950s, the definition of a manager had already changed to one who "is responsible for the performance of people." Today, we know that is also too narrow a definition. The right definition of a manager is one who "is responsible for the application and performance of knowledge."[3]

Notice that Drucker's definition of the role of a manager is meant to be inclusive of the definitions that it supersedes. Managers enjoy rank and power, are responsible for the performance of people, and are responsible for the application of and performance of knowledge. In each of these roles, managers have distinct obligations. Insofar as they enjoy rank and power in the context of organizational internal decision structures, managers wield significant power over corporate policies and practices. The higher ranking the manager, the greater the power to effect positive (or negative) moral change. Insofar as they are responsible for the employees who work for them, managers are morally responsible for their employees' welfare and productivity. Finally, managers are responsible for both specialized and general knowledge. They are responsible for the specialized knowledge particular to their field of expertise (whether marketing, information technology, finance, human resources, sales, operations, or another specialty). They are also responsible for general knowledge of the organization's internal decision structures, its policies, and its goals. The internal decision structure of an organization comprises its offices and levels of responsibility, together with the rules that allow managers to differentiate between enterprise-level decisions and the decisions of individual employees.[4] A knowledge of these features of an organization is necessary if a manager is to become part of the organization's policy-making process.

One feature of the specialized knowledge for which managers are responsible concerns the moral complexities of the tasks with which they and the employees under their supervision are charged. Likewise, one feature of the general knowledge for which managers are responsible concerns the organization's ethics policies and practices. An innovative manager is one who introduces new ideas, methods, or practices. A *morally* innovative manager is thus one who introduces new ideas, methods, or practices of a distinctly moral nature.

The primary moral obligation of a manager of a business enterprise is to serve the interests of his or her employer by helping to produce and sell a product or service. This is not, however, the only obligation of a manager. Managers must balance this obligation with other obligations such as respect for the law and respect for core moral norms. The central moral problem in a business enterprise is not then "right against wrong" but is instead "right against right."[5] Managers must balance their legitimate obligation to the owners of the business with equally legitimate obligations to other stakeholders.

THE MORAL POINT OF VIEW

Suppose that an American MNE sourcing manager must choose between two offshore factories that wish to serve as suppliers. Both suppliers operate factories in a developing nation with an emerging democracy that has completed two rounds of free and fair elections. Workers in this nation have recently become entitled to freedom of association, collective bargaining, and a national health care program funded by social security payroll deductions. However, the ability of both federal and local officials to enforce these laws is minimal. Federal enforcement agencies are underfunded and understaffed, while residual corruption undermines the local enforcement of labor laws. Furthermore, there is a well-grounded concern on the part of federal officials that the enforcement of existing labor laws will result in higher costs for MNEs and that because of that, MNEs will place fewer orders in the domestic manufacturing sector.

The two suppliers submit bids, together with product samples. Both sets of samples meet minimum quality standards; however, the bid of supplier A is 20 percent more than the bid of supplier B. The bid differential is attributable to the fact that supplier A has substantially higher employee costs than supplier B. Supplier A provides workers with legally required overtime pay, deducts and pays to the government social security payroll taxes, provides bonuses for meeting specified quality standards, provides annual pay raises; provides opportunities to workers for promotion, and has invested in health and safety measures to prevent basic risks to the lives and health of employees while at work. Employees of supplier A who work 50 to 60 hours per week are able to avoid conditions of overall poverty as defined by the United Nations (see figure 4.1).

Supplier B, on the other hand, does not pay workers as required for overtime, deducts but does not turn over social security payroll taxes to the government, provides no bonuses or regular pay raises, provides no opportunities for promotion (instead making exclusive use of foreign nationals as supervisors), and has taken no measures to prevent basic risks to the lives and health of employees. Employees of supplier B who work 50 to 60 hours per week, typically live in conditions of extreme poverty as defined by the United Nations.

Figure 4.1
Types of Poverty

Types of Poverty	Deficiencies	Measures
Extreme Poverty (also known as Absolute Poverty)	Lack of income necessary to satisfy basic food needs	Minimum caloric intake and a food basket that meets that requirement
Overall Poverty (also known as Relative Poverty)	Lack of income necessary to satisfy basic non-food needs	Ability to secure shelter, energy, transportation, and basic health care, e.g.
Human Poverty	Lack of basic human capabilities	Access to goods, services, and infrastructure, e.g.

Source: United Nations Development Programme, *Poverty Report 2000: Overcoming Human Poverty* (New York: United Nations Development Programme, 2000).

It is platitudinous, but necessary, to observe that different individuals may agree that the correct choice is obvious, yet disagree about *which* choice is correct. Various interested parties—factory workers, economists, MNE shareholders, customers, and so on—will each have their own distinct perspectives. For example, some labor or human rights activists, or individuals sympathetic to the arguments put forth by such activists, might reason as follows: "The very existence of supplier A is unusual, as most factories in developing countries better fit the description of supplier B. The opportunity to work with supplier A should be embraced by the MNE, since doing so will promote human and labor rights. The additional costs are minimal for an American MNE." Some MNE sourcing managers or individuals sympathetic to the arguments put forth by such managers might reason as follows: "Supplier B is the norm in nearly all developing countries. It is the responsibility of national governments to enforce existing labor laws uniformly. When governments do not enforce such laws uniformly, an MNE cannot be expected to bear the costs of adhering to local labor laws, let alone the costs of providing the comfortable working conditions and high wages present in supplier A. To do so would place the MNE at a competitive disadvantage."

The disagreement between the MNE manager and the human rights activist may be usefully broken down into two distinct components. First, there may be empirical disagreements. For example, there may be disagreements about whether or not North American consumers are willing to pay higher prices to cover the costs of improved working conditions and higher employee wages; or disagreements about the significance of added labor costs relative to revenues; or disagreements about what formula ought to be employed to determine an appropriate hourly or weekly wage. Empirical disagreements can be resolved only by objective scrutiny of the best available data.[6] Empirical matters are of obvious and significant importance for the purposes of assessing the moral legitimacy of different global labor practices. However, empirical disagreements concerning global labor practices are not the primary concern of this chapter; such matters are taken up elsewhere in this book (see, especially, chapters 2 and 3).

Second, there may be normative disagreements about the moral norms that ought to guide the decisions of managers. For example, there may be disagreements concerning those to whom managers have obligations; or disagreements concerning the nature of those obligations; or disagreements concerning how those obligations ought to be prioritized. Normative disagreements differ from empirical disagreements in that disputants of the former variety may embrace different, sometimes incompatible, moral stances. The resolution of such disagreements can be resolved only by reference to the moral point of view or to the principles derived from the moral point of view.

The moral point of view may be understood as the point of view of every person. Here the term *person* is used in a technical sense to denote rational, self-governing beings. When we take the moral point of view, we seek to adjudicate disputes rationally, we assume that other persons are neither more nor less important than ourselves, and we assume that our own claims will be considered alongside those of others in an impartial manner. These three components of the moral point of view are respectively concerned with rationality, universalizability, and impartiality. They may be summarized as follows:

1. **Rationality.** The moral point of view is rational in the sense that it involves the application of reason rather than feeling or mere inclination. Moral issues frequently invoke a strong emotional response in individuals. The attempt to justify a moral stance by appeal to reasons that may be considered and evaluated by other persons facilitates a process whereby individuals with distinctly different emotional responses to a moral issue may seek mutual understanding and perhaps agreement.

2. **Universalizability.** The moral point of view is universal in the sense that the principles or propositions ascertained therefrom apply to all persons and to all relevantly similar circumstances. Thus, if a moral principle or proposition is valid, no persons are exempt from its strictures.

3. **Impartiality.** The moral point of view is impartial in the sense that principles or propositions ascertained therefrom apply to persons irrespective of arbitrary considerations. This impartiality may involve the application of a specific principle that purposively ignores the circumstances of individual lives, or it may involve an unbiased evaluation of the particular reality of individual persons and an assessment of the needs and preferences of individual persons in light of the needs and preferences of others. In any case, it requires that characteristics such as a person's race, sex, nationality, and economic circumstances, for example, cannot be regarded as a legitimate basis for treating persons differently from other persons when there are no good reasons for thinking such considerations relevant.

It is important to note that the moral point of view does not exclude partiality. Favoring the interests of one party over another is justified when there are overriding reasons for ranking the specific interests of one party over another. This is especially so when one has familial, professional, or contractual responsibilities. This point is of obvious relevance to business managers who have distinct moral and legal obligations to their employers. The challenge for moral managers is to determine when the interests of their employers trump those of other stakeholders and when the interests of those stakeholders override the interests of the managers' employers.

The idea of the moral point of view may seem commonplace, but it is an idea with deep theoretical foundations. In the eighteenth century Immanuel Kant, the great Enlightenment philosopher, argued that one should always treat other persons as an end unto themselves and never as a means only. Persons are free and rational creatures and as such, argued Kant, all persons have intrinsic value that must be respected. This means that the desires, goals, and aspirations of persons other than ourselves must be given due consideration. Kant did not merely assert that persons are entitled to due consideration, he provided a compelling argument for that conclusion. The interests of all persons ought to be given due consideration because persons have dignity. For Kant, a being that has dignity is beyond price. Persons have a dignity that mere objects lack. They have dignity because they are autonomous, responsible beings capable of rational activity, that is, they are moral beings. Reason requires that any moral principle must be rational in the sense that it is universal. The fact that persons have this capability means that they possess dignity. As a matter of consistency, persons who recognize themselves as moral beings must ascribe dignity and accord due respect to anyone who, like themselves, is a moral being.

How can using the moral point of view help us to adjudicate the normative disagreement between the MNE manager and the human rights activist? The most obvious way in which it can do so is by providing a minimal set of conditions with which both the manager and the activist must operate. These conditions are those of rationality, universality, and impartiality. A moral manager will not shirk operating from the perspective of the moral point of view. And a human rights activist who embraces the moral point of view will acknowledge the distinct obligations managers have to the owners of a business enterprise.

If the MNE manager takes the moral point of view, then which supplier should he or she choose? From the descriptions provided, it is clear that supplier A has made a concerted effort to treat workers with the respect and dignity that they deserve as persons. Supplier A has, in other words, made a concerted effort to honor the basic rights of workers. Supplier B appears to have made no such effort. The moral manager should therefore choose supplier A. The added cost of using supplier A, rather than supplier B, is a significant concern that needs to be addressed. However, it should not constitute an insurmountable obstacle for the moral manager for at least two reasons. First, it has been assumed for the sake of argument that honoring the basic rights of workers will result in higher costs. However, as will be argued in a later section of this chapter, that is not always so. Second, in cases such as the example discussed above—cases in which respecting workers' rights does produce greater labor costs—numerous options for balancing these costs are available to morally innovative MNE managers. Some of these options are discussed below. From the moral point of view, however, these costs must be regarded as a necessary condition of doing business.

What is a moral manager to do when, as is frequently the case, suppliers who honor the basic rights of workers are unavailable? One solution is to aid suppliers in developing labor practices that respect such rights. Examples of such initiatives are provided in Part II of this book. Moral managers overseeing company-owned factories in developing nations will, of course, also need to ensure that the basic rights of employees are respected. But what *specific* rights must be protected? To answer that question in a non-question-begging manner, it is necessary to provide a justification and explanation of basic human rights. It is to this task that we now turn.

THE JUSTIFICATION OF HUMAN RIGHTS

To think about human rights in a meaningful way, it is necessary to answer certain philosophical questions about their nature. The following are three of the most basic questions: How can human rights be justified? What specific human rights exist? How do human rights differ from other rights, such as legal rights? Let us consider each question in turn.

Human rights are rights enjoyed by humans not because we are members of the species *Homo sapiens,* but because fully functional members of our species are persons. Personhood is a metaphysical category that may or may not be unique to *Homo sapiens.* To be a person one must be capable of reflecting on one's desires at a second-order level, and one must be capable of acting in a manner consistent with one's considered preferences.[7] First-order desires are the assortment of desires that occupy one's conscious mind and compete for one's attention. Second-order desires are desires about those first-order desires. When one embraces a particular first-order desire at a second-order level, it becomes a preference. A mundane example will help to illustrate this concept. All of us are likely to have found ourselves staring at a bedside clock after having turned off an early-morning alarm. Lying comfortably in bed, we might reflect on our immediate desires: to get up and go for a run, to get up and prepare for an early morning meeting, or to roll over and return to sleep. The process of reflecting on these competing desires takes place at a second-order level of consciousness. It is the capacity to reflect on one's competing desires and to act in a manner consistent with one's second-order preferences that distinguishes persons from mere animals. This is not to say that one cannot sometimes fail to act in a manner consistent with one's better judgment and still be regarded as a person. Indeed, most of us are intimately familiar with such weakness of the will. The point is that we enjoy this capacity, and we are capable of acting in a manner consistent with this capacity. Furthermore, if humans were constitutionally incapable of acting in a manner consistent with their second-order preferences, they would not be properly described as persons.[8] It is in this sense that the idea of personhood is properly understood as metaphysical rather than biological.[9]

The derivation of human rights from the concept of personhood is a complex endeavor and one of the most important accomplishments of twentieth-century philosophy. Some of the most important work on this topic has been produced by the philosopher Alan Gewirth. In his influential book *Reason and Morality*, Gewirth provides a rigorous and detailed justification of human rights.[10] Since it is sometimes argued that human rights cannot be justified without appealing to specific religious or legal traditions, it is necessary to provide a summary of Gewirth's philosophical defense of human rights.

Gewirth begins with the idea that all people regard their purposes as good according to their own criteria. By rising each morning and pursuing their own individual goals, people demonstrate in a practical way those things that they value.[11] Such actions are possible only insofar as the necessary conditions of their acting to achieve their purposes are satisfied. In other words, via the act of pursuing their individual aims, people demonstrate that they value the necessary conditions of action. The necessary conditions of action are freedom and well-being. Without freedom and well-being, people cannot pursue those things that they value. Freedom is here understood as controlling one's behavior by one's unforced choice while having knowledge of relevant circumstances. Possessing well-being entails having the general abilities and conditions required to be able to act in a manner consistent with one's considered, or second-order, preferences. Anyone who pursues a particular good must, on pain of contradiction, claim to have a right to freedom and well-being. As such, all people must accept that others have rights to freedom and well-being. Gewirth expresses the matter this way:

Since the agent [or person] regards as necessary goods the freedom and well-being that constitute the generic features of his successful action, he logically must hold that he has rights to these generic features, and he implicitly makes a corresponding rights claim.[12]

Gewirth is not arguing, as some might think, that because persons require freedom and well-being to function, they are thereby entitled to freedom and well-being.[13] Such an argument, one grounded in *empirical necessity*, would not be convincing because having a right to something does not follow from the fact that one requires that thing. While Gewirth's argument does have an empirical component, it is properly understood as a transcendental argument in the Kantian tradition. A transcendental argument is one that establishes the truth of a proposition by appealing to necessary conditions of human experience. Gewirth's argument is that, as a matter of *rational consistency*, persons must acknowledge that they are purposive beings and that the pursuit of their ends requires freedom and well-being. Hence they must claim a right to freedom and well-being. To do otherwise would be irrational. Because all other persons share these qualities, they must—again, as a matter of rational consistency—ascribe these rights to all other beings. To deny that persons have the right to freedom and well-being is to deny that one is a purposive being. Since the denial is a purposive act, it contradicts the proposition being asserted. In this way, Gewirth provides a deep and satisfying justification for human rights. Because the justification is grounded in rational reflection on the human condition, it can be embraced by individuals of diverse religious faiths and different cultural identities.

At this point in our discussion it is worthwhile to consider an objection to the foregoing argument concerning human rights. This criticism stems from the observation that the idea of human rights emerged from the Western philosophical tradition, but is taken to be universal in its applicability. The claim is then made that human rights are of less importance in the value systems of other cultures. For example, it is argued that Asian values emphasize order, discipline, and social harmony, as opposed to individual rights. In this view, the freedom and well-being of individuals should not be allowed to interfere with the harmony of the community, as might be the case, for example, when workers engage in disruptive collective action in an effort to secure their rights. This view might also be used to defend the claim that the moral norms that govern Asian factory operations should emphasize order and discipline, not freedom and well-being.

Several points may be made in reply to that objection. First, Asia is a large region with a vast and heterogeneous population. As Amartya Sen and others have argued, to claim that all, or even most, Asians share a uniform set of values is to impose a level of uniformity that does not exist at present and has not existed in the past.[14] Second, in secular, democratic Asian societies such as India, respect for individual rights has a long tradition. Indeed, there are significant antecedents in the history of the civilizations of the Indian subcontinent that emphasize individual freedom and well-being. For example, in the third century B.C.E. the emperor Ashoka granted his citizens the freedom to embrace whatever religious or philosophical system they might choose, while he emphasized the importance of tolerance and respect for philosophical and religious beliefs different from one's own.[15] Third, even if it was the case that Asian cultures shared a uniform set of values that de-emphasized human rights, that would not by itself provide good reasons for denying or disrespecting the rights to freedom and well-being. This is because the justification of human rights provided above is grounded in rational arguments that are valid across cultures. Jack Donnely makes a similar point in his recent defense of universal human rights.

One of the things that makes us human is our capacity to create and change our culture. Cultural diversity has in recent years increasingly come to be valued in itself. Westerners have in recent centuries been especially insensitive in their approach to such differences. Nonetheless, the essential insight of human rights is that the worlds we make for ourselves, intentionally and unintentionally, must conform to relatively universal requirements that rest on our common humanity and seek to guarantee equal concern and respect from the state for every person.[16]

The critic is likely to retort that such a view reflects Western prejudices grounded in Enlightenment ideals. However, that response is unpersuasive. Diverse intellectual traditions have emphasized the importance of values derived from reason, rather than mythology, traditionalism, mere sentiment, or some other source. For example, in the sixteenth century the Moghul emperor Akbar wrote:

The pursuit of reason and rejection of traditionalism are so brilliantly patent as to be above the need for argument. If traditionalism were proper, the prophets would merely have followed their own elders (and not come with new messages).[17]

Akbar arranged to have philosophers representing diverse religious and philosophical beliefs engage in rational discussions regarding the merits of their competing views, and sought to identify the most persuasive features of each view. In so doing, Akbar was able to emphasize the power and force of rational analysis. Given that a similar emphasis on rational analysis concerning values may be found in the histories of other non-Western cultures, the claim that such analysis is uniquely Western is unpersuasive.

Human rights are moral rights that apply to all persons in all nations, regardless of whether the nation in which a person resides acknowledges and protects those rights. It is in this sense that human rights are said to be *inalienable*. Human rights differ from legal rights in that, unlike legal rights, the existence of human rights is not contingent on any institution. Many nations grant their citizens certain constitutional or legal rights via foundational documents or legal precedent. However, the rights that are protected vary among nations. Some nations ensure that the rights of citizens are protected by effective policing and an independent judiciary. Frequently, however, poor citizens and disfavored groups are not provided with the same level of protection for their legal rights as the economic and political elite. Persons who are deprived of their rights do not thereby cease to have those rights. As A. I. Melden has argued,

the complaint that persons are deprived of their human rights when, for example, they are subjected to forced indenture by their employers, is a complaint that their rights have been violated and implies, clearly, that they have rights they are unjustly prevented from exercising. If one were deprived of one's rights in the sense in which one would be deprived of things in one's physical possession by having them taken away, one would no longer have the rights, and there would be no grounds for the complaint. So it is with the denial of a person's right—this does not consist in denying that he has the right but, rather, in denying him, by withholding from him, that to which he has the right or the means or opportunity for its exercise.[18]

Employers may deny employees their inalienable right to freedom and well-being, whether or not local governments are complicit, but in doing so they in no way diminish the legitimacy of the claims of their employees to those rights. However, by virtue of their failure to operate from the moral point of view, such employers succeed in diminishing their own standing in the community of rights holders.

HUMAN RIGHTS AND LABOR PRACTICES

We have seen how a right to freedom and a right to well-being can be justified. If persons have a right to freedom and well-being, then at a minimum other persons have an obligation to refrain from interfering with those rights. It is in this sense that rights entail corresponding duties on the part of other persons. What are the specific obligations or duties of MNE managers with respect to the freedom and well-being of employees, and how are these obligations to be balanced against the obligations of managers to their employers?

Because freedom and well-being are basic rights, the obligation to respect those rights are equally basic. As such, no labor practices may be undertaken that will violate a worker's right to freedom and well-being. MNEs are in a unique position to ensure that basic rights are respected in the workplace by virtue of their power and the vast resources under their command. In the words of the United Nations, "Society no longer accepts the view that the conduct of global corporations is bound only by the laws of the country they operate in. By virtue of their global influence and power, they must accept responsibility and be accountable for upholding high human rights standards."[19] As was noted above, MNEs typically have well-defined internal decision structures that provide an internal mechanism for enforcing human rights standards. For that reason, morally innovative managers are well positioned to play a constructive role in ensuring that the rights of workers in developing nations are respected.[20]

MNE managers should regard respect for their employees' rights to freedom and well-being as constraints on the activities they undertake on behalf of their employers. However, the rights to freedom and well-being are very general. Greater specificity regarding the content of these rights must be provided.

Let us begin with freedom. Previously we characterized freedom as controlling one's behavior via one's unforced choice while having knowledge of relevant circumstances. Gewirth provides a helpful summary of the content of the right to freedom:

This consists in a person's controlling his actions and his participation in transactions by his own unforced choice or consent and with knowledge of relevant circumstances, so that his behavior is neither compelled nor prevented by the actions of other persons. Hence, a person's right to freedom is violated if he is subjected to violence, coercion, deception, or any other procedures that attack or remove his informed control of his behavior by his own unforced choice. This right includes having a sphere of personal autonomy and privacy whereby one is let alone by others unless and until he unforcedly consents to undergo their action.[21]

Possessing freedom entails having the general abilities and conditions required to be able to act in a manner consistent with one's second-order preferences. A right to freedom, then, involves the right to pursue one's own goals and preferences without interference from others. Specifically, it includes control over one's own physical integrity, freedom of belief and expression, and freedom of association. Traditionally, the right to freedom is thought to be as extensive as is compatible with a like right to freedom for all. Such freedom is not, however, unlimited. It may be rightfully curtailed if one's actions illegitimately infringe on the freedom or well-being of others.

The rights one enjoys as a human being are not unlimited in the sense that one is free to exercise all of them under any circumstances. Legitimate restrictions may be placed on the exercise of one's rights by both the state and private enterprise. It is, for example, not an illegitimate infringement of one's right to freedom of belief and expression if an employer prohibits proselytizing on behalf of one's religious convictions while at work. Such activity is typically disruptive and as such incompatible with the purposes for which employees are hired. Furthermore, employees are free to engage in such activity when they are not working. Restricting employee activity in this manner does not infringe on an employee's dignity as a person. There are, however, certain restrictions on employee freedom that always violate human dignity because they treat the employee as a tool rather than as a person. Control over one's physical integrity is one such example. This freedom could, for example, be violated by a rule that permitted only one bathroom break each day.

Several international covenants and conventions are available to MNEs interested in specific guidance with respect to their global labor practices. For example, the Articles of the United Nations Universal Declaration of Human Rights (1948) provide specific examples of what it means to respect an employee's right to freedom at work (see below). Articles 3, 4, and 5 provide a basis for the prohibition of all forced labor, indentured servitude, corporeal punishment of employees by supervisors, and seriously unsafe working conditions. Article 23, section 4, provides a basis for the prohibition of the termination of employees for organizing or joining a trade union:

Article 3

Everyone has the right to life, liberty, and security of person.

Article 4

No one shall be held in slavery or servitude; slavery and the slave trade shall be prohibited in all their forms.

Article 5

No one shall be subjected to torture or to cruel, inhuman or degrading treatment or punishment.

Article 23, Section 4

Everyone has the right to form and to join trade unions for the protection of his interests.[22]

Now let us turn to well-being. As we have seen, well-being entails a person's having the general abilities and conditions required to be able to act autonomously. The most important component of well-being, and the one that we shall focus on here, is basic goods. Basic goods are the general physical and psychological capabilities necessary for human functioning. In recent years the relationship between well-being and human functioning has received a great deal of attention from economists and philosophers. Some of the most important work on this topic has been produced by Amartya Sen and Martha Nussbaum. Their distinctive variety of quality-of-life assessment, known as the capabilities approach, has become increasingly influential. That is partly due to the fact that it has been adapted by the United Nations Development Programme (UNDP) and has been incorporated into the UNDP Human Development Reports since 1993. The relationship between human functioning and well-being is usefully articulated by Sen:

The primary feature of well-being can be seen in terms of how a person can "function," taking that term in a very broad sense. I shall refer to various doings and beings that come into this assessment as functionings. These could be activities (like eating or reading or seeing), or states of existence or being, e.g., being well nourished, being free from malaria, not being ashamed by the poverty of one's clothing or shoes (to go back to a question that Adam Smith discussed in his *Wealth of Nations*).[23]

It is important to note that not all persons will have the same capacity to function well with the same goods. Variations in the transformation of goods into constituent elements of well-being will vary significantly among persons.

Take, for example, the consumption of food, on the one hand, and the functioning of being well nourished, on the other. The relationship between them varies with (1) metabolic rates, (2) body size, (3) age, (4) sex (and if a woman, whether pregnant or lactating), (5) activity levels, (6) medical services, (7) nutritional knowledge, and other influences.[24]

Access to the basic goods necessary for human functioning does not mean that a person who enjoys the basic goods necessary to function well will do so. Two individuals may have access to the same goods necessary for each of them to achieve the same level of well-being, yet fail to do so because one of them made choices that reduced his or her ability to function well. For that reason it is necessary to emphasize an individual's *capability* to function. What are these capabilities?

Nussbaum identifies 10 capabilities as necessary for humans to enjoy well-being: life; bodily health; bodily integrity; senses, imagination, and thought; emotion; practical reason; affiliation; other species; play; and control over one's environment.[25] The list is itself the product of years of cross-cultural study and discussion and represents a sort of overlapping consensus on the part of individuals with widely disparate views of human life. Nussbaum is careful to point out both that the list is open-ended and that items on the list may be interpreted somewhat differently in different societies. However, each item on the list is of central importance and, as such, when a person falls below any one of the central areas, it must be regarded as a significant loss. The claim being defended here is not that MNE managers have an obligation to ensure that all of their employees function well. Instead, the claim is that MNE managers have an obligation to ensure that the right of their employees to basic goods is respected at work. By ensuring that these basic needs are met, managers will meet their moral obligation to provide their employees with the capability to function well.

The Articles of the United Nations Universal Declaration of Human Rights provide a valuable resource for determining what it means for an employer to respect an employee's right to well-being (see below). Article 23, section 2, provides a basis for the prohibition of discrimination based on arbitrary characteristics such as race or sex. Article 23, section 2, and article 25, section 1, provide a basis for paying employees wages that are consistent with living with dignity. They also provide a basis for thinking that it is the responsibility of MNEs to ensure that social security and other taxes are paid to appropriate governmental authorities. Article 24 provides a basis for the view that employees are entitled to wages adequate for a dignified standard of living without working extensive overtime hours:

Article 23

(2) Everyone, without any discrimination, has the right to equal pay for equal work.

(3) Everyone who works has the right to just and favorable remuneration ensuring for himself and his family an existence worthy of human dignity, and supplemented, if necessary, by other means of social protection.

Article 24

Everyone has the right to rest and leisure, including reasonable limitation of working hours and periodic holidays with pay.

Article 25

(1) Everyone has the right to a standard of living adequate for health and well-being of himself and of his family, including food, clothing, housing and medical care and necessary social services, and the right to security in the event of unemployment, sickness, disability, widowhood, old age or other lack of livelihood in circumstances beyond his control.[26]

Some individuals who are very much concerned with the welfare of workers in developing nations will disagree with the conclusion that MNE labor practices must not violate a worker's right to freedom and well-being. The claim is frequently made, with varying degrees of sophistication, that respecting employee rights will result in greater harm than good. For example, in a recent monograph—a monograph endorsed by *The Economist*[27]—David Henderson argues that the expenditure by MNEs of corporate resources in the interest of "human rights" or "social justice" will result in workers being made worse off.

In so far as managers down the line, in the pursuit of such goals, are made subject to company-wide specific instructions governing hiring, selection, promotion, dismissal and permitted terms and conditions of employment, freedom of contract is liable to be curtailed. A range of mutually advantageous deals may be precluded. Not only will such enforced uniformity of practices tend to raise enterprise costs, but also, like economy-wide regulations or restrictive agreements of the kind referred to above, it prevents labour markets from functioning freely, and hence deprives ordinary people of opportunities to make themselves better off.[28]

Henderson's conclusion is shared by Ian Maitland who claims that "attempts to improve on market outcomes may have unforeseen tragic consequences" for workers in developing nations.[29] The core argument of both Henderson and Maitland, as it pertains to formal sector workers in developing nations, is that the imposition of wages or labor standards greater than those demanded by the market will increase costs, and that this will inevitably lead to layoffs and higher unemployment. How persuasive is that argument?

To see that voluntarily improving employee wages and working conditions will not inevitably lead to the "tragic consequences" that Henderson and Maitland predict, consider the following points.[30] First, with regard to the lowest-paid formal-sector wage earners in developing countries, the assumption that productivity is independent of wage levels is mistaken. Put simply, workers whose minimum daily dietary requirements are met and who have basic nonfood needs met, will have more energy and better attitudes at work; will be less likely to come to work ill; and will be absent less frequently. Workers are thus likely to be more productive and loyal. Increased productivity resulting from better nutrition and increased employee loyalty alone may offset the cost of higher wages.[31] Second, it is economically feasible for MNEs to raise wages and improve working conditions in factories in developing economies without causing increases in unemployment. MNEs may *choose* to improve wages and working conditions while maintaining existing employment levels. Profit margins vary among products. For the manufacturers of brand-name retail goods, a significant increase in labor costs may be readily absorbed as an operating expense. Indeed, the expense may be offset by the value added to the good insofar as consumers demonstrate a preference for products produced under conditions in which the rights of workers are respected. Third, there may be cases in which increased labor costs are not offset by greater productivity and in which the increase in costs cannot be readily absorbed as an operating expense. For example, manufacturers of generic goods with low profit margins *may* find it difficult to simply absorb the cost of increased labor expenses. In such cases, the added cost of labor may instead be balanced by internal cost-cutting measures;[32] or it may be passed on to consumers via higher prices,[33] or it may be passed on to the owners of the business enterprise via lower return on equity.[34]

MORAL IMAGINATION AND INNOVATION

As we have seen, the Universal Declaration of Human Rights provides a valuable resource for moral managers who wish to respect the rights of employees. In addition, the International Labour Organization's (ILO) carefully developed conventions and recommendations on safety and health provide a detailed template for minimum safety standards. Both the UN and the ILO provide specific guidance to MNEs via the ILO's Tripartite Declaration of Principles concerning Multinational Enterprises and Social Policy (1977) and the United Nations Global Compact (1999).

However, knowledge of specific examples of the rights to freedom and well-being is not by itself sufficient for the moral manager to ensure that employee rights are respected. Something more is needed. Managers must be capable of innovative moral decision making.

The claim that managers must be capable of innovative strategic decision making is so common as to be passé. However, the claim that managers qua managers must also be capable of innovative *moral* decision making has only recently been the subject of serious study. In an important recent book, Patricia Werhane provides a sustained defense of the thesis that moral imagination is a necessary condition of innovative managerial moral decision making.[35] Werhane defines the functioning of moral imagination in the following terms. First, managers must have an *awareness of the particular* that includes the following:

1. Awareness of the character, context, situation, event, and dilemma at issue.
2. Awareness of the script . . . in that context and role relationships entailed in that context.
3. Awareness of possible moral conflicts or dilemmas that might arise in that situation, including dilemmas created at least in part by the dominating script or the situation itself.[36]

Second, managers must have a *capacity for productive imagination.* A productive moral imagination involves an awareness of an "incomplete, perhaps even limiting or distorting script" and a willingness to challenge that script. Third, managers must have a *capacity for creativity* that will enable them to "envision and actualize novel, morally justifiable possibilities through a fresh point of view or conceptual scheme."[37] Managers must, in other words, be capable of understanding, evaluating, and rewriting the script.

That managers can assess an existing script regarding labor practices, recognize the limitations of that script, and produce a new script is well illustrated by the case of Mattel, Inc. In 1997 senior executives at Mattel, the world's largest manufacturer of toys, assessed their existing script concerning global labor practices and determined it to be morally unsatisfactory. In that same year Mattel announced the creation of its Global Manufacturing Principles (GMP) and the establishment of an independent monitoring council to ensure compliance with the GMP at the 20+ factories that are owned or controlled by Mattel, and at the 300+ production facilities with which Mattel contracts.[38] According to S. Prakash Sethi, Chair of Mattel's Independent Monitoring Council for Global Manufacturing Principles, this was the first time that a major MNE "voluntarily committed itself to independent monitoring by outside observers with complete authority to make their findings available to the public."[39] Sethi reports Mattel's progress to date has been commendable:

Mattel has already completed extensive in-house audits to ensure that its own plants, and those of the company's major suppliers, are in compliance with Mattel's Global Manufacturing Principles. Where necessary, it has also worked closely with the company's suppliers to help them improve their operations so as to meet Mattel's standards—frequently at Mattel's expense. And, in a number of cases, where suppliers have been unable or unwilling to make such an effort, Mattel has discontinued its business relationship with those suppliers.

Mattel has been quite responsive to the needs of the communities where it has major plants and other types of operations. The company has committed itself to a program of coordinated activities that would (1) help the communities where it has operations, and (2) further strengthen and expand programs that would help workers—through education and training—develop non-job related skills that would enhance their productivity and income once they leave Mattel and pursue other employment and career options. Mattel has also committed the company to establishing higher standards of work and living environments for its workers in overseas operations, both in all new facilities that it would build in the future, and through upgrading of its current facilities.[40]

Mattel's efforts to substantially improve its global labor practices demonstrate both respect for the rights of employees and moral imagination. The case studies included in Part II of this book include previously undocumented examples of company programs that, to one degree or another, demonstrate similar moral innovation in their global labor practices.

CONCLUSION

As has been noted in previous chapters, the vast majority of workers in most developing nations operate outside or at the periphery of formal employment relations. As formal sector employment increases in these nations, MNEs that demonstrate respect for the rights of workers can be expected to have an influence on the local norms governing labor practices disproportionate to the number of workers that they actually employ. This is because they, together with morally innovative indigenous employers, will be setting the standard against which other employers must be measured. The result will be a substantially improved quality of life for the growing ranks of workers in the formal sector. Correspondingly, morally innovative MNEs and their suppliers can be expected to enjoy the most productive and loyal indigenous workers since they will be ranked among the most desirable employers. Furthermore, as increasing numbers of workers leave the informal sector in pursuit of better opportunities in the formal sector, less pressure will be exerted on the scarce productive resources of the informal sector. This should permit an enhanced standard of living for those remaining in the informal sector.

It has been argued that freedom and well-being are rights that all persons enjoy qua persons, and that MNEs have an obligation to ensure that these rights are properly respected in their factories and in those of their subcontractors. If such rights *are* recognized, how are they to be protected? The remaining two chapters of Part I of this book provide answers to that question. In chapter 5 Michael Santoro discusses the roles nongovernmental organizations can play in helping to ensure that worker rights are protected. In chapter 6 Sandra Waddock and Charles Bodwell present a systems approach that may be employed by MNE managers to ensure that the rights of workers are protected. It is hoped that these contributions will provide practical guidance for those interested in protecting human rights globally.

NOTES

1. See chapters 2 and 3 for an in-depth discussion of these issues.

2. An important set of arguments concerning the obligations of MNEs regarding human rights may be found in Thomas Donaldson, *The Ethics of International Business* (New York: Oxford University Press, 1989). For helpful discussions of the morally appropriate stances that MNEs should take toward repressive regimes, see John R. Schermerhorn Jr., "Terms of Global Business Engagement in Ethically Challenged Environments: Applications to Burma," *Business Ethics Quarterly* 9 (July 1999): pp. 485–505; S. Prakash Sethi and Oliver F. Williams, *Economic Imperatives and Ethical Values in Global Business: The South African Experience and International Codes Today* (Dordrecht: Kluwer Academic Publishers, 2000); and Michael A. Santoro, *Profits and Principles: Global Capitalism and Human Rights in China* (Ithaca, N.Y.: Cornell University Press, 2000).

3. Peter F. Drucker, *Post-Capitalist Society* (New York: HarperCollins, 1993), p. 44.

4. The idea of an organizational internal decision structure was first articulated by Peter French nearly 25 years ago in his essay "The Corporation as a Moral Person," *American Philosophical Quarterly* 16 (1979): pp. 207–17. For a statement of his current views on the subject see his *Corporate Ethics* (Fort Worth, Tex.: Harcourt Brace, 1995).

5. See Drucker, *Post-Capitalist Society*, p. 99.

6. The question of what constitutes objectivity is complicated. For helpful discussions of this issue see Harold I. Brown, *Perception, Theory, and Commitment* (Chicago, Ill.: University of Chicago Press, 1977); and Helen Logino, *Science as Social Knowledge* (Princeton, N.J.: Princeton University Press, 1990).

7. For a defense of this account of personhood see Harry G. Frankfurt, *The Importance of What We Care About* (Cambridge, U.K.: Cambridge University Press, 1988); see also Gerald Dworkin, *The Theory and Practice of Autonomy* (Cambridge, U.K.: Cambridge University Press, 1988).

8. Not surprisingly, the question of what rights humans with severe mental impairment may be said to have is a complex one. Addressing this important topic is, however, beyond the scope of this essay.

9. For an important discussion of the relationship of personhood to rights, see A. I. Melden, *Rights and Persons* (Berkeley, Calif.: University of California Press, 1977).

10. Alan Gewirth, *Reason and Morality* (Chicago, Ill.: University of Chicago Press, 1978).

11. One might object to this view on the grounds that some people pursue ends that they themselves do not regard as valuable. Such an objection fails to undermine Gewirth's point since, on his account, one demonstrates that one regards some ends as valuable insofar as one pursues that end. Here Gewirth's position may be regarded as consistent with those social scientists who are interested in studying not what people say they value, but what they demonstrate they value through their actions.

12. Gewirth, *Reason and Morality*, p. 63.

13. For example, Alasdair MacIntyre mistakenly interprets Gewirth in this manner. See Alasdair MacIntyre, *After Virtue*, 2E (Notre Dame, Ind.: University of Notre Dame Press, 1984), pp. 66–67.

14. See Amartya Sen, "Human Rights and Asian Values," in *Business Ethics in the Global Marketplace*, ed. Tibor R. Machan (Stanford, Calif.: Hoover Institution Press, 1999), pp. 37–62; and "East and West: The Reach of Reason," *The New York Review of Books* (July 20, 2000), pp. 33–38. Much of my discussion of these issues follows that of Sen. See also Inoue Tatsuo, "Liberal Democracy and Asian Orientalism," in *The East Asian Challenge for Human Rights*, ed. Joanne R. Bauer and Daniel A. Bell (Cambridge, U.K.: Cambridge University Press, 1999), pp. 27–59; and Jack Donnely, "Human Rights and Asian Values: A Defense of 'Western' Universalism," in *The East Asian Challenge for Human Rights*, ed. Joanne R. Bauer and Daniel A. Bell (Cambridge, U.K.: Cambridge University Press, 1999), pp. 60–87.

15. Sen, "Human Rights and Asian Values," pp. 48–53.

16. Donnely. "Human Rights and Asian Values, p. 87.

17. Quoted in Sen, "East and West: The Reach of Reason," p. 37.

18. Melden, *Rights and Persons*, pp. 167–68.

19. United Nations Development Programme, *Human Development Report 2000* (New York: Oxford University Press, 2000), p. 80.

20. Henry Shue argues that to make an exception on the part of MNEs with respect to the duty of not depriving other persons of their rights would be to effectively deny the existence of those rights. See Shue, *Basic Rights* (Princeton, N.J.: Princeton University Press, 1980), p. 170.

21. Alan Gewirth, *Human Rights: Essays on Justification and Applications* (Chicago, Ill.: University of Chicago Press, 1982), pp. 56–57.

22. United Nations Department of Public Information, "Universal Declaration of Human Rights," http://www.unhchr.ch/udhr/lang/eng.htm (accessed 31 July 2002).

23. Amartya Sen, "Well-Being, Agency and Freedom: The Dewey Lectures 1984," *Journal of Philosophy* 82 (April 1985), pp. 197–98.

24. Sen, "Well-Being, Agency and Freedom," pp. 198–9.

25. Central Human Functional Capabilities:

1. Life. Being able to live to the end of a human life of normal length; not dying prematurely, or before one's life is so reduced as to not be worth living.

2. Bodily health. Being able to have good health, including reproductive health; to be adequately nourished; to have adequate shelter.

3. Body integrity. Being able to move freely from place to place; having one's bodily boundaries treated as sovereign, that is, being able to be secure against assault, including sexual assault, child sexual abuse, and domestic violence; having opportunities for sexual satisfaction and for choice in matters of reproduction.

4. Senses, imagination, and thought. Being able to use the senses, to imagine, think, and reason—and to do these things in a "truly human" way, a way informed and cultivated by an adequate education, including, but by no means limited to, literacy and basic mathematical and scientific training. Being able to use imagination and thought in connection with experiencing and producing self-expressive works and events of one's own choice—religious, literary, musical, and so forth. Being able to use one's mind in ways protected by guarantees of freedom of expression with respect to both political and artistic speech, and freedom of religious exercise. Being able to have pleasurable experiences and to avoid unnecessary pain.

5. Emotion. Being able to have attachments to things and people outside of ourselves; to love those who love and care for us, to grieve at their absence; in general, to love, to grieve, to experience longing, gratitude, and justified anger. Not having one's emotional development blighted by overwhelming fear and anxiety or by traumatic events of abuse or neglect. (Supporting this capability means supporting forms of human association that can be shown to be crucial in their development.)

6. Practical reason. Being able to form a conception of the good and to engage in critical reflection about the planning of one's life. (This entails protection of the liberty of conscience.)

7. Affiliation.

    A. Being able to live with and toward others, to recognize and show concern for other human beings, to engage in various forms of social interaction; to be able to imagine the situation of another and have compassion for that situation; to have the capability for both justice and friendship. (Protecting this capability means protecting institutions that constitute and nourish such forms of affiliation and also protecting the freedom of assembly and political speech.)

    B. Having the social bases of self-respect and nonhumiliation; being able to be treated as a dignified being whose worth is equal to that of others. This entails, at a minimum, protections against discrimination on the basis of race, sex, sexual orientation, religion, caste, ethnicity, or national origin. In work, being able to work as a human being, exercising practical reason and entering into meaningful relationships of mutual recognition with other workers.

8. Other species. Being able to live with concern for and in relation to animals, plants, and the world of nature.

9. Play. Being able to laugh, to play, to enjoy recreational activities.

10. Control over one's environment.

    A. Political. Being able to participate effectively in political choices that govern one's life; having the right of political participation, protections of free speech and free association.

    B. Material. Being able to hold property (both land and movable goods), not just formally but in terms of real opportunity; having property rights on an equal basis with others; having the right to seek employment on an

equal basis with others; having the freedom from unwarranted search and seizure.
Martha Nussbaum, *Women and Human Development* (New York: Cambridge University Press, 2001), pp. 78–80.

26. United Nations Department of Public Information, "Universal Declaration of Human Rights," http://www.unhchr.ch/udhr/lang/eng.htm (accessed 31 July 2002).

27. "Curse of the Ethical Executive," *The Economist* (17 November 2001): p. 70.

28. David Henderson, *Misguided Virtue: False Notions of Corporate Social Responsibility* (London: Institute for Economic Affairs, 2001), http://www.iea.org.uk/record.php?type=publication&ID=143 (accessed 10 September 2002).

29. Ian Maitland, "The Great Non-Debate Over International Sweatshops," in *Ethical Theory and Business,* 6th ed., ed. Tom L. Beauchamp and Norman E. Bowie (Englewood Cliffs: Prentice Hall, 2001), p. 603.

30. For a more thorough reply to this objection, see Denis G. Arnold and Norman E. Bowie, "Sweatshops and Respect for Persons," *Business Ethics Quarterly* 13 (2003).

31. The wage that, if reduced, would make the firm worse off because of a decrease in worker productivity is known as the efficiency wage. Firms that pay employees at rates higher than the efficiency wage may enjoy other economic advantages such as reduced training costs as a result of greater employee loyalty. For theoretical and empirical discussions of efficiency wages, see C. J. Bliss and N. H. Stern, "Productivity, Wages, and Nutrition, 1: The Theory," *Journal of Development Economics* 5 (1978), pp. 331–62; and C. J. Bliss and N. H. Stern, "Productivity, Wages, and Nutrition, 2: Some Observations," *Journal of Development Economics* 5 (1978), pp. 363–98.

32. One set of obvious targets for expense reduction is the cost of supporting significant numbers of home country managers in the country of the supplier. While some presence may be necessary, it will often be more cost effective to employ host country nationals in this capacity. Another attractive set of targets is executive perks. While such perks vary significantly among firms, it does appear morally inconsistent to argue that improving the welfare of factory workers is cost prohibitive while executive perks remain substantial.

33. Given the frequently fierce competition among the manufacturers of generic products targeted at cost-conscious consumers, it may be difficult for one retailer to remain competitive while raising prices to cover increased labor costs, while others do not. For this reason, industry-wide standards concerning labor practices may prove valuable as a way of distributing costs equitably.

34. To keep investors informed regarding such policies it will be important to report on efforts to protect worker rights in annual reports and other appropriate MNE communications.

35. Patricia H. Werhane, *Moral Imagination and Management Decision Making* (New York: Oxford University Press, 1999).

36. Ibid., p. 103.

37. Ibid., p. 104.

38. S. Prakash Sethi, "Codes of Conduct for Multinational Corporations: An Idea Whose Time Has Come," *Business and Society Review* 104, no. 3 (1999): pp. 225–41.

39. Sethi, "Codes of Conduct," pp. 237–38.

40. Sethi, "Codes of Conduct," pp. 239–40.

CHAPTER 5

Philosophy Applied I: How Nongovernmental Organizations and Multinational Enterprises Can Work Together to Protect Global Labor Rights[1]

Michael A. Santoro [2]

The movement to hold multinational enterprises (MNEs) responsible for labor and human rights has largely been channeled through nongovernmental organizations (NGOs). Many NGOs are cooperating with MNEs to improve labor and human rights conditions in Third World factories. However, many human rights NGOs remain ambivalent about whether the better course is to confront or to cooperate with MNEs. Using interviews with managers of global marketing companies and NGO leaders, this chapter examines the strategic choices behind cooperative labor rights efforts as well as the reasons why many NGOs choose instead to pursue confrontational tactics.

We're having a big discussion within our internal business group. . . . The big question is: When do you move from a promotional, friendly relationship with a company to an oppositional relationship. . . . There are Amnesty members who probably say the only way you can deal with business is on the barricades. Others say the best way is to go and speak with the board. There will also be a range of views between the two extremes.

Irene Kahn, Secretary-General, Amnesty International, June 12, 2002[3]

ESTABLISHING ACCOUNTABILITY FOR LABOR AND HUMAN RIGHTS IN THE GLOBAL ECONOMY

Because multinational enterprises (MNEs) wield such conspicuous power and wealth, critics and activists seek to hold them responsible for a myriad of social problems resulting from the increased international trade and investment that characterize globalization.[4] Many have called for greater social responsibility from MNEs on issues ranging from the environment to combating the scourge of AIDS.[5] Among other things, global marketing firms are being asked to provide transparent assurance that their subcontractors and suppliers in Third World nations honor the rights of workers to a living wage, overtime pay, safe and healthy working conditions, and free association.[6]

For a number of reasons, the movement to hold MNEs responsible for labor and human rights has largely been channeled through nongovernmental organizations (NGOs). Many of the activities and transactions of MNEs are geographically dispersed and fast moving. As a result, they elude the governing will and capacity of both the developed countries in which MNEs are based and the developing countries in which manufacturing operations are located. In developing countries the competition to attract foreign capital and corruption both contribute to lax enforcement of local labor laws in a phenomenon that some have called a "race to the bottom." At the same time that national governments have failed to regulate global labor practices of MNEs, international institutions have yet to acquire sufficient power and global support to do so.[7] Legislators have from time to time considered imposing national and international legal obligations on MNEs operating in foreign countries.[8] To date, however, these efforts have not proved to be fruitful.

NGOs, along with labor unions, have stepped into the power vacuum to become the most conspicuous and vociferous critics of MNEs on labor and human rights.[9] In the United States, public attention first focused on sweatshop issues in the mid-1990s when the National Labor Committee, led by Charles Kernaghan, spearheaded a highly effective media campaign exposing labor violations at the licensees of a clothing label associated with television personality Kathy Lee Gifford.[10] In Europe consumer activism on global labor rights issues presaged the movement in the United States. In the early 1990s the Clean Clothes Campaign began in the Netherlands. A decade later, there were Clean Clothes Campaigns in 10 Western European countries pressuring retailers to use their purchasing power to improve global labor conditions.[11] Some critics of NGOs argue that valuable corporate resources are wasted when MNEs are forced to respond to NGO criticism about labor practices.[12] As Denis Arnold argues in chapter 4, however, MNEs have a moral obligation to ensure the basic rights of workers. NGOs, by default, are the primary channel for exerting pressure on MNEs to meet this moral obligation.

Not surprisingly, the watchdog human and labor rights role staked out by NGOs has engendered significant tension with MNEs. This tension over worker rights reflects a broader trend of mutual distrust. A 1998 Notre Dame–PricewaterhouseCoopers study authored by Georges En-

derle and Glen Peters found that 41 percent of NGOs concerned with
international social issues regarded their relationship with MNEs as "antagonistic," and another 47 percent said it was "ambivalent." Moreover,
the same survey found that 62 percent of NGOs believe that MNEs do
not care about ethical standards. Looking to the future, however, opti-
mism prevails. Sixty-one percent foresee a time when relations between
them will be "cooperative." Although only 30 percent of NGOs surveyed
had actually cooperated with MNEs, 80 percent thought it was possible
to do so.[13]

As the twenty-first century begins, many—though decidedly not all—
NGOs are cooperating with MNEs to improve labor and human rights
conditions in Third World factories. As the comments of Amnesty International's Irene Kahn poignantly illustrate, however, many human rights
NGOs remain ambivalent, if not downright confused, about whether the
better course is to confront or cooperate with MNEs. Using data gathered
from interviews with managers from global marketing companies and
NGO leaders concerned with global labor rights, this chapter examines
the strategic choices behind collaborative efforts as well as the reasons
why many NGOs remain deeply skeptical of the motivations of MNEs
and choose instead to pursue confrontational tactics. The chapter also offers various suggestions for how the effectiveness of this cooperation may
be enhanced.

CONFRONTATION AND COOPERATION: VARYING STRATEGIC OBJECTIVES AND TACTICS OF LABOR RIGHTS NGOs

The voluntary workplace code of conduct has become a cynosure in the
struggle for labor and human rights in the global economy.[14] Responding
to pressure from student groups, labor rights activists, and NGOs, many
retailing and manufacturing companies have adopted voluntary codes to
govern their own manufacturing operations and those of their subcontractors and suppliers in Third World nations.[15]

NGOs have had varied responses to the voluntary efforts of MNEs to
adopt and enforce codes of conduct. Some have encouraged these voluntary efforts and worked cooperatively with MNEs in the hopes of
achieving sustainable and systemic—albeit incremental—improvements
in the protection of global labor and human rights. For example, NGOs
such as Social Accountability International (SAI), the Fair Labor Association (FLA), and the Ethical Trading Initiative (ETI) have developed standardized voluntary codes of conduct for adoption by participating
companies. These NGOs have also engaged MNEs in a wide array of
collaborative efforts to monitor compliance with voluntary codes and improve labor conditions in Third World factories. By contrast, NGOs such

as the United Students Against Sweatshops (USAS) and Global Exchange, working in tandem with unions such as the Union of Needletrades, Industrial and Textile Employees (UNITE), have maintained a skeptical attitude and, in large measure, confrontational approach toward MNEs. These groups continue to keep the pressure on MNEs through muckraking investigations and publicity campaigns that expose egregious practices in selected manufacturing facilities throughout the world.

While this chapter concerns global labor rights, a mixture of cooperation and confrontation between NGOs and MNEs can also be observed in regard to other human rights and other social issues. Moreover, government can sometimes play a useful role in facilitating such cooperation. Perhaps the most successful example of such government facilitation can be found in the creation, in the last year of the Clinton administration, of the Voluntary Principles on Security and Human Rights, for which the U.S. State Department and the U.K. Foreign Office brought together human rights NGOs and several large oil, mining, and energy companies.[16]

EMBRACING COOPERATION WHOLEHEARTEDLY: SAI, FLA, AND ETI

SAI, a multistakeholder NGO with participation from industry and labor, started operations in 1997. It was founded by The Council on Economic Priorities to improve on existing supply chain code of conduct programs.[17] Its verification system is modeled after International Organization for Standardization (ISO) methodology. The SA8000 standard is designed to function either as a substitute for or as a complement to a company's own voluntary code.

SAI oversees a standardized global system enabling MNEs to monitor the labor practices of their suppliers and subcontractors. It accredits and trains third-party monitoring firms to conduct social certification audits of facilities in nine categories—child labor, forced labor, health and safety, freedom of association, discrimination, disciplinary practices, working hours, management oversight, and compensation (including a living-wage provision). In many countries, SAI also partners with international trade unions, local NGOs, and others to provide worker training, supplier training, and auditor training. The SA8000 standard is derived, as are most voluntary codes, from existing human rights instruments, including the Universal Declaration of Human Rights, the United Nations Convention on the Rights of the Child, and various conventions of the International Labour Organization.

By early 2002, eight auditing organizations had been accredited to conduct SA8000 certification audits. Certification had been earned by 133 facilities, employing over 69,000 workers, in 26 countries, including China, Italy, the United States, Vietnam, Brazil, Turkey, Malaysia, and Pakistan.

Once certified, a facility is subject to semiannual audits verifying continual compliance and successful implementation of corrective actions. In addition, SAI reports that more than 2,000 workplaces had been monitored to evaluate their "audit readiness."

The SA8000 auditing process has had some notable glitches, requiring use of its complaint and appeal system. For example, in 2000, the Christian Industrial Committee, a Hong Kong–based labor rights organization, charged that the Yongsheng shoe factory in southern China was in violation of the SA8000 standard and was improperly certified by the Norwegian social auditing firm, Det Norske Veritas. After investigation of the complaint, the factory's certification was suspended.[18] In 2001, certification was withdrawn from the Lizhan Chinese shoe factory where investigators from the U.S.–based National Labor Committee (NLC) found dormitory rooms packed with up to 28 people and employees working 12-hour work-shifts. (The SA8000 standard limits work time to 48 hours of regular shifts and 12 hours of overtime per week.) The NLC also found that workers were coached to lie to SA8000 inspectors.[19] Eileen Kaufman, SAI's executive director, cites these decertifications as evidence that the SA8000 system is working. "The fact that certification is public," says Kaufman, "provides structure for anyone with evidence of noncompliance to trigger an investigation leading to corrective actions or suspension or revocation of certification. Complaints have also led to changes to improve audit procedures."[20]

Companies committed to SA8000 have total annual revenues of over $100 billion. They include Avon, Cutter & Buck, Toys 'R Us, and Dole from the United States; Switzerland's Vogele and Amana; Italy's Coop Italia; Dutch WE Europe; and Germany's Otto Versand. Tom Deluca, vice president for product development and compliance at Toys 'R Us, has stated that eventually all of its five thousand suppliers will be required to obtain certification under SA8000.[21]

Perhaps the most significant potential marketplace impact of SA8000 is its certification mark. Workplaces determined to be in compliance with SA8000 will be entitled to use the SA8000 certification mark. It is designed to signal to consumers that the company's factories respect labor and human rights. When they do, consumers will be in a position to make morally informed choices about the goods they buy. It will be interesting to see whether, given the choice in the marketplace, consumers will exhibit a preference for goods manufactured by certified factories.

Consumers' marketplace preferences will constitute a critical factor in the long-run success of the global labor rights movement. Though proponents of codes of conduct argue, sometimes with anecdotal evidence, that the benefits of such programs in the form of increased efficiency and decreased worker turnover outweigh the costs of implementation, to date there has been no comprehensive and convincing study demonstrating such cost-effectiveness. It would seem inevitable that raising labor standards will increase production costs. Any increased production cost attributable to maintaining labor standards will ultimately be passed along to consumers. The willingness of consumers to absorb the costs of upholding labor rights is critical, therefore, to the effectiveness and sustainability of corporate codes of conduct.

There is some evidence suggesting that consumers are willing to pay more to uphold labor rights, but this evidence is not conclusive. A survey conducted by Marymount University in Arlington, Virginia, found that 86 percent of Americans surveyed said that they would pay an extra $1 on a $20 garment if they knew it was made in a "legitimate" shop, that is, one that respected human rights.[22] However, only marketplace experience will establish conclusively whether consumers actually will behave in accordance with the avowed preferences in the survey or whether, faced with the prospect of paying higher prices for certified goods, they will purchase with their budgets rather than their consciences in mind. For that reason, consumer reaction to the SA8000 mark will be an important telltale. If consumers accord no marketplace value to the SA8000 mark, it will be a significant impediment to the global labor rights movement. In effect, this will mean that "good" companies that maintain labor standards will suffer a competitive disadvantage vis-à-vis "bad" companies that don't.[23]

The FLA offers an alternative code of conduct and monitoring system.[24] As does SAI, the FLA accredits third-party monitors to conduct audits. However, it does not have a certification mark. Prior to charter amendments adopted by the FLA board of directors in April 2002, to qualify for participation in the FLA, a firm had to have 30 percent of its suppliers and subcontractors inspected by external third-party monitors over the initial implementation period, which could be as long as three years, at the company's election. Additionally, the company itself must follow certain internal procedures, such as ensuring that a code of conduct is posted and communicated to all factories within a two-year period. Even if one could be assured of the reliability of all the third-party audits, the FLA system thus depends substantially on the effectiveness of internal checks, a feature that critics decry as unreliable.

As a result of the April 2002 charter amendments, the FLA will employ external monitors to inspect a random statistical sampling of member companies' manufacturing facilities. In most cases, according to the estimates of statisticians hired by the FLA, this will mean that less than 5 percent of any given company's facilities will be inspected each year. All such inspections will be unannounced and conducted by monitors selected by the FLA. The inspection results will be posted on the FLA Web site.

FLA member companies include adidas-Salomon, Gear, Levi Strauss,

Liz Claiborne, Nike, Patagonia, Reebok, Eddie Bauer, and Polo Ralph Lauren. Over 170 colleges and universities are also members of the FLA. These schools require all of their licensees manufacturing clothing and other goods bearing university logos to follow the FLA Code of Conduct.

Some European-based labor rights NGOs have also adopted a strategy of cooperation with MNEs. For example, the United Kingdom–based ETI is a tripartite alliance of companies, NGOs, and trade unions working collaboratively to "ensure that the working conditions of employees in companies that supply goods to consumers in the UK meet or exceed international standards."[25] The ETI has a "base code" derived from ILO principles that participating companies may either adopt verbatim or incorporate into their own codes. At the beginning of 2002, the ETI had 26 corporate members, including Marks & Spencer, The Body Shop, and Tesco.

The ETI has no certification or accreditation programs. Instead, it emphasizes learning, research, and sharing information about implementing codes of conduct in global supply chains. A central mission of the ETI is to produce reports, analyses of labor conditions, and surveys of "best practices" in particular industries that can be shared with participating companies. For example, one ETI pilot project in India is investigating ways to effectively identify and remedy child labor problems.[26]

NGOs EMPHASIZING CONFRONTATION: UNITE, USAS, AND GLOBAL EXCHANGE

Despite the rapid proliferation of voluntary codes in recent years, some labor rights advocates remain deeply skeptical about the integrity of self-monitoring and assert that external monitoring systems such as those offered by SAI and the FLA are unreliable, serving only to cosmetically cover up deep and systemic problems. On a broad level these critics worry that the emphasis on voluntary codes undermines the growth of trade unions and governmental interventions, both of which the critics view as more reliable and effective than voluntary codes. In particular, the criticism has been aimed at both the standards required for certification and the monitoring procedures employed to ensure compliance. Controversy has arisen, for example, about whether codes should require workers to be paid a "living wage"[27] and whether participating companies should be required to engage in collective bargaining with independent trade unions. There also has been considerable debate over issues such as the frequency of factory inspections and the need for unannounced inspections.

As a result of such concerns, student groups, NGOs, and labor unions such as USAS, Global Exchange, and UNITE have chosen to address global labor issues by targeting prominent name-brand companies for muckraking investigations. By subjecting a few well-known companies to public embarrassment and condemnation, these groups hope to generate a public outcry and thereby pressure image-conscious companies into adopting significant reforms in the way they conduct global manufacturing operations.

In the Christmas shopping season of 2001, for example, UNITE announced a publicity and demonstration campaign against 10 retailers. As Christmas approached, UNITE targeted fewer and fewer retailers, based in part on the willingness of each company to negotiate with UNITE. UNITE's goal was to exact concessions from retailers on a living wage, a prohibition against child labor, safe working conditions, and the right of workers to organize a union. Bruce Raynor, UNITE president, explained the union's intentions: "Retailers know if a seam is one-eighth inch off, but they say they don't know it's made with child labor. Bullshit. They know exactly what's going on, and we'll hold them accountable."[28]

Following a somewhat different strategy, USAS has proposed a code of conduct program, termed the Workers Rights Consortium (WRC), whose substantive provisions are in certain respects more rigorous that those required by SAI and the FLA. The WRC is mostly intended to address the practices of companies that manufacture apparel and other licensed products for the collegiate market. It is funded through annual fees—1 percent of licensing revenues—collected from member schools.[29]

Among other things, the WRC's Model Code requires the licensees of its collegiate members to manufacture only in factories that pay a living wage and bargain collectively with independent trade unions. In effect, this means that when licensees operate in China, where all trade unions are by law under the control of the All China Confederation of Trade Unions, they will technically be in violation of the WRC code. As of mid-2002 more than 100 schools had joined the WRC. However, according to Marybeth Schmutz, a member of the Board of Directors of the Association of Collegiate Licensing Administrators, "very few were requiring their licensees to comply with the 'living wage' and collective bargaining provisions of the WRC code."[30]

The WRC makes no pretense of creating a system of monitoring and compliance analogous to those offered by SAI and the FLA. In essence, the WRC Code of Conduct is really a platform for conducting a limited number of targeted investigations that, according to Scott Nova, the WRC's executive director, "are designed to take an in-depth look at key factories and determine whether the brands' internal monitoring is getting the job done."[31] Rather than attempting to set up a systematic third-party monitoring system covering thousands of factories, Nova says that the WRC uses the prospect of negative publicity to "create a permanent incentive for multinationals to upgrade conditions in their factories." As the WRC Web site proclaims, "instead of attempting to create a comprehensive monitoring regime in order to certify companies, the WRC will use limited but carefully targeted investigatory resources to hold companies accountable. . . . Coupled with broad-based public disclosure, spot investigations force each licensee to recognize that any plant located around the world can bring negative exposure at any time."[32]

Other NGOs also continue to follow primarily confrontational strategies in their approach to global labor rights. While these NGOs eschew cooperation with MNEs, they often take advantage of the information sharing made possible by the Internet and global professional networks to work in tandem. Global Exchange, for example, is a San Francisco-based NGO active in a broad array of "environmental, political and social justice" global issues. Working in partnership with like-minded NGOs around the world, Global Exchange's anti-sweatshop Clean Clothes Campaign seeks to highlight abusive practices by targeted brand-name companies. In March 2002 Global Exchange collaborated with Oxfam Community Aid Abroad to issue a report criticizing abusive labor practices by Nike and adidas in selected factories in Indonesia.[33]

GOOD COP, BAD COP: COOPERATION AND CONFRONTATION AS COMPLEMENTARY NGO STRATEGIES

In certain respects the cooperative approaches of NGOs such as SAI and the FLA work at cross-purposes with the confrontational tactics of USAS, UNITE, and Global Exchange. Nowhere is the heat of this opposition felt more keenly than among the beleaguered college administrators caught in the middle of the battle between the two groups. Conscious of their own image and ethical responsibilities, college administrators are anxious to take some action to help ensure that products manufactured by their licensees (T-shirts, mugs, baseball caps, etc.) are in conformity with minimal global labor standards. For college administrators, participation by their licensees in programs such as the FLA and SAI is comforting, as it represents a palpable, albeit flawed, step toward the ideal goal of ensuring that all licensed goods be manufactured with respect for labor and human rights. The best intentions of administrators have not, however, been rewarded. USAS has been highly effective in training and organizing student representatives to lambaste administrators who adopt the imperfect and incremental solutions that the FLA and SAI represent. Many college administrators—some simply to avoid unpleasant encounters with radicalized students and others because they recognize the merits of complementary strategies—have decided to join both the FLA and the WRC initiative introduced by USAS.

Although they sometimes work at cross-purposes, the carrot-and-stick tactics variously employed by NGOs can also work in a complementary fashion. Confrontational tactics have been very successful in shining a spotlight onto the issue of labor abuse and in scaring the heck out of MNEs. Moreover, USAS, UNITE, and other like-minded groups have been very influential in pushing the envelope on what is considered possible. For example, when USAS first suggested that companies manufacturing under collegiate licenses disclose the locations of all of their subcontractors in developing countries, they were met with incredulous denial. "Impossible," they were told. "That is a valuable trade secret," many companies asserted. But after years of pressing on the issue by USAS, nearly all the companies participating in FLA-monitored collegiate licensing programs have agreed to make such disclosure widely available.

Buoyed by such successes, student groups continue to exert pressure on the FLA to put more teeth into the third-party monitoring process. The WRC's Scott Nova emphasizes how investigative tactics complement the monitoring process: "The WRC's targeted, in-depth investigations provide a level of information about key factories that is not available from other groups, and, by finding problems other monitors may miss, create an incentive for companies to improve their more systematic compliance efforts. Thus, schools can look to the FLA for broader scope and the WRC for its essential watchdog function."

Although they have been successful in focusing attention and pushing the frontiers of the agenda, the bad cop groups such as the WRC and UNITE have not sought to develop comprehensive, independent supply chain monitoring systems. That has been the strong suit of good cops such as SAI, which have cooperated with MNEs to fashion workplace codes of conduct, and to accomplish the formidable task of setting up reliable, sustainable, comprehensive global systems for monitoring compliance with those codes throughout the supply chain. Despite the publicity accorded to the embarrassing missteps in the implementation of internal and third-party monitoring programs, they nevertheless constitute an indispensable element of any serious solution to the global sweatshop problem. NGOs such as SAI have invested significant time and resources to position themselves as trustworthy "honest brokers" that will work cooperatively with companies to improve the way such systems work.

The radically divergent tactics of confrontation and cooperation thus prove, on closer inspection, to be highly complementary. Neither tactic would be as effective without the other. It is interesting to note that while some individual NGOs are exclusively cooperative and others are exclusively confrontational, some are attempting the yin-yang task of pursuing the two tactics simultaneously. The WRC, for example, is putting increasing emphasis on working with companies to develop solutions to the problems it uncovers. The WRC's watershed experience was its investigation of Mexmode—a factory in Mexico that supplied college sweatshirts to Nike and Reebok. Marcela Munoz, a seamstress, and other workers were fired for boycotting the cafeteria because they were angered to find worms in their salads. The WRC, after initially emphasizing public pressure as a tactic, made a conscious effort to work with Nike, Reebok, and the factory operators to improve conditions in the factory.[34] Encouraged by such successes, the WRC's Scott Nova says, "There is no point in exposing violations at a factory if you are not committed to doing the work necessary to eliminate those abuses. In some cases that requires public censure. In others the best approach is cooperative engagement. This is the tactic we are employing at the PT Dada factory, a major stuffed animal and cap factory in Indonesia."

From a public policy perspective there is room in the global labor rights movement for all sorts of NGOs that do their jobs effectively and with integrity—those that are fully cooperative with MNEs, those that are wholly confrontational, and those that try to be a little bit of both. The important thing is that the movement as a whole continues both to cooperate with MNEs when progress can be made that way and to challenge MNEs when that is required. As successful as the WRC has been in particular instances such as Mexmode, however, such efforts cannot by themselves create global, systemic, and sustainable change. There are literally hundreds of thousands of factories scattered throughout the globe where brand-name companies manufacture their goods for export to Europe, the United States, and other economically advanced countries. Though cooperative programs such as those promulgated by SAI are flawed, they do, through sustained engagement with MNEs, offer the promise of addressing global labor rights issues at the required scale. They also offer extensive resources for organizational and policy changes in MNEs. Alas, such systemic and global changes proceed imperfectly and at a glacial pace. There will, therefore, continue to be for the foreseeable future an equally important watchdog role for NGOs such as the WRC.

The debt owed to the more confrontational NGOs is not lost on the cooperative NGOs. The FLA's executive director, Auret Van Heerdeen, credits the more confrontational NGOs with the "ability to uncover problems." In explaining why the FLA chooses to go the cooperative route, however, Van Heerdeen explains that "once you've uncovered a problem, the question becomes how to fix it. To do that you need access to manufacturing facilities and to the brand name companies that have the leverage to achieve change in those facilities." Van Heerdeen goes on to say that "whereas other NGOs might see their role as investigatory, our role is to be programmatic and consistent—to get contractors and brands to sign on to a multi-year compliance program."[35] SAI's executive director, Eileen Kaufman, agrees: "There are many different roles to play in the struggle for labor rights. We don't try to play every role. Our mission is to achieve change by means of implementing multi-stakeholder consensus." The WRC's Scott Nova envisions the WRC's role as changing perceptions about what is possible to achieve by homing in on particular cases: "Our job is to pinpoint abuses and get the problems fixed, while encouraging companies to take the positive lessons they learn from remediation efforts at one factory and begin to apply them across the board."

THE FRUITS OF COOPERATION FOR MNEs:
PUBLIC EXPECTATIONS, CREDIBILITY, ACCESS
TO RESOURCES, AND LEVERAGE

Many global marketing companies have eagerly seized the olive branch extended by some elements of the NGO community. They have joined collaborative programs such as the FLA, SAI, and the ETI to bolster their own codes of conduct and monitoring efforts. Although the benefits of working cooperatively with NGOs are manifest, executives of MNEs must be thoughtful about the way they approach such relationships. One key to working effectively with NGOs is to choose NGO collaborators carefully. As Doug Cahn of Reebok expresses it, "We can't participate in every NGO labor rights system. There are enough different models that it would be burdensome to adopt each system. Each has their benefits and costs." For Tom Deluca of Toys-R-Us, SAI's multi-industry approach is an important attraction: "We are more than a toy company. We sell apparel and baby products too. Working with a cross industry standard like SA8000 means that we don't have to work with three separate programs."

MNEs perceive a number of benefits from cooperating with NGOs. The most important are gauging public expectations of their behavior, gaining credibility for their efforts, securing access to resources, and achieving greater leverage with their contractors. At a minimum, it behooves MNEs to keep in close communication with NGOs because NGOs offer the most effective way for MNEs to understand what the public expects from them. As Doug Cahn, Vice President for Human Rights Programs at Reebok, notes, "A company cannot afford to be blind to what NGOs expect and the standards to which we will be held because those expectations, when the NGOs have representation from the labor rights communities, often approximate the expectations of the community."[36] Moreover, cooperation with NGOs can offer a kind of safe harbor from the often uncertain and unpredictable spotlight of public opinion. As SAI's Eileen Kaufman expresses it, "Companies working with us will have the benefit of a clear and well-developed system. We have a definite standard and a well-defined program of certification."

NGOs are also a potential source of credibility for MNEs seeking to promote a global brand. Many NGOs, particularly those in which labor rights advocates have a voice, have established credibility with stakeholders that are crucial for MNEs, for example, the press, students, workers, and consumers. By working cooperatively with such NGOs, MNEs are better able to establish their own bona fides in addressing worker rights. Doug Cahn of Reebok notes, "As a global brand, we need to demonstrate transparency in our labor rights efforts. We need to demonstrate to a broad audience that we are doing our job. When companies and NGOs collaborate on a project that truly benefits workers, the credibility of a company's labor compliance program is almost always enhanced."[37]

The credibility benefits of working with NGOs become pronounced when the integrity of an MNE is challenged. For example, when Global Exchange issued a report criticizing Nike's labor practices in Indonesia, Nike immediately issued a rebuttal that referenced Nike's cooperative efforts with other NGOs: "Nike is well aware of the issues raised in the report (based on interviews with 35 workers) because we engaged in a transparent assessment of our Indonesia operations with an independent entity, the Global Alliance for Workers and Communities, that involved interviews with 4,000 workers." Nike also cited its work with the FLA: "If there are further specific issues of concern they can be freely raised through the Fair Labor Association grievance process to ensure their swift and fair resolution. . . . In Indonesia and around the world, Nike participates in independent monitoring through the FLA."[38]

NGOs also offer a plethora of informational and training resources that can help MNEs to implement their human rights programs more effectively. Apart from having model codes of conduct, some NGOs such as SAI and the FLA have independent monitoring systems that can help MNEs measure the effectiveness of their internal effort. Moreover, NGOs are the repository of significant expertise and networks of influence into which MNEs can tap. For example, when Reebok was having trouble with some of its suppliers in a Southeast Asian country, an NGO helped the company to identify local NGOs that provided training in local labor laws to its factory operators. Seeking a credible independent monitor for its factories, Liz Claiborne worked with the International Labor Rights Fund and Business for Social Responsibility as project facilitators, to identify a suitable NGO. This process helped lead to the formation of the Commission for the Verification of Corporate Codes of Conduct (COVERCO). Liz Claiborne began working with COVERCO in Guatemala on a pilot project with two goals—(1) to get an in-depth look at conditions in one factory and to help the company to formulate solutions to those problems and (2) to experiment with how it might make its labor compliance program more publicly transparent. Tom Deluca of Toys 'R Us even enrolled in one of SAI's training programs for independent monitors. "I wanted to see for myself how good the training was and what the auditors needed to learn to be certified. Knowing about the training process helps me when I talk with factory operators about what it will take them to come into compliance with the SA8000 standard."[39]

The FLA's Van Heerdeen notes that companies may not be cognizant of all the value-added programs the FLA makes available, for example, a third-party complaint system in which the FLA will independently investigate allegations of abuse and a crisis management program for particularly egregious factory violations that need to be addressed speedily. Eileen Kaufman of SAI also touts the consultative capacities of her NGO in terms that speak to the bottom line concerns of business managers: "We help companies to achieve continuous improvement, to meet and exceed minimum standards," Kaufman says, "working with SA8000 can help firms to achieve efficiency gains." She cites as an example the way that a Thai factory addressed the problem of excessive overtime: "What began as an inquiry into how to lower work hours to comply with SA8000," says Kaufman, "ended up as a reengineering effort which also evidently replaced a traditional assembly production process with a quality circle manufacturing operation that increased productivity and maintained compensation levels at the plant." Similarly, in India, Kaufman reports, "a government case study of a textile factory reported synergies among SA8000, ISO9000 and ISO14000 certification efforts that resulted in reduced effluent, input savings and a halving of overtime."[40]

A final benefit of cooperating with NGOs is that it enables MNEs to leverage influence over their contractors and suppliers through collaborations with other companies. In most cases, when an MNE contracts with a supplier, the MNE represents only a fraction of that supplier's business. This makes it difficult to impress on that supplier the urgency of operating a factory in a manner that respects the labor and human rights of workers. However, by working in collaborative initiatives with NGOs and labor rights advocates, MNEs can coordinate their own efforts in particular factories with those of other companies and thereby increase their leverage over their suppliers. As Reebok's Doug Cahn expresses it, "We may be only 20 percent of a particular supplier's business and thus have little influence, but when we can combine with two other companies that each have 20 percent, we can leverage our influence over that factory operator." Auret Van Heerdeen of the FLA concurs, adding "there are benefits to an association which go beyond the sum of the parts."

Once the decision is made to cooperate with NGOs, the collaboration cannot be half-hearted and may involve more openness and transparency than a company is used to showing to the public. Liz Claiborne's Vice President for Human Rights Compliance, Daryl Brown, emphasizes the importance of embracing openness, wherever it might lead. Referring to public documents issued by COVERCO about a plant in Guatemala, Ms. Brown said that "the reports were candid and at times reported on issues that were disturbing to all. But this is what transparency and credibility are all about."[41] The FLA's Van Heerdeen observes that "many companies, because of their corporate culture find it hard to embrace transparency with open arms, but it's ultimately in the company's interest to do so."

CONCLUSION

There will always be some degree of tension between NGOs and MNEs. This is inevitable in ongoing relations between organizations with different aims—profit for stockholders versus advocacy of labor and human rights.[42] As Van Heerdeen observes, "After all, our responsibility is ultimately to the public." Indeed, some in the NGO community worry that too close an association with MNEs will compromise the NGO's objectivity. Because MNEs and NGOs have different ultimate objectives, they will never be perfect partners. There will always be some areas of disagreement between them. The fact that there will always be tension in the relationship, however, does not mean that the relationship must always be antagonistic. As we have seen, both NGOs and MNEs have much to gain from cooperating with one another. These benefits constitute a compelling incentive for NGOs and MNEs to take steps to enhance the effectiveness of this cooperation. For both sides, there is understandable ambivalence about such cooperation. Ultimately, however, the most important reason for seeking effective cooperation is that it can lead to real improvements in the lives of low-wage workers in developing countries.

NOTES

1. Adapted from an article originally published in the *Brown Journal of World Affairs* 9, no. 2 (Fall 2002).

2. The author gratefully acknowledges a research grant from the Aspen Institute's Initiative for Social Innovation Through Business.

3. Alison Maitland, "Human Rights and Accountability," *The Financial Times,* 12 June 2002, p. 15.

4. See generally Debora L. Spar, "The Spotlight and the Bottom Line," *Foreign Affairs* 77, no. 2 (March/April 1998), pp. 7–13.

5. One watershed of the accountability being demanded by the world community is United Nations General Secretary Kofi Annan's call for MNEs to pledge adherence to a "Global Compact" on social concerns. See "Global Compact," http://65.214.34.30/un/gc/unweb.nsf/content/thenine.htm (accessed 12 August 2002).

6. See generally David S. Weissbrodt, "Human Rights Principles and Responsibilities for Transnational Corporations and Other Business Enterprises," U.N. Doc. E/CN.4/Sub.2/2002/XX/Add.1, E/CN.4/Sub.2/2002/WG.2/WP.1/Add.1 (2002), http://www1.umn.edu/humanrts/introduction05–01–02finalhtml (accessed 24 July 2002). For an analysis of child labor issues, see Kaushik Basu, "International Labor Standards and Child Labor," *Challenge* 42, no. 5 (September/October 1999): 80–93. The ethical and public policy issues concerning multina-

tional enterprises and human rights are addressed in Michael A. Santoro, *Profits and Principles: Global Capitalism and Human Rights in China* (Ithaca, N.Y.: Cornell University Press, 2000). For an ethical analysis of corporate responsibility for worker rights violations, see Laura P. Hartman, Bill Shaw, and Rodney Stevenson, "Exploring the Ethics and Economics of Global Labor Standards," and Denis G. Arnold and Norman E. Bowie, "Sweatshops and Respect for Persons," both in volume 13, no. 2 of *Business Ethics Quarterly* (2003).

7. For an analysis of the reasons behind the limited power of existing international institutions such as the Human Rights Commission and the International Labor Organization, see Santoro, *Profits and Principles*.

8. In a White Paper published in July 2002, the European Commission rejected a regulatory approach to corporate social responsibility issues, including global labor rights, in favor of continued emphasis on voluntary efforts. European Commission, "Corporate Social Responsibility: A Business Contribution to Sustainable Development" (2 July 2002), http://europa.eu.int/comm/employment_social/soc-dial/csr/csr2002_en.pdf (accessed 26 July 2002). For an analysis of the legality of such proposals under U.S. law, see Diane Orentlicher and T. Gelatt, "Public Law, Private Actors: The Impact of Human Rights on Business Investment in China," *Northwestern Journal of International Law and Business* 66 (1993): p. 14. For an argument that international human rights instruments and treaties might create legal obligations for private companies, see International Council on Human Rights, "Beyond Voluntarism: Human Rights and the Developing International Legal Obligations of Companies" (2002), http://www.ichrp.org/cgi-bin/show?what=project&id=107 (accessed 12 August 2002). See generally European Union Committee on Development and Cooperation, "Report on EU standards for European Enterprises operating in developing countries: Toward a European Code of Conduct" (17 December 1998), http://www.cleanclothes.org/codes/howit.htm (accessed 29 July 2002).

9. The "instant classic" analysis of the rise of nonstate actors in the global system is Jessica T. Mathews, "Power Shift," *Foreign Affairs* 77, no. 1 (January/February 1977): pp. 50–66; see generally *NGOs and the Universal Declaration of Human Rights: A Curious Grapevine* (New York: Palgrave MacMillan, 1998); Claude Welch, ed., *International Non-governmental Human Rights Organizations: Making a Difference?* (Philadelphia: University of Pennsylvania Press, 2000); see also Debora Spar and James Dail, "Of Measurement and Mission: Accounting for Performance in Non-Governmental Organizations," *Chicago Journal of International Law* 3, no.1 (spring 2002).

10. Information about the National Labor Committee and the Kathy Lee Gifford campaign can be found at www.nlcnet.org (accessed 29 July 2002).

11. Information about the Clean Clothes Campaign can be found at www.cleanclothes.org (accessed 29 July 2002).

12. See, for example, David Henderson, "Misguided Virtue: False Notions of Corporate Social Responsibility," Hobart Paper no. 142 (London: Institute for Economic Affairs, 2001) (5 November 2001), Institute of Economic Affairs, http://www.iea.org.uk/record.php?type=publicatiion&ID=143 (accessed 7 August 2002). This criticism is addressed further in chapter 4.

13. Georges Enderle and Glen Peters, "A Strange Affair? The Emerging Rela-

tionship Between NGOs and Transnational Companies" (1998), http://www.pwcglobal.com (accessed 29 July 2002).

14. See Oliver Williams, ed., *Global Codes of Conduct: An Idea Whose Time Has Come* (South Bend, Ind.: University of Notre Dame Press, 2000).

15. For an account of the challenges of implementing a global code of conduct, see Stephen J. Frenkel and Duncan Scott, "Compliance, Cooperation, and Codes of Labor Practice: Inside adidas" (*California Management Review,* forthcoming); see generally Gary Gereffi, Ronnie Garcia-Johnson, and Erika Sasser, "The NGO-Industrial Complex," *Foreign Policy* (July/August 2001): 56–66.

16. United States Department of State, "Voluntary Principles on Security and Human Rights," http://www.state.gov/www/global/human_rights/001220_fsdrl_principles.html (accessed 29 July 2002); see Bennett Freeman, "Drilling for Common Ground," *Foreign Policy* 125 (July/August 2001): p. 50 and Bennett Freeman et al., "A New Approach to Corporate Responsibility: The Voluntary Principles on Security and Human Rights," *Hastings International and Comparative Law Review* 24, no. 3 (spring 2001): 423–49.

17. Information about Social Accountability International can be found on its Web site www.sa-intl.org (accessed 29 July 2002).

18. Jennifer Ehrlich, "Sweatshop Swindlers," *South China Morning Post,* 18 December 2000, http://www.1worldcommunication.org/labornews.htm—Sweatshop%20Swindlers (accessed 12 August 2002).

19. Bruce Gilley, "Sweating it Out," *Far Eastern Economic Review* 164, no. 18 (10 May 2001): 40–41.

20. Interview by author with Eileen Kaufman, 12 March 2002.

21. Interview by author with Tom Deluca, 19 March 2002.

22. "The Consumer and Sweatshops" (November 1999), available at Marymount University Center for Ethical Concerns, www.marymount.edu/news/garmentstudy/findings.html (accessed 29 July 2003). See Santoro, *Profits and Principles,* pp. 162–66.

23. "The Consumer and Sweatshops."

24. Information about the Fair Labor Association can be found on its Web site www.fairlabor.org (accessed 29 July 2002).

25. Information about the Ethical Trade Initiative can be found on its Web site www.ethicaltrade.org (accessed 29 July 2002).

26. See www.ethicaltrade.org/pub/activities/pilots/cildlab0102/index.shtml (accessed 26 August 2002).

27. For a discussion of the "living wage" debate, see the Lafollette Institute of the University of Wisconsin "Report on the Living Wage Symposium," available at www.lafollette.wisc.edu/livingwage/Final_Report/report.htm (accessed 29 July 2002).

28. David Moberg, "Never Let Them See You Sweat," *InTheseTimes.com* (15 October 2001), www.inthesetimes.com/web2523/moberg2523a.html (accessed 29 July 2002).

29. Information about WRC can be found at www.nlcnet.org/elsalvador/wrcandes.html (accessed 29 July 2002).

30. Interview by author with Marybeth Schmutz, 15 January 2002.

31. Interview by author with Scott Nova, 3 July 2002.

32. www.nlcnet.org/elsalvador/wrcandes.html (accessed 29 July 2002).

33. Global Exchange, "We Are Not Machines," available at http://www. globalexchange.org/economy/corporations/nike/machines/ (accessed 29 July 2002); see Reuters, "Report Says Nike, Adidas Factories Still Sweatshops," 7 March 2002.

34. Ginger Thompson, "Mexican Labor Protest Gets Result," *New York Times,* 8 October 2001, p. A3.

35. Interview by author with Auret Van Heerdeen, 13 March 2002.

36. Interview by author with Doug Cahn, 26 February 2002.

37. Cahn, interview.

38. Nike, Inc., "Nike Statement Regarding Indonesia Report," Company Press Release (7 March 2002), http://www.nike.com/nikebiz/news/pressrelease. jhtml?year = 2002&month = 03&letter = c (accessed 7 August 2002). The press release also noted that, "in 2001, the FLA accredited eleven monitoring organizations to conduct independent external monitoring of participating companies' factories. Accredited monitoring organizations have already conducted external audits in Thailand, China, the Philippines, Indonesia, Malaysia, India, Bangladesh, Guatemala, Mexico, and in the United States." However, the press release did not specify whether any of these organizations conducted external audits of Nike factories in any of these countries.

39. Interview by author with Tom Deluca, 19 March 2002.

40. Interview by author with Eileen Kaufman, 19 March 2002.

41. Interview by author with Daryl Brown, 19 March 2002.

42. It should be noted that, although, as a matter of corporation law, directors and officers owe a fiduciary duty to stockholders to run the corporation for stockholder benefit, there remains considerable disagreement among ethical thinkers as to which stakeholders are owed moral duties by directors and officers. The pioneering work on stakeholder theory is R. Edward Freeman, *Strategic Management: A Stakeholder Approach* (Boston, Mass.: Pitman, 1984). In the legal literature, there is a long-standing debate over whether the corporation should be managed exclusively for the benefit of shareholders. Compare A. A. Berle Jr., "Corporate Powers as Powers in Trust," *Harvard Law Review* 44 (1931): 1049; A. A. Berle Jr., "For Whom Corporate Managers Are Trustees: A Note," *Harvard Law Review* 45 (1932): 1365 with E. Merrick Dodd Jr., "For Whom Are Corporate Managers Trustees?" *Harvard Law Review* 45 (1932): 1145. See also Thomas W. Dunfee, "Corporate Governance in a Market with Morality," *Law & Contemporary Problems* 62 (summer 1999): p. 129. The classic economic case for managing a corporation solely in the interests of shareholders is Milton Friedman, "The Social Responsibility of Business Is to Increase its Profits," *New York Times Magazine,* 13 September 1970, p. 32.

CHAPTER 6

Philosophy Applied II: Total Responsibility Management

Sandra Waddock and Charles Bodwell[1]

This chapter discusses responsibility management through the lens of the total responsibility management (TRM) approach, which is emerging in multinational firms as a way for the firms to manage their labor practices through the implementation of their codes of conduct. TRM approaches are, like quality management systems, systemic, holistic, and process-oriented. The TRM approach provides a framework consisting of three core elements or processes that can be used to guide the implementation of codes. These general processes are (1) *inspiration* or vision-setting and leadership-commitment processes; (2) *integration* of the vision and values established into strategy, human resource, and operating practices; and (3) *innovation* processes, which involve establishing indicators that measure responsibility performance and provide a basis for improvements, remediation where necessary, and learning. Transparency and accountability for impacts and outcomes are also essential elements of TRM approaches, particularly with respect to labor.

There are many possible ways to analyze the types of initiatives that companies are taking to respond to global labor challenges, which are described elsewhere in this book. One approach that many companies find useful for avoiding reputational and management difficulties associated with labor problems is to develop systems for managing employee- and other stakeholder-related (and environmental) responsibilities. Much as companies developed systems for managing quality during the 1980s and 1990s and, in some instances, for managing their use of the natural environment in the 1990s, companies today are undertaking these responsibility management approaches as a way of meeting the insistent and sometimes urgent demands from different constituencies or stakeholders. Building on the quality movement's success in developing management processes, we will call these systems total responsibility management systems, or TRM (modeling the language of total quality management— TQM). In this chapter we will define and describe the process of TRM. The case studies in Part II will provide examples of its application and implementation.

TRM systems enable companies to define the responsibility goals and to develop appropriate management, measurement, and integration processes to help them to meet those goals. Managing responsibility is more important than ever in a world in which activists, consumers, employees, and the media are demanding more responsible corporate performance, more transparency, and more accountability from companies. TRM approaches, like the quality management approaches that came before them, are holistic ways of running a business responsibly through systemic management approaches that define, implement, measure, and reward responsible practice, as the cases in this book illustrate.[2]

The TRM approach to responsibility management is premised on the emerging realization that it is, in fact, possible to measure and to improve a company's commitment to responsible practice, much as awareness emerged in the 1980s that quality could be measured and improved on. Responsibility management is thus a *process* or a system of specific goals and vision, an articulation of values, and a *process* of continual improvements in building employee capacity and integration into management systems throughout the company. TRM provides a framework for understanding what is needed and a set of tools for making improvements that help to satisfy critical stakeholders' demands for more responsible practices. Because TRM approaches are also premised on agreed-upon foundational values or standards promulgated by international bodies such as the United Nations, they provide, at a minimum, a baseline of expected standards and behaviors. Because they are systemic, responsibility management systems require securing commitment from top management, recognizing the importance of managing responsibility in achieving the company's long-term objectives, building positive relationships with important stakeholders, and generating positive returns. But they can, as the cases in the chapters that follow illustrate, be initiated at any level of the enterprise.

There is a significant lesson to be learned about responsibility management from the quality movement, which has now become so fundamental to business operations that it is in some respects no longer a movement. *Managing responsibility is no different from managing any other system in the company.* True, contrary to some corporate systems, responsibility management pervades all activities, strategies, operating practices, and relationships that a company develops with its stakeholders and the natural environment, but the same can be said of quality management, and managing quality is now an accepted reality of corporate life.

Some level of quality is present in every product or service a company produces. Quality can be low or high; but it is there. Similarly, the reality is that some degree of responsibility—or irresponsibility—*is* present in any relationship, practice, or behavior in a company. Responsibility is particularly evident in relationships with employees, whether a company or manager is aware of it or not, because the interactions with and treatment of employees are essential to producing the goods and services that are the lifeblood of any economic system. TRM approaches mean working to build trusting, interactive, and ongoing relationships with key stakeholders, such as employees, customers, suppliers, and communities and developing mutually beneficial practices and ways of interacting. Trust is at the core of these relationships—especially trust between management and employees—wherever they are in the supply chain, because it is on the basis of employee–management relationships that all of the company's other relationships are built.

TRM approaches simply provide a *framework* for considering the integrated systems required to manage and integrate responsibility into corporate practices, paying particular attention to employee and labor practices in the supply chains of global companies. Such TRM approaches need to be matched to companies' specific strategies, goals, and operating cultures, as well as their unique operating conditions and competitive environment. By ensuring that they adhere to baseline foundational standards throughout their supply chains, companies can incorporate local national labor standards, while meeting or exceeding the global labor standards and expectations of external stakeholders, which were discussed in earlier chapters.

As the cases in this book illustrate, TRM approaches can be developed at the project or unit level, at the plant or divisional level, through training programs, as well as company-wide. Many times TRM approaches evolve out of efforts to implement codes of conduct—to make these codes as real in practice as they are on paper, especially in companies such as the ones studied here, in which supply chains are long and responsibilities apparently diffuse. And many times, of course, at least the initial attempts to build responsibility management systems are, as with quality management systems, far from "total" in that they cover only certain aspects of a company's activities. Thus, TRM approaches can be implemented at the company level, divisional level, plant, or even functional level. They can be suffused through supply chains under the leadership of a corporate responsibility officer or they can be project-based, as many of the cases in this study are.

The case studies also illustrate that the practices that managers develop to cope with labor and employee issues carry with them either a positive willingness to engage with employees, share mutual concerns, and make positive changes to cope—or not. Thus, some level of responsibility—or irresponsibility—will be present in any situation. Further, in today's connected world, if day-to-day practice veers toward the irresponsible side of the continuum, external stakeholders, such as NGO and labor activists, employees, the media, and other critical observers, will surely sound their alarms. Companies' figurative feet are held to the fire of public observations, demands for transparency and accountability, and expectations of good treatment of internal and external stakeholders as never before.

Moreover, never has it been easier for reporters, activists, nongovernmental organizations (NGOs), community members, and other critical observers to find fault with companies and their subsidiaries. A problem identified in a remote region today can virtually instantaneously be transmitted around the world at the click of a mouse. Complicating matters further, companies today find that outsiders seldom make distinctions between a multinational company (MNE) itself and members of its supply and distribution chains, believing instead that the MNE can and should be held responsible for whatever happens throughout its supply and distribution system. Virtually every global company and many domestic companies as well have experienced criticism and activism of one sort or another. The click of a mouse or posting to a Web site is all it takes for negative images of a company's treatment of its workforce to be spread globally.

Today such dynamics all operate simultaneously to create significant pressures on companies to manage responsibility. Partly the choice to manage responsibility constitutes self-protection so companies can avoid reputational damage, criticisms, and a consequent loss of business. Partly it could represent a proactive attempt to achieve competitive advantage through reputational benefits, becoming an employer or neighbor of choice, or being a "green" or "sweatshop-free" company so as to attract customers, investors, and employees. As the cases in this book clearly demonstrate, responsibility management throughout a company's supply and distribution chain is rapidly becoming the business imperative of the early twenty-first century, much as quality management became the business imperative of the late twentieth century.

This chapter provides a framework outlining the ways in which companies are systemically approaching issues of responsibility management today, a framework that can be applied to the cases in ensuing chapters as we think about how companies approach issues of responsibility management. The TRM approach we outline can be applied in different units, divisions, plants, or facilities of a company or across the whole company. We will see various aspects of TRM approaches surface in the cases, as companies struggle to improve working conditions in factories; establish better employee relations; implement training programs; and proactively (even interactively) avoid controversies with critical external stakeholders, employees, and labor unions.

In the following sections, we will explore each of these elements in more detail, especially as they relate to the cases that follow.

MANAGING CORPORATE RESPONSIBILITY: THE TRM APPROACH

Companies that have developed responsibility management systems are not perfect. But when problems develop, as they inevitably will, companies with these systems in place have a base of responsible practice; an understanding of the interests and perspectives of their stakeholders, particularly employees; and systems in place to provide for innovation and improvements—and remediation where needed. They have established processes for identifying problem areas and for moving forward toward a solution when problems arise. (See figure 6.1.)

Figure 6.1
Total Responsibility Management System

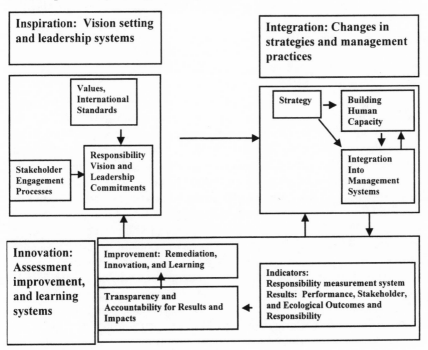

In many cases, these processes engage stakeholders in an interactive "conversation," or dialogue, with company management so that solutions achieved are amenable to all. Such mutually engaged *relationships* with key stakeholders, particularly employees, enable companies to problem solve *with* stakeholders from a basis of trust rather than a more adversarial base. They also create relatively more equality in relationships, since there is an expectation of mutuality of input, trust, and at least some degree (often small) of power sharing within the project. With responsibility management systems in place, company leaders can work problems out with stakeholders, rather than allowing those problems to damage both the company and its stakeholders or the relationships they have established.

Improvement and Innovation, But Not Perfection . . .

TRM is not about perfection; it is about improvement. It is about relationships with different stakeholders. It is about processes of engagement, involvement, and interaction built on mutual regard and a foundation of trust. It is about establishing—and sticking to—standards, goals, and objectives and doing business responsibly today so that the company maintains its license to operate tomorrow. TRM approaches help a company establish and maintain its integrity in the eyes of employees, customers, communities, and others. These efforts at improving facilities, local working conditions, and labor standards are exactly the types of initiatives we will visit in Part II of this book.

Inspiration

TRM approaches start with *inspiration*. *Inspiration* is about establishing and ensuring that management makes a commitment to a company's vision and the values that underpin that vision. In TRM approaches, inspiration involves integrating into the company's strategic vision and competitive strategies a perspective (and an associated set of values) on the way the company will interact with its stakeholders. The vision delineates the company's long-term goals and objectives, its strategies, and the ways in which it will develop its operating practices to accomplish those strategies. Many times, these values are articulated in the company's code of conduct. But simply having the code is insufficient to improve a company's practices; as the cases in this book demonstrate vividly, the code must be supported and known by management and employees, and be seriously implemented, not just hang on the factory wall.

Inspiration is also about ensuring that top management is committed to the vision and that individuals in leadership positions throughout the organization understand and are equally committed to making that vision real in practice. Inspiration is also about determining the ways in which the company will engage with its stakeholders and share and even de-velop that inspiration—vision—with them. Finding the right inspiration in the complex conditions faced in global supply chains is not always easy or straightforward. For example, at adidas-Salomon, the inspiration or fundamental vision supporting a response to child labor was far from simple, as the alternatives to children's work are not always positive or beneficial. Such complex situations require inputs from multiple stake-holders of differing perspectives or visions to reach productive, ethical resolutions.

Inspiration, or vision-setting and leadership systems, involves three ma-jor activities:

1. Responsibility, Vision, and Leadership Commitment: Creating a company- or unit-wide vision, which includes the company's responsibilities with and to stakeholders; securing the commitment of top managers and leaders through-out the enterprise to that vision; and ensuring that the vision is part of the corporate culture, mythology, and strategies. Enrolling relevant stakeholders, especially employees, in the vision (or, ideally, co-creating it with them) and empowering them to work toward achieving it.

2. Foundational Values: Articulating the company's core values and the ways in which those values link to the bedrock of internationally agreed-on foundation values that provide a floor of acceptable practice. (Consider the discussion of universal principles from chap. 5.) Frequently these values are articulated in the company's vision or mission statement and code of conduct. With suppliers, sometimes these values can be found in statements about the terms of engagement.

3. Stakeholder Engagement Processes: Developing processes for interactively working with stakeholders to allow them a forum for input, interaction, and airing of—and action on—their concerns, and providing feedback and inputs necessary to shape the company's long-term vision and strategies.

Inspirational visions help create meaning for the company's key stake-holders, particularly the employees who carry out the vision through their daily efforts. An inspirational vision inspires because it incorporates the company's ideas about how the world will be better off as a result of the work that is being done. In a responsibility vision, the company may well articulate types of relationships that it hopes to develop with its stake-holders, thereby fostering a sense of purpose, both individual and com-munity, that can be widely shared throughout the organization. Vision matters because it guides the organization going forward and provides a way for people involved with the company to know what is important to it. Properly articulated and widely shared, vision can create a sense of community, of belonging.

Vision is frequently linked to values, whether those are company-based values or foundational values, that is, those values generally agreed to be important by the international community. TRM approaches ensure that foundational values are spelled out clearly because they provide the baseline under which the company may run into ethical problems, as we have heard about continuously in the press. For example, the footwear giant adidas-Salomon (chap. 8) has a long-term vision of having its suppliers achieve strong self-governance and sustainability. One way that the company does this is by striving to incorporate core values—foundational values—into its suppliers' decisions through its Standards of Engagement. Where successful, the firm then develops processes, described in the case on adidas-Salomon, to ensure that suppliers are living up to those Standards of Engagement.

In the labor arena foundational values are frequently based on the International Labour Organization's four fundamental conventions (see below). These principles include freedom of association and the effective recognition of the right to collective bargaining, elimination of all forms of forced and compulsory labor, the effective abolition of child labor, and the elimination of discrimination in employment and occupation. Generally agreed-on human rights and environmental protection or (increasingly) sustainability are also frequent foundational values. Although adidas-Salomon found it unacceptable to have child labor in its supplier factories, based on foundational and company values articulated in its Standards of Engagement, determining what to do about it was not easy.

Declaration of Fundamental Principles and Rights at Work

The Declaration of Fundamental Principles and Rights at Work provide four general principles, identified as "conventions." The ILO introduction to these principles explains:

Globalization—economic integration characterized by open international trade, investment, and capital flows—requires a universal social pillar that supports democracy, transparency, equity, and development. There is a growing recognition that, unless questions of unfairness and inequality are systematically addressed by the world community, the process of international integration itself may be rejected by increasing numbers of countries and people.

The International Labour Organisation's Declaration of Fundamental Principles and Rights at Work is a vital piece of that social pillar. It is a reinvigorated commitment by the ILO to the values of its Constitution.

A universal consensus now exists that all countries, regardless of their level of economic development, cultural values, or number of the ILO Conventions ratified, have an obligation to respect, promote, and realize the following fundamental principles and rights:

- Freedom of association and the effective recognition of the right to collective bargaining
- Elimination of all forms of forced or compulsory labor
- Effective abolition of child labor
- Elimination of discrimination in respect to employment and occupation

The Declaration is a promotional tool that may not be used for protectionist purposes. It is accompanied by a meaningful, promotional follow-up reporting mechanism whose primary aim is to focus technical cooperation efforts on helping countries achieve the principles and rights as a basis for development, democracy, and equity.[3]

Stakeholder engagement is an interactive, dialogue-based, and mutual process of engagement around issues of mutual interest that occurs between companies and their stakeholders. Stakeholder engagement explicitly recognizes the mutuality of interests and possible responses. A stakeholder engagement process is mutual in that information, exchanges and, to some extent, input on relevant decisions go two ways. Companies can take one of three types of stances toward their stakeholders: reactive, proactive, or interactive.[4] Reactive stances mean that the company is simply reacting to problems as they occur. Proactive stances suggest that the company has created some sort of boundary-spanning function to plan how it engages with stakeholders (for example, a human, labor, or community relations function). Interactive stances, in which stakeholder engagement processes can be classified, mean that the company develops systems and processes of mutual engagement, interaction, and communication in which inputs are sought on company decisions and, indeed, in which those inputs are taken seriously.

Companies that have stakeholder engagement processes have implicitly or explicitly recognized that mutual benefits are possible when information, insights, and ideas are exchanged. New ideas for cooperation, improvements, or innovation, for example, with employees, can sometimes be generated through such interactions. Nike, for example, focused on improving its relationships with employees through the education programs discussed in chapter 7, in part, as a way of improving its reputation with its constituencies.

Stakeholder engagement processes mean that not only do stakeholders' voices get heard in new ways, but sometimes the company itself has to change as well. Active engagement or interaction means that stakeholders sometimes need to change their attitudes, opinions, requests, or demands. But because the process is interactive, the company itself will also sometimes have to change its own practices, strategies, or systems in responding to issues raised by stakeholders.

Cultural differences, as well as differences in power, status, and type of relationship to the company, create the need for systems of stakeholder engagement that work interactively to draw out ideas, insights, differences, and points of agreement so that company actions are effective in particular situations. As chapter 7 indicates with regard to Nike's microenterprise loan or cultural sensitivity programs, sometimes it is important for company managers to work together with representatives of the local community to determine what the real interests and needs are, so that programs can be developed that meet those needs.

Integration

Integration in TRM approaches means that companies are paying close attention to how well the responsibility vision, values, and stakeholder engagement processes they have developed are actually integrated into strategies, human resource systems that affect employees, and operating practices that affect other stakeholders and the natural environment. The integration process thus involves three major components: integration into company strategies for achieving the corporate vision and purposes; integration into employee policies and practices, because, after all, it is the employee who actually accomplishes the work of the organization; and integration into functional areas that deal with other stakeholders and into management systems, in particular the reward system. The ILO's Factory Improvement Program (chap. 12) illustrates one way that training programs can be developed and implemented to make the integration process real for managers and employees at the plant level (see figure 6.2).

TRM approaches mean paying attention to a wide range of stakeholders, that is, those who can affect or are affected by the activities of the firm.[5] Employees; customers; suppliers and distributors; other allies and partners; communities in which the company locates facilities (or the supply chain members are located); owners and investors; creditors; and local, regional, and national governments are among the stakeholders to whom it makes sense to pay attention, given the pressures companies face today. Companies that recognize the importance of developing interactive systems to build positive relationships with all of these stakeholders know that integration of the company's stated responsibility vision and values into operating practices is a critical component of gaining credibility with them.

Integration into Strategy

Company strategy defines the overall direction of a business by asking (and answering) the questions: What business(es) are we in? and How do we compete? Putting responsibility management systems in place means incorporating into corporate systems and strategies a third type of ques-

Figure 6.2
Integrated Model of Total Responsibility Management (TRM)

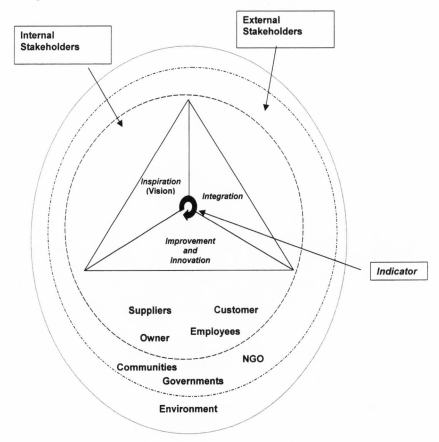

tion, what scholars R. Edward Freeman and Dan Gilbert call the "enterprise strategy" question: What do we stand for?[6]

Answering these questions involves linking the way a company competes to the core values and the responsibility vision that have been identified and ensuring that operating practices, including labor standards, reflect the vision and values. To do this well means expanding the company's traditional focus beyond simply "maximizing shareholder wealth," to understanding the investments, commitments, risks, and ties or bonds that other stakeholders have with respect to the company. A critically important group of stakeholders is workers or employees, who actually make or deliver the products and services that provide the basis for strategy and competition in the first place. Other key stakeholders are owners (shareholders), customers, suppliers, communities in which the company has operations, and governments of the countries in which the company operates. Responsibility strategies need to be developed with all of these stakeholders firmly in mind. Nike's reputational problems around labor issues, for example, created significant strategic difficulties for the company with respect to socially aware customers and investors. These types of reputational problems also made other footwear producers, such as adidas-Salomon, aware of the need for creating interactive programs to deal with these issues (see chap. 8).

Building Human Resource Capacity

A critical step in developing a TRM approach is building human resource capacity, as the cases readily illustrate. Employees/workers, after all, are responsible for day-to-day production of the company's goods or services. TRM approaches pay significant attention to employee policies because of the central role that employees play in any company and, in particular, to whether workers are being treated with dignity and respect. In the global context, as the cases illustrate, it is critically important for company management to pay attention to international labor standards as a baseline for treating employees responsibly.

TRM approaches recognize the value that employees or workers bring to creating success for the company. As is made abundantly clear from significant amounts of academic research, employees do their best when their efforts are valued and when they feel empowered with respect to their jobs, that is, when they are respected. Poor treatment of employees, lack of respect, and abusive situations lead not only to reputational problems for the company (e.g., what Nike has experienced in the past), but also to lower productivity than could otherwise be expected.[7]

Management theorist Jeffrey Pfeffer suggests that successful companies employ seven practices with respect to employees:

- Employment security
- Selective hiring of new personnel
- Self-managed teams and decentralization of decision making as the basic principles of organizational design
- Comparatively high compensation contingent on organizational performance
- Extensive training
- Reduced status distinctions and barriers, including dress, language, office arrangements, and wage differences across levels
- Extensive sharing of financial and performance information throughout the organization[8]

Clearly, in global supply chains, the application of these practices needs to be undertaken in a culturally sensitive way and specifically tailored to the unique situations faced in different nations and cultures and with employees from different ethnic backgrounds. The approach adidas-Salomon takes to child labor, for example, forced the firm to think through what made the most sense in the particular contexts in which child labor might be problematic.

Attaining excellence in company productivity is based on a wider array of values embedded in employee-related practices than simply the foundational principles articulated in the ILO conventions or human rights agreements. Work by scholar Jeanne Liedtka[9] points the way not only to good employee practices, but also to successful efforts to improve productivity (see figure 6.3), many of which can be seen in the cases in this book. Liedtka studied various systemic approaches to improving performance and found that they shared a number of common themes that can be used in thinking through TRM approaches.

Liedtka notes that creating shared purpose and meaning is important, as well as developing a broader—systems—perspective in all employees so that they can understand their roles and the way those roles relate to each other. As figure 6.3 indicates, it is also important to empower employees to make relevant decisions regarding their own work and to focus on work processes, rather than on individual tasks. Sharing information with workers also helps productivity, as does providing extensive opportunities for training and development, and working through dialogue processes rather than hierarchical or less respectful mechanisms. When projects to improve a factory or to work with a foundational standard (e.g., child labor problems) are undertaken with recognition of cultural differences, when all voices can be heard equally and with input from workers familiar with local customs, solutions to otherwise difficult issues can be found. Nike's experience with the after-hours education program in Ho Chi Minh City is one example of a collaborative, employee-centered, and empowered approach (chap. 7).

Integration into Management Systems

Developing employee systems and building human resource capacity alone are insufficient for implementation of holistic TRM approaches. Incorporating the responsibility vision and values into other management systems, particularly the reward, information, and communications systems, as well as into all stakeholder-related functions, is also critical. Responsibility management approaches need to be systemic if they are to be effective because companies are organic systems in which changes in one part of the company produce ripple effects throughout the whole entity. Once the decision is made to manage responsibility, the company needs to pay close attention to all the systems that support its productive pro-

Figure 6.3

Values-Based Management Practices in Systems Approaches to Managing

Shared Themes	Relevant Values-Based Practices
Create a shared sense of meaning, vision, and purpose that connects the personal to the organizational.	• Values community without subordinating the individual • Sees community purpose as flowing from individuals
Develop a systems perspective in all--a view held by each individual of him- or herself as embedded within a larger system.	• Seeks to serve other community members and ecosystem partners
Emphasize business processes, rather than hierarchy or structure.	• Believes work itself has intrinsic value • Belief in quality of both ends and means
Localize decision making around work processes.	• Responsibility for actions • Primacy of reach, with needed support
Leverage information within the system.	• Truth telling (honesty--integrity) • Full access to accurate and complete information
Focus on development, at both personal and organizational levels	• Value the individual as an end • Focus on learning and growth, at both individual and organizational levels
Encourage dialogue	• Freedom and responsibility to speak and to listen • Commitment to find higher ground through exchange of diverse views
Foster the capacity to take multiple perspectives simultaneously.	• Willingness to understand and work with the perspectives of others, rather than imposing own views
Create a sense of commitment and ownership.	• Promise keeping • Sense of urgency • Engagement rather than detachment

Sources: Adapted from Jeanne M. Liedtka, "Constructing an Ethic for Business Practice: Competing Effectively and Doing Good," in *Leading Corporate Citizens: Vision, Values, Value Added,* Sandra Waddock (Burr Ridge: McGraw-Hill, 2002).

cesses, as well as its employees, customers, communities, owners, suppliers, and other stakeholders.

The integration of TRM requires that leaders take a systemic approach, considering all of a company's practices and resulting impact. Thus, integration of responsibility into management systems can mean rethinking how the company relates to all of its internal and external stakeholders, how effective and efficient its resource use, production processes, and distribution systems are, as well as how well the company is living up to its stated values.

Figure 6.4 highlights some of the critical functional areas and related practices that companies consider as they think holistically about implementing systems for responsibility management. Key functions are those that span the boundary between management and other stakeholders, particularly employees, through the human resource function, training

Figure 6.4
Areas in Which Integration Responsibility Is Integrated into
Stakeholder-Related Practices

Functional area	Practices: Processes and Policies
Human Resources	Hiring and recruitment
	Appraisal, assessment, performance review
	Dismissal and layoff policies
	Promotion
	Training and development programs
	Working conditions, safety
	Management style, employee empowerment
	Implementation of code of conduct
Marketing	Product design
	Public relations
	Product quality, impacts, safety
	Advertising and promotional strategies
	Customer relationships
Finance/Investor Relations	Sources and uses of capital
Accounting and Control	Responsibility measurement system
	Multiple (triple) bottom line assessment
Operations	Production processes
	Labor and working standards
	Lighting
	Safety systems
Supplier Relationships	Contractual obligations
	Code of conduct implementation
	Environment management systems
	Employee/labor requirements and conditions
Management Information Systems	Control and dissemination of key information
	Use of information gathered
	Employee communication system
	External communication system
Environmental Management System	Waste disposal, pollution control
	Environmental, health & safety practices
	Packaging and production considerations
	Resource reuse, reduction, recycling
Community Relations	Neighbor of choice practices

Source: Charles Bodwell and Sandra Waddock, "Managing Corporate Responsibility," working paper, Boston College, 2001.

programs, and employee policies. Also important, however, are customer relationships developed through customer-related practices such as the nature and quality of the product; marketing and other types of communications; and customer relationship systems, investor relations, and operations. As the cases in this book highlight, to meet global labor standards, it is critically important to build constructive relationships with suppliers and, increasingly, to apply and expect the same standards as one does with company-operated facilities. Of particular relevance is the development of accounting and control systems to measure the responsibility management systems in place and the management information systems used to provide for transparency and accountability for the results of company activities.

One of the stickier areas for the integration of TRM systems in multinational companies is in the increasingly long supply chains that many of these companies have established in the effort to be globally competitive and to achieve low-cost production. A study by the International Labour Organization[10] of global supply chains, focused on how leading firms, which are under the greatest pressures to improve labor practices in their suppliers, have progressed from denying responsibility for conditions in supplier factories to embracing this responsibility. Indeed, they are rolling up their sleeves and taking on the challenge of improving labor, human rights, and environmental practices, as well as the overall integrity of their systems through implementation of strict codes of conduct and responsibility standards, that is, TRM approaches.

As will become obvious in reading the cases, it is not an easy decision for a firm to accept responsibilities beyond those typically viewed as being within the borders of the firm. It is one thing to say, "We make our suppliers sign a code of conduct and we expect them to follow it." It is entirely another thing to say, "We expect our suppliers to follow our code. We work with them to help them meet the code. We check to ensure they do, and if they don't then we don't work with them any longer." Yet these decisions, difficult as they are, are exactly the ones that the companies studied are making every day.

Creating a code of conduct is challenging, but not nearly as challenging as accepting responsibility down the chain and introducing all the management systems necessary to make adherence to the code possible. The firms studied here have realized that taking this second step requires systemic approaches, not simply narrow consideration of purchasing and compliance functions. Implementing the code, truly ensuring that global labor standards are met, means taking responsibility for the labor practices of distant suppliers. Of course, meeting global labor standards requires not only a broad-based consideration of how the responsibility goals of the organization can be met, but also ways to innovate and improve when problems are discovered.

Innovation and Improvement

TRM approaches foster innovation and improvement in management systems by carefully designing responsibility objectives for each of the company's core stakeholders, starting with the sine qua non stakeholder group—a company's employees. An important part of the innovation and improvement process is ensuring that companies and their suppliers achieve global labor standards. Innovations and improvements in various operating practices that affect different stakeholders, boost performance, and improve results are a consistent feature of TRM approaches. Nike's approach to cultural sensitivity training (chap. 7) is an example of a situation in which continual improvements have resulted in a better program over time.

Leaders can accomplish the objective of continual improvement in TRM by carefully designing improvement directly into the system. A firm must recognize that, in many ways, it needs to always strive for improvement in its stakeholder relationships and the effects or outcomes of its activities. The innovation and improvement component of TRM approaches includes indicators or a responsibility measurement system and transparency and accountability for results and impacts. The improvements then must be made on a continual basis over time to generate remediation, innovation, and learning. The ILO's Factory Improvement Program, discussed in chapter 12, will work with managers to develop measurement systems that indicate progress along important dimensions of labor standards.

As with TQM, taking a TRM approach to managing labor standards in the global context is dependent on integration of responsibility management into labor practices and day-to-day operations throughout the supply chain. Indicators in a TRM system that are linked closely to other measurement systems, such as financial, productivity, and quality systems, can provide a baseline for future action to improve the company's responsibility management and, it is hoped, its productivity and financial bottom line as well. Thus, to accomplish the improvements and innovations, TRM approaches use key performance indicators, measurement systems that assess how well the company is performing not just along the financial line, but also along multiple bottom lines. Typically, this approach focuses on the triple bottom lines of economic, social, and environment (see figure 6.5).[11]

Global labor standards, such as the ILO's key fundamental conventions, also provide guidance as to the kinds of indicators that are relevant to TRM approaches. In the United States, Social Accountability International is working to develop SA8000, a measurement and reporting system focused specifically on labor standards.[12] The SA8000 standard establishes a uniform labor standard designed to be audited and verified by third

Figure 6.5
Multiple Bottom Line Performance Indicators

Ten Measures of Business Success	Ten Dimensions of Corporate Sustainable Development Performance
Financial Performance 1. Shareholder value 2. Revenue 3. Operational efficiency 4. Access to capital **Financial Drivers** 5. Customer attraction 6. Brand value and reputation 7. Human and intellectual capital 8. Risk profile 9. Innovation 10. License to operate	**Governance** 1. Ethics, values and principles 2. Accountability and transparency **General** 3. Triple bottom line commitment **Environment** 4. Environmental process focus 5. Environmental product focus **Socio-Economic** 6. Socio-economic development 7. Human rights 8. Workplace conditions **Stakeholder Engagement** 9. Engaging business partners 10. Engaging non-business partners

Source: van Heel, John Elkington, Shelly Fennell, and Franceska van Dijk, *Buried Treasure: Uncovering the Business Case for Corporate Sustainability* (London: Sustainability, 2001).

parties. Based on the ILO's four fundamental conventions, plus conventions relevant to other possible areas of abuse, the SA8000 standards define accountability requirements and possible indicators that can be audited regularly in the following areas:

- Child labor
- Forced labor
- Health and safety
- Freedom of association and right to collective bargaining
- Discrimination
- Disciplinary practices
- Working hours
- Remuneration
- Management systems

It is worth noting that management systems related to labor standards, as established by SA8000, represent a complex array of company practices. The designation *management systems* encompasses company policy for taking into consideration social accountability and labor conditions, conducting management review, engaging with company representatives, planning and implementing new practices, controlling suppliers/subcontractors and subsuppliers, addressing concerns and taking corrective action, conducting outside communication, obtaining access for verification, and maintaining records.[13]

Implementing a responsibility vision is an ongoing, cyclical process of continual innovation, not a once-and-done event. That is, TRM approaches use iterative processes focused on making all of the company's stakeholder relationships and impacts better over time. The innovation and improvement components of TRM involve establishing processes for remediation of wrongs; improvement where needed; innovation of new ideas, processes, and practices; and ongoing organizational learning. Data from indicators in the measurement and accountability system provide managers with the feedback to create needed innovations and improvements in management practices and systems.

Accountability for impacts on stakeholders, particularly employees, is critical in today's networks of suppliers, distributors, and multinational firms, particularly given the connectivity of external activists and other concerned observers. One of the constant demands facing multinationals these days is for transparency with respect to results and stakeholder impacts. Companies taking TRM approaches recognize this need for both accountability and transparency as an essential element of building trust internally with employees and externally with other stakeholders. Communicating the results of initiatives to concerned and relevant stakeholders is a key to success. For certain practices (e.g., some labor situations, working conditions, and employee-related problems), external verification by outside (social) auditors may also be important.

As the cases in this book remind us, once problems are discovered, they need to be fixed. Remediation involves fixing what is wrong. Obviously, the first step toward TRM is to identify problem areas. But identifying the problem is not the end of the process; it is only the beginning. More important is figuring out how to resolve the identified problems, addressing concerns raised by stakeholders through the stakeholder dialogue process, or reducing gaps between espoused values and goals and realized ones. This resolution process is the remediation process.

TRM AND GLOBAL LABOR CHALLENGES

In this chapter we have presented a generic model of the types of approaches that companies are using to manage responsibilities with respect to labor challenges. Appendix 6.1 presents an overview of the key elements of TRM approaches, while figures 6.4 and 6.5 illustrate the ways in which components of TRM are integrated with each other. As we will see in the following chapters, there are many ways in which approaches to responsibility management evolve and many different types of situations to which such approaches apply. TRM approaches can help companies better cope with challenges to their labor standards when those standards are consistently developed and applied, and when there is a sincere effort to improve situations once problems are discovered. In the chapters that follow, we shall see example after example of just such approaches.

NOTES

1. The responsibility for opinions expressed in this chapter rests solely with the authors, and publication does not constitute an endorsement by Boston College or the International Labour Office.

2. See, for example, Sandra Waddock and Charles Bodwell, "From TQM to TRM: The Emerging Evolution of Responsibility Management Systems," *Journal of Corporate Citizenship*, Autumn 2 (7): 113–126; Sandra Waddock, Charles Bodwell, and Samuel B. Graves, "Responsibility: The New Business Imperative," *Academy of Management Executive* 16 (2): 132–148; and Sandra Waddock and Charles Bodwell, "Foundation Principles for Making Corporate Citizenship Real," Working paper, Boston College (2001). Some of the ideas and language in this chapter are adapted from Charles Bodwell and Sandra Waddock, "Managing Corporate Responsibility," Working paper, Boston College (2001).

3. http://www.ilo.org/public/english/standards/decl/declaration/index.htm

4. Lee E. Preston and James E. Post, *Private Management and Public Policy* (New York: Prentice-Hall, 1975).

5. R. Edward Freeman, *Strategic Management: A Stakeholder Approach* (Boston: Pitman, 1984).

6. R. Edward Freeman and Daniel R. Gilbert Jr., *Corporate Strategy and the Search for Ethics* (Englewood Cliffs, N.J.: Prentice Hall, 1988).

7. See Jeffrey Pfeffer, "Seven Practices of Successful Organizations," *California Management Review* 40, no. 2 (winter 1998): pp. 96–124. See also, Jeffrey Pfeffer and John F. Veiga, "Putting People First for Organizational Success," *Academy of Management Executive* 13, no. 2 (May 1999): 37–48.

8. See Pfeffer, "Seven Practices of Successful Organizations," p. 96.

9. Jeanne M. Liedtka, "Constructing an Ethic for Business Practice: Competing Effectively and Doing Good," *Business and Society* 37, no. 3 (September 1998): 254–80.

10. Ivanka Mamic, *Business and Code of Conduct Implementation: How Firms Use Management Systems for Social Performance* (Geneva: International Labour Office, 2003). For additional examples see also Laura P. Hartman et al., "Program Analyses: Exploration of Management Alternatives to Global Labor Challenges," *Ethics Resource Center Working Paper* (2001).

11. John Elkington, *Cannibals with Forks: The Triple Bottom Line of Sustainability* (Gabriola Island: New Society Publishers, 1988).

12. See http://www.cepaa.org/SA8000%20Standard.htm for the current standards (accessed 15 July 2002).

13. Social Accountability International, SA8000, International Standard 2001, http://www.cepaa.org/SA8000%20Standard.htm (accessed 15 July 2002).

Total Responsibility Management Approaches: Framework for Understanding Approaches to Responsibility Management

Inspiration: Vision Setting and Leadership Systems

1. **Stakeholder Engagement Processes.** Stakeholder engagement means developing dialogue, communication, and mutuality with important stakeholders to inform operating practices and strategies. The company determines "What is our impact on stakeholders?" and "How do we appropriately incorporate the views of key stakeholders into our responsibility vision and leadership?" through its stakeholder engagement processes. Stakeholders include primary stakeholders, that is, employees, owners, suppliers/allies, and customers as well as critical secondary stakeholders, that is, communities and governments. Specific other stakeholders may also be included, depending on the company's situation and industry.

2. **Foundational Values, International Standards.** Articulating the company's core values and the ways in which those values link to the bedrock of internationally agreed foundation values that provide a floor of acceptable practice. Frequently these values are articulated in the company's vision or mission statement and code of conduct. With suppliers, sometimes these values can be found in statements about the terms of engagement.

3. **Responsibility Vision and Leadership Commitments.** Each firm determines its own vision for responsible practice and leadership, based on a foundation of generally agreed-on global standards articulated by international bodies. The company determines "What do we stand for?" in developing a responsible vision, leadership commitments, and core values that underpin all of its activities.

Integration: Changes in Strategies and Management Practices

4. **Strategy.** Having determined its responsibility vision and stakeholder engagement strategy, a company then develops an overall strategy for achieving its vision, leadership, and corporate goals in a responsible manner. The company asks, "How do we match our vision and what we stand for with the reality of what we do and are?" and "How do we achieve our corporate goals and objectives?"

5. **Building Human Resource Capacity.** It is people who are organized in organizations. It is people who implement the company's vision and leadership and particularly determine how responsibly the company operates. People involved with a company, whether directly as employees or in the supply chain for a company, deserve to be treated responsibly, that is, with dignity and respect. Responsibility for human resource practices thus stretches beyond a company's formal boundaries to include other companies taking part in a focal company's value chain. Responsibility for human resources includes key elements of training; performance appraisal; recruitment; retention and dismissal policies; wage and salary policies consistent with local conditions; working conditions; and employee development, communication, and empowerment practices.

6. **Integration into Management Systems.** Responsibility is integral to corporate practices, impacts, and relationships. This integration means that corporate practices and relations are either responsible—or they are not. Recognizing this reality, TRM companies develop management systems that explicitly and deliberately integrate an understanding and implementation of responsibility into all management systems as well as corporate strategies. Key systems include reward systems; information and communication systems; operating, production, and delivery systems; purchasing, accounting, and financial systems; environmental systems; marketing and sales systems; human resource systems; other corporate systems; supplier/ally relationships; and others as relevant.

Innovation: Assessment, Improvement, and Learning Systems

7. **Indicators: Responsibility Measurement System.** Measurement of the impacts and responsibility of both the processes and results of systems and corporate practices in a multiple (at least triple, i.e., economic, social, and ecological) bottom-line framework is a critical component of implementing and understanding a responsibility vision. Responsible companies know that their effects on stakeholders and stakeholder relationships can and need to be measured regularly and consistently so that results can be reported both internally and externally and improvements can be made where necessary. Measurement systems evaluate stakeholder impacts and performance through strategic and functional area assessments. Data gathered through measurement procedures, information technology systems, and responsibility auditing practices provide a baseline for continually improving operating practices, highlighting urgent situations, providing feedback on progress, and fostering accountability to internal and external stakeholders through valid and reliable assessment/auditing practices.

8. **Transparency and Accountability for Results and Impacts.** The responsible company knows that it needs to be accountable for its stakeholder and ecological impacts and results, and also to report those impacts and its operating results transparently through at least a triple bottom line framework (economic, societal, and ecological). Data from the responsibility measurement system are used to produce responsibility reports addressing internal and external practices and the effects of corporate activities. Companies determine how to develop trust with external and internal stakeholders through dialogue and how to ensure the validity and reliability of their accountability systems in a cost-effective way.

9. **Improvement: Remediation, Innovation, and Learning.** Implementing a responsibility vision is an ongoing, cyclical process of continual improvement, innovation, organizational learning, and remediation for wrongs. Data from the measurement and accountability systems provide managers with guidance and structures that encourage responsible practices and provide an emphasis on continued organizational learning and development toward ever-more-responsible practice. Remediation links to both the foundational values agreed on by the international community and the specific responsibility vision of the corporation, focusing on continually learning and improving practices that are generally responsible but could be performed better, while immediately eliminating practices that are intolerable under the foundational values. The stakeholder dialogue process also provides key data for process, standards, and system improvements.

PART II

Program Studies of Innovation in the Management of Global Labor Challenges

CHAPTER 7

Nike, Inc.: Corporate Social Responsibility and Workplace Standard Initiatives in Vietnam

Laura P. Hartman and Richard E. Wokutch

CORPORATE OVERVIEW

Though the purpose of these case studies is not to showcase an entire firm, but rather to highlight specific model programs, it is helpful to understand the context in which these programs exist and are implemented. To that end, this chapter provides factual information about Nike with regard to its work environment and relates its operating environment to the globalization factors discussed in Part I of this book.

Nike was founded in 1964 by Philip H. Knight as "BRS (Blue Ribbon Sports)"; in 1972 the name was changed to "Nike." Phil Knight remains Nike's owner, chairman, and CEO today. Nike, based in Beaverton, Oregon, has more than 22,000 and over 800 contracted suppliers in about 52 countries throughout the world, employing more than 550,000 workers on any given day creating sports and fitness footwear, apparel, equipment, and accessories for worldwide distribution (over 400 of these suppliers are located in Asia).[1] Approximately 175 million pairs of shoes are manufactured each year for Nike, contributing in part to Nike's annual revenue for 2001, which totaled almost $10 billion.[2] Nike's Code of Conduct, first sent out to manufacturers in 1992 and the second code to be developed in the entire industry,[3] binds all Nike contract manufacturers and requires that all "manufacturing partners must post this Code in all major workspaces, translated into the language of the worker, and must endeavor to train workers on their rights and obligations as defined by this Code and applicable labor laws."[4] (The code is reprinted following this chapter as appendix 7.1.) In its code, Nike sets a standard for its partnerships by seeking contractors who are committed to best practices and continuous improvement in the following areas:

- Employing management practices that respect the rights of all employees, including the right to free association and collective bargaining
- Minimizing the impact on the environment
- Providing a safe and healthy workplace
- Promoting the health and well-being of all employees

Specifically, Nike's code binds its partners to core standards of conduct concerning the following issues:

1. Forced labor.
2. Child labor.
3. Compensation.
4. Benefits.
5. Hours of work/overtime.
6. Environment, safety, and health: The Nike Corporate Responsibility Compliance Production SHAPE (Safety, Health, Attitude of Management, People Investment & Environment). Assessment Form follows this chapter as appendix 7.2, and a description of the management program for Environment, Safety and Health (MESH) follows this chapter as appendix 7.3.
7. Documentation and inspection.[5]

When Nike chooses to establish a relationship with a new production factory, it requires that the factory agree to, pay for, and undergo a presourcing audit conducted by a third party, as well as a Nike internal SHAPE inspection.[6] The goal is that SHAPE inspections will take place at least four times a year for footwear factories and twice a year for each apparel or equipment factory. For the relationship to continue or for an order to be placed, both of the inspections described above must conclude that the factory is in "substantial compliance" with the Nike code of conduct. If not, the factory may choose to resubmit at a later date, striving toward compliance at that time. The entire monitoring process strives to achieve the following schedule of events:

- Factory identified by Nike production/sourcing staff
- SHAPE inspection carried out by production and/or LP manager
- Presourcing monitoring visit conducted by Global Social Compliance/ PricewaterhouseCoopers (PwC)
- Factory approved by vice president of compliance
- Production begins in the factory

- SHAPE inspections carried out quarterly for footwear manufacturers and bi-annually for apparel and equipment manufacturers
- When noncompliance issues identified, recommended action plan compiled for factory by Nike labor practice department working in conjunction with Nike production staff
- Follow-up monitoring visit done to measure corrective action taken by factory

Nike has developed a new management audit designed to quantitatively measure a contract factory's compliance with Nike management standards concerning pay, wage, benefits, forced labor, nondiscrimination, age, freedom of association, and the treatment of workers. This new instrument is in-depth, and Nike is focusing on global consistency, striving to find ways to link performance on this audit with sourcing decisions and incentive schemes. The audit evaluates contract factories on the basis of four areas of risk assessment: country location, size of factory, type of operation, and factory-specific historical compliance performance record. In conjunction with the development of the audit, Nike's president Mark Parker approved the hiring of 21 new internal labor compliance auditors for the compliance department. On the basis of Nike's assessment of its contract factories, these auditors will categorize them as high, medium, and low risk. Each year, using this tool, Nike plans to audit 100 percent of high-risk factories, 50 percent of medium-risk factories, and 10 percent of low-risk factories.[7]

Evolution of Nike's Approach to Global Labor Issues

Attention to the labor practices of Nike's suppliers began about 1988 when journalists focused several news stories on the situation in Nike's Jakarta, Indonesia, suppliers. USAID then funded a large-scale survey to document wage law violations that was later supported by a study of the Indonesian shoe industry. Between 1988 and 1996 the minimum wage rate in Indonesia rose more than 300 percent (from $.86 to $2.46 per day), in large part due to this attention and efforts by large MNEs such as Nike.[8] The rate of inflation in Indonesia for the same time period was 205 percent.[9] On May 12, 1998, Nike CEO Phil Knight delivered a speech at the National Press Club that became a turning point in Nike's approach to the issues facing its suppliers.[10] In that speech, Knight accepted responsibility at the corporate level for the labor activities of Nike's suppliers by establishing six initiatives for the firm. Knight explained that, as of that day, Nike committed to the following:

- Increasing the minimum age of new footwear factory workers to 18, and the minimum age for all other new light-manufacturing workers (apparel, accessories, equipment) to 16.

- Adopting the personal exposure limits (PEL) of the U.S. Occupational Safety and Health Administration (OSHA) as the standard for indoor air quality for all footwear factories.

- Funding university research and open forums to explore issues related to global manufacturing and responsible business practices such as independent monitoring and air quality standards.

- Expanding worker education programs, including middle and high school equivalency courses, for workers in all Nike footwear factories.

- Increasing support of its current microenterprise loan program to 1,000 families each in Vietnam, Indonesia, Pakistan, and Thailand; expanding its current independent monitoring programs to include nongovernmental organizations (NGOs), foundations, and educational institutions; and making summaries of the findings public.

- Involving NGOs in the process of factory monitoring, with summaries released to the public.[11] (See appendix 7.4 following this chapter for full text of speech.)

The *New York Times* applauded Knight's commitments, claiming that they "set a standard that other companies should match."[12] To the contrary, however, some critics chastised Knight for not including several other commitments, including the protection of whistle-blowers in the factories, Nike-directed worker rights education programs, guarantee of living wages and reasonable working hours, and protection of workers' right to freedom of association.[13]

Since the time of Knight's pronouncement, Nike has developed a system of comprehensive monitoring and remediation.[14] This includes a health management and safety audit program and a significant global labor practice team that visits factories on an everyday basis[15] and conducts training and awareness initiatives. In connection with auditing programs, not only has Nike coordinated these activities from inside, but it has also engaged external auditors, as well as NGOs, to monitor, audit, and report on ongoing activities from an external perspective. Nike is also a founding member of the Fair Labor Association and has committed to external independent monitoring throughout its factory base. Though many have praised these efforts,[16] not all of Nike's critics have been pacified by them, as is specifically evidenced by scholar Dara O'Rourke's critique of the PwC labor-monitoring program, in which he claims not only that PwC failed to catch and assess several violations, but also that it allowed for management bias in the audits and failed to effectively gather information.[17]

In 2001 Nike invited Global Alliance for Workers and Communities (GA) to evaluate challenges existing in its suppliers' factories in Indonesia, Thailand, and Vietnam. Though some have questioned the validity and credibility of GA's work as a result of its relationship with Nike (along with The Gap, St. John's University, Kent State University, the World Bank, and the John D. and Catherine T. MacArthur Foundation, Nike has contributed funds to GA),[18] GA maintains strict standards relating to conflicts of interest and autonomy of its research. As a result of Nike's invitation, GA produced a report titled "Workers' Voices: An Interim Report on Workers' Needs and Aspirations in Nine Nike Contract Factories in Indonesia." The report was based on interviews with more than 4,450 workers at nine Nike supplier factories.[19] Currently, GA is engaged with Nike in a tailored training program focused on supervisory skills in Thailand, Indonesia, Vietnam, India, and China.

Most recently, in September 2001, Knight and Nike's board of directors created a Corporate Responsibility Committee of the Board. The committee's responsibility is to review, report, and make recommendations to the full board regarding Nike's alignment with corporate responsibility commitments. Issues to be addressed include labor compliance initiatives, environmental practices, community affairs programs, human resources, diversity issues, and philanthropic efforts.

Vietnam Operations

Nike has been manufacturing in Vietnam through factory partners since 1995, currently employing more than 43,000 workers making 22 million shoes annually and exporting apparel totaling over $450 million. Nike production accounts for 8 percent of Vietnam's manufactured exports and 32 percent of its footwear exports.[20]

Based in Ho Chi Minh City, Vietnam, American Chris Helzer served as Nike's director of government affairs for Southeast Asia and Australia for two and a half years. Lalit Monteiro is the general manager of Nike-Vietnam and works on ethics-related issues with Steve Hewitt, the corporate responsibility and compliance manager. As a modification to Nike's earlier compliance structure, the vice president for apparel sourcing now has the oversight for corporate responsibility and may veto any given source as a result of its failure to comply with corporate responsibility standards.

Leverage toward compliance is much greater in the Vietnam footwear industry than in apparel or other industries since most footwear factories serve Nike 100 percent and since there is little, if any, slow season. Of Nike's more than 850 supplier factories worldwide, 68 are footwear factories (5 footwear and 7 apparel factories are located in Vietnam). Nike has 46,000 workers in Vietnam with a current turnover of only 1 percent,[21] which is usually due to lack of desire on the part of female workers to return after pregnancy or marriage. As the largest employer in Vietnam, Nike has a significant impact on the Vietnamese economy. While the discussion above evidences prior challenges, even one of Nike's harshest critics, Medea Benjamin of Global Exchange, notes that "things are changing for the better"[22] and that the firm has made an "astounding turn-around."[23] (See photos 7.1 and 7.2 of Nike's Vietnam operations.)

NIKE, INC.—PROGRAM ANALYSES

Program 1: After-Hours Education Program

Inspiration and Vision Setting: Idea Generation/Inception

The inspiration or vision-setting process for the Nike after-hours education program began during one of the ongoing meetings with suppliers coordinated by Nike when Dae Shin, the Korean owner of a supplier located in Vietnam, noted that the workers have requested and would benefit from an education program that could be attended after working hours. It was determined by this supplier and others interested that the best program would be one that balanced worker interest, slots available, and the nature of the educational need. In his May 1998 initiatives speech, Knight made the education program a Nike standard, promising that by the end of 2001 Nike would order footwear only from manufacturers that offer a "Jobs + Education" program to workers.

Integration: The Approval Process

The approval process for this project was informal. A group of individuals involved in supply chain compliance and integrity at Nike, including CEO Phil Knight and President Dave Taylor, sat down to explore how Nike might be able to best support this project. During this stage of the project's establishment, group members discussed the parameters of their corporate responsibility as well as the investment that they hoped to make, not only in these suppliers, but also in the workers and the countries in which they lived, highlighting the importance of top management commitment to the responsibility vision Nike was establishing. It was determined that the most effective program would be one that was coordinated in partnership with the Ministry of Education to ensure GED compliance where desired by the students. (GED-equivalent is the norm for Vietnam. However, in other countries, workers were more interested in obtaining life and other skills. Thus, education programs in some countries do not necessarily result in granting of GED equivalency.)

Integration, Establishment, and Implementation

The supplier, in partnership with Nike and the Ministry of Education, worked together in the integration process and established GED programs by hiring teachers and renting classrooms in local educational facilities

Photo 7.1 Line at Nike supplier factory. *Source:* Laura Hartman

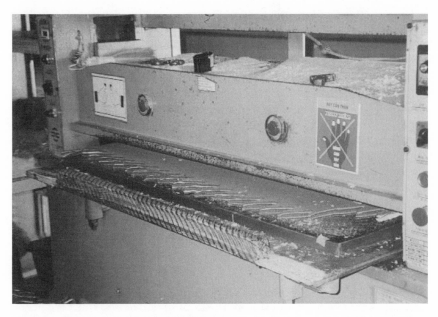

Photo 7.2 Two-handed press (modification to include two required buttons reduces injuries). *Source:* Laura Hartman

near the factories. The program covers the expenses of each student including books and other supplies and a meal allowance. Nike currently
participates in the after-hours education program by funding 50 percent
of the cost of the program to each supplier. All Nike footwear suppliers
in Vietnam currently have active education programs in accordance with
this model. One of the factory owners involved identifies the program as
a foundation for personal development, "We would like to be able to
promote from within and can only do that once these workers have additional educations." In fact, this owner has already promoted several
Vietnamese workers to line management positions on completion of the
education program. He explains that he and his firm "want to go beyond
compliance, both for the business relationship with Nike as well as for its
own impact on the workers and our organization. To achieve our profits,
we have to address the employees from an emotional perspective, as
well."

As these practices are integrated into Nike's training programs, they
serve as a foundation for long-term relationships,[24] Dusty Kidd, Nike's
Vice President for Compliance, explains that these programs are valuable
not just as a gesture of Nike's commitment to the workforce and the supplier's future, they are valuable because they also result in long-term ef-
ficiencies that can be realized by investing in education. By investing
matching funds ranging on average from $15,000 to $20,000 per supplier,
Nike "can touch 300 people for a lifetime."[25] To date, over 10,000 contract
workers have participated in these programs. The education program at
one factory, Cheng Shin, is currently the largest program, with 400 students having originally enrolled and an 85 percent completion rate, which
are important indicators of success that provide a basis for improvement
and innovation (see photo 7.3). In addition, the Chang Shin Vietnam factory suggested a literacy program for the workers, jointly funded with
Nike, Chang Shin Vietnam, and the local government, to which Nike
agreed. Chang Shin Vietnam also offers "livelihood training" for interested workers, coordinating sessions on hand-knitting, embroidery, and
other skills that the workers can then also teach their relatives. It is hoped
that this program might offer the workers' families skills that they could
use for additional income.

Though the subjects vary depending on worker demand and interest,
the programs themselves range from high school equivalency, to vocational, to short-term education programs on specific subjects such as personal health or financial management. After-hours education programs
now exist in Korea, Vietnam, Taiwan, China, Thailand, and Indonesia.
Educators are generally hired from the local region to best meet the needs
of the workers and to comply with education regulations of the education
ministries in various countries.

Photo 7.3 Education program at Nike supplier. *Source:* **Laura Hartman**

Indicators: Continued Program Assessment

For program assessment, Nike considers the following factors as important indicators that help measure performance during its biannual audit visit:

- Are students remaining in the classes? If not, is it because of lack of interest, lack of time from work, the level or quality of the instruction, or other variables? (In one situation, Nike learned that the students did not feel that the quality of instruction was good, so the company worked with local programs to find more high-quality instructors and a better curriculum.)
- Are the students able to learn from and complete the coursework?
- What is the absentee rate? Why?
- Are the programs offered at appropriate times? Appropriate, accessible locations?
- What does our monitoring program report in connection with these programs? What do we learn from pretests and posttests or GED completion rates?

Since the workers have expressed a great deal of satisfaction with this program and encourage its continuation, Nike has encouraged its suppliers and suppliers of other companies from Vietnam and throughout Southeast Asia to visit the factory and learn about the program. To date, factory owners and others from adidas, Fujitsu, and Nike itself have visited the program. Nike has institutionalized these types of visits to allow its suppliers to share best practices, providing a basis for ongoing improvement initiatives. Once a month, general managers from each factory come together in a different factory and discuss accomplishments and challenges. Every six months this same group travels to factories in other countries to learn about their processes (with Nike financial support).

As of June, 1999, there were 20 separate education programs in the factories of 37 Asian Nike footwear contractors, including five footwear factories in Vietnam, six footwear factories in Indonesia, six in China, and three in Thailand. In Vietnam, this program has been extended to include two contract apparel factories, and a third will begin participating soon.

Exit Strategy

In terms of an exit strategy, Nike expects that it will remain as long as necessary or as long as it has a relationship with that supplier. However, by participating in this program, Nike also hopes that it might affect the general standard of education in that country such that the supplemental programs are no longer necessary, as regional education programs are enhanced.

Program 2: The Nike Jobs and Microenterprise Program

Inspiration and Vision Setting: Idea Generation/Inception

Conceived in 1997 and beginning in 1998, Nike established a microenterprise loan program to provide some support for women in the communities surrounding its suppliers. The inspiration or vision for the program originated in Vietnam and was later expanded to include Thailand and Indonesia. The purpose of the program is to allow women a chance to build small businesses that will ultimately boost their family's economic well-being, as well as contribute to the community's overall development. Though there is no direct financial gain for Nike, "the microloan program helps to create a more healthy community, which then provides other sources of income in the community, better workers, and additional sources of support for the families of current workers, raising the whole village's standard of living," says Helzer.

Microloans respond to another difficult challenge in the Southeast Asian region. Nike has a global prohibition against any at-home work. However, this might have the impact of discriminating against women who, for social and cultural reasons, have either chosen not to work or are not allowed to work outside of the home. Therefore, because of the prohibition against any at-home outsourcing, these women may not have any financial means to protect their rights in other areas. The microloan program can provide this financial stability without outsourcing Nike manufacturing.

Photo 7.4 Nike supplier factory in Vietnam. *Source:* **Laura Hartman**

Integration, Establishment, and Implementation

In each country in which the program is located, Nike has teamed with local NGOs in an effort to ensure that ongoing support is available for borrowers and that the programs are well integrated. The Vietnam programs were established as a joint effort between Nike, Colorado-based Friendship Bridge (an NGO devoted to creating loan programs for developing economies that was involved in the first three years of the program), and the local Vietnamese Women's Unions (who notify and solicit the borrowers). Currently, there have been approximately 3,200 loans in place, with the average loan standing at approximately $65 [maximum loan = 1 million Vietnamese Dong (VND) (≈U.S.$75), and the minimum loan = 500,000 VND (≈U.S.$37)]. Total Nike investment to date has been approximately 3.5 billion VND (U.S.$244,755), which includes an administrative fee paid to Friendship Bridge. Usually women will borrow the minimum amount for their first loan and increase the amounts for subsequent loans.

The Vietnam program includes potential borrowers within a 30-mile radius of Nike suppliers. The loan program currently operates in 6 villages in the Dong Nai province and 12 villages in the Cu Chi province. The borrowers must submit a business plan and go through basic business training and health seminars before the plans and loans are approved. The business plan must include a provision for saving a part of the money earned, and miniclasses are available to borrowers regarding good saving habits. An additional component of the program requires children of borrowers to remain in school.

Those receiving the loans included groups of women who team together to borrow funding to raise small livestock, to produce incense sticks and other basic manufactured items (garments), or to tend to rice fields in the production of rice paper for spring rolls. More than 2,300 rural women and former workers have received funds to help them in creating small businesses and, in Vietnam specifically, there have been no defaults on the loans.[26]

The loans are granted in a "trust bank" format to teams of individuals to build in a support structure to the program. The 5 to 20 team members of each trust bank guarantee each other's loans. The borrowers meet weekly or monthly to make loan repayments, share business tips, address community concerns, and receive training in business topics such as financial management as well as personal subjects such as nutrition, hygiene, child care, and so on. After repaying loans, trust bank members can qualify for larger loans, and their payments are recycled to others in the form of new loans. Trust Bank clients have maintained an average repayment rate of 97 percent or better. (See figure 7.1.)

Photo 7.5 Rice paper drying outside home. *Source:* **Laura Hartman**

Figure 7.1
Steps in the Trust Bank Cycle

Steps in the Trust Bank Cycle	
1. Feasibility study	to select a community where Trust Banks can make a difference
2. Promotional meeting	to explain the Trust Bank program to interested entrepreneurs
3. Eight to ten weekly meetings	to build group solidarity, strengthen leadership skills, develop business plans, and train clients in managing their own loan repayments
4. Verbal examination	to assess readiness of group to take on a loan commitment and guarantee each other's loans
5. Loan disbursement	
6. Beginning of first loan cycle (usually 16-20 weeks)	with weekly meetings for collecting repayments and savings, trading business tips, and discussing family and community concerns. Trust Bank members elect their own leaders, who plan and conduct the meetings.
7. Final repayment of the loans	
8. Beginning of a new loan cycle, with clients receiving larger loans	

Source: Women's Opportunity Fund, http://www.womensopportunityfund.org/Pages/main_what.html, reprinted with permission of the Women's Opportunity Fund.

In Indonesia the microenterprise loan program is offered in conjunction with Opportunity International, an NGO whose primary goal is fighting global poverty. The basis of the program is the belief that a very small loan (such as less than U.S.$100) may allow individuals to expand their inventory or to buy their raw materials in bulk, so that they can increase their profit margin, improve their business, and perhaps begin to accumulate savings.

Through a partnership with an NGO called the Population and Community Development Association and Union Footwear, Nike also supports a microenterprise program in northeastern Thailand, where it helped to establish a rural village stitching center and surrounding infrastructure, such as a vegetable bank, a tree bank, a school, and a women's empowerment center. Nike invested to build cash crop projects, to provide jobs, and to support the rural development of the region, which reversed migration to the city, By providing this kind of small business loan assistance, Nike can potentially put thousands of individuals to work. Significant local community improvement and innovation efforts are associated with the program.

Case Example: In conducting research for this report, one author visited the home of one of the Vietnamese microloan borrowers in the Cu Chi province. This young woman had borrowed money from the program each year for the past four years and had used the funds to purchase equipment to create rice paper. Before her involvement in the program, this woman engaged in a variety of domestic services in neighboring communities but never held a stable job until she began this work for herself. Currently, she produces between 10 and 20 kilograms a day of rice paper (depending on the weather) and is the sole support for her family of four. Although her youngest child is still in school, her husband and daughter assist in the production. With proceeds from the sale of her rice paper, this woman was able to rebuild her house using a brick structure and has been able to repay each of the four loans on time. Admittedly, although she earns significantly more money than she would earn in a factory working the same hours, she has no benefits available to her and is joined in her work by other family members.

Indicators: Continued Program Assessment

Until the program reaches self-sufficiency, Nike receives quarterly or biannual reports from the program coordinators as indicators of progress.

Exit Strategy

The program was developed and structured with the intent of self-sufficiency within several years. On the basis of interest charged and re-investment of capital, the program will soon be able to afford its loans with no additional infusion of capital from Nike.

Program 3: Nike Cultural Sensitivity Training Program

Inspiration and Vision Setting: Idea Generation/Inception

Nike's Office of Labor Practices (now called Corporate Responsibility Compliance) was established in 1996. At that time one of the more pressing issues revolved around a culture gap apparent in Vietnamese Korean- and Taiwanese-owned factories between the Vietnam nationals and the foreign supervisors. The Korean- and Taiwanese-owned suppliers used local labor in Vietnam and found that they were faced with significant management challenges in connection with cultural issues.

In early 1997 Nike asked Andrew Young to visit the factories in China, Indonesia, and Vietnam for purposes of assessing how well Nike's code of conduct was being implemented. Young also reported on the cultural gap between the workers and the managers in these particular factories and identified specific areas of challenge in connection with cultural differences. He suggested that special human relations and cultural sensitiv-ity programs should be designed and organized and that participation should be mandatory for all expatriate management.[27] His report, com-bined with the earlier identification of the problem, served as the inspi-ration for the vision-setting process that was to occur at Nike.

It should be noted that Young's report was not received without criti-cism. Critics contended that Young avoided the main issues and used a flawed research method that did not uncover the facts about conditions facing workers who produce Nike products. He was criticized for relying in part on previous, purportedly imprecise Ernst & Young audit reports; for failing to meet with certain NGO's; for spending insufficient time in various factories; and for issuing vague recommendations.[28] However, other investigators reported agreement with Young's findings.[29]

In response to Young's report on cultural challenges, Nike determined that it should assist the factories in bridging the cultural divide by as-signing human resource expert Fukumi Hauser as its global training man-ager. (Hauser is currently Nike director of global compliance, monitoring, and training.) These findings were also later supported by the work of the Center for Economic and Social Applications (CESAIS, now Truong Doan), which visited seven Vietnamese footwear factories in 1999. They found that one of the primary issues facing these Vietnamese workers was better relations between workers and managers.[30] Hauser visited the fac-tories herself and identified several specific hurdles she might be able to help the suppliers overcome.

First, on the most basic level, there were language differences. These differences in language served to exacerbate other differences because of a general inability to communicate. Second, the Taiwanese and Korean supervisors managed the Vietnamese workers according to their home standards, rather than those in place in Vietnam. However, when the Viet-namese workers were displeased, they did not come forward for fear of losing their jobs or because sharing concerns was not encouraged. Other cultural management differences abounded. A specific example related to Taiwanese culture is the Taiwanese response to illness. If Taiwanese people are sick, they will often look to their ancestors, their graves, their ancestral homes, to determine whether something is amiss, perceiving the illness to be a sign that the ancestors are disturbed. The Vietnamese culture does not share that perception and therefore would consider medicinal reme-dies instead to mend the illness if a worker were sick. Understanding these distinctions was vital to working together.

Third, the Vietnamese workers were accustomed to a rural, self-paced agricultural work routine and found it hard to adjust to a regimented factory routine with thousands of co-workers. Fourth, the Vietnamese workers did not have a great deal of education and therefore were not aware of their basic worker rights. This naïveté discouraged them from coming forward to assert their rights, as they did not know the parameters of those rights.

When an expectation gap resulting from different management styles is merged with a language barrier that prevents free-flowing communication, a power differential, and a lack of awareness regarding rights, the result is lower productivity, higher attrition, a possible abridgement of rights, and a consequent low sense of morale in the workplace. These conditions, obviously, make stakeholder engagement difficult.

Integration, Establishment, and Implementation: Cultural Sensitivity Training

Confronted with these significant barriers to healthy working relationships, Hauser considered her options. In lieu of asking the Vietnamese workers to modify their perceptions and to learn new communication skills, Hauser concluded that those in power had the responsibility to learn about those with whom they worked. Hauser developed an awareness campaign and, after training the top management staff from Nike footwear supplier sites in Vietnam, Indonesia, and China (and simultaneously creating top management commitment), she was asked to go to the home offices of the suppliers in Korea and Taiwan. Currently, the cultural training program has been integrated into Nike's monitoring program, which is called SHAPE ("Safety, Health, Attitude of Management, People Investment, Environment").

The cultural sensitivity campaign encompassed three segments. The training began by exploring the nature of a "culture." What is culture? We all are part of some culture, but how do we define those cultures beyond simply food and language distinctions to differences in respect, relationships, communication styles, and so on? For example, cultures differ based on whether they are future-oriented or past-oriented. This is critical to understand since a past-oriented culture will place great weight on how a person has acted, while a future-oriented culture will place great weight on how a person modifies her or his actions. The second segment of the training asked the participants to identify for themselves their own particular culture and its specific components. Finally, Hauser explores with the participants the nature of Vietnamese culture to allow them to better understand their subordinates.

She explains the impact of this type of awareness by referring to American culture and its impact on American workers. For instance, in the United States, we often hear about "The American Dream," insinuating that anything is possible; if a person just reaches for a goal, it can be attained. However, consider the implications of these messages for American workers. Where a supervisor manages workers on the basis of this cultural belief system, workers' failure must only be their own. If a person can do anything, the failure to do something is also the person's responsibility.

Moreover, if someone has a problem, that person is expected to speak up and voice the problem in an attempt to solve it. In other cultures, speaking up causes conflicts in two areas. First, it may be viewed as dull-witted since silence connotes wisdom and understanding. Second, in certain cultures, individuals with a problem expect the manager to know their problem, even if they have not voiced it. By voicing a problem, a person may be implying that the manager did not know enough to be aware of that issue. Therefore, it may be insulting to the manager if a person raises a problem—not a good result. Also specifically "American" are the concepts of individualism and freedom of choice. As with those discussed above, these values are not necessarily considered to be "positive" values in some other cultures. In a culture that focuses its attention on the past and is slow to forgive, mistakes such as these are not easily forgotten.

Hauser relates this to the Vietnamese situation by sharing the following example. One issue of cultural conflict has to do with the basic sounds of the different languages. Vietnamese is a language that is spoken in a soft, somewhat singsong, tone that has been compared to "birds chirping." Korean, on the other hand, is spoken quite boisterously. There were bound to be instances in which, as a result of the language barrier, the Vietnamese workers misinterpreted a Korean manager's statement to be full of anger when it was simply basic speech.

Issues of age and respect also play a role in creating possible workplace conflicts. In Vietnam, no matter one's position, the younger worker owes strong respect to an older worker. Consequently, in instances in which a younger foreign supervisor manages an older Vietnamese line worker, the older worker may respond indignantly if the manager does not respect the cultural mores connected with age.

Another example of distinction refers to communication styles, as opposed to the words or sounds that are used. Hauser explains that the Korean and Taiwanese managers expressed concern that the Vietnamese workers were making mistakes but refused to accept responsibility for them. "They would deny it and I would ask them to admit it." They then found that the workers would giggle and laugh at them as they continued to try to get the worker to own up to his or her mistake. The managers explain that all they wanted was for the worker to accept responsibility and things would be all right.

Hauser was able to diffuse this type of conflict by explaining to the managers that, in Vietnamese culture, (1) reproach should be handled in private, (2) public reproach is the source of shame and embarrassment, (3) workers smile or giggle when they are embarrassed or ashamed, and (4) Vietnamese expect to have to pay harshly for their mistakes. Therefore, the managers learned that the more they reproached the individual for not accepting responsibility, the more likely it was that the worker would smile or laugh. As the manager would get more and more angry, the worker would continue to be ashamed and, therefore, smile. It was also very difficult for the Vietnamese workers to trust that they would not be fired when a manager expresses anger at a mistake.

As a resolution of this issue, Hauser did not suggest that the managers refrain from pointing out mistakes; instead she suggested through her training program that the reproach take place in a private area and that the trust would grow as workers were able to see that every mistake did not result in a termination. The response: "Aha! We had no idea!" Thus by explaining differences, Hauser was able to allow for greater understanding and compassion, and these improvements could be integrated into daily management practice.

Finally, cultural differences exist in connection with reporting violations. Predictably, when people feel that they are not protected by promises of due process, reporting a supervisor's violation is an extremely risky venture. Moreover, when that retribution may be inordinately more severe than the violation, people are discouraged from bearing that responsibility. In one instance, a journalist reported a violation by a Vietnamese line supervisor but refused to offer the person's name for fear of inappropriate punishment. In that situation, Nike resorted to retraining all management in this particular area.

Integration, Establishment, and Implementation: Management Training

It is critical that these suppliers be able to promote from within to management positions because not only do expatriate managers often choose to return home after a stint overseas, but also because fewer and fewer managers choose to go into this industry and accept foreign postings. Consider today's young Taiwanese and Koreans. As education standards in their own countries have increased, these individuals are less likely to go into footwear manufacturing but instead will gravitate toward other, more attractive and lucrative industries such as those in the hi-tech arena. Therefore, there is a shortage of possible managers, and these Korean- and Taiwanese-owned firms must be able to recruit management and supervisors from within their Vietnamese ranks.

As a result, while there was improved communication between expatriate managers and the Vietnamese workers, there was one additional challenge in connection with training that had been left unsolved. During newly implemented exit interviews, the suppliers were finding that Vietnamese workers who were promoted to first-level supervisory roles found themselves in those roles with no management training. Therefore, they simply replicated some of the original management styles of the Korean and Taiwanese managers who first supervised them. They were often under the impression that this was what was expected of a manager and, if their style failed to resemble the foreign management style, they might be fired.

To create a management training program appropriate for the Vietnamese workers, Hauser enlisted the assistance of a Vietnamese-American trainer named Tuan Nguyen, who was experienced in management training through Levi Straus and other firms in the United States. Together, Hauser and Nguyen created and coordinated a five-day supervisor training program for Vietnamese workers. The training program was designed to improve management abilities by enhancing self-awareness, improving communication skills, and working with cultural differences. Nike paid fully for a pilot of the weeklong program, first with five workers from each factory. After responding to feedback from the pilot effort, Nguyen returned for 22 weeks, training 100 supervisors from each of the five participating factories. For this segment of the training, Nike covered two-thirds of the cost, with the supplier covering one-third.

The aim of the program was to create a self-sustaining system in which trainers were available in each factory, and training materials were tailored for each factory's needs, so that later training could be initiated and be fully paid for by the supplier. This integration into factory-specific systems allows individual factories to develop the improvement process needed for their specific situation.

Currently, managers in many of Nike's suppliers receive support materials regarding some of these issues on joining the factory. For instance, expatriate managers in one factory received a booklet titled "Vietnamese Language for Daily Communication." In this way, though all foreign managers or supervisors are required to learn the local language, they also have additional support tools to help in day-to-day operations. In one factory, Vietnamese line managers and above are chosen to participate in the factory's "Innovation School," in which additional business skills are developed.

Indicators: Continued Program Assessment

Currently, each footwear factory in Vietnam conducts its own ongoing supervisor training using the modified material. Continued regular dialogues with workers, departmental representatives, and the trade unions; surveys; suggestion boxes; and self-reviews provide indicators that allow Nike both to ascertain the efficacy of the programs and to identify areas that continue to need to be addressed. (In fact, one firm receives thousands of suggestions each month.) For instance, during one review, a problem was identified about gift giving. It seems that Vietnamese culture dictates small gifts on certain occasions, holidays, accomplishments, and so on. The factory owner, a Korean, was unfamiliar with this practice, so the workers simply believed that he chose not to do so. Once notified of this error, he instituted certain awards or benefits such as calendars, raincoats, or token amounts of money on appropriate occasions. The same challenge proved surmountable when one Korean factory president, C. T. Park, realized that female workers no longer spoke to him and some even sneered at him from time to time. Later he learned that this "snub" treatment was the result of his failure to attend or even respond to their wedding invitations—a major cultural faux pas and one that could be easily ameliorated.[31]

One unexpected consequence of the training, however, is that workers are confused by the modified behavior. Hauser reports that workers have asked their supervisors, "Why are you like this now? Why are you treating me differently?" When asked to create additional training materials to help them to "integrate" into the workplace, Hauser responded that what was needed was not more training, but more problem-solving sessions that would empower the workers and the supervisors to jointly explore challenges and resolve issues on their own.

NOTES

1. Nike, Inc., "Corporate Responsibility Report, 2001," p. 1; see also Amanda Tucker, Nike director of compliance for the Americas, presentation transcribed in Richard Wokutch, "Nike and Its Critics," *Organization & Environment* 14, no. 2 (June 2001): 207–37, 212.

2. "Nike Annual Report 2001," http://www.nike.com/nikebiz/invest/reports/ar_01/pdfs/financials.pdf (accessed 15 July 2002).

3. Nike's code was second behind Levi Strauss, which disseminated its code in December 1991.

4. Nike, "Code of Conduct," http://www.nike.com/nikebiz/nikebiz.jhtml?page=25&cat=compliance&subcat=code (accessed 15 July 2002).

5. Nike, "Code of Conduct."

6. For Nike's explanation of this and other processes, as well as a Nike-produced visual tour inside one Nike contract supplier, see Nike, Inc., "An Online Look: Inside Nike's Contract Factories," http://www.nike.com/nikebiz/nikebiz.jhtml?page = 25&cat = overview&subcat = factorytour.

7. Discussion with Amanda Tucker, Director of Compliance, Nike, Inc., and Fukumi Hauser, Director of Global Compliance, Monitoring, and Training (4 November 2002) and e-mail from Amanda Tucker (26 July 2002).

8. Jeff Ballinger, "Once Again, Nike's Voice Looms Larger than That of Its Workers," www.BehindTheLabel.org, http://www.behindthelabel.org/oped.php?story_id = 22 (accessed 15 July 2002).

9. The World Bank International Economics Department, Development Data Group, *World Development Indicators* (1999).

10. http://www.nike.com/nikebiz/news/pressrelease.jhtml?year = 2001&

month = 05&letter = g (accessed 15 July 2002) (link to speech at bottom of page). See also, http://cbae.nmsu.edu/~dboje/NIKphilspeech.html (accessed 15 July 2002).

11. http://cbae.nmsu.edu/~dboje/NIKphilspeech.html (accessed 15 July 2002); see also http://www.nikebiz.com/labor/time.shtml.

12. Tim Connor, *Still Waiting for Nike To Do It* (San Francisco, Calif.: Global Exchange, 2001), http://www.globalexchange.org/economy/corporations/nike/stillwaiting.html (accessed 15 July 2002), p. 1.

13. Ibid, p. 5.

14. For Nike's overview of the challenges and successes of these initiatives to date, see http://www.nike.com/nikebiz/news/pr/2001/p_challenges.jhtml (accessed 28 July 2002).

15. Currently, there are over 100 individuals in Nike's compliance department, including more than 20 people permanently housed overseas.

16. Daniel Akst, "Nike in Indonesia, Through a Different Lens," *New York Times,* 4 March 2001, sec. 3, p. 4; "Smelly Sneakers," *The Asian Wall Street Journal,* 2 March 2001, editorial, p. 6; "Knight Speaks Out on Improving Globalization," *Financial Times,* 1 August 2000, p. 15; Holger Jensen, "A Tale of Two Swooshes in Indonesia," Rockymountainnews.com, 2 July 2000 [related article in the *San Jose Mercury News,* 5 July 2000, p. B6]; David Lamb, "Economic Program Revitalizing Thailand's Countryside," *Los Angeles Times,* 27 February 2000, p. A34; "Indonesian Workers to Get Boost in Entry-Level Wages," *Wall Street Journal,* 24 March 1999, business brief, p. B2; "For Citizens of Vietnam, Nike is the Place to Work," *Oregonian,* 6 March 1999, editorial, p. C7.

17. Dara O'Rourke, "Monitoring the Monitors: A Critique of PricewaterhouseCoopers Labor Monitoring," September 2000, http://web.mit.edu/dorourke/www/PDF/pwc.pdf (accessed 15 July 2002).

18. Jeff Ballinger, "Once Again, Nike's Voice Looms Larger than That of Its Workers."

19. Results of the report can be found at http://www.theglobalalliance.org/section.cfm/6/30 (accessed 15 July 2002).

20. "Envoy Defends Nike's Practices in Vietnam," *Financial Times,* 12 April 1999, p. 4.

21. Interview with Steve Hewitt, Nike–Vietnam, corporate responsibility manager, 6 July 2001.

22. Ibid.

23. "Nike Critic Praises Gains in Air Quality at Vietnam Factory," *New York Times,* 12 March 1999, p. C3.

24. Nike has done business with many of the same Vietnamese suppliers for over 25 years.

25. Conversation with Dusty Kidd, 27 April 2001.

26. Phil Knight, "New Labor Initiatives," 12 May 1998, text at http://cbae.nmsu.edu/~dboje/NIKphilspeech.html (accessed 15 July 2002), also reported in PBS *Newshour,* http://www.pbs.org/newshour/forum/may98/nike.html (accessed 15 July 2002) (confirmed in discussions with Dusty Kidd). For additional information on the loan program, see http://www.nike.com/nikebiz/nikebiz.jhtml?page = 26&item = asia (accessed 15 July 2002) and http://www.nike.com/

nikebiz/nikebiz.jhtml?page=25&cat=communityprograms&subcat=smbizloans (accessed 15 July 2002).

27. GoodWorks International, LLC, "Report: The Nike Code of Conduct," 1997, pp. 33, 47–8.

28. Tim Connor, "A Response to Andrew Young's Report into Nike's Code of Conduct," The NikeWatch Campaign at Oxfam Community Aid Abroad, http://www.caa.org.au/campaigns/nike/young.html (accessed 15 July 2002); Campaign for Labor Rights, "The Andrew Young/Good Works Report on Nike," *Labor Alerts* (28 June 1997), http://www.hartford-hwp.com/archives/26/004.html (accessed 15 July 2002); Eric Lourmand, "Nike Drops the Ball: The Andrew Young Report," http://www-personal.umich.edu/~lormand/poli/nike/nike101–5.htm (accessed 15 July 2002).

29. Lynn Kahle, et al., "Good Morning, Vietnam: An Ethical Analysis of Nike Activities in Southeast Asia," *Sport Marketing Quarterly* 9, no. 1 (2000): pp. 43–52.

30. Nike, Inc., "Corporate Responsibility Report, 2001," p. 35.

31. Samantha Marshall, "Executive Action: Cultural Sensitivity on the Assembly Line," *Asian Wall Street Journal*, 25 February 2000.

Nike, Inc. Code of Conduct

Nike, Inc. was founded on a handshake.

Implicit in that act was the determination that we would build our business with all of our partners based on trust, teamwork, honesty and mutual respect. We expect all of our business partners to operate on the same principles.

At the core of the NIKE corporate ethic is the belief that we are a company comprising many different kinds of people, appreciating individual diversity, and dedicated to equal opportunity for each individual.

NIKE designs, manufactures, and markets products for sports and fitness consumers. At every step in that process, we are driven to do not only what is required by law, but what is expected of a leader. We expect our business partners to do the same. NIKE partners with contractors who share our commitment to best practices and continuous improvement in the following areas:

1. Employing management practices that respect the rights of all employees, including the right to free association and collective bargaining
2. Minimizing our impact on the environment
3. Providing a safe and healthy workplace
4. Promoting the health and well-being of all employees

Contractors must recognize the dignity of each employee, and the right to a workplace free of harassment, abuse or corporal punishment. Decisions on hiring, salary, benefits, advancement, termination or retirement must be based solely on the employee's ability to do the job. There shall be no discrimination based on race, creed, gender, marital or maternity status, religious or political beliefs, age or sexual orientation.

Wherever NIKE operates around the globe we are guided by this Code of Conduct and we bind our contractors to these principles. Contractors must post this Code in all major workspaces, translated into the language of the employee, and must train employees on their rights and obligations as defined by this Code and applicable local laws.

While these principles establish the spirit of our partnerships, we also bind our partners to specific standards of conduct. The core standards are set forth below.

FORCED LABOR

The contractor does not use forced labor in any form—prison, indentured, bonded or otherwise.

CHILD LABOR

The contractor does not employ any person below the age of 18 to produce footwear. The contractor does not employ any person below the age of 16 to produce apparel, accessories or equipment. If at the time Nike production begins, the contractor employs people of the legal working age who are at least 15, that employment may continue, but the contractor will not hire any person going forward who is younger than the Nike or legal age limit, whichever is higher. To further ensure these age standards are complied with, the contractor does not use any form of homework for Nike production.

COMPENSATION

The contractor provides each employee at least the minimum wage, or the prevailing industry wage, whichever is higher; provides each employee a clear, written accounting for every pay period; and does not deduct from employee pay for disciplinary infractions.

BENEFITS

The contractor provides each employee all legally mandated benefits.

HOURS OF WORK/OVERTIME

The contractor complies with legally mandated work hours; uses overtime only when each employee is fully compensated according to local law; informs each employee at the time of hiring if mandatory overtime is a condition of employment; and on a regularly scheduled basis provides one day off in seven, and requires no more than 60 hours of work per week on a regularly scheduled basis, or complies with local limits if they are lower.

ENVIRONMENT, SAFETY AND HEALTH (ES&H)

From suppliers to factories to distributors and to retailers, Nike considers every member of our supply chain as partners in our business.

DOCUMENTATION AND INSPECTION

The contractor maintains on file all documentation needed to demonstrate compliance with this Code of Conduct and required laws; agrees to make these documents available for Nike or its designated monitor; and agrees to submit to inspections with or without prior notice.

Source: http://www.nike.com/nikebiz/nikebiz.jhtml?page = 25&cat = compliance&subcat = code (as updated by Paula Valero, Director, Compliance Systems & Services, Nike, Inc.). Reprinted with permission of Nike Inc.

APPENDIX 7.2

Nike Corporate Responsibility Compliance Production SHAPE Assessment Form

Nike Corporate Responsibility Compliance
Production SHAPE Assessment Form
Safety, Health, Attitude, People & Environment

Contractor Name:	
Contractor Code:	
Contractor City:	
Contractor Country:	

	First Name:	Last Name/Surname:
NIKE Representative Name:		
NIKE Representative Title:		

	First Name:	Last Name/Surname:
Employee Representative Name:		
Contractor Representative Name:		
Contractor Representative Title:		
Date:		

S	0
H	0
A	0
P	0
E	0
Total	0
%	0%

How to Evaluate Training Guidance:

Training

1. Documented signature sheet including name of employee and signature, date of training and signature of designated trainer.

2. Documented curriculum of each training subject and a picture or two of the training session.

3. Observation of employees skills and behaviors.

How to Evaluate Documentation Guidance:

Policy & Manuals:

1. Must be written in the language of the employees, managers, supervisors and in English

2. Must be "posted" in a public area (Contractor bulletin board), given to the employee (employee handbook) or available to employee upon request

3. Must be reviewed and updated once each year, signed by President Director

How to score the SHAPE Inspection

	Score	Comments
YES	1	100% compliant at time of inspection
NO	0	Not 100% compliant
Not Applicable	N/A	Please note "why" marked N/A in Locations / Comments section (be sure to mark N/A in score column)

* = documentation check

171

SAFETY

Item		Direction	Score	Max	Locations / Comments
Safety Practices					
1*	Contractor has a written Safety & Health Policy that is current (within the last 12 months), signed by the President Director and is posted (Policy should reflect commitment of top management, state overall S&H objectives, commitment to improving S&H performance, committment to continuous improvement, commitment to comply with local country laws and other requirements to which the contractor subscribes, available to the public; reviewed periodically and communicated to employees)	See Documentation Guidance		1	
2*	Contractor has documented new employee orientation training (training should include review of policies, rules & regulations, emergency procedures and any special condition specific to his / her working environment)	See Documentation Guidance		1	
3*	Contractor has documented training that employees are trained on the standard operating procedures for their individual work areas, to include all specific and general hazards that relate to that work area and their surrounding work environment	See Documentation Guidance		1	
4	Employees and supervisors wear the required Personal Protective Equipment (PPE) as posted	Examples: safety glasses, hearing protection, respirators		1	
5*	Contractor has documented PPE training	See Training Guidance		1	
6	Machines engineered for two-hand activation are working properly	2 hands used		1	
Emergency Action					
7*	Contractor has a written emergency action plan that is accessible (i.e. posted and / or centrally located) to employees, supervisors and management to include, at a minimum, escape procedures, escape route assignments and roll-call	See Documentation Guidance		1	
8*	Contractor has a written medical and first-aid program to include, at a minimum, location and availability of medical facilities and emergency services, availability of medical personnel, first aid kit locations & contents and types of accidents that could reasonably occur	See Documentation Guidance		1	

#	Item	Guidance		Score
9	Contractor has **posted** emergency contact numbers by telephones or employee bulletin boards and other conspicuous locations			1
10*	Contractor has annual evacuation drills (drills can be conducted in the larger contractors so that all employees have done at least one drill every year)	check documentation that drills have been done		1
11	Exits are unlocked from the inside during working hours			1
12	Alarm systems are provided to warn employees of necessary action to be taken	alarm must be seen or heard		1
13	Manually activated alarm systems (i.e. pull box stations) are unobstructed, marked and accessible			1
14	First aid kits are accessible to each work area, kitchen / canteen and dorm area with necessary supplies available	approved by consulting physician/nurse or person competent in first aid and who's knowledgeable of factory workplace hazards		1
Fire Prevention				
15*	Contractor has documented fire extinguisher training	See Training Guidance		1
16	Fire extinguishers are accessible and free of obstructions			1
17	Fire extinguishers are mounted	minimum of 4 inches off the ground		1
18	Fire extinguishers are marked (demarcated to be seen at eye level)			1
19	Fire extinguishers are inspected monthly (tracking system evident)			1
20	Contractor has emergency lighting (all exits and stairways)	not powered by main power supply		1
21	Fire exits marked with an illuminated exit sign by a reliable light source			1
22	Contractor has fire systems in place (sprinklers, fire hoses, fire brigade)	one will count		1

			Score	Max	
Electrical					
23	Flexible cords and cables free of splices, frayed wiring or deteriorated insulation	no bare wires		1	
24	Individual equipment such as sewing machines, buffing machines and cutting machines are wired so as not to interfere with work or employees			1	
25	Disconnecting switches and circuit breakers (electrical panel) are labeled to indicate their use or equipment served	Example: breaker #6-lights/ Switch 1C- Rubbermill #2		1	
26	Electrical enclosures (i.e. switches, receptacles, junction boxes, etc.) are provided with tight fitting covers or plates			1	
27	Electrical equipment (i.e. electrical panels, fuse/breaker boxes) are accessible and free of obstructions	marked with floor lines at least 1 meter/3 feet clearance on all sides		1	
Material Handling, Lighting, Housekeeping					
28	Storage areas (materials and finished goods) are uncluttered and accessible	local		1	
29	Floors & aisles are clean, marked & kept clear of obstructions	floor lines		1	
30	Stairs have railings (with 4 or more risers, 1 side minimum, never an "open" side)	waist height is best		1	
31	Stairs are illuminated (top to bottom)			1	
32	Stairs are clear of obstructions and are in good condition			1	
33	Lifts have a door or gate on the opening to the lift shaft			1	
34	Lifts cannot be "activated" if the door or gate is in the open position	critical: interlocked with safety device		1	
	Safety Total Score		0	34	

		Direction	Score	Max	Location/Comments
HEALTH					
	Item				
Sanitation – All Spaces					
35	Employees are provided with individual drinkable water	cups or fountain		1	

#	Item		
36	Drinking water is easily accessible to employees in each work area		1
37	Toilets facilities have soap	liquid is preferred	1
38	Toilets have paper towels or hand dryers	local	1
39	Toilets have washing basins	local	1
40	Toilets have running water	local	1
41	Toilets have water flushing system	some countries using scoop water flush system	1
42	All toilet spaces are adequately ventilated	local	1
43	All toilet spaces have adequate enclosed drainage	local	1
44	Deodorant tablets used in urinals & toilet areas	local	1
45	Toilets and floors are cleaned daily with disinfectant	local	1
46	Covered rubbish bins are in each toilet area	local	1
47	Rubbish bins are cleared daily, as necessary	local	1

Kitchen, Canteen or Catered Food Service

#	Item		
48*	Food service employees receive medical checks every six months and individual health certificates are posted by factory clinic	locally relevant check	1
49	Functioning cold room, freezer or refrigeration system used	local	1
50	Functioning cold room, freezer or refrigeration system is sanitary	local	1
51	Dishes cleaned with hot water and liquid detergent	local	1
52	Floors and drains are clean	local	1
53	Tabletops are clean	local	1
54	Food is stored off of ground	local	1
55	Kitchen area has a clean water basin, running water and soap that is accessible to foodhandlers		1
56	Kitchen / canteen area is sanitary / free of flies, rodents, and cats		
57	Food is covered		1
58	Food handlers wear hairnets / hats and aprons when preparing meals	local	1
59	Food servers wear hairnets / hats, aprons and gloves when serving	local	1

Clinics or Emergency Health Treatment

#	Item		
60	If more than 1,000 employees. Contractor has on-site clinic	local	1
61	Clinic has at least one clean, screened bed per 1,000 employees	local	1

175

			Score	Max	
62	Contractor has one full-time doctor, two nurses on-site for every 5,000 employees during all Contractor working hours, including all overtime	local		1	
63	Clinic is air conditioned / heated to maintain a "comfortable" level	21 - 28 C range		1	
64*	Clinic has computerized health records for every employee	local		1	
65	Clinic has database to track illnesses and injuries	local		1	
66	If less than 1,000 employees, Contractor has posted names of dedicated emergency responders in each work area	local		1	
	Worker Dormitories				
67	All spaces are sanitary (toilets, showers, halls, kitchen / canteen, etc.)	local		1	
68	All spaces have adequate heating and ventilation	local		1	
69	All spaces have adequate lighting	local		1	
70	Washing areas & toilets are adequate for number of employees			1	
71	Living quarters for men & women are appropriately separated	local		1	
72	Contractor provides dormitory security at all times (24 hours)	local		1	
73	Dormitories have emergency lighting	local		1	
74	Dormitories have illuminated emergency exits marked by visible signs and exits are free of obstructions	local		1	
75	Living space doors are unlocked for fire evacuation safety	local		1	
	Health Total Score		0	41	

Attitude of Management					
Item		Direction	Score	Max	Locations/Comments
Employee Hours					
76*	Contractor has a mechanical / electrical timekeeping system (timecards or computerized system)			1	
77	Contractor has overtime policy posted in language of worker, management and English				
78	Based on 10 randomly selected time cards, where the law allows more than 60 hrs/week, employees are compliant with local OT limits	complying with NIKE OT Policy		1	
79*	Based on 10 randomly selected time cards, where the law allows more than 60 hrs/week, employees are signing statements to voluntarily work overtime per the NIKE OT Policy	complying with NIKE OT Policy		1	

176

	Item	Direction	Score	Max	Locations/Comments
80*	Based on 10 randomly selected time cards, employees are receiving one day off in seven on a regularly scheduled basis	25% of a given period		1	
81*	Contractor maintains weekly OT summary by department	all departments		1	
Culture of Respect					
82*	Contractor has documented training for expatriate management about the culture of their employees	See Training Guidance		1	
83*	All managers and workers have documented training in local labor law, NIKE Code and Harassment & Abuse Policy	See Training Guidance		1	
84	No work disruptions in past six months (i.e. strikes, walkouts, etc.)			1	
85	Current NIKE Code of Conduct is posted in all major work areas in the language of the employees, management and English	all areas		1	
86*	All Employees and management have received Code of Conduct cards in language of the employees and management respectively	all employees and supervisors		1	
87	Labor rights (wages, hours of work, benefits, holidays) are posted	all work spaces		1	
88	Contractor has employee-management communication systems (i.e. union, employee reps, employee committees) which consists of regular communication between management and employee reps at least once a month and related information is posted	one will count		1	
89	Contractor has confidential grievance/feedback system	example: suggestion boxes, ombudsmen offices		1	
90	Contractor posts management responses to employee feedback and concerns at least on a quarterly basis	all areas		1	
Attitude Total Score			0	15	
People					
	Item	Direction	Score	Max	Locations/Comments
91	Contractor offers educational opportunities (vocation, language training, scholarships) for employees	any 1 will count		1	
92	Contractor posts culturally appropriate information on drug abuse, AIDS awareness, family planning, related life skills topics, etc.	any 1 will count		1	

#	Item	Direction	Score	Max	Locations/Comments
93	Contractor provides employees with cultural/recreational activities and/or childcare services	any 1 will count		1	
94	Contractor has system in place to recognize top performing employees (visible evidence)	local		1	
95	Contractor provides free/subsidized transportation	local		1	
96	Contractor provides free/subsidized meals	local		1	
97	Contractor involved with community outreach programs	local		1	
	People Total Score		0	7	

Environment

Item	Direction	Score	Max	Locations/Comments
Environmental Practices				
98* Contractor has a written Environmental Policy that is current (within the last 12 months), signed by President Director and is **posted** (Policy should reflect commitment of top management, state overall Environmental objectives, commitment to improving Environmental performance, commitment to continuous improvement, commitment to comply with local country law and other requirements to which the contractor subscribes, available to the public, reviewed periodically and communicated to employees)	See Documentation Guidance		1	
Chemical Storage, Use and Handling				
99 Material Safety Data Sheets (MSDS) are available in the language of the employees, management and english	where chemicals are used		1	
100* Contractor has documented MSDS training	See Training Guidance		1	
101 Chemical containers are in good condition	not crushed, dented, rusted or leaking		1	
102 Chemical containers are labeled (including secondary containers)	should include name of product, hazards, PPE, etc.		1	
103 Chemical containers are kept closed except when removing / adding product (including secondary containers)			1	

#	Item	Value	
104	Chemical storage areas are neat / orderly	local	1
105	Chemical storage areas are separated from production areas	walled off area	1
106	Chemical storage areas are ventilated	not enclosed/good air flow	1
107	Chemical storage areas have fire safety protection	nearby	1
108	Chemical storage areas have secondary containment barriers in place to keep spills from entering environment	example: self-contained room, concrete berm	1
109	Chemical storage areas are covered with a roof		1
	Hazardous Waste Storage		
110	Hazardous waste storage areas are neat / orderly	local	1
111	Hazardous waste storage areas are separated from production areas	walled off area	1
112	Hazardous waste storage areas are ventilated	not enclosed/good air flow	1
113	Hazardous waste storage areas have fire safety protection	nearby	1
114	Hazardous waste storage areas are covered with a roof		1
115	Hazardous waste storage areas have secondary containment barriers in place to keep spills from entering environment	self-contained room, concrete berm	1
116	Contractor has posted signs that prohibit eating near chemical storage and hazardous waste storage areas	local	1
117	Contractor has posted signs that prohibit drinking near chemical storage and hazardous waste storage areas	local	1
118	Contractor has posted signs that prohibit smoking near chemical storage and hazardous waste storage areas	local	1
	Non-Hazardous Waste Storage		
119	Non-hazardous waste storage areas are neat/orderly	material scraps, organic waste, office paper	1
120	Non-hazardous waste storage areas are covered with a roof		1
121	Non-hazardous waste storage areas are separated from production areas	walled off area	1
122	Non-hazardous waste storage areas have fire safety protection	nearby	1

Aboveground Storage Tanks

123	Aboveground storage tanks are labeled with contents and associated hazards	Example: diesel fuel, propane		1
124	Aboveground storage tanks have secondary containment	concrete berm		1
125	Contractor has posted aboveground storage tank filling procedures	local		1
126	Aboveground storage tanks have barriers in place to protect against accidental damage due to contact with vehicles or machinery	concrete wall, guardrails, concrete posts		1
Environment Total Score			0	29

Safety		0	34
Health		0	41
Attitude		0	15
People		0	7
Environment		0	29
Score Totals		**0**	**126**
Percentage	0%		

GENERAL REMARKS

Signatures

NIKE Representative   Date

Employee Representative   Date

Contractor Representative   Date

APPENDIX 7.3

Nike Manufacturing Practices, MESH

From suppliers to factories to distributors and to retailers, Nike considers every member of our supply chain as partners in our business.

As such, we've worked with our Asian footwear partners to achieve specific environmental, health and safety goals, beginning with a program called MESH (Management of Environment, Safety and Health).

Nike launched MESH in June 1998 to help our Asian footwear business relationships develop objectives and to manage all aspects of global corporate citizenship. The program was developed closely with two external consultants—The Gauntlett Group of California and Environmental Resources Management (ERM) of Hong Kong. Originally intended as an environmental safety and health system, MESH was expanded to encompass all non-product management issues, including manufacturing practices, community affairs, environmental management and health/ nutrition programs. It employs extensive educational forums conducted with our contract footwear manufacturers to help them develop, implement, and monitor the MESH program.

The functioning MESH system goes well beyond the requirements of ISO 14001, a system of compliance standards designed to apply to all types and sizes of organizations with diverse geographical, cultural and social conditions. It was the basic international environmental management standard on which Nike originally based its program. MESH includes those issues, and much more.

CHALLENGES

This wasn't easy. There were challenges along the way, namely the language barrier. Bahasa, English, Korean, Mandarin, Filipino, and Vietnamese were all represented in the mix of Nike nationals and contract factories. To ease the process, Nike provided verbal translation and documents translated into five languages. Moreover, while the interactive nature of the workshops was extremely helpful to some, the interaction could be intimidating for others. These exercises were intended to break down traditional barriers and encourage cooperation and understanding. The positive results come from each factory's sincere commitment to improvement.

With MESH workshops, we were able to educate and to assist the footwear factories in building their own management system—element by element.

Source: http://www.nike.com/nikebiz/nikebiz.jhtml?page = 25&cat = compliance&subcat = mesh (as updated by Paula Valero, Director, Compliance Systems & Services, Nike, Inc.), reprinted with permission of Nike, Inc.

Text of "New Labor Initiatives" Speech by Nike Chairman and CEO Phil Knight (May 12, 1998)

On May 12, 1998, Nike CEO Philip H. Knight announced a series of new initiatives to further improve factory working conditions worldwide and provide increased opportunities for people who manufacture Nike products.

In his remarks at the National Press Club, Knight said, "We are committed to improving working conditions for the 500,000 people who make our products. The initiatives we are announcing today build upon input from factory workers, factory partners, non-governmental organizations, health and safety specialists, academics, religious groups, President Clinton's Apparel Industry Partnership (AIP) and our auditors.

"Effective today, Nike commits to

- Increasing the minimum age of new footwear factory workers to 18, and the minimum age for all other new light-manufacturing workers (apparel, accessories, equipment) to 16
- Adopting the personal exposure limits (PEL) of the U.S. Occupational Safety and Health Administration (OSHA) as the standard for indoor air quality for all footwear factories
- Funding university research and open forums to explore issues related to global manufacturing and responsible business practices such as independent monitoring and air quality standards
- Expanding education programs, including middle and high school equivalency courses, for workers in all Nike footwear factories
- Increasing support of its current microenterprise loan program to 1,000 families each in Vietnam, Indonesia, Pakistan, and Thailand;

- Expanding its current independent monitoring programs to include nongovernmental organizations (NGOs), foundations, and educational institutions and making summaries of the findings public"

Over the past 13 months, there has been a lot of progress made. What follows is an internal memo to Phil Knight that provides an update on the initiatives he announced:

Age Limits

We have effectively changed our minimum age limits from the ILO standards of 15 in most countries and 14 in developing countries to 18 in all footwear manufacturing and 16 in all other types of manufacturing (apparel, accessories, and equipment.). Existing workers legally employed under the former limits were grandfathered into the new requirements. Our partners indicated they were able to meet the new standards with their newly hired employees. Our independent auditors certify on an ongoing basis that these new standards are being met.

During the past 13 months we have moved to a 100 percent factory audit scheme, where every Nike contract factory will receive an annual check by PricewaterhouseCoopers teams who are specially trained on our Code of Conduct Owner's Manual and audit/monitoring procedures. To date they have performed about 300 such monitoring visits. In a few instances in apparel factories they have found workers under our age standards. Those factories have been required to raise their standards to 17 years of age, to require three documents certifying age, and to redouble their efforts to ensure workers meet those standards through interviews and records checks.

Environmental Health and Safety/Sustainable Design

This initiative has three components: Indoor air quality; sustainable business practices and design; and Management-Environment-Safety-Health (MESH) systems for all footwear factories.

Indoor Air

Our goal was to ensure workers around the globe are protected by requiring factories to have no workers exposed to levels above those mandated by the permissible exposure limits (PELs) for chemicals prescribed in the OSHA indoor air quality standards.

The number one priority in this initiative is to eliminate the source of potential health hazards from the workplace, specifically, petroleum-based solutions that are commonly used in the production of athletic shoes. We noted in May 1998 that nine out of ten Nike shoes were manufactured using water-based adhesives. Some shoe types (soccer and baseball, for example) initially did not perform well using water-based adhesives, but we have since had further success. We are closer now to 95 out of 100 shoes (or 95%) made with water-based adhesives. There is still some work to do. In parallel, we have succeeded in reducing the use of the petroleum-based solvents significantly. From 1995 through 1998, solvent usage was reduced 73%. We expect the next quarterly report to indicate the total reduction is more than 80%. Each succeeding reduction becomes harder and harder to achieve as we work toward the margins of the issue. But the remaining 20% is primarily in the priming area, and today we are already running trials on water-based primers, which are showing encouraging results. In the meantime any worker using these solvents will be protected to OSHA levels or better using improved ventilation and personal protective equipment (PPE).

Our second priority was to assess the actual quality of indoor air in our footwear factories, and then make corrections. Independent certified industrial hygienists and other health professionals from Reliance Insurance, one of the country's largest and most respected commercial risk assessment consultants, has overseen indoor air quality tests in all of our Asian footwear manufacturing factories. We tested the factories in Italy.

The results are encouraging, but the most important aspect of that work is to pinpoint areas in factories where improvements should be made. We shared this information, as well as our water-base work and conversion, with the rest of the athletic footwear industry at an open forum in Bangkok in November 1998.

To provide a better sense of what we are finding and the steps we are taking in all countries of manufacture, here are some top-line results from one country, Vietnam, where we have five footwear manufacturing partners. Here is what the studies found there:

Testing began in December 1997, and continued through 1998, with additional retesting in 1999. There are a combined 40,000 workers in these five factories. Of that number, testing indicated about 50 people potentially may have been exposed above the OSHA permissible exposure levels (PELs). It is important to note that in those limited areas where chemical exposures still exceed the OSHA PELs, Nike factory workers can still be adequately protected through the mandatory use of appropriate personal protective equipment (PPE). When such equipment is properly used, the overexposure potential is eliminated.

So long as one worker faces an issue of overexposure, our work is not complete. As we continue to upgrade our processes, the factories have been directed to take the necessary steps to achieve levels at or below OSHA-prescribed PELs. These steps include ventilation equipment upgrades, mandated PPE use, and changes in work practices to accomplish our compliance objectives.

Throughout the last year, these tests and retests, conducted by Reliance Insurance, have verified the findings using laboratories in the United States certified by the American Industrial Hygiene Association (AIHA).

On the administrative front, OSHA administrators encourage or in some cases mandate certain procedures for dealing with overexposure issues in manufacturing facilities within the United States. We have taken the same steps in Vietnam and other Asian source countries. These steps, which are ongoing, include the following:

- Elimination of toxic source chemicals (e.g. methylene chloride and toluene) which may affect the overall health and safety of workers. Substitution of water-based compounds, which do not give off potentially harmful vapors.
- Implementation of better administrative controls, including rotating work shifts and duties of persons to limit their long-term exposure to certain chemical agents; also, altering the positioning and containment of chemicals at individual work stations.
- Implementation of engineering controls, including materially upgrading the work stations and ventilation systems of factories through new equipment. Plexiglas booths and hooded ventilation systems have been effective in clearing potentially harmful vapors from the workplace.
- Ensure through managerial controls and training that workers receive the proper personal protective equipment (PPE), including safety glasses, goggles, gloves, earplugs, and appropriate respiratory protection.

In addition to the installation of new ventilation equipment, the factories have also increased their medical facilities to treat respiratory conditions, regardless of whether they are lung infections and viruses common among the general population of Vietnam or conditions potentially triggered by factory work. Tae Kwang Vina, for example, has tripled the capacity of its medical facilities and doubled the size of the medical staff during the past year. We are working now with three different NGOs to evaluate the wellness of workers through studies and standards in nutrition, workplace safety, the use of personal protective equipment, and the quality of health care and health education provided by the factory clinics.

MESH (Management-Environment-Safety-Health)

A second environmental program we committed to was to require all footwear factories to adopt an Environmental Health and Safety Management System. Using outside consultants Gauntlett Group of San Francisco and Environmental Resource Management (ERM) of Hong Kong, in June and August 1998, we inaugurated the first of the EHSMS workshops for factories in China. In the fall and winter of 1998 and into spring of 1999 these workshops and follow-up brought the concepts and workshops to factories in Korea, Taiwan, Thailand, Vietnam, and Indonesia. This year we decided to expand MESH to encompass all corporate responsibility programs, including labor practices and community affairs (management), environmental programs (environment), and the worker wellness programs (safety and health.) Although MESH will be a work in progress for years to come, we believe it will have a marked impact on worker populations, factory impacts and the basic quality of management of these issues across the board.

Sustainable Business

The third of the environmental initiatives was adoption of the goal of sustainable business practices. We have engaged McDonough Braungart Design Chemistry on the first element of that concept, sustainable product design. On September 9, 1998, we inaugurated a new Nike Environmental Policy. We have also committed to eliminate polyvinyl chloride (PVC) from all of our business activities.

Forums/Rising Tides

In May 1998 we committed to a policy of open communications on corporate responsibility issues. In the spirit of sharing our knowledge and continued challenges on improving indoor air quality, Nike hosted our first open forum on factory environmental issues on November 26, 1998, in Bangkok, Thailand. On the following day, we invited representatives from the footwear industry, governmental health officials, and nongovernmental organization (NGOs) representatives to a tour of our Thailand factories.

The objective of the forum and factory tours was to share knowledge and best practices on worker health and safety issues that will primarily benefit the footwear industry and perhaps other global companies seeking to export measurable standards to their contractors abroad.

We published a compendium of results of that forum, including complete results of all air quality testing and information on water-based compounds. We have also developed from that work a manual for air quality correction.

In addition to forums, the second of which we are exploring now, we also committed to fund university studies of corporate responsibility issues. To date, the Tuck School of Business at Dartmouth College has undertaken wage and spending surveys of workers in factories in Vietnam and Indonesia and will continue that work for us. The University of North Carolina's School of Public Health is working with us to develop a long-term study of health impacts and training in footwear factories.

Education

On May 12, 1998, we committed Nike to work with manufacturers who take a leading interest in their worker welfare. A key component of that commitment is that every Nike contract footwear factory must have a supplemental worker education program. To date, such programs are up and operating in about half of the footwear factory base, or 20 factories, in four countries (China, Thailand, Vietnam, and Indonesia). Our goal in this fiscal year is to add 10 more factories to that list and to ensure through the Global Alliance, World Vision, and other outside resources that the existing programs are operated to standards of best practice.

Each factory produces its own program guides based on our standard (the Jobs & Education Program guide), local requirements, and advice and counsel from outside resources. In Indonesia, factories who have started education programs have done so in conjunction with the Ministry of Education, using certified teachers and curriculum. Three of those factories have been formally recognized by the Indonesian government for their contributions to literacy.

In China, our partner is the Washington State–based NGO World Vision, which through its World Vision Hong Kong and World Vision China organizations has conducted worker surveys to see what programs are desired, designed a program concept that encompasses academic as well as life skills components, and then staffed the programs with trainers and managers.

In Vietnam and Thailand the factories have developed programs using local teachers and facilities.

Microloans

In May 1998 we committed to providing small business loans to women in Vietnam and three other Asian countries. In the intervening year the Vietnam program through the Vietnam Women's Union and the Colorado-based NGO Friendship Bridge has been expanded to also include workers who lost jobs. To date, more than 2,300 rural women and former workers have created small businesses in Vietnam, and the success rate has been absolutely amazing. Thus far there have been no defaults on loans, and business borrowers have come back to expand businesses with second and third loans. The typical business involves raising pigs, ducks, or chickens, the production of rice paper for spring rolls, or the production of incense sticks and other basic manufactured goods.

In Indonesia, our NGO partner Opportunity International (OI) has launched a microloan program using Nike working capital that is targeted at an area of Jakarta where many people have lost jobs as a result of the economic downturn. OI projects several thousand businesses will be created from this program in the coming 3 to 5 years.

In Thailand, our partners, the local NGO called Population and Community Development Association (PDA) and Union Footwear, have collaborated with Nike to establish a rural village stitching center around which a number of related programs will be built, including a microenterprise cooperative, a vegetable bank, tree bank, school, and women's empowerment center. The concept is to create a center for enterprise and education that keeps jobs in the countryside, reverses migration to the city, and builds reforestation and cash crop projects. Although it is small in scale, we hope the village concept will stimulate similar efforts on the part of other businesses.

We are investigating a microloan program in Pakistan, but to date have not come to resolution as to a partner or program.

Independent Monitoring

On May 12, 1998, we committed Nike to involve NGOs in the process of monitoring our factories. In the past year we have expanded our program in Vietnam with the University of Economics, which conducts worker focus groups; we have engaged one NGO in Indonesia to work alongside Nike auditors in factory oversight; and, most important, we have joined as a charter member in the Global Alliance, what will eventually be a global system of engaging local NGOs to survey workers in factories, report those results, and help us and our factory partners to devise programs that address issues that are raised and prioritized by the workers themselves.

The Global Alliance for Workers and Communities has been established by the International Youth Foundation (IYF), with participation from the World Bank, the John D. and Catherine T. MacArthur Foundation, Nike, and Mattel. Our goal for this fiscal year is to have assessment and feedback from workers in factories in four countries, which all together have 100,000 workers, or about 20% of our total contract labor force. Assessment begins in the first factories in July or August.

The White House Apparel Industry Partnership since May 12, 1998, has come to agreement on principles of monitoring and is working now to establish a Fair Labor Association, which would manage the oversight of each member company's monitoring process. In addition to the seven member companies, the FLA also has the commitment of more than 80 universities that have their logos licensed to apparel manufacturers like Nike. Many of the schools with which we have licensing agreements have joined the FLA. Our hope is that this program will be operating by fall 1999.

Source: Link located at: http://www.nike.com/nikebiz/news/press release.jhtml?year = 2001&month = 05&letter = g, reprinted with permission of Nike, Inc.

CHAPTER 8

adidas-Salomon: Child Labor and Health and Safety Initiatives in Vietnam and Brazil

*Laura P. Hartman, Richard E. Wokutch,
and J. Lawrence French*

CORPORATE ENVIRONMENT

adidas-Salomon, formerly called adidas, was founded in 1949 and named after its founder Adolf (Adi for short) Dassler.[1] It produces primarily athletic shoes, apparel lines, and sports equipment.[2] The company was nearly bankrupt until it shifted production to Asia in the early 1980s and strengthened its budget for marketing.[3] In the 1990s, under CEO Robert Louis-Dreyfus, adidas-Salomon shifted from being primarily a manufacturing company to primarily a marketing company, getting most of its production from contractors. In 1995 the firm went public.[4] Its purchase of French ski, golf, and bike gear maker Salomon steered the company into the equipment arena but has left it with integration challenges.[5] From a financial perspective, the Salomon purchase put an 8 percent decline of profits on the books in 1998. However, despite a decline in the growth of the global market in these goods, adidas-Salomon increased net sales in that year by 48 percent to U.S.$5.5 billion. In the year ending December 31, 2001, adidas-Salomon had net income of 208 million euros (approximately U.S.$183 million) on net sales of 6.11 billion euros (approximately U.S.$5.35 billion).[6] Footwear accounted for approximately 44 percent of sales and apparel for 36 percent during that year.[7]

Worldwide, adidas-Salomon contracts with approximately 950 factories.[8] For the adidas brand alone adidas-Salomon contracted with 570 factories in 2000, of which 267 were in Asia, 122 were in North and South

America, and 181 were in Europe.[9] While adidas-Salomon composes only a small percentage of many of the apparel factories' business, most of its footwear suppliers produce almost exclusively for adidas-Salomon. This allows them greater leverage in those circumstances to request modifications with regard to labor practices or issues surrounding safety, health, and the environment. Given its leverage with suppliers, adidas-Salomon has conceded that "outsourcing supply does not mean outsourcing social responsibility."[10] The number of adidas-Salomon contractors is declining over time as adidas-Salomon consolidates its supplier base.

While "quality" was the primary focus of the 1980s and 1990s, that focus has expanded to now include broader concerns about the social implications of operations, notably including working conditions in contractors' factories. Decisions at adidas-Salomon require "triple signatures" from the Social & Environmental Affairs Department, the adidas-Salomon Country Manager, and the Director of adidas-Salomon Apparel Operations. The quote from the adidas-Salomon Global Director, Social and Environmental Affairs, David Husselbee, that opens the following section establishes the challenge faced by any multinational firm choosing to source from a global market. Currently, according to Husselbee, adidas-Salomon (no. 7) and Nike (no. 4) are named in a list of the top 10 global brands compiled by Young & Rubicam and, with Calvin Klein (no. 9), constitute the representation of the footwear and apparel industries.

Codes and Principles: adidas-Salomon's Standards of Engagement

> "People like to be linked with brands which embody unique ideas and the passion and energy to change the world."
> —David Husselbee in June 26, 2001 presentation,
> quoting Young & Rubicam

As mentioned earlier in this text, many firms have created and published codes of conduct and other like statements subsequent to targeted attacks by activists. adidas-Salomon had been subject to similar attacks but also had discovered through its own internal mechanisms that some of its supplier operations were not operated at the same standards as its own operations. In 1998 adidas-Salomon published its Standards of Engagement (SoE) (see below) with the aim of ensuring that all of its suppliers' factories are safe, fair places to work. Updated in 2001 the SoE are patterned after the ILO conventions and the model code of conduct of the World Federation of Sporting Goods Industries and reflect attention to the following labor, safety, health, and environmental issues:

- Forced labor
- Child labor

- Discrimination
- Wages and benefits
- Hours of work
- Freedom of association and collective bargaining
- Disciplinary practices
- Health and safety
- Environmental requirements
- Community involvement

The following constitutes adidas' Standards of Engagement:

Authenticity. Inspiration. Commitment. Honesty.

These are some of the core values of the adidas brand. We measure ourselves by these values, and we measure our business partners in the same way.

Consistent with these brand values, we expect our partners—contractors, sub-contractors, suppliers, and others—to conduct themselves with the utmost fairness, honesty, and responsibility in all aspects of their business.

These Standards of Engagement are tools that assist us in selecting and retaining business partners that follow workplace standards and business practices consistent with our policies and values. As a set of guiding principles, they also help identify potential problems so that we can work with our business partners to address issues of concern as they arise.

Specifically, we expect our business partners to operate workplaces where the following standards and practices are followed:

I. General Principle Business partners shall comply fully with all legal requirements relevant to the conduct of their businesses.

II. Employment Standards We will only do business with partners who treat their employees fairly and legally with regard to wages, benefits, and working conditions. In particular, the following guidelines apply:

Forced Labor: Business partners shall not employ forced labor, whether in the form of prison labor, indentured labor, bonded labor, or otherwise.

Child Labor: Business partners shall not employ children who are less than 15 years old (or 14 years old where the law of the country of manufacture allows), or who are younger than the age for completing compulsory education in the country of manufacture where such age is higher than 15.

Discrimination: While we recognize and respect cultural differences, we believe that workers should be employed on the basis of their ability to do the job, rather than on the basis of personal characteristics or beliefs. We will seek business partners that share this value, and that do not discriminate in hiring and employment practices on grounds of race, national origin, gender, religion, age, disability, sexual orientation, or political opinion.

Wages and Benefits: Business partners shall pay their employees the minimum wage required by law or the prevailing industry wage, whichever is higher, and shall provide legally mandated benefits. Wages shall be paid directly to the employee in cash or check or the equivalent, and information relating to wages shall be provided to employees in a form they understand. Advances and deductions from wages shall be carefully monitored, and shall comply with law.

Hours of Work: Employees shall not be required to work more than sixty hours per week, including overtime, on a regular basis and shall be compensated for overtime according to law. Employees shall be allowed at least 24 consecutive hours off per week, and should receive paid annual leave.

Right of Association: Business partners shall recognize and respect the right of workers to join and organize associations of their own choosing.

Disciplinary Practices: Every employee shall be treated with respect and dignity. No employee shall be subject to any physical, sexual, psychological or verbal harassment or abuse.

III. Health and Safety Business partners shall provide a safe and healthy working environment, including protection from fire, accidents, and toxic substances. Lighting, heating and ventilation systems should be adequate. Employees should have access at all times to sanitary facilities, which should be adequate and clean. When residential facilities are provided for employees, the same standards should apply.

IV. Environmental Requirements Business partners shall comply with all applicable environmental laws and regulations.

V. Community Involvement We will favor business partners who make efforts to contribute to improving conditions in the countries and communities in which they operate.[11]

The SoE Program

The general counsel for adidas-Salomon, North America, Susheela Jayapal, is generally credited with having spearheaded the establishment of the Standards of Engagement at the corporate level in 1997.[12] Interest in developing these standards stemmed from a controversy regarding the use of child labor in stitching soccer balls in Pakistan that tarnished the reputations of several firms in the sporting goods and apparel industry, including adidas-Salomon. Around 1997, adidas-Salomon, Nike, and Reebok were identified in the popular media as violating child labor standards in the production of their soccer balls. These companies or their direct contractors did not directly employ the child workers, but they were employed by subcontractors, who, as is the custom in the production of soccer balls, performed the stitching operations. Although Nike received more of the criticism for this in the United States, adidas-Salomon, as a European company, was more heavily criticized in Europe. Given adidas-Salomon's strong identification with soccer, this controversy posed a particular challenge for the company.

This episode was viewed as an embarrassment to the company; the use of child labor in its products, an unsavory labor practice, conflicted with company values and principles and adidas-Salomon did not want to be involved with it. As a result, adidas-Salomon worked together with Nike, Reebok, and the nongovernmental organization (NGO) Save the Children to put an end to the use of child labor in this operation. This resolution involved putting an end to the illegal employment of children in these operations and making an effort to ensure that these children went to school. They endeavored to do this by compensating the children and their families for lost income and by guaranteeing employment at the completion of schooling and the attainment of legal working age. In addition, an effort was made to move subcontracting out of home-based workshops into factory-based stitching centers so that child labor could be more easily prevented.

After this experience Susheela Jayapal took the initiative to propose the establishment of the Standards of Engagement to ensure that other contractors would be acting in a socially responsible way with respect to employment practices and working conditions. The proposed Standards of Engagement were approved quickly by the board of directors of adidas-Salomon and then chaired by CEO Robert Louis-Dreyfus. They went into effect in 1998. The quick approval of these standards reflected a recognition that the current business environment required firms to ensure humane working conditions not only in their own factories but also, to the extent possible, in the supplier and contractor firms with which they work.

It is noteworthy that the impetus for the labor component of the SoE seems to have come primarily from the American side of adidas-Salomon, whereas the health, safety, and environment (HSE) component came primarily from the European side. The European members of adidas-Salomon were reportedly somewhat more focused on HSE issues, in part because labor concerns in Europe, like the rights of association, are taken as a given. In Germany, for example, where adidas-Salomon has its headquarters, laws dictate trade union representation on boards of directors. In contrast, the Green movement in Germany has been very aggressive in pushing firms to take steps to protect the environment. The American concern for labor issues and the European concern for HSE reportedly dovetailed well in the formulation of the SoE.

With reference to the continuum of standard-setting initiatives and practices, adidas-Salomon has guiding principles supported by its SoE, as well as reporting and certification initiatives supported by procedures established by the SoE team.

SoE Global Administrative Structure

The SoE management team comprises 29 people from 13 countries with responsibilities for Asia, the Americas, and Europe. As shown in the organization chart (figure 8.1), adidas-Salomon's SoE teams are organized globally by region: Asia, Europe, and the Americas. The three regional

Figure 8.1
Global Standards of Engagement Team Structure

The adidas-Salomon Global Standards of Engagement Team

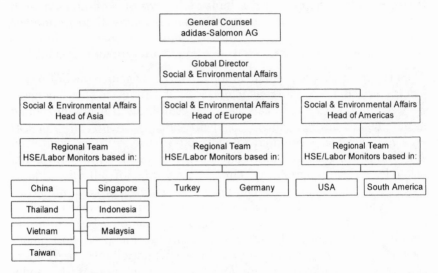

Source: Adapted from adidas-Salomon SoE, 2001, reprinted with permission of adidas-Salomon.

directors of Social and Environmental Affairs are William Anderson (Asia), Gregg Nebel (Americas), and Frank Henke (Europe). They report to David Husselbee, who serves as the Global Vice-President of Social and Environmental Affairs. Husselbee, in turn, reports to Manfred Ihle, Global General Counsel and a member of the board of directors. The SoE team members have very diverse disciplinary backgrounds. David Husselbee and William Anderson both have previous experience working with NGOs, and several SoE team members have labor law backgrounds. Husselbee had been working as the Managing Director of Save the Children in Pakistan when it cooperated with adidas-Salomon in resolving the Pakistani child labor problem. There are also a chemical engineer and an environmental specialist on staff as well as people with backgrounds in manufacturing, quality control, sourcing, socioeconomic development, and urban planning.

The SoE team members have a high level of commitment to the Standards of Engagement from production personnel. In fact, the former head of SoE in Asia is Duncan Scott, who is now in charge of footwear production globally. According to the SoE staff, this is helpful in many ways, particularly with respect to enhancing their organizational credibility and their leverage to get things done.

Typical issues raised by auditors in the various countries and regions are delineated in the adidas-Salomon "Our World" report and can be seen in figure 8.2. According to the report, the most widely encountered problems in Asian supplier factories are the payment of recruitment fees (noted as a concern in five countries), poor age documentation (seven countries), wages lower than minimum wage (five countries), maximum working hours ignored (eight countries), working rules not published (six countries), wages docked as punishment for violating working rules (five countries), confiscation of passports (three countries), abuse of migrant workers (three countries), and illegal status of unions (three countries).[13]

adidas-Salomon sources from fewer suppliers and fewer countries in the Americas. There are suppliers for international sales in only four countries (Brazil, El Salvador, Canada, and Mexico) in the Americas. (As indicated below, more suppliers in more countries are involved when production for local markets and production for other adidas-Salomon group brands are considered.) The most common problems cited for these international suppliers' operations are gender, race, and age discrimination (two countries), delayed payment of wages (one country), unclear piece-rate system/time recording (one country), and discrimination against union members (one country).[14]

Figure 8.2a
Typical Issues Raised by Auditors in the Various Countries and Regions: Asia

	Cambodia	China	India	Indonesia	Japan	Korea	Lao PDR	Malaysia	Pakistan	Philippines	Singapore	Sri Lanka	Taiwan	Thailand	Vietnam
Forced labor															
Recruitment fees	☑	☑						☑		☑			☑		
Confiscated passport								☑		☑			☑		
Temporary Contracts			☑							☑					
Trainee Wages										☑					
Forced Savings		☑											☑		
Child labor															
Poor age documentation	☑		☑	☑			☑	☑				☑			☑
Under-18 rights ignored															
Discrimination															
Gender, race, age															
Migrant workers				☑									☑	☑	
Wages and benefits															
Delayed payment															
Less than minimum wage	☑		☑							☑				☑	☑
Unclear piece-rate system/time recording			☑												
No benefits					☑									☑	
Local Licensing of Foreign-owned factories															☑
No pay slips															
Hours of work															
Maximum working hours ignored	☑			☑				☑		☑	☑		☑	☑	☑
Poor record-keeping		☑											☑		
Unpaid overtime									☑						
Rights of association															
Unions illegal	☑	☑								☑					
Union members discriminated				☑											
Disciplinary practices															
Rules not published	☑	☑	☑			☑				☑					☑
Wages docked as punished		☑		☑		☑				☑					☑

Figure 8.2b
Typical Issues Raised by Auditors in the Various Countries and Regions: Europe and the Americas

	Albania	Brazil	Bulgaria	Canada	El Salvador	Macedonia	Mexico	Turkey
Forced labor								
Recruitment fees								
Confiscated passport			☑					
Temporary Contracts								
Trainee Wages								
Forced Savings								
Child labor								
Poor age documentation								
Under-18 rights ignored								☑
Discrimination								
Gender, race, age		☑					☑	
Migrant workers								
Wages and benefits								
Delayed payment		☑				☑		
Less than minimum wage								
Unclear piece-rate system/time recording			☑	☑		☑		
No benefits								☑
Local Licensing of Foreign-owned factories								
No pay slips	☑							
Hours of work								
Maximum working hours ignored								☑
Poor record-keeping				☑				☑
Unpaid overtime								☑
Rights of association								
Unions illegal								
Union members discriminated			☑		☑			
Disciplinary practices								
Rules not published								
Wages docked as punished								

Note: The adidas SoE team has assessed which issues arise in suppliers' factories. Each tick represents a typical reason for suppliers in that country failing to met adidas's SoE. Only countries with significant problems are listed.
Source: Adapted from adidas-Salomon, "Our World: Social and Environmental Report 2000," p. 21, 26–27, reprinted with permission from adidas-Salomon.

Apparel factories reportedly represent more of a challenge to adidas-Salomon's inspection monitoring program than do footwear factories because adidas-Salomon accounts for a much smaller share of production of the individual apparel factories than is the case with footwear factories and thus has less leverage over each apparel supplier. Also, problems that arise in these suppliers might stem from production demands other brands place on them, leaving these suppliers in a difficult position.

As the program studies documented in this report originate in Asia and in the Americas, a brief overview of SoE responsibility and implementation in those regions follows.

Asian SoE Operations

adidas-Salomon has been sourcing in Asia for over 30 years, originally with German managers using Asian agents to develop partnerships. Asia currently represents the most important source of both footwear and apparel for adidas-Salomon, with 227 of its total of 328 first-tier supplier factories in Asia and 40 of its total of 242 second-tier supplier factories in Asia (figures for adidas brand only). These supplier factories are located in: Cambodia, China, Hong Kong, India, Indonesia, Japan, Korea, Laos, Macao, Malaysia, Mauritius, Pakistan, Philippines, Singapore, Sri Lanka, Taiwan, Thailand, and Vietnam, representing a very wide geographic area that encompasses significant economic, social, political, and cultural differences.

There are a total of 19 SoE staff members including two administrative assistants in the Asia region. In addition to the head of the department, William Anderson, the Social and Environmental Affairs staff includes Eric Mo, Regional Manager, Social and Environmental Affairs, Greater China; Barry Tang, Regional Manager, Social and Environmental Affairs, North Asia; and Kitty Potter, Regional Manager, Social and Environmental Affairs, South Asia. Asia region headquarters are located in Hong Kong, and these managers operate from there, but they travel extensively throughout the Asia region visiting suppliers. Other SoE staff members are located near suppliers in China, Vietnam, Indonesia, Singapore, Malaysia, Korea, Taiwan, and Thailand.

Previously, the SoE staff working in Asia were divided between those working with apparel suppliers and those working with footwear suppliers. The footwear team was further divided into labor monitors and health, safety, and environment monitors (apparel monitors covered both labor issues and health, safety, and environment). Now however, footwear and apparel monitoring operations are being merged, and there will be integrated teams covering all aspects of SoE, visiting both footwear and apparel factories.

The Americas SoE Operations

In the Americas region, adidas-Salomon has contractors located in Argentina, Brazil, Canada, Colombia, El Salvador, Honduras, Mexico, Peru, the United States, Uruguay, and Guatemala, representing a large geographic region as well as a very broad range of socioeconomic, regulatory, and cultural conditions. As of 2000 there were 64 first-tier adidas-Salomon suppliers in this region, and 58 second-tier suppliers (figures for adidas brand only).[15] That includes several factories in Uruguay and Guatemala that produce solely for the local markets. The number of first-tier and second-tier suppliers was smaller in 2001. This is a result of reduced production demand, consolidation of programs for multiple suppliers, compliance problems, and subpar performance by suppliers in terms of delivery and quality. Reduction in the supplier base is also related to the implementation of a new adilean program through which SoE field staff work with suppliers to promote lean production in the suppliers' facilities. To the extent that the adilean program is successful, it will allow adidas-Salomon to focus on fewer suppliers with larger production volumes. The adilean program is being progressively implemented; as of the end of 2001, not all suppliers had become involved with it.

Gregg Nebel, the Regional Head for Social and Environmental Affairs for Region Americas, is based in adidas-Salomon's Portland, Oregon, regional headquarters. His team is charged with implementing the SoE in the Americas region. Nebel originally joined adidas-Salomon in 1992 to work in the sourcing area. He was named to this current position when the SoE were approved in 1997. Working with him in the implementation of the SoE throughout this region is one full-time field auditor/manager, Corey Sebastian, and six part-time assistant auditors located regionally in the product integrity office and subsidiary offices. These part-timers work full time for adidas-Salomon, but only part of their work is in the enforcement of the SoE.

As in other regions, workers in South American contractor factories are involved in the implementation of the SoE to the extent that they have been notified of the existence of the SoE through posters and other forms of communications. Also, when factory audits are conducted one principal part of the process is interviewing workers to get information independent from the information that is provided by management regarding the work issues covered in the SoE. Nebel, however, is not sure how workers feel overall about the importance of the SoE to them personally. In his view, worker awareness of the company's compliance process is probably the weakest part of the program. He believes this is the case for similar programs operated by other firms in the industry as well. adidas-Salomon is attempting to address this concern through encouraging effective labor-management communications and the establishment of labor relations councils, health and safety councils, and other worker-participation groups in the workplace.

The SoE team in the Americas addresses the same general work issues (wages and hours of work, safety and health, environmental issues, discrimination, and so on) with suppliers, as do adidas-Salomon SoE members elsewhere. However, as they move from country to country— according to Nebel he is on the road traveling to contractors about 250 days per year—the nature of the particular problem areas changes as does the focus of audits. As an example of this, Nebel noted that in some countries, free unions (in the sense that we know them in the United States) are not permitted. In such cases, the SoE team focuses on remediation plans that encourage the development of a constructive labor-management dialogue that could promote workers' interests until a time when genuine rights of association are available. At the same time adidas-Salomon might quietly lobby in the background, along with the appropriate governmental parties, NGOs, and special interest groups knowledgeable about freedom of association compliance. In doing so, adidas-Salomon is neither advocating nor working against the formation of a union, but is simply supporting the workers' right to choose for themselves.

According to Nebel the SoE team in Region Americas is currently spending more time on some of the grayer areas of labor compliance, such as rights of association, discrimination, and the "living wage," as opposed to more often visited concrete and quantifiable compliance standards like health and safety. Nebel feels these grayer areas are more challenging to address, and often factory managers, many of whom have engineering backgrounds, are more comfortable with the quantifiability of health, safety, and environment standards. Nevertheless, his team has developed some expertise in these gray areas, and he feels they can offer the most help there.

According to Nebel there were no real barriers to implementation of the SoE in the Americas. There was a great deal of support in the company, and external stakeholders were also supportive of the initiative. Many factory owners were neither surprised by nor opposed to the implementation of the program. Implementation was made more interesting, though, because of the nature of the footwear and apparel industries. Some of these suppliers contract with several firms in the industry, and a given factory might be visited by inspectors from several different companies. According to Nebel some of the contractors were initially surprised at the comprehensiveness of the audit reviews conducted by adidas-Salomon. According to him these contractors indicated that the audits were considerably more comprehensive than those conducted by other firms in the industry.

Management Processes, Reporting, and Certification

When the SoE was first established in 1997, adidas-Salomon was already doing a certain amount of factory auditing of principal contractors, but passage of the SoE broadened this function and provided a more formal mandate for it. To implement the SoE, they needed to (1) identify subcontractors lower down in the supply chain, (2) develop audit tools (one for health, safety, and environment and one for labor issues), and (3) hire a staff and build a budget to support it. Gregg Nebel and Luke O'Conner started implementing the SoE in the field during the fourth quarter of 1997. Nebel was working primarily with apparel factories in the Americas, and Luke O'Conner was working primarily with footwear factories in Asia. By March 1998 there were a half dozen SoE field workers.

The SoE team provides training to contractors on the various elements of the Standards of Engagement, but the focus and nature of that training vary a great deal from country to country. All contractors are provided with general training on the Standards of Engagement addressing certain issues: What are the standards? What do they mean? What is the legal precedent? What are some case studies? When a factory does something wrong, what should they do? What are some common areas of noncompliance? What are ways to resolve those areas of noncompliance?

The auditing process is also considered to be part of the training process. When problems are discovered, remediation measures will be suggested and training can be provided so as to avoid these problems in the future. During these audit visits the SoE team also provides "best practice training." Thus, even though a factory is in compliance with existing standards, factory representatives are trained in the use of state-of-the-art techniques to address the work issue in question. The application of continuous improvement techniques to safety, health, and environment and labor standards is one example of this.

Over the course of years the team has found that there is a need for greater description and definition of the principles identified in the SoE. Consequently, adidas-Salomon began discussing the institution of a labor manual for contractors as a guideline for implementing the SoE and as a support for the training function of the SoE team. In June 2001 members of the adidas-Salomon SoE team met with the leadership of the company's global apparel, accessories, and footwear operations and its complete global audit team to begin the design, review, and global launch of the labor manual for all suppliers. The first draft of the *Guidelines on Employment Standards* strives to put into plain language the implementation expectations articulated in the SoE for suppliers.

In fact, it is adidas-Salomon's long-term vision to allow its suppliers to achieve strong self-governance and sustainability through the SoE cycle shown in figure 8.3.

adidas-Salomon ensures compliance through an internal global team of auditors, and to assist in these efforts it has also engaged the services of external independent auditors such as Verité, a nongovernmental organization that focuses on human rights and standards in global outsourcing. adidas-Salomon now belongs to the Fair Labor Association (FLA), which also contracts with independent auditors who visit adidas-Salomon factories and use the FLA's auditing tools, methodology, and standards.

Once informed by its sourcing division that adidas-Salomon will be using a new supplier, the company's SoE division schedules a first-time compliance audit. At the conclusion of this or other annual audits, suppliers are informed about areas needing attention, are given performance ratings for (1) health, safety, and environment and (2) labor standards and are ranked using the adidas-Salomon 5-star approach described in its report "Clearer: Social and Environmental Report 2001." (See figure 8.4 for the supplier scoring system.)

Figure 8.3
The Cycle of SoE

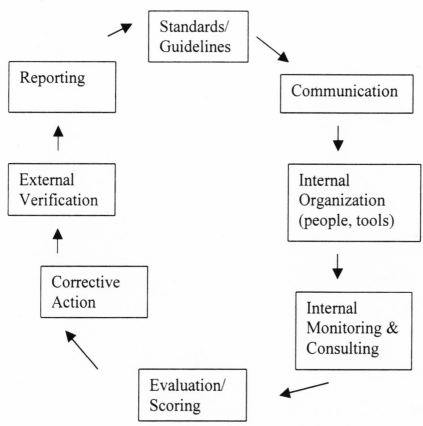

Source: Adapted by the authors from materials from adidas-Salomon.

Figure 8.5 contains data on the rated status of the factories of adidas-Salomon's suppliers as of 2001. The table summarizes the performance of suppliers against both adidas labor standards and adidas HSE standards. The table uses the supplier scoring system described above to compare performance.

Efforts Toward Sustainability

It is critical for the success of any adidas-Salomon-requested modification or program that factory owners and management "buy into" the effort. While this cannot always be achieved, it is more likely when management or the factory owners feel that they are a part of any change process. To encourage the factory to own the program for itself, in an effort

Figure 8.4
Standards of Engagement Supplier Scoring System

★☆☆☆☆	There are numerous severe non-compliance issues. The factory has been given notice that business will be terminated unless there is immediate improvement
★★☆☆☆	There are some non-compliance issues and the factory is responding to the action plan slowly or with reluctance. The factory is monitored regularly.
★★★☆☆	There are minor non-compliance issues, and there are some best practices in place, confirmed in documentation.
★★★★☆	Generally there are non-compliance issues, and there are some best practices in place, confirmed in documentation.
★★★★★	There are no non-compliance issues and all of the factory's management system and practices are in place, confirmed in documentation.

Source: adidas-Salomon, "Clearer: Social and Environmental Report 2001," p. 25.

toward self-governance and self-sustainability, factory owners participate fully in the factory visits, are encouraged to offer feedback regarding the audit, engage in training programs arranged by adidas-Salomon for factory groups, attend "supplier summits," engage in e-mail communications with the adidas-Salomon SoE team for consultancies, participate in follow-up visits, engage in costing negotiations with adidas-Salomon (which may relate to SoE compliance), and allow worker interviews.

Where suppliers are not in full compliance with the SoE, including the labor as well as the health, safety, and environment provisions, the auditor will work with the supplier to develop a plan for moving toward full compliance. One of the challenges for this program, however, is the difficulty of determining when a supplier is sufficiently out of compliance to cancel all contractual relations. During 2001 adidas-Salomon termi-

Figure 8.5
Number of Factories Rated by adidas Supplier Scoring System, by Region

International Sourcing

Apparel				Footwear			
Labour Standards	Asia	America	Europe	Labour Standards	Asia	America	Europe
★☆☆☆☆	12	0	0	★☆☆☆☆	3	0	0
★★☆☆☆	44	2	13	★★☆☆☆	2	0	0
★★★☆☆	70	38	83	★★★☆☆	8	0	4
★★★★☆	12	9	4	★★★★☆	5	0	1
★★★★★	1	0	0	★★★★★	1	0	1
Total Audited to Date	139	49	100	Total Audited to Date	19	0	6
Total Audited in 2001	94	44	68	Total Audited in 2001	19	0	3
Total Factories in Region	146	100	140	Total Factories in Region	19	0	6

nated 21 suppliers in Asia and 32 suppliers worldwide on the basis of noncompliance/nonperformance relative to the SoE. This is about 3 percent of its supplier base. The general policy is that adidas-Salomon engages the factory and strives to work with it to bring it into compliance. If, after a period of time, it is clear that there is insufficient management commitment to meet basic levels of compliance, the relationship will be terminated. Decisions are made on a case-by-case basis after adidas-Salomon weighs the compliance history of the specific factory and the level or areas of nonconformance. Accordingly, terminating a contract is not the intended result of noncompliance. The termination of a supplier's contract, in effect, also terminates any leverage that adidas-Salomon might have to effect wide-scale change in that particular factory. Of course a careful balancing act is required. Allowing contractors to continue supplying to adidas-Salomon in the face of protracted serious violations of the SoE would undercut the credibility of the company's enforcement, both with that supplier and with others.

While this chapter outlines specific programs in place at adidas-Salomon's Vietnamese, Thai, and Brazilian suppliers, there are additional activities that also should be noted. For instance, many adidas-Salomon suppliers maintain suggestion boxes on-site and reward employees for suggestions that are put into place. For example, in one supplier, noise reduction was a tremendous challenge as workers would lift the rubber press molds and allow them to fall backward against the presses, all of which were made of steel. One employee suggested that scrap rubber be used to act as a buffer between the steel surfaces. The noise problem from that particular source was completely eliminated (see photos 8.1 and 8.2).

Evaluation

Activities related to the Standards of Engagement are evaluated in several ways. The SoE team reports to the board of directors of adidas-Salomon through Manfred Ihle, and the board evaluates performance on an ongoing basis. In addition, adidas-Salomon's first social and environmental report was published in 2001 and the second in 2002;[16] these serve an important internal evaluation function for the operation of the Standards of Engagement. This annual report also provides a mechanism to communicate information about activities in these areas externally to various corporate stakeholders.

In an effort to ensure that this annual report effectively addresses issues of concern and interest to its stakeholders, adidas engaged Business for Social Responsibility (BSR) to conduct a "stakeholder dialogue" on the 2002 report. BSR invited representative adidas stakeholders to a day-long discussion that sought to critically analyze the direction and activities of adidas's social programs in the past and coming years. Though these dialogues took place in each of adidas's three regions (Asia, the Americas, and Europe[17]), participants at the Americas dialogue included represen-

Photo 8.1 Red rubber noise reducer for presses. *Source:* **Laura Hartman**

Photo 8.2 Red rubber noise reducer for presses. *Source:* Laura Hartman

tatives from academia; from NGOs such as CARE, Coverco, FLA, Workers Rights Consortium, and Lawyers Committee on Human Rights; and from values-based investments such as Walden Asset Management.[18] Stakeholder dialogues such as this are strongly encouraged by NGOs, government entities, and private-sector organizations, alike, such as the World Business Council for Sustainable Development, which claims that the dialogues are important since an MNE "[cannot] operate successfully without the tacit consent of its customers, the local community and society at large. A 'license to operate' must be obtained and renewed over time."[19]

In addition to a general solicitation for input, adidas-Salomon's involvement in FLA provides some external validation of its activities. FLA evaluates the performance of member firms as corporate entities in terms of their handling of health, safety, environment, and labor issues in their supply chain factories. FLA member firms agree to match or exceed these standards. The initial FLA evaluations of corporate compliance with its standards will be issued for member firms annually and will start by the end of 2003. As noted, adidas-Salomon on occasion has also contracted with NGOs such as Verite' to provide external monitoring of conditions in contractor factories.

adidas-Salomon is also rated on the Dow Jones Sustainability Index (DSJI). In 2000 it was ranked fourth in its industry on this index, and in 2001 the company moved up to first in the industry. Much of this improvement is attributed to the compliance work the company is doing with its international suppliers. Moreover, public awareness of that work including the improvement on the DSJI has been enhanced by the publication of the *2001 Social and Environmental Report*, a first for the sporting goods industry.

Given stakeholder demands for greater transparency in corporate contracting procedures,[20] the publication of these reports must be viewed favorably from that perspective. Stakeholder groups and critics of adidas-Salomon who, in the past, had been concerned about adidas-Salomon's activities in the areas covered by the SoE have found their ability to stay informed about performance in these areas improved by the publication of this report.

SoE Case Example: Implementation in Thailand

It was not possible in the course of this research to document the implementation of the SoE in the wide region covered by adidas-Salomon contractor relationships in all of Asia. Instead, this case example and the one following are presented to show SoE implementation in two particular countries, Thailand and Brazil.

Thailand is an interesting national context in which to consider the implementation of the SoE. It is more mature in terms of industrial development than other countries such as Vietnam or Indonesia, but not nearly so far along as Japan, Singapore, or Taiwan. There are many more individual freedoms than are found in China or Vietnam, for example; but labor leaders decry the barriers to effective union organizing and worker representation that undercut efforts to raise the standard of living and promote workers' interests in Thailand.[21] A more in-depth discussion of the social, economic, and political climate in Thailand is provided at http://pres.depaul.edu/hartman/beyondsweatshops/countryreports.

Thai SoE Structure

adidas-Salomon's sourcing operations in Thailand are directed by Johannes Schuller, a German national. Approximately 60 people work in the

Bangkok Liaison Office of adidas-Salomon, and production, primarily of apparel, is sourced to approximately 30 factories in Thailand, most of which are located in the general vicinity of Bangkok.

Songpon Pengchamsri is the SoE Manager for Thailand and has responsibility for overseeing supplier compliance in Laos, India, Sri Lanka, and Pakistan, in addition to Thailand. A lawyer by training, Pengchamsri joined adidas-Salomon in January 2000 to work with the SoE team. Previously, he worked with an adidas-Salomon supplier firm, Bangkok Rubber Company, first in the Personnel Department and then heading the company's R&D Department. Pengchamsri visits each of the supplier factories in Thailand approximately two to three times per year. In the period since he has been working with adidas-Salomon, Pengchamsri has focused on explaining the SoE program to suppliers; training them in how to meet the standards; and, in so doing, showing them how they can enhance their profitability. According to Pengchamsri he has worked with suppliers to help them organize their records so that compliance with these standards can be readily checked. He also discusses benefit issues and encourages managers to have regular monthly meetings with workers' committees. These worker committees, required by law where no union exists, are supposed to discuss health and safety issues as well as various other aspects of wages, benefits, and working conditions. During the visits Pengchamsri will meet with each factory's SoE coordinator, its safety and health manager, as well as worker committee representatives and individual workers (at least one from each department) to discuss issues of concern. He will also conduct general factory inspections, looking for workplace safety and health problems.

Critical Issues of Concern

As can be seen in figure 8.2, the typical concerns in adidas-Salomon Thai subcontractor factories are (1) exploitation of migrant workers, (2) payment of less than the minimum wage, (3) nonpayment of benefits, and (4) the ignoring of maximum working hours. Pengchamsri also mentioned age discrimination as a concern. He noted that some managers prefer workers in the 18 to 25 age range, on the assumption that these workers have the most manual dexterity and are easier to control. Some factory managers will not hire workers older than this, and some factory managers will let current workers go when they exceed this age range. Pengchamsri has been attempting to encourage managers to hire and retain workers on the basis of ability and to test for this through time and motion studies or other measures of performance rather than relying on age as an employment criterion. Interestingly, exercises using Parcheesi games are used for these tests. During factory visits Pengchamsri also attempts to pay close attention to potential violations of minimum age standards. In Thailand the legal minimum working age was recently raised from 15 years of age to 18. However, workers 15 to 18 years of age were "grandfathered" in when this change was made and were permitted to continue working.

With regard to the issue of migrant workers mentioned above, the concern is that migrant workers are often the most vulnerable group of workers in supplier factories. As explained by Kitty Potter, migrant workers are often exploited by recruitment agents in their home and work countries; are discriminated against in the workplace (when compared with local workers); suffer serious language and communication problems; are required to live in poor and sometimes dangerous accommodations; and receive little support from the unions and governments of both the home and work country. Because of this, special attention is paid when migrant workers are employed by a contractor factory. It is noteworthy that Thailand itself is a source of migrant labor for other parts of Asia. Pengchamsri, for example, has interviewed Thai workers in factories in Taiwan to address concerns over the fees payable to agents and middlemen in Thailand.

Issues in Monitoring

One of the challenges with any inspection or monitoring system is ensuring that factory problems that do exist are uncovered during the inspections. Currently, factory managers are given 24 hours notice of an inspection, creating the potential for managers to cover up certain problems to make the factory more presentable for an inspection. According to Pengchamsri this 24-hour notice provision is being changed, and "surprise" inspections will be much more common in the future. Under the manufacturing agreement between adidas and its suppliers, suppliers must allow the SoE team access to factories at any time of the day or night, with or without notice. adidas-Salomon does not however invoke this provision very often. The SoE team believes it is more useful to develop cooperative relations with factory managers and their staff. In addition, there is concern that if suppliers are not notified of an impending visit, travel and work time can be wasted. Surprise visits might mean that the inspection team will arrive to discover that the management or department heads are not available for meetings, documents are not accessible, or production is down due to power failures or some other unforeseen circumstance. If there is suspicion of coaching or intimidation of workers, SoE team members will conduct impromptu interviews with workers off-site. Also if they have concerns over excessive overtime they will on occasion monitor the operating hours and arrange to meet with workers outside the factory gate. Under the FLA auditing system, to which adidas-Salomon is a party, independent auditing visits are unannounced unless notification is required for logistical or security reasons. If in the judgment of the independent monitor practical conditions dictate notification, the factory will receive a one-day notice of the forthcoming inspection.

One additional concern about the inspection and monitoring system is whether workers will feel free or comfortable in airing their grievances with inspectors. Although Thai labor law has provisions for the protection of workers who file complaints, labor advocates are skeptical of their enforcement and they believe that filing of grievances is effectively discouraged by the low rate of unionization and the resulting lack of union protection. They contend that managers will make note of workers who talk to the inspectors or who even spend too much time looking at posted working condition standards like adidas-Salomon's Standards of Engagement.

According to Pengchamsri he can tell which workers would like to speak with him about concerns regarding working conditions because they are the ones who will make eye contact with him. He will meet with these workers privately so that managers will not hear their concerns directly. Nevertheless, he acknowledges that some of the workers with concerns do not want to be seen talking with him directly. As a result, he will on occasion attempt to meet with workers off-site before or after work to learn what grievances they might have about workplace conditions.

According to Kitty Potter trust is very much a factor in workers' willingness to talk with SoE staff. It makes a difference whether the SoE staff member is on his or her first visit to a factory or the 120th visit; and it makes a difference whether there have been any prior incidents of the factory managers disciplining or firing a worker who has complained about some aspect of work to an inspector. In general, according to Potter, the young women who predominantly staff the adidas-Salomon supplier factories are probably more comfortable talking with other young women. The SoE team has in her view a good gender mix—six females and seven males—reflecting a wide range of skills. She believes that an interviewer must at least speak the local language of the workers, and it is her experience that it often is easier to obtain truthful information about working conditions if the interview is conducted off-site or outside work hours. This technique has also been promoted widely by the nongovernmental organization Verite'.

While visiting adidas-Salomon operations in Thailand, the researcher had the opportunity to accompany Pengchamsri on a visit to a supplier factory, the Oriental Garment Co., located on the outskirts of Bangkok. This supplier, with approximately 1,500 employees and U.S.$25 million in sales annually, manufactures a variety of apparel including jackets, coats, jogging suits, and pants, with the majority (65 percent) of the production targeted for men. Entry-level workers make the minimum wage for the Bangkok region, 162 baht/day (about $4).[22] The overtime rate is one and a half times the minimum wage, and work on scheduled rest days is two times the minimum rate. Skilled workers make up to 222 baht/day (about $4.50). Although no figures were provided, it was clear that most of the production workers in this factory were young women. Three out of 5 members of the board of directors and 9 of 17 members of executive management are also women. The majority of the company's product is exported to the United States and Europe. In addition to producing for adidas-Salomon, the Oriental Garment Co. produces for a variety of other brands including Tommy-Hilfiger, Columbia, Next, and Polo Ralph Lauren. Codes of conduct for the various brands adorn the walls of the stairwells.

Many of the workers at this factory operate sewing machines (see photo 8.3), performing work that can be tedious and that potentially poses safety and health risks. The needles on these machines operate very fast and with much force, so one of the hazards related to this sort of work is the occasional broken needle that could do damage to the worker, particularly if it hit her in the eye. To protect workers from this hazard, needle guards have been installed on sewing machines at the Oriental Garment Company. Interestingly, in studies undertaken since these needle guards have been installed at this factory, it has been learned that the safety measure also enables sewers to work faster and more efficiently because they are no longer worried about needle wounds. To protect the customers metal

Photo 8.3 Sewing machine operations. *Source:* **Richard Wokutch**

detector machines were also used to detect broken needle parts in apparel before it is shipped.

Factory managers of the Oriental Garment Company were apparently eager to show the researcher around the factory. They were proud to point to new construction that was taking place. They also took considerable pride in showing the factory's ISO 9002 and ISO 14001 certification. In their view, this certification not only ensures quality products for the customers but it also helps provide job stability and opportunities for advancement for the workers.

Implementation Challenges

Several challenges to the implementation of the SoE in Asia in general and in Thailand in particular have been noted above. These include potential worker reluctance to air grievances to inspectors, particularly if, as is typically the case in Thailand, workers do not have union representation and therefore are less knowledgeable about their rights and entitlements. Still it has been the experience of SoE team members that Thai workers are generally cooperative and candid even with strangers.

The conflicting demands of other brands sourcing from a given supplier (particularly in apparel) can create problems. This is especially problematic with respect to working hours when factory management has multiple orders and deadlines. However, social and HSE compliance is one key area in which brands do not compete with one another. William Anderson notes that adidas-Salomon's SoE team members will speak to and collaborate with their counterparts in Nike, Reebok, and other firms. This may take the form of sharing or agreeing on common actions for a single shared supplier.

Another issue is the potential cost to the employer for achieving compliance with the Standards of Engagement. It is recognized that although some standards (such as eliminating discrimination) can have economic benefits for the suppliers, others can impose costs and cut margins for suppliers, at least in the short run. But, according to Anderson, the majority of code requirements are in fact already covered by local laws. He concedes that these laws often lack enforcement, but they exist nonetheless. In addition, in cases in which adidas-Salomon has standards that are higher than local regulations demand, say for fire safety, he contends that this has a real and measurable benefit for the factory, which cannot be judged against margin—it protects physical assets, as well as the lives of the workers.

In a few cases in which additional costs have been imposed, adidas-Salomon has on occasion paid more to the suppliers for products. This has happened only in the footwear side of the business, in which there is a very detailed breakdown of the cost of making a particular model and the price adidas-Salomon will pay for it. If the contractor can demonstrate transparently that its labor costs have increased because of, for instance, a rise in the national minimum wage or increased contributions to the national social security scheme, then adidas-Salomon will pay an increased amount for the labor component in the price. The lean manufacturing program (discussed above) is intended to address this concern by helping suppliers make their production processes more efficient. It is also felt that, by adhering to the SoE, suppliers can help themselves achieve more surety of orders over the long run from adidas-Salomon and others.

SoE Case Example: Implementation in Brazil

As of 2000 adidas-Salomon had 24 main factory suppliers and 1 subcontractor in Brazil.[23] Of these suppliers, 18 supply apparel and 7 supply footwear. The numbers of suppliers and subcontractors are said to be fairly fluid, with a general trend toward consolidation into fewer and larger ones. Three of the footwear suppliers are located in (or in the vicinity of) Franca, a city of about 290,000 in São Paulo state. Franca is one of the principal centers of men's leather dress shoe production in Brazil. Athletic shoes such as those made for adidas-Salomon by Franca area suppliers constitute a relatively small proportion of shoe production in the region. The researchers had the opportunity to visit one of these Franca area suppliers, Dharma-Casual, in early 2002.

During the visit to adidas-Salomon sourcing offices in Franca, the researchers met with a production manager, Volnei Cipriano, and an information technology manager, Marcus Tadeu Ferreira.[24] Cipriano was working as a part-time SoE staff member along with another adidas-Salomon employee who had since been reassigned overseas. Ferreira is currently being trained to be a part-time SoE manager along with Jim Tandy. Cipriano and Ferreira have both worked for adidas-Salomon for about three years.

The Standards of Engagement were initially implemented before either Volnei or Ferreira came to work with adidas-Salomon in Franca, but they both arrived shortly after the implementation began. According to them, the implementation of the SoE among adidas-Salomon suppliers in Franca was described as "not too difficult." Suppliers were not particularly enthusiastic about the program but have been told that they would need to comply with the standards if they wanted to remain an adidas-Salomon supplier. Where investments in new machinery or processes were required, attempts have been made to convince suppliers that these will pay off in terms of increased sales and greater profitability in the long run. Apparently though the results of these efforts have been mixed. According to Nebel there has been considerable difficulty in convincing suppliers to provide adequate ventilation and extraction equipment. The suppliers have also had difficulty in getting workers to use required personal protective equipment. In addition, enforcement by government regulators of requirements pertaining to the use of personal protective equipment is virtually nonexistent. Because compliance with rules on the use of this equipment has been spotty, the adidas-Salomon staff has decided to try a different approach to encourage workers to use these devices. The staff intends to use posters with graphic pictures of workers involved in accidents or suffering illnesses resulting from failure to follow such rules.

The difficulties in convincing suppliers to improve ventilation and extraction and the inconsistent use of personal protective equipment are, of course, related problems. The recommended ventilation and extraction equipment will reduce, but not eliminate, the need for personal protective equipment. Delays in the installation of the recommended equipment compound the problems associated with the inconsistent use of the personal equipment.

Dharma-Casual has its main offices and an adjacent factory in the town of Franca. It has a second factory, the one we visited, located in the neighboring state of Minas Gerais in a small town called Claraval. It is about 15 to 20 minutes away by car from Franca. When asked what the motivation was for locating this factory here, the owners quickly pointed out that there are significant tax advantages to producing in Minas Gerais relative to the neighboring São Paulo state. The proximity of Franca to the Minas Gerais border made the decision to locate there easy.

Dharma-Casual employs approximately 115 workers at the Claraval plant and approximately the same number at the Franca plant. About 60 percent of the workers at the Claraval plant are women, and 40 percent are men. It was said that approximately 50 percent of the workers commute on a company bus, and wage rates are roughly the same as in Franca. Workers make a minimum of R$248 per month (about U.S.$100, approximately 25 percent of the workforce makes that amount), and the most skilled workers, leather cutters, earn R$700–$800 (U.S.$280–$320). The average is about R$450 (U.S.$180) per month. By way of comparison, the minimum wage in Brazil is R$180 (U.S.$72) per month. Workers are paid an hourly wage with various incentives for meeting production targets, attendance standards, and so on. The typical workweek at this plant is 44 hours, with the one and only shift starting at 6:55 A.M. and ending at 4:30 P.M., with a 1-hour break for lunch. Thus, the typical worker earns about U.S.$1 per hour. The hourly labor cost to the employers is approximately twice that, however, as the employer pays about 100 percent of the wages to the government for social security and medical insurance programs.

Dharma-Casual is owned and managed by three brothers who live in Franca and who, like many of the workers at the factory, commute daily to Claraval. Dharma-Casual produces for adidas-Salomon as well as for the company's own local Brazilian brand called Dharma (the company does not supply any other international company however). About 40,000 pairs of athletic shoes are produced per month, comprising about 4 or 5 models. The company also owns a retail chain that sells Dharma shoes and apparel. The plant originally started as a sewing center (or *banca*), providing subcontracted labor to other shoe companies, but it grew to its present size and is now a primary contractor. According to the owners/ managers, the firm does not itself subcontract out any of its work.

The production of athletic shoes consists of four primary tasks: cutting, gluing, sewing, and finishing. Of these tasks, sewing and gluing pose the most hazards from a safety and health perspective. The sewing can be hazardous because of the possibility of a worker getting a finger punctured by a needle or sustaining an eye injury from a needle break. Perhaps even more problematic is the gluing operation. This is because of the toxic substances (solvents) that have historically been used with or contained in the glue, and the pervasiveness of the fumes.

It is clear that there are some real challenges for the implementation of adidas-Salomon's Standards of Engagement at Dharma-Casual. This is a very small plant compared with the Oriental Garment Company apparel plant in Thailand. It is also very small compared with three athletic footwear factories supplying to other brands that have been visited by one of the authors (Wokutch) while taking students to China on study-abroad programs in recent years. Production methods and safety, health, and environment measures seem to lag far behind these other larger factories. Much of the equipment and machines appeared to be old, and the factory work areas were rather dirty and noisy. In the part of the factory in which gluing operations were taking place, the smell of fumes from the glue being used was very strong. It was later explained to the researchers that these fumes contained acetone and methyl ethyl kentone (MEK). It was also noted that workers in this area, especially those who worked directly with the glue in areas scheduled to have a new ventilation/fume extraction system installed, should be wearing masks. Clearly though the fumes from the glue were quite strong throughout this entire work area, and all the workers there would benefit from wearing masks under these circumstances. The use of the masks was, however, inconsistent. We estimated that only about half of the workers in this part of the plant used the protective masks. The use of the ear plugs for hearing protection seemed more extensive, although managers noted that the Brazilian government had recently relaxed regulations on the use of hearing protection.

adidas-Salomon's SoE staff recognizes the problems here and is attempting to address them. According to Nebel the performance of this factory is one of the poorest on the health, safety, and environment dimension in adidas-Salomon's network of suppliers. In 2001 this plant was audited and given a grade of 2 stars for health and safety and 3 stars for labor issues on adidas-Salomon's 5-star scale. According to the adidas-

Salomon rating system, the health and safety score means that the factory has been audited, there are some serous noncompliance issues, there is an action plan in place, the factory is responding to the action plan slowly or with reluctance, and the factory is being monitored on a regular basis.[25] The adidas-Salomon SoE staff members have prioritized action plans for remediation of a number of safety, health, and environmental problems at this plant into three categories:

Priority 1:

A. Use water-based adhesive in assembly and in sole preparation.

B. Identify and replace solvent-based products with non-solvent-based products.

C. Ensure compliance with prohibited substances list.

D. Install exhaust systems for any remaining solvent-based application.

E. Install or maintain dust-extraction systems.

Priority 2:

A. Install needle guards and belt protectors on stitching machines; install belt guards and protective devices and warning signs on other machines.

B. Check electrical wiring and bring into compliance with safety standards.

Priority 3:

A. Bring chemical storage area into compliance.

B. Put into place emergency exits, exit signs, and evacuation plan.

Addressing these safety, health, and environmental problems at Dharma-Casual poses a difficult challenge to adidas-Salomon. According to Nebel, Dharma-Casual had been supplying adidas-Salomon for several years before the enactment of the Standards of Engagement. He noted that the company would not be accepted as a new supplier today because of the inferior safety and health conditions; yet adidas-Salomon feels an obligation to help Dharma-Casual improve conditions because of the historic relationship it has had with the company. The difficult part of this is to exert sufficient pressure on the owners/managers to have them make the necessary changes without pressing so hard that Dharma either gives up trying to improve and quits supplying to adidas-Salomon or is driven into bankruptcy. The practice of prioritizing the changes to focus attention on the most important concerns first is considered an important part of this process.

One of the most important concerns was the discovery of toluene on factory premises at Dharma Casual (priority 1, item C above). Toluene, a carcinogenic substance, is a solvent that was formerly used extensively in the glue used in the manufacture of athletic shoes. However, due to health concerns, the major brands have prohibited its use and have been replacing it with other solvents in their supplier factories. (Solvents are used with rubber to form cement/glue or to clean cement and glue.) According to Nebel the presence of the toluene at a Dharma Casual plant was a cause of serious concern. The amounts of acetone and MEK in glues have also been reduced but, so far, it has not been possible to eliminate them entirely. Thus, ventilation/extraction equipment and personal protection devices are used to limit exposure to these chemicals. However, as noted above, the ventilation/extraction equipment has not yet been completely installed, and the use of personal protection devices is inconsistent.

The owners/managers were asked about the changes in production and the work environment that have resulted from adidas-Salomon's implementation of the SoE. According to them the emphasis on safety, health, and environment has been the biggest change. They noted that, although the Brazilian government has many laws pertaining to these dimensions, they are rarely enforced. No one could recall a government safety and health inspector ever visiting the plant. In contrast, they see adidas-Salomon people four to five times per day. (In the past Nebel has been able to get to this plant only every six months because of visa difficulties that had limited his entry to Brazil to two times per year. However, this visa issue has been resolved, and he expects to visit there more frequently in the future. He also now has two part-time SoE assistants, including Jim Tandy, the manager of adidas-Salomon's Franca office.)

The owners/managers further noted that ensuring worker use of personal protective devices, such as the masks discussed above, has been the most challenging aspect of the SoE program. They complained that disciplining workers who did not comply with these regulations was difficult because of likely union opposition and legal challenges. When asked if it would be possible to discipline or dock the pay of a worker who repeatedly failed to use personal protective equipment when necessary, the answer was a straightforward "no." Instead, they just keep reminding workers of the need to use these devices. adidas-Salomon personnel have not encouraged the use of disciplinary procedures to achieve compliance with requirements regarding the use of personal protective devices for fear that there could be some negative consequences associated with this tactic. Rather, they are now making use of the new graphic pictures/posters to encourage compliance. This is viewed as the most viable interim solution until the engineering solutions alluded to above are fully implemented, that is, providing better extraction/ventilation and moving toward the use of solvents and adhesives that don't pose as many health problems. It is also worth noting that this approach to the problem—trying to make workers use personal protective equipment rather than fixing the underlying problem—may hold appeal to the owners/managers, who may view this as a cheaper alternative than the engineering controls. This approach is consistent with a behavioral approach to occupational safety and health and is open to all of the criticisms that have been raised against that orientation.[26]

One of the major changes in the production system that the SoE have brought about in adidas-Salomon suppliers is the consolidation of operations in first-tier suppliers. Formerly a large part of the stitching operation was subcontracted to sewing centers, or *bancas*. These are often home-based workshops that are inherently difficult to monitor with respect to labor practices. Surveys and interviews of adolescents in Franca schools[27] indicate that much of the child labor that takes place in this community takes place in *bancas*. Indications are that even inspections by the Pro Child Institute (see chap. 11) intended to weed out child labor practices in the shoe industry in Brazil fail to catch most of the child labor that takes place in *bancas*. Other labor practices are equally difficult to monitor there, so the centralization of these activities into regular factories through the SoE improves adidas-Salomon's ability to monitor and control labor practices.

Clearly there are serious concerns regarding safety and health issues at this plant. This may well be atypical. As the reader will recall, according to Gregg Nebel, SoE enforcement has focused more on "grayer" areas of labor compliance, such as rights of association, discrimination, and the "living wage," but at this plant safety and health issues seem to be the concerns. Moreover, there do seem to be some real costs to this supplier associated with compliance with SoE safety and health standards. From a strictly financial standpoint, it is understandable that the owners/managers may prefer to try to have workers wear protective devices rather than make the necessary engineering improvements; this is a cheaper alternative.

As adidas-Salomon is in the process of consolidating production into a smaller number of larger, more-efficient factories, clearly Dharma-Casual is a prime candidate for the reallocation of orders. Another producer with fewer safety and health problems could be found. It will certainly be a challenge for the SoE staff to see whether or not they are able to help bring about sufficient changes in Dharma-Casual to allow it to remain a supplier without violating adidas-Salomon's own standards for suppliers. If Dharma-Casual is unable or unwilling to bring about the prescribed improvements, one might speculate on whether suspending contracts with the company might send a useful message to it, and other suppliers as well, that failure to adhere to SoE standards has serious consequences. One might also speculate about whether adidas-Salomon should bear some of the cost of the safety and health improvements. From a financial resource standpoint, adidas-Salomon would certainly seem to be more capable of bearing additional costs than would this supplier.

ADIDAS-SALOMON—PROGRAM ANALYSES

Program 1: Health, Safety, and Environment Program—Prince of Wales International Business Leaders Forum, Business Links Initiative (Ho Chi Minh City)

Inspiration and Vision Setting: Idea Generation/Inception

The following program is one example of how competitor partnerships can create a better environment for all involved and how commitment to growing the social capital of a country can have resulting benefits to the firms involved. In this phase of program development in a Total Responsibility Management (TRM) approach, the initial idea or *inspiration* is formulated, providing a basis for later determination of values and the ways in which the company engages its stakeholders. In 1990 the Prince of Wales issued an invitation to more than 100 international chief executives from 13 countries to join him in a discussion about the role of businesses as corporate citizens. The discussion resulted in the formation of the Prince of Wales International Business Leaders Forum, a network of senior executives from 30 countries committed to operating responsibly, to seeking innovative partnerships, and to sharing their knowledge and experience of good practice. The mission statement identifies its goals as follows: "To advance education and research in business management with specific reference to the development of corporate social responsibilities and community involvement of industry and commerce."

Identification of the Need for a Comprehensive Joint Program In early 1999 the Pentland Group (retailers of Speedo and LaCoste brands) completed a study and produced a report on the use of hazardous chemicals in the footwear industry in Vietnam. The report concluded that employees were at risk from hazardous chemicals, poor ventilation, inadequate safety equipment, and a lack of training. As a result of this report the U.K. Department for International Development (DfID) partially funded a follow-up project on specific non-MNE-contracting factories, directing that the program cover hazardous chemicals issues as well as general health and safety issues in the footwear production industry. DfID appointed the International Business Leaders Forum (IBLF) to draw up a workable, collaborative action plan to address those issues.

In December 1999 IBLF approached adidas, Nike, and others to help to fund a three-year project—The Vietnam Footwear Industry Business Links Initiative. (See participant list and management structure following this chapter as appendixes 8.1 and 8.2.)[28] Since the factories in need of assistance were those who were not currently engaged in contracts with multinationals (as those were already subject to higher standards and enforcement by the MNEs themselves), including both state-owned and privately owned operations, those became the focus of the IBLF's program plan. Nike, adidas, and the Pentland Group agreed to participate in part to support the general social structure of a country in which they currently had suppliers, but also to create more supplier options with higher standards of HSE to support expanded Vietnamese operations. Moreover, by participating in the project jointly with a number of Vietnamese governmental units, Nike, adidas, and the Pentland Group also benefited from the close working relationships and increased trust that were bound to develop with these units.

The IBLF has long been an advocate of building partnerships to create sustainable development in developing economies. However, these partnerships must be based on standards of good practice for them to have lasting impact. The IBLF has defined these good practice standards as follows:

- Ensuring clear and common goals based on mutual benefit
- Articulating the role of and providing intermediary leadership
- Understanding and consulting with beneficiaries and stakeholders
- Ensuring clarity of roles and responsibilities
- Understanding resource needs and capacities
- Instituting clear communication
- Evaluating and celebrating progress
- Ensuring continuous learning and adaptation[29]

The IBLF played a critical role in ensuring the success of the partnership on these bases.

Motivation for Involvement From adidas's perspective, interest in the project was stimulated by Husselbee's commitment to working toward social sustainability in the countries in which adidas operated. This commitment translated into approval for two days a week input by one adidas representative (in later phases reduced to two days per month). Since the program's inception, that representative has been Niall Middlehurst, adidas's Manager of Health, Safety and Environment for Vietnam. Nike and Pentland contributed financial resources of approximately 25,000 British pounds each and meeting time of its representatives. The British government, through its Department of International Development, contributed 50,000 British pounds. The desired result of the project was to put into place a system for raising the HSE standards in Vietnamese suppliers, overall, and for transferring the management of the program entirely to Vietnamese government departments to ensure greater sustainability. (The program named a Vietnamese Program Director in summer 2001. Since that time, there has been a substantial increase in cooperation and involvement from the Vietnamese partners.) adidas committed to a three-year involvement, working toward this self-sustainability objective by beginning in an active role, then converting to an advisory role before its ultimate anticipated exit.

Establishment and Implementation

The first phase of the project was to learn what the others were doing, and then to identify the nature and extent of the problem in noncontracting factories. To do so, Middlehurst, the IBLF Program Coordinator, and Representatives from the Vietnam Chamber of Commerce and Industry conducted extensive visits to over 40 factories in northern Vietnam chosen at random by geographical area. They made presentations to factory owners about the project and explained the potential benefits of participation. These attempts to involve and gain commitment from key suppliers represent part of the stakeholder engagement process identified above as part of TRM approaches. Middlehurst and others explained that, if HSE in the factory can be improved, there will be fewer accidents, injuries, and fatalities; thus workers will stay longer and there will be less turnover; thus more experienced workers with lower training costs; thus higher productivity and higher quality; thus an increase in income.

Recognizing the financial limitations of the subject factories (recall that these are factories that did not currently have MNE contracts), the objective of the visits was also to identify low-cost solutions for ameliorating the HSE challenges in the factories. When asked about the standards in place at these factories compared with those currently under contract with adidas, Middlehurst explained that the conditions were "much worse than in MNE-contracted factories. It was like HSE standards from the 1920s! Long-term planning just didn't seem to exist." The visitors saw the chemical benzene standing in open cans, with nearby workers exposed to dangerous fumes and the potential for easy spillage; toluene-based substances instead of the now-standard water-based substances; and unsafe, outdated machinery, among other imminently dangerous conditions. The problems cited fell generally into the following categories:

- Fire issues (prevention and control)
- Emergency escape routes
- Handling and use of hazardous substances
- First aid
- Hazards involving cutting machines
- Hazards involving sewing machines (lack of needle/belt guards)
- Finishing areas such as industrial steam irons
- No flammability data on any of the raw materials used

Working with the factory, Middlehurst and others helped to catalog and then prioritize the action items and, as the TRM approach indicates, *integrate* them into practice. "Factory management were keen to join and to begin these pilot projects. No one had previously visited with these factories to highlight a better way of doing things."[30] To the contrary, however, during this early phase of the program, the most resistance came from the Vietnamese government departments, themselves. They failed to speak up during the development of the project, yet later criticized the firms involved for treating the suppliers "like they were working for MNEs" and demanded to be compensated for attending meetings, contrary to the guidelines for participation originally discussed.

Also as part of this early phase, Middlehurst spearheaded an effort to develop supporting documents, standards, and guidelines to be used in moving forward with the program titled the Management Support System (MSS). Included in the appendixes that follow this chapter are the Middlehurst/IBLF-prepared introduction to the training materials for the MSS (appendix 8.3) as well as the introduction to the adidas training materials (appendix 8.4). These materials represent Middlehurst's and the IBLF's effort to create clearer, more transparent, modern, user-friendly standards with guidelines for implementation designed particularly for the issues faced by these suppliers in this industry. The MSS has also been submitted to the Vietnamese authorities for approval as the official HSE documentation for the Vietnamese footwear industry. Training programs using these materials have already begun, and three have taken place in Hanoi, Ho Chi Minh City, and Hai Phong. The most recent training session in Ho Chi Minh City had 47 representatives from local factories, the previous one in Hai Phong had 35, and the next one planned in Hai Phong already has over 30 wanting to attend. The training courses, which will now continue on a monthly basis in the major footwear regions, represent part of the continual improvement and innovation effort.

On the basis of these supporting materials and the results of their visits, the participants identified one factory in which to attempt a pilot project that would assess the effectiveness of their project process. The subject operation was a family-owned factory led by a woman who was extremely interested in the project and willing to participate. Some of the early activities with this factory involved cleaning the factory; painting aisle markers, exit alleys, and storage areas; and physically organizing the operation. These safety-oriented upgrades, though seemingly cosmetic, had the potential of having a significant impact on the workers as well as the plant management, thus increasing the level of receptivity of all parties for later modifications and upgrades.

The second phase of the project is to put this type of action plan into place with additional factories by devising project programs designed to allow them to move toward a more healthy and safe environment for their workers. The program is designed to jointly identify several appropriate high-priority projects from which the factory will choose so that the factory has some amount of self-determination in connection with these efforts. (See Pilot Projects, appendix 8.5.) In general, these factories are anxious to begin the second phase because the program offers them cost-free consulting services, as well as a review, discussion, and report on their own facilities, which has not before been available to them. The least receptive of the factories involved have been the government-owned operations because they have little, if any, discretionary funding for even these low-cost projects.

During this phase program representatives would meet with representatives from each factory to devise action plans for short-term, midterm, and long-term objectives. Examples of short-term projects might include the most visible quick-fix activities such as those mentioned above. Midterm solutions included activities such as installing or improving the guard protections on machines, while long-term plans might include installing or improving the extraction systems for air quality control, new chemical storage facilities, or new containment systems. To fund these projects, the program participants stressed their low-cost nature but also advised the factories to discuss the issues with their customers. They were urged to explain to customers (in a process of continuing commitment to the vision and stakeholder engagement, this time with customers) that they had decided to stop using banned chemicals and to create a safer workplace for their employees.

The third phase of the project will begin as soon as several projects have been completed at various factories. The program envisions sharing sessions in which factories can model their improvements from which other factories can learn and move forward in those areas on their own. Also vital to this phase is the establishment of a train-the-trainer program for steering committee participants, which is critical to the emphasis on continued improvement inherent in TRM approaches. It is expected that Middlehurst will conduct model training programs for the committee participants, who will then be able to train factory representatives, who will then be able to train workers at each factory regarding a variety of HSE topics.

The final phase of the project is to work with regional universities in connection with teaching HSE. Though students take 40 hours on the federal labor code, there is very little, if any, discussion of HSE. The project also seeks links with overseas universities to encourage more practical HSE application in the programs that supply managers and monitors in Vietnam (for instance, most petrochemical engineering programs have no discussion of workplace HSE).

Continued Program Assessment

When asked whether there were "competitive" hurdles to overcome in participating in a partnership with one's direct competitor, Middlehurst responded, "If you're doing this HSE seriously, you care about the issue. You share the information. On HSE issues, there is no competition. We just want to improve HSE standards overall."[31] In fact, as three MNE representatives working with a large number of representatives from other types of entities, Middlehurst and his Nike and Pentland colleagues found it was often necessary for them to work together as a cohesive unit to move forward and to defend each other when needed.

In terms of general program challenges, as a result of training in another language, those involved experienced minor difficulties in translating documents and in trying to simplify concepts to make them understandable to the managers and workers. Both management and workers, however, have found the training sessions to be valuable nonetheless. The grasp of HSE problems was the slightly greater challenge, but time has generally resolved that issue as well. In fact, many of the managers were aware that there were problems but did not have the knowledge or resources to correct them. The visits and basically free HSE consultation by Middlehurst seemed to set them on the right track or gave them ammunition to use against less enthusiastic senior managers.

Moreover, in many developing economies, there is a conflict regarding self-governance when a multinational offers guidance on human rights or safety issues in factories with which it has no financial relationship.[32] (In fact, that latter factor was not always so clear. Middlehurst commented that, as long as he was identified as coming from adidas, he was often viewed first as a potential purchaser. It was critical that he made clear that there was no guarantee of an adidas contract if the supplier chose to make the necessary HSE changes.) To avoid this possible conflict, it was critical for Middlehurst and his colleagues to explain the "why" of each improvement and justify it objectively using indicators that provide a means of assessment rather than relying on a common understanding. In other words, the end results needed to be evidenced rather than simply implied. This same concept of "knowledge as power" played a role in the relationship between the MNEs and the government units involved in the program. "The concept of a partnership really didn't play out for them."

As a result, Middlehurst recommends that the local "national" organizations that are used should be allowed a stronger management role right from the start of the project. There has been a very noticeable change in participation since the change of management from the IBLF to the Vietnamese, not only in connection with the factories but also with the government departments involved. Middlehurst felt that there was initial resentment stemming from a perception that foreigners were being critical of the industry and the Vietnamese legal systems, and that the Vietnamese had no control over what the IBLF program participants did. This perception seems to have lessened at present. One example of this lessening is the fact that the Vietnamese are considering using the material that

Middlehurst wrote as the basis for a national standard document for the industry.

Program 2: Responding to the Challenge of Child Labor in Supplier Factories (Ho Chi Minh City)

Introduction to the Issue

One of the most challenging issues any MNE might face is what to do about child labor found at a supplier or vendor. First, let's be clear about terminology. For purposes of this study, *child labor* refers to paid workers who are under 16 years of age. *Juvenile labor* refers to paid workers between the ages of 16 and 18. *Youth workers* refers to any worker under 18, grouping together the two previous subgroups.[33] The ILO Convention No. 182, against the Worst Forms of Child Labour, came into force on November 19, 2000. That convention defines *child* to be anyone younger than 18 years of age. According to the new ILO estimates, there are some 250 million children 5 to 14 years old who are toiling in economic activity in developing countries, with almost half working on a full-time basis.[34] Even economically developed countries currently employ child and juvenile labor, albeit with restrictions, and so one should carefully review the social and economic structure in which the labor exists. (See chap. 11 for a further discussion of child labor issues.)

While the easy, black-and-white answer may be to rid all factories of all workers under 18 years of age, that is generally not the best answer for the children or the families involved. This is because alternative activities such as full-time education programs or child care are not universally available, forcing these youths to perhaps engage in less desirable, though profitable, activities such as prostitution or drug dealing.[35] Moreover, notwithstanding the possible educational alternatives in some environments, this proposed solution completely ignores the financial effects of terminating the employment of a youth worker. The income generated by the youth worker may, at the very least, assist in supporting that particular youth's fundamental needs (food, clothing, and shelter) and, at the very most, it may be critical in supporting the entire family. The following discussion of the negative impact of current responses to child labor was created by the Indian Consumer Unity & Trust Society (CUTS), which was established in 1983 as a consumer protection organization in Rajasthan, India. Currently they operate out of four centers in India and one in Africa.

In 1995 the United States stopped the import of garments made by children below 15. Bangladesh, one of the world's poorest countries, was the first to be hit. Garment makers had to send home at least 50,000 children that they employed. Families that depended on this source of income from child wage earners were thrown into the streets, exacerbating their poverty and social disintegration and leading to a higher crime rate, child prostitution, and other social consequences. The nation too felt the pinch. For garments account for 55 percent of Bangladesh's export earnings, and it earned $700 million from exports to the United States alone in 1994. Garment makers had agreed to phase out child labor by 1997, but the Washington-based Child Labour Coalition would have none of this. It called for a boycott of Bangladesh garments in the United States.[36] As is evidenced by this one example, an alternative solution other than immediate termination of the relationship between employer and youth worker must be found.

Inspiration and Vision Setting: Idea Generation/Inception

Children Found in Factory adidas found itself facing this particularly challenging dilemma when it performed a first-time audit of a footwear supplier in Vietnam. On her audit of the factory, the auditor found documents that did not seem to make sense and confirmed these inconsistencies through worker interviews. She would ask some of the workers how old they were and would hear an appropriate (i.e., compliant) answer. However, as a follow-up, she would ask the worker what their "animal year" was (a fact known by all Vietnamese in accordance with the Vietnamese zodiac calendar), and they would not be able to respond immediately, without taking time to figure it out. Given this information, the auditor continued her investigation and later identified just under 200 of the factory's 2,000 workers as underage, according to adidas's SoE.

The auditor found both child workers as well as juveniles. Both groups were subject to the same responsibilities, pay, hours, and overtime requirements as other workers, in violation of adidas's SoE. According to the SoE and its Guidelines on Employment Standards, child laborers are not permitted at all; business partners may not employ children who are younger than 15 or who are younger than the age for completing compulsory education in the country of manufacture where such age is higher than 15. adidas also requires that juvenile workers be assigned to age-appropriate, safe duties, with a maximum of seven hours per day with no overtime.[37]

Next Steps After reporting this information, Kitty Potter, adidas's Regional Labour Manager—Asia, realized that the solution was more complicated than simply letting all of these youths leave the workplace. In this *inspiration or vision-setting* situation, however, while the SoE division was contemplating its response, several dozen child workers were immediately terminated, sometimes accompanied by threats should they return, without the knowledge of adidas at the time. adidas SoE staff now knew that something must be done—and quickly—to avoid losing contact with other youth workers, forcing these kids to consider alternatives far worse than the work environment they were made to leave.

Potter and senior adidas production staff immediately told the factory manager that no more youths could be encouraged to leave, under any circumstances. adidas felt incredible pressure to act without delay in establishing some parameters for the situation, even though a more drawn-out process might have resulted in greater buy-in and participation from the factory and a longer consultation period with the youths. adidas contacted an NGO called Verité (a nongovernmental organization that focuses on human rights and standards in global outsourcing) for assistance. Verité recommended a Vietnamese education coordinator. At the same time adidas drafted some basic notices to the children on behalf of the factory. The notices explained that the factory would offer a program of educational classes and vocational training to the workers under 18. The students had to decide whether they would commit to the program. The notice required them to discuss the issue with family members and give their consent to enter into the program. It was clear to the adidas SoE team members that most of the students did not have a full understanding of what was going to happen, and many of them were naturally suspicious.

Possible Solutions? Working with Verité and an education coordinator, adidas was able to develop what later became its global policy for managing similar situations, that is, a global vision:

The supplier meets with the worker and tries to persuade them to go back to school. If the worker agrees to return to school, schooling fees and other costs are paid for by the factory until the worker completes compulsory education. Any continued employment is conditional on enrolling the worker in a work study program of continued education.

The factory continues to pay the average monthly wage for the worker until the worker finishes school. This will make up for any lost income that the worker's family depends on in order to cover the basic needs of the family. The worker is required to provide the personnel manager proof of enrollment in school in order to continue receiving the monthly salary and school payments.

Finally, the factory agrees to provide a job for the worker once the worker has completed compulsory education.[38]

Motivation for Response Part of the motivation behind this standard is that if a supplier chooses to use children as laborers and that supplier is caught, it must pay the children plus send them to school; it is therefore a negative incentive. In implementing this standard, adidas was *integrating* its policies into operating practices with its suppliers. adidas monitors the payments to the youths in both programs to ensure that they all receive payment equal to their average monthly wages over the year preceding the introduction of the program. In the case of juvenile workers who will continue to work on a reduced shift, this has a significant impact since those individuals were originally paid on a piece-rate basis (i.e., based on productivity). The juvenile workers will accordingly produce less since they can work only seven hours a day; yet they will be paid based on their average wage from the previous year during which, of course, they were able to produce more in an eight-hour shift.

For children up to 16 years of age, in cooperation with teachers from the local government schools, the factory put into place a full-day education program with coverage similar to that of local schools. Topics included math, literature, chemistry, physics, biology, and history. Children would arrive and depart from the factory at the same times they originally traveled, but would spend the workday in a large classroom in a space specifically designated for the program by the factory. Preprogram assessments were completed to accurately place each student in an education-appropriate program, and teachers were hired to conduct the classes from a local province.

For juveniles 16 and 17 years old, adidas felt it was important to offer continuing education programs in lifestyle skills subjects, such as computer skills, the Vietnamese Labor Code, the environment, safety (both personal and in the workplace, with a focus on fire safety), AIDS/HIV, sexual education, and hygiene. Not only would these programs assist the juveniles in areas of personal development, but adidas felt that it was necessary to occupy the workers in the afternoons so they wouldn't go find other work in alternate factories, thus subverting the current efforts.

Integration, Establishment, and Implementation

When the program began, 13 students were enrolled in the younger program and 133 students in the juvenile program. As of June 2001, only 56 students remained involved in the program since many had already reached the age of 18. Eleven of these students are younger than 16 (following an academic program equivalent to the 6th, 7th, and 8th grade levels), 43 are juveniles participating in the lifestyle education programs, and two are older workers who have chosen to participate in these latter courses.

It was determined that the education programs would take place at a location right at the factory itself. This would reduce any possible transportation problems in actually going to the program (since the youths could already get to the factory). In addition, by installing the program on-site, adidas was better equipped to monitor the program and the youths' compensation than if the youths attended programs in their communities.

While adidas was of tremendous assistance in the establishment of the programs, themselves, it did not contribute to the programs on a financial level. "We wanted them to know that we believed this was their responsibility and not a 'rescue,'" says Potter. To facilitate payments, and because it was Verité's policy to enter into a contractual relationship with the multinational rather than the factory (to ensure payments and ensure leverage between the MNE and the factory), adidas paid to Verité a quarterly advance for the work anticipated while the factory paid adidas retrospectively on a monthly basis for work performed. Under these arrangements, the risk was carried in full by adidas, but this arrangement also afforded adidas the leverage it needed to ensure compliance by the factory. In the final months of the program, an assessment by another NGO and local Vietnamese researchers will be conducted. The assessment will be fully funded by adidas, but the results of, and any recommendations in, the assessment will be available to all parties involved in the program.

Continued Program Assessment

This was adidas's first experience with child labor of this magnitude. Therefore, there was a great deal of innovation, improvement, and learning that was accomplished in connection with this particular program regarding education programs, juvenile development programs, and the employment of youths. In this situation it was evidently vital to have a program in place as soon as possible to prevent greater harms. However, if adidas and Verité were to begin this process again, both would prefer to have a longer advance time to prepare the program. Under normal circumstances the organizations would have been able to develop a comprehensive needs assessment, to test the participants for appropriate placements, and to develop programming that would meet the needs of the students. Unfortunately, oftentimes it is impossible to plan for these circumstances, as they arise unexpectedly and demand immediate attention and crisis management.

The best method for advance preparation, therefore, is to determine exactly how the firm would respond under this scenario and to have in place as much of the preparation as possible so that it can be activated in a short time span. Under current circumstances adidas and Verité had to "launch and learn" at the same time and only afterward make corrections based on some of the challenges that later arose (see below).

Moreover, one of the indicators, attendance, has been an issue in the programs. The factory experienced some attrition from the program after the students' annual leave time, which one of the supplier's education coordinators explained might be due to the fact that "they're tired of school; they would rather just come back and make money."

Both Potter and Heather White of Verité suggest that, as discussed above, innovation and improvement are possible with more lead time. For example, a program could be designed based on subject demand rather than expert recommendations. In other words, perhaps the prospective students (especially in the juvenile lifestyles program) could be consulted regarding the precise topics of which they seek a greater understanding. In that way, the factory would be providing the educations that these youths want, rather than (or in addition to) that which is determined to be what they should have. For instance, a survey conducted after the program had begun revealed that the two most alluring topics for these older students were family life issues and family planning.

Potter also notes that a greater, more in-depth understanding of each individual youth's family and social situation might have allowed adidas and the factory to have engaged in a more effective, "holistic" approach to each person's particular circumstances. Perhaps by reviewing these circumstances, adidas and the factory could ameliorate some of the pressures that had led to the youth in the workplace in the first place.

There remain other challenges, as well. Students have noted the lack of interactivity in the classes, particularly the afternoon classes for the juvenile workers. These juveniles would have worked a seven-hour shift before coming to class. It is crucial, therefore, that these classes draw the students out through interaction and participatory teaching styles. "They just want to go home," explains Thuy Duong Le, the adidas labor auditor for this supplier. The objective is therefore to marry cultural values with modern, sophisticated teaching methods. In this way the class becomes more attractive, and the students are better able to learn in these circumstances. adidas engaged the services of an additional individual representing Verité named Minh Phuoc to respond to these issues by creating a training program for the teachers involved.

Attendance, however, is a tricky balance. Those in developed countries generally consider the value of any education to be tremendous and, when compensated, the opportunity to go to school in lieu of work to be an easy choice. To the contrary, however, in this situation in Vietnam, many of these students would have preferred to work (or as in the case of the juvenile workers, to work longer hours) and to earn more money than to go to school at all. Unfortunately, there are woefully few examples of peer workers who have received their education and thereby excelled or succeeded in the workplace. Young factory workers in Vietnam do not look to their immediate supervisors or line managers above them and see educated Vietnamese colleagues. Instead, the leadership of these factories, from the president level down to the supervisors and line managers, is foreign-based expatriates. For example, in each of the factories this author visited, the ownership and management rested abroad, either in Taiwan or Korea. Therefore, without internal management programs or leadership training, the Vietnamese youth see no advantage at all in pursuing an education when they could otherwise be earning more money.[39]

Connecting this lack of role models to the attendance issue, the factories need to walk the fine line between requiring the young worker to attend school or lifestyle programs and asking too much of a worker, thereby encouraging that young person to quit and work for a factory that would allow them to work more and not place these demands on them. Consider the impact of this struggle on the education program itself. Testing and grading are not necessarily part of the program because you would not want students to "drop out." The program must be sufficiently interesting to encourage students to remain, even if they foresee no economic benefit from doing so. And, as long as the labor law prohibiting workers under 16 and limiting the hours and types of work for 16- and 17-year-olds is not strictly enforced, these youths *will* have alternative employment to which they can turn.

Finally, both Verité and adidas suggest that the program could be more successful if they would have had the time to involve the factory management in a more significant way from the start. As it was, adidas had no choice but to move quickly and hire outside consultants, who then created a program to implement immediately. Given a longer time frame, factory management would have been able to play a greater role and might thereby have "bought into" the program a bit more from its very inception, as well as been able to sell it a bit more strongly on the factory floor. In so doing, perhaps both adidas and the factory management would have been able to link this program into larger economic initiatives, thus planning for greater self-sustainability.

NOTES

1. Note: adidas-Salomon customarily uses a lower-case "a" to begin its name.

2. http://www.adidas-salomon.com/en/overview/.

3. Hoovers Online, "adidas-Salomon: (Capsule)," http://www.hoovers.com/co/capsule/2/0,2163,92632,00.html.

4. adidas-Salomon, "Overview, History," http://www.adidas-salomon.com/en/overview/.

5. adidas-Salomon, "Overview, History."

6. adidas-Salomon, "Overview, History."

7. adidas-Salomon, "Overview, History."

8. adidas-Salomon, "Clearer: Social and Environmental Report 2001" (Herzogenaurach, Germany: adidas-Salomon, 2000), p. 20.

9. adidas-Salomon, "Our World: Social and Environmental Report 2000" (Herzogenaurach, Germany: adidas-Salomon, 1999), pp. 22–23. These figures are for export production only. Additional factories supply production for sale in local markets only.

10. adidas-Salomon, "Our World," p. 14.

11. adidas-Salomon, "Clearer: Social and Environmental Report 2001," p. 19. Reprinted with permission of adidas-Salomon.

12. The operations department headed by Glenn Bennett, the only American board member, also took a leading role.

13. adidas-Salomon, "Our World," pp. 26–27.

14. Note, these figures are for international sales of adidas products. When production for local markets and production of other brands in the adidas-Salomon group are taken into account there are more suppliers and more countries represented.

15. adidas-Salomon, "Our World."

16. adidas-Salomon, "Our World." and adidas-Salomon, "Clearer: Social and Environmental Report 2001."

17. The first dialogue was held in Hong Kong; the second was held in Washington, D.C., and is discussed in this section in greater detail. The third dialogue was held in Brussels later during the same year. adidas regional head for social and environmental affairs for region Americas, Gregg Nebel, explains that this will be a regular process during their stakeholder reviews that will take place each year.

18. Author Hartman also participated on the invitation of BSR.

19. World Business Council for Sustainable Development, "Capacity Building," http://www.wbcsd.ch/projects/tools_dialogues.htm (accessed 31 July 2002).

20. This was a key concern relative to MNC activity in general raised in a 31 May 2001 meeting with members of the Asia Monitor Resource Council, a group that tracks MNC sourcing activity in Asia.

21. This point was made very strongly in interviews conducted in Bangkok with Phil Robertson of the AFL-CIO (29 November 2001) and Junya Yiprasert (Lek) of the Thai Labour Campaign (30 November 2001).

22. Gregory Schoepfle, U.S. Department of Labor, "Wages, Benefits, Poverty Line, and Meeting Workers' Needs in the Apparel and Footwear Industries of Selected Countries," http://www2.dol.gov/ILAB/reports/oiea/wagestudy/FS-Thailand.htm (accessed 28 July 2002).

23. adidas-Salomon, "Clearer: Social and Environmental Report 2001."

24. The visit to adidas-Salomon offices in Franca was originally scheduled for mid-September 2001, but had to be rescheduled due to the September 11 terrorist attacks. The researchers visited adidas-Salomon offices in Franca during the New Year 2002 holiday season and were therefore unable to meet with the head of the office, Jim Tandy, who was in the United States for the holidays.

25. adidas-Salomon, "Our World," p. 24.

26. For a review of criticisms of behaviorally based occupational safety and health approaches, see Richard E. Wokutch and Craig VanSandt, "The Role of Occupational Health and Safety Management in the United States and Japan: The duPont Model and the Toyota Model," in *Systematic Occupational Health and Safety Management: Perspectives on an international development*, ed. Kaj Frick, Per Langaa Jensen, Michael Quinlan, and Ton Witlhagen (Oxford, U.K.: Elsevier Science, 2000), pp. 367–89.

27. Lawrence French and Richard E. Wokutch, "Child Labor and International Business Ethics: The Case of the Brazilian Shoe Industry," paper presented at the Academy of Management Annual Meeting, Denver, Colo., August 2002.

28. Nike has chosen to play a role in the program as a result of the perceived gap between existing standards of health and safety and industry standards in more developed countries. In conjunction with this external outreach, Nike instituted a program in 1998 titled "Management-Environment-Safety-Health (MESH)," which comprises education workshops and assessment in Vietnam, as

well as Indonesia, Korea, Taiwan, and Thailand. This program is designed to build on its previous SHAPE ("Safety, Health, Attitude of Management, People Investment, Environment") Program.

29. J. Nelson, Prince of Wales Business Leaders Forum, *Business as Partners in Development: Creating Wealth for Countries, Companies and Communities* (London: Prince of Wales Business Leaders Forum, 1996), pp. 275–77. These same types of factors were echoed in a 1999 article by Rosabeth Moss Kanter wherein she discusses six characteristics of successful partnerships: a clear business agenda, strong partners committed to change, investment by both parties, rootedness in the user community, links to other community organizations, and a long-term commitment to sustain and replicate the results. "From Spare Change to Real Change: The Social Sector as Beta Site for Business Innovation," *Harvard Business Review* (May–June 1999): p. 126.

30. Interview by author with Niall Middlehurst, 3 July 2001, Ho Chi Minh City, Vietnam

31. Interview by author with Niall Middlehurst, 3 July 2001, Ho Chi Minh City, Vietnam.

32. On the other hand, Middlehurst notes that some suppliers immediately saw this project as an opportunity for free consulting services and welcomed any and all suggestions from the project participants.

33. The Global Reporting Initiative uses the term *young workers* and defines it as "a person who is above the applicable minimum working age and younger than 18 years of age." Global Reporting Initiative, Child Labour Protocol, Draft for Public Comment (17 May 2002).

34. Kebebew Ashagrie, "Statistics on Working Children and Hazardous Child Labor in Brief" (Geneva: ILO, 1998), http://www.ilo.org/public/english/standards/ipec/simpoc/stats/child/stats.htm (accessed 15 July 2002).

35. However, some advocacy groups fail to consider all perspectives. For example, the Global Reporting Initiative's discussion on its Child Labour Indicators fails to take into account the impact of the termination of children beyond their removal from the workplace.

36. CUTS-India, "Textiles and Clothing—Who Gains, Who Loses, and Why!" http://www.cuts-india.org/1997–5.htm (May 1997) (accessed 15 July 2002).

37. adidas-Salomon, "Guidelines on Employment Standards," (2001), part 2, chapter 3, p. 1–8.

38. adidas-Salomon, "Guidelines on Employment Standards," p. 5.

39. These same circumstances also provide no incentive for the factory to supply additional education or management or leadership training, since the Vietnamese workers are not expected to manage the factory.

APPENDIX 8.1

Vietnam Footwear Industry Business Links Initiative— Participant List

ActionAid Vietnam

adidas-Salomon

Department for International Development—U.K. Government

Directorate for Standards and Quality

Environmental Resources Management

Friedrich Ebert Stiftung

Institute for Environmental Research—Hanoi Polytechnics University

International Federation of Red Cross and Red Crescent Societies

International Finance Corp.

Mekong Project Development Facility

Ministry of Health

Ministry of Industry

Ministry of Labour Invalids and Social Affairs

Ministry of Planning and Investment

Ministry of Science, Technology and Environment—Directorate for Standards and Quality

Ministry of Science, Technology and Environment—STAMEQ Vietnam Standard Centre

Ministry of Science, Technology and Environment—Vietnam Standards Institute

Ministry of Trade

National Institute of Labour Protection

National Institute of Occupational & Environmental Health

National Office for Appraisal of Technology and Environment of Investment Projects

Nike, Inc.

Pentland Group PLC

Prince of Wales Business Leaders Forum

SGS Vietnam Ltd.

Vietnam Chamber of Commerce and Industry

Vietnam General Confederation of Labour

Vietnam Leather and Footwear Association

Vietnam National Leather and Footwear Association

Source: adidas-Salomon, reprinted with permission.

APPENDIX 8.2

Vietnam Footwear Industry Business Links Initiative— Management Structure

VBLI	Vietnam Footwear Industry Business Links Initiative and the Confirmed Action Programme
DEFINITIONS	
Participating Organizations:	Organizations who agreed to support BLI
IBLF	Prince of Wales International Business Leaders Forum
VCCI	Vietnam Chamber of Commerce and Industry

STRUCTURE

Steering Committee	The Steering Committee shall monitor the implementation of the Programme and review the reports from the Programme Director. Members are appointed by the participating organization they are representing. The Steering Committee is chaired by the VCCI.
Management Committee	The Management Committee shall act as a regular liaison with the Programme Director and VCCI. Its members are nominated by the Steering Committee.

Programme Director

The Programme Director shall be responsible for the overall management of the Programme, reporting to the Steering Committee. The Programme Director will be appointed by the Management Committee.

Advisory Groups

The Advisory Groups shall assist the Programme Director with the various aspects of the Programme. The members shall be appointed by the Programme Director in consultation with the Management Committee and selected from Participating Organizations and third parties. The Programme Director shall chair the meetings.

Special Committees

The Special Committees may be required to deal with or advise on particular aspects of the Programme from time to time. They will be temporary and will be dissolved when they have served their purpose. Special Committees will be established by the Programme Director in consultation with the Management Committee and where relevant with Advisory Groups.

Financial Management

The IBLF shall keep all funds and collect all monies on behalf of the VBLI. The IBLF shall disburse funds to the Programme Director based on budgets submitted to and approved by the IBLF. The financial arrangements of the Programme will be audited and financial statements will be submitted to the Steering Committee at each of its meetings.

APPENDIX 8.3

Training Materials for the Management Support System

VIETNAM FOOTWEAR INDUSTRY BUSINESS LINKS INITIATIVE MANAGEMENT SUPPORT SYSTEM

INTRODUCTION TO HEALTH AND SAFETY

Implementing International Health and Safety standards demonstrated a company's commitment to a safe working environment and to protecting employees against injuries at work. In the Footwear Industry, one of the more sensitive areas is Chemical Safety, including the selection, storage, handling, use and disposal of chemicals used to manufacture footwear and this area was chosen as the fundamental cornerstone in improving worker safety.

However the Vietnam Footwear Industry—Business Links Initiative has recognized that there are other as vital concerns and has concentrated efforts on including international best practise in regards to the reduction of noise, fumes and dust, hence providing a healthier and safer environment for workers in the footwear industry.

This Management Support System has been developed as a compilation of International Best Practises to address these safety concerns and has been reviewed by relevant Vietnamese government agencies. It is not designed as scripture, but is designed to provide Management in the Vietnam Footwear Industry with practical tools that can be implemented and further developed to meet the national and international growing concerns in regards to worker safety in the Footwear Industry and to comply with National Legislation.

In brief the Management Support System will cover the following areas:

- Occupational Health and Safety (OHS) Management
- Hazardous Substances at Work
- First Aid at Work
- Material Safety Data Sheets
- Machinery Guarding
- Safety Signs
- OHS Training
- Waste Management
- Sanitation & Hygiene
- Storage of Hazardous Chemicals
- Compressed Gases
- Compressed Air Systems
- Housekeeping
- Warehouses and Materials Storage
- Overview of National Legislation

GLOBALIZATION AND THE EXPECTATIONS FOR HEALTH AND SAFETY

Today, as never before, customers are coming under pressure to assure the products they purchase from Vietnam are not only of suitable quality but also manufactured in a socially responsible environment. An environment that ensures issues such as worker health and safety are paramount and the rights of the workers are protected.

The challenges of globalisation include our customers managing their public image as an asset that must be developed and protected to the maximum and suppliers to these companies are expected to adopt a more systematic approach to health and safety as part of the global Social Accountability.

Vietnamese suppliers that accept the challenges of globalisation will be in a much stronger position and will thrive and prosper in the competitive world of international trade.

But business practice and supply chain issues—whether in the developing or developed world—have the potential to undermine consumer confidence in a company and damage brand credibility. Effective health and safety practices by suppliers are a signal to the end consumer that your business is taking health and safety obligations seriously.

THE BENEFITS FROM IMPLEMENTING THE HEALTH AND SAFETY MANAGEMENT SUPPORT SYSTEM

The Management Support System is aimed at the reduction and prevention of accidents and accident-related loss of lives, equipment and time. It focused company management on its processes, practices, materials and products. It will also:

• Support a company in identifying regulatory requirements for compliance with legislation
• Help to identify hazards and manage risks
• Enhance the overall appearance of health and safety issues within the company
• Provide the framework for training and foster teamwork through improved communication on all levels of the company, with relevant business partners and third parties.

The Management Support System will also be a platform from which a company can move to certification of their Health and Safety Management System to international standards such as OHSAS 18001. It will also help companies to save money, maintain a good reputation and be in a position to secure their share of international and domestic contracts.

Other benefits from implementing a systematic approach to health and safety include:

• Regulators will recognize the implementation of this support system as a commitment to safe working conditions and to continuous improvement.
• Acts as a promotional tool: healthier and safer operations have an obvious impact on the quality and reliability of suppliers.
• Acts as a potential basis for attracting more investors and proving due diligence to the marketplace as a whole.
• Improves management controls through implementing a documented system that is auditable.

IMPLEMENTING THE HEALTH AND SAFETY MANAGEMENT SUPPORT SYSTEM

The implementation of the Health and Safety Management Support System begins with senior management's commitment and support for the Health and Safety Management Support System and the appointment of a person with the overall responsibility for the development of the Health and Safety Management Support System will be required. This person should preferably become the Health and Safety Management Representative" and will be the person to oversee the development and implementation of the Health and Safety Management System.

Appraisal and Planning

The company will firstly need to establish the scope of the project, as in what areas of the operations will be covered by the Health and Safety Management System and identify the business process within the proposed project. A comparison of current practices then needs to be done to the appropriate sections of the Management Support System and Legislation.

Results of the comparison should be carefully documented and should highlight deficiencies in terms of the areas that need further development, and additional procedures and controls required. From these results, develop an action plan. Define which areas of the Management Support System will be implemented first, include time-scales, responsibilities and actions to be carried out. Identify resource requirements including the people and skills required for the development of the Health and Safety Management System and report the findings to senior management to gain their commitment to the project.

Without an implementation action plan, particularly without set time-scales, the development process could drift aimlessly from month to month with no sense of purpose or targets to achieve.

You may wish to consider setting up a Health and Safety Management System Committee with representatives of departments concerned with the Health and Safety Management System. A committee approach has some distinct advantages, namely each member can be assigned one or more of the specific tasks required in the development and implementation of your Health and Safety Management System, hence spreading the workload. You will also find a greater consensus of opinion can be obtained and each member normally provides a sense of ownership on behalf of his or her department.

Documenting the System

The development of your Health and Safety Management System is the actual creation of the forms and, where needed, procedures. In this process you will need to document and circulate a Health and Safety Management Policy and chart and define organizational responsibilities in regards to the Health and Safety Management System.

You will need to draft and circulate your developing documentation and begin to develop any required procedures or changes to working practices. Some of the development tasks may be delegated by the committee to those with line responsibilities; however, the committee must ensure that these tasks are accomplished.

If the development of a Health and Safety Management System is to be successful, it must:

- Build on the good parts of your existing system.
- Begin with an easier or defined area, perhaps the chemical store.
- Aim to achieve compliance with a minimum of documentation.
- Ensure that responsibilities and actions are clearly identified.
- Ensure that the system complies to the legislation and suits your company and its business processes.

Operational Implementation

The implementation of your Health and Safety Management System is the actual operational development or implementation of the Health and Safety Management System. The implementation may overlap with the actual development of the Health and Safety Management System. Whatever happens, you must ensure that staff are fully involved in the implementation process.

All employees concerned with the Health and Safety Management System should be made aware of the development program and what their contribution to this and the Health and Safety Management System will be. It is a good idea to hold a series of staff awareness seminars, preferably on a departmental basis to discuss and explain the purpose of establishing a formal Health and Safety Management System, its benefits to the organization and to the employees. You need to confirm senior management's policies and commitment, the Health and Safety Management System development program and their involvement. Also, it is a good idea to overview the changing requirements to their particular tasks.

The awareness sessions are good opportunities to obtain individual contributions and are essential in eliminating fears and misunderstandings.

During this operational implementation, it is a good idea to give new or modified procedures, controls or associated forms a trial run for specific periods, followed by a formal review and feedback to the committee.

Remember, the best procedures are those which are followed by habit; therefore, the sooner these are implemented the better. There will of course be some resistance but provided the procedure, forms, etc. are not "over the top" and good sound reasons can be given as to why they are needed, they will in time be accepted.

Some of the major sources of difficulty in the implementation of a Health and Safety Management System that you should be aware of include:

- Inadequate or insufficient documentation and records.
- Inadequate training of management and employees.
- Lack of a written Health and Safety Management Policy.
- Inadequate or no systematic management review of the Health and Safety Management System.

- Lack of formal and complete corrective and preventive action procedures.
- Poor planning of the system and its implementation.
- No monitoring and review process and no responsibilities for Health and Safety Management assigned.

AFTER IMPLEMENTATION

After the implementation you need to begin a periodic assessment to ensure that the procedures, processes and forms that you have developed and implemented are in fact being followed. There will not be any benefits in implementing your Health and Safety Management System if management and staff are not following it.

The Health and Safety Management Representative or Trained Auditors must conduct regular reviews to ensure that your Health and Safety Management System is being followed and where necessary update procedures, processes and forms in accordance with your changing business needs and local legislation or international best practices.

Source: adidas-Salomon, reprinted with permission.

APPENDIX 8.4

Introduction to the adidas Training Materials

SAFETY FOR MANAGERS
INTRODUCTION

As a manager or supervisor you should ensure that the following tasks are carried out.

You may do them all yourself or delegate the tasks where appropriate.

- Provide written, up-to-date health and safety policy.
- Carry out risk assessments, and record the main findings and your arrangements for health and safety.
- Display current copies of any certificates or inspections reports that may be required by local legislation or regulations.
- Display appropriate health and safety notices, posters or information for employees.
- Notify the relevant authorities of any specific injuries, illness or disease.
- Consult with other managers, supervisors, union representatives and employees on health and safety issues.

Good health and safety policy starts the commitment and co-operation of people, and good examples and leadership by managers and supervisors generate that initially.

Managers and supervisors have a responsibility to their company, employees, shareholders and customers to manage *safely*. Failure to do so carries consequences and penalties, as well as in some cases legal fines and even imprisonment in some instances. Poor health and safety can result in accidents and injuries, lower production, increased sickness and absenteeism and costly breakages and mistakes.

Although at first it may seem daunting, implementing health and safety is actually quite straightforward and mainly common sense that can be summarized in four simple steps.

- Know and understand your safety policy and procedures;
- Plan ways to reduce risk and remove hazards;
- Organise people and resources to create a safe working environment and safe systems of work.
- Measure your safety performance by statistics and discussions with employees. Investigate accidents fully.

SET YOUR POLICY

Your health and safety policy should be a written statement and should include the key elements listed below. It should also include any specific preventative measures needed and any individual responsibilities.

The key elements are:

- Identifying hazards (something with the potential to cause harm);
- Reducing risks (the chance of that harm happening);
- Deciding what precautions can be taken;
- Putting procedures and controls in place.

The same types of mistakes that can cause injuries and illness can also cause property damage, interrupt production and generally have a detrimental effect on your business. Because of this, you should aim to control all accidental losses by identifying hazards, assessing the associated risks and by deciding what precautions are needed, implementing them and checking their effectiveness.

Your health and safety policy should influence all activities of your company including the:

- Staff selection;
- Equipment and material selection and purchasing;
- Design of work areas;
- Work practices and methods.

Having a written statement of your health and safety policy, and its associated organization, implementation and monitoring arrangements, shows your staff and your customers that hazards have been identified, risks assessed, and the means to either eliminate or control the risks implemented.

It also shows your employees, customers and suppliers that the management of health and safety is considered to be as important as any of the company's other business functions.

Source: Niall Middlehurst, adidas-Salomon, reprinted with permission.

APPENDIX 8.5

Vietnam Footwear Industry Business Links Initiative— Pilot Projects

Project	Factories										
Location	Hanoi	Hanoi	Hai Phong	Hai Phong	Da Nang	Ho Chi Minh City	HCMC	HCMC	HCMC	Binh Duong Province	
Project	Thang Long Shoes	Joint Stock Co.: Nam Thang	Thanh Hung Co.	Hai Phong Leather & Footwear Co.	Hunexco	Tan Binh Import Expert Corp.	Cong Ty 32 (ASECO)	Fulam	Thein Loc Shoes Co., Ltd.	Thai Binh Co.	**Completion Date**
General HSE			X					X			
Chemical Handling				X			X	X		X	
Chemical Information				X	X		X	X		X	
Chemical Labeling				X	X		X			X	
Chemical Storage				X	X	X	X	X			
Chemical Training				X	X					X	
Color Coding											
Dust Control	X										
Electrical			X				X				
Emergency/Fire/Evacuation					X	X					
First Aid			X								
Health Survey Statistics						X			X		
Housekeeping			X								
HSE Signs			X			X					
LEV Systems				X					X		
Machinery Guarding	X						X				
Noise											
PPE											
Sanitation/ Hygiene			X								
Warehouse, Materials Storage											
	July 2000		Sept. 2000		Sept. 2000	Sept. 2000	Sept. 2000			Sept. 2000	

Source: adidas-Salomon, reprinted with permission.

CHAPTER 9

Levi Strauss & Co.: Implementation of Global Sourcing and Operating Guidelines in Latin America

Tara J. Radin

In 1991, Levi Strauss & Co. (LS&CO) became the first multinational enterprise (MNE) to establish comprehensive global sourcing and operating guidelines, the Terms of Engagement (ToE).[1] During the past decade LS&CO has influenced international labor practices by enforcing compliance with these guidelines around the world. In Latin America, for example, LS&CO has developed a number of positive relationships with sourcing partners who demonstrate how the ToE influence their treatment of workers, in creating change (Mexico), in influencing value-based management from the ground up (El Salvador), in supporting continuous improvement (Mexico), and in sustaining a competitive advantage (Guatemala). The case also describes LS&CO's other efforts to improve global labor practices, such as through government advocacy and sourcing grants.

LS&CO, creator of "blue jeans," has demonstrated that it is also creative in labor practices. In enforcing the ToE and demonstrating that they are more than words on paper, LS&CO has helped to ignite ripples of change in international labor practices. LS&CO has both influenced the mind-sets of sourcing partners to prompt creation of initiatives that respect workers, and has encouraged other companies to establish codes and global labor standards.

This case underscores the influence of sourcing guidelines in shaping supplier behavior. Each of the contractors described reflects a different dimension of the implementation of the ToE: identifying where values are needed in a formerly agnostic organization, assisting in developing value-based systems and procedures from the ground up in a nascent organization, supporting programs to promote growth for a midsized organization, and creating a sustainable competitive advantage for a mature organization endeavoring to compete globally. This case also describes LS&CO's other efforts to improve working conditions around the world, such as its government advocacy and sourcing grants programs.

APPAREL AND FOOTWEAR INDUSTRIES[2]

The apparel and footwear industries now span the globe, with centralized operations in Asia and Latin America, among other locations. A number of companies, such as adidas-Salomon and Nike, maintain a strong presence in Asia. MNEs such as LS&CO have also developed a strong presence in Latin America. Both regions are preferable to the United States as a result of wage, benefits, and regulatory considerations. A number of governments in Latin America provide tax and tariff incentives to MNEs and outsourcing partners. El Salvador, for example, has created "free zones," which are free from local taxes and government restrictions to attract foreign investment.

During recent decades, the apparel and footwear industries have become susceptible to "sweatshop" labor conditions.[3] While some companies have taken gross advantage of local labor conditions, the entire industry now operates under the taint that belongs primarily to those culprits.[4] A number of companies have traditionally respected workers.[5] Many employers have treated workers in developing countries with respect by offering reasonable compensation and benefits, and they have still managed to achieve significant cost savings.[6]

In the highly saturated apparel and footwear markets, the challenge of overcoming intense competition and low profit margins has largely been accomplished by reducing overhead costs. As more production takes place in developing and emerging countries, more workers are involved, which increases the magnitude of the negative effects. The situation is complicated by the practice of outsourcing. Instead of operating their own plants in developing and emerging countries, many manufacturers choose to engage in outsourcing relationships with local contractors. Local contractors are not always inherently in touch with the same values that guide business practices in developed countries.[7] This imposes on the manufacturers the burden of training those contractors and monitoring their efforts. Manufacturers who do not pay careful enough attention to working conditions in their contractors' factories have found that they are held accountable for contractors' wrongdoing.[8]

Costs of Outsourcing

The trend toward outsourcing has resulted in a 30 percent decline in the number of clothing workers employed in the United States between the mid-1970s and the early 1990s.[9] During that time the market share of imported clothing climbed from 28 percent to 66 percent.[10] Such staggering figures have prompted considerable criticism that the industry is abandoning its domestic employees and has given rise to assumptions that manufacturers must be engaging in unethical business practices to achieve reported cost savings.[11]

While the practice of outsourcing labor has arguably had a negative impact on the shrinking American apparel manufacturing industry, it has nevertheless made a clear positive contribution to the global workplace, where an increasing number of laborers, particularly in developing or emerging countries, are finding suitable jobs where few or none previously existed.[12]

LS&CO has recently become a prominent player in this debate. The company has been outsourcing operations for more than 15 years, but it has only recently dramatically shifted the balance between domestic and outsourced operations. A longtime mainstay in the San Francisco area, LS&CO announced in April 2002 its decision to shut down six domestic manufacturing plants and cut back 3,300 jobs in favor of moving operations to contractor facilities in other countries, including Latin America.[13]

Latin America

As manufacturers shut plants down and relocate or outsource, significant questions remain as to the impact on the domestic labor pool in the United States and the perpetuation of potentially exploitative measures against laborers in the maquiladoras in Latin America.

Maquiladora, from the Spanish word *multure* (fee for grain), is the term originally used to refer to assembly plants in Mexico.[14] Although a large amount of production has been outsourced to Asia as a result of the skilled worker population available at extremely low costs, a significant amount of production is also sourced to contractors in Latin America, beginning with the birth of the maquiladoras in Mexico in 1965, when duty-free export assembly operations first began to become popular.[15] In 20 years maquiladoras turned a closed society into the 13th largest exporter in the world.[16] They began as low-end garment or small-appliance assembly outfits, but have developed into high-end manufacturers.[17] In 2001 maquiladoras shipped goods worth $76.8 billion. This constituted more than half of Mexico's total merchandise exports.[18] Growth has stalled, though, both because of the slowdown in the United States following September 11, 2001,[19] and the fact that many MNEs have been stripped of the benefits of doing business in Mexico.[20] In 2001 alone 350 maquiladoras were closed.[21]

While *maquiladora* refers generally to manufacturing facilities for items for export to be sold in foreign markets, the connotation of the word maquiladora is often synonymous with "sweatshop."[22] It is often assumed that working conditions in maquiladoras must be poor to provide manufacturers with enticing cost savings.

The term maquiladora was initially used to describe manufacturing plants on or near the border between Mexico and the United States. These plants were offered tariff breaks on items imported for assembly before being sold in foreign markets to attract foreign business.[23] During recent years, particularly as other Latin American countries have attempted to attract foreign investment, the term has been extended to describe similar operations throughout Latin America and sometimes in Asia as well.

It is important to view the maquiladoras in the distinct cultural context in which they emerged. A product of the traditionally "machismo," male-dominated Latin American society, the maquiladoras have historically profited through the employment and exploitation of women and child laborers. These benefits enjoyed by MNEs are often tempered by poor conditions, hours that range from 50 to 80 hours per week and wages ranging from \$.56 to \$.77 per hour in plants such as the Doall maquiladora plant in El Salvador.[24]

A lack of parity exists between the role of women in maquiladoras, where they are frequently mistreated, and their role at home. Women are deprived of many of the advantages that men enjoy.[25] It is more difficult for women to obtain jobs or education to prepare them for desirable jobs. At the same time, the family is clearly maternalistic. Mothers are revered and respected.[26] In fact, in Guatemala, Koramsa, one of the largest textile factories in the region, hosts a Mother's Day celebration every year.[27]

Korean Presence in Latin America

Culture plays a prominent role in international labor practices. In Asia, for example, many practices are culturally embedded. MNEs have also confronted cultural differences in Latin America. Koreans, for example, have developed a controversial presence, and have acquired a reputation for operating factories with poor working conditions, including long hours, physical abuse, and discrimination. Korean maquiladora owners and operators have long been perceived to maintain the poorest working conditions and longest hours and are known to resort to physical abuse and discrimination.[28]

This reputation is fueled by conflicting cultural perspectives on work and workplace customs. An additional reluctance by Korean managers to adapt practices and policies to local work customs, or even allow locals to have involvement in management decision-making processes, has exacerbated the situation. Instead of evaluating methodologies and management relationships that have worked on a localized level, Korean operators continue to insist on imposing their own workplace customs.[29]

A Mexican manager noted, "We have neither authority nor respect as managers. Decisions have already been made at the top management level. We only know what to do to meet the goal, but not why we are doing it. . . . Mexican managers know better how to control their own employees and manage them. Korean managers treat us not as managers but as subordinates."[30]

Such treatment is not the sole province of the Koreans, but they are identified by workers and competitors as prone to mistreating workers.[31] A number of factories in Guatemala have closed to prevent union organization; many of these factories were Korean.[32] The commonly held perceptions of Korean workplaces has led the EU to adopt a resolution condemning the exploitation of workers by Koreans.[33]

Role of NGOs

Nongovernmental organizations (NGOs) have traditionally endured antagonistic relationships with MNEs. Thomas Donaldson nevertheless argues that the tension between NGOs and companies is likely to prove transient. He notes a study conducted by Georges Enderle and Glen Peters that reveals that NGOs are optimistic about the future of their relationship with MNEs. While only 10 percent of NGOs view relationships currently as "cooperative," nearly 60 percent anticipate that future relationships will be cooperative.[34]

White House Apparel Industry Partnership

The American retail markets for apparel and footwear remained relatively unchallenged by external critics until the early 1990s, when they were bombarded with accusations of routine exposure of foreign workers to unfair treatment, including unsanitary and unsafe working conditions, low wages, and long hours. Public outcries against such conditions prompted political action.

In 1996 then-president Bill Clinton invited a group of leading apparel manufacturers, labor associations, and independent human rights organizations to form the White House Apparel Industry Partnership in an attempt to address growing global concerns with sweatshop labor. During the next two years they endeavored to strike an accord that would put guidelines in place to regulate and monitor workplace conditions.

The White House Apparel Industry Partnership agreement was ultimately conceived and signed in November 1998, but it was greeted by only a lukewarm reception. It ended up polarizing the public, in that it divided the concerned population into one group who supported and signed the pact and championed it as a step in the right direction[35] and another group who refused to endorse it and instead criticized it for its failure to address every critical issue.[36] Even though the groups shared similar concerns, they failed to agree on appropriate mechanisms for resolving them.

Fair Labor Association

International labor practices is becoming an important item on the public agenda. This has been evidenced by the emergence of organizations such as the Fair Labor Association (FLA), an NGO comprised of major manufacturers and retailers, labor and human rights groups, and universities, with an underlying goal of protecting workers' rights through the institutionalization of a uniform code of workplace regulations, conduct, and monitoring procedures.

The FLA was convened by then-president Clinton in the late 1990s.[37] Its influence today encompasses 3,000 firms in 80 countries, with sales totaling $30 billion through the membership of adidas-Salomon, Eddie Bauer, GEAR for Sports, Jostens, Joy Athletic, Liz Claiborne, LS&CO,[38] Nike, Patagonia, Phillips-Van Heusen Corp., Polo Ralph Lauren Corp., and Reebok International.[39]

The FLA has multiple functions. One contribution of the organization has been a code of conduct to guide member companies.[40] In addition, the FLA has created a process through which independent monitors could be accredited, and it soon approved its first external monitor, Verité, based in Amherst, Massachusetts, to monitor factories in 14 countries.[41] According to then-president Clinton, such initiatives "put a more human face on the global economy by protecting workers, children, and families from abusive and unfair labor practices."[42] He pledged $750,000 to the FLA on behalf of the United States.[43]

Although the FLA has developed a strong international presence, the organization has been criticized as ineffective. It has traditionally depended largely on internal monitoring and has required only "independent external monitors accredited by the the FLA to conduct periodic inspections of 30 percent of the company's applicable facilities."[44] The requirement of members to abide by local "minimum wage laws,"[45] as opposed to mandating a "cost of living" wage, also seemingly leaves the door open for worker exploitation, in that minimum wage requirements in many Latin American countries do not sufficiently cover a laborer's basic living needs.[46] Additional skepticism has been raised about the FLA being funded by the very corporations who belong to the organization.[47] Further, the organization has displayed little openness, accountability, or transparency. In its first five years of existence, not a single report—negative, positive, or neutral—was published by the FLA regarding monitoring.[48]

Although criticism of the organization continues, the FLA has acquired a definite presence in the global marketplace, and it serves to connect MNEs, NGOs, and other interested groups. Its reach extends beyond the apparel and footwear industries and now includes universities, monitors, and other industries.[49] In addition, the FLA has recently expanded its role in the monitoring process.[50] On April 9, 2002, the organization adjusted its structure to involve itself in the monitoring process, to mandate external monitoring, and to compel disclosure.[51]

Worker Rights Consortium

Concerns about the efficacy of the FLA have manifested themselves in the public spectrum through vehicles such as the Worker Rights Consortium (WRC), an NGO that unites efforts of college and university administrations, students, and labor rights experts to assist in the enforcement of manufacturing codes of conduct designed by colleges and universities.[52] The codes are designed to ensure that any factories used to produce clothing and goods for the schools respect basic workers' rights.[53]

Attempting to serve as an independent monitor and watchdog, the WRC has not only established its own factory assessment program, but has also pressured the FLA and non-FLA members to make appropriate improvements by threatening to cancel contracts and conduct boycotts. This was most recently accomplished in a public battle between Ohio State University, the University of Iowa, and other schools against New Era Cap Company, after the WRC released a report that detailed allegations of human rights violations in the PT Dada factory in Indonesia that included "physical, sexual, and racial harassment, and discriminatory religious practices. The factory also allegedly forced employees to work without pay and placed workers who spoke up against such abuses in solitary confinement."[54] The result has led New Era to pledge to make changes, beginning with the ratification of a new contract with the Communications Workers of America Union, to ensure that specific guidelines and standards are followed in regard to health, safety, wages, productivity, and absenteeism.[55]

Looking Forward

Abundant criticism targets MNEs that commit harm, but there is little notice of companies who engage in fair labor practices and contribute positively to the global workplace. Most MNEs have adopted codes and instituted processes and procedures that protect workers' rights. While they do so to varying degrees, more and more companies are realizing the importance of recognizing basic rights—not just in the United States but in developing and emerging countries as well. LS&CO illustrates the positive role MNEs can play in influencing international labor practices.

LS&CO CORPORATE ENVIRONMENT

The year 2003 will mark 150 years in business for LS&CO. Levi Strauss first opened a dry-goods house in San Francisco, California, in 1853 as a branch of his brother's New York operation. Strauss spent the next 20 years developing a prosperous business as he made a name for himself as both a respected businessman and a concerned philanthropist. Jacob Davis, a customer, created a product—a type of riveted pants—that he was anxious to sell. Concerned about protecting his creation, he recognized that he needed a business partner, and so he approached Strauss. They applied for a patent together and received it on May 20, 1873–considered the "birthday" of blue jeans.[56] LS&CO has been selling jeans, in addition to other clothing merchandise, ever since.[57]

With worldwide sales greater than $4 billion in 2001, LS&CO, a privately held business, stands among the world's largest brand-name apparel manufacturers.[58] The company has remained family-owned since its founding, except for a brief period in 1971 when LS&CO went public. Under the leadership of Robert Haas, CEO from 1984 to 1999, LS&CO went private again in 1985.[59]

LS&CO has a significant global presence, with sales in more than 100 countries. The Levi's® trademark is registered in 160 countries.[60] Levi Strauss—the Americas (LSA) accounted for 67 percent of worldwide sales in 2001.[61] LS&CO employs approximately 15,200 workers worldwide, with 1,400 people based at its headquarters in San Francisco.[62]

The past several years have witnessed a significant downturn in the apparel market, particularly in the jeans and casual pants market. LS&CO has felt this downturn along with many other companies, with sales still sliding.[63] Although LS&CO remains third in the apparel market,[64] sales have been on a steady decline since the mid-1990s, when LS&CO surpassed $7 billion.[65]

LS&CO Values

Despite falling sales, LS&CO remains committed to its underlying values. In fact, in the 2001 annual report, President and CEO Philip A. Marineau reiterated the company's commitment and assured the public that LS&CO's success will always be connected to its values, as illustrated through "The LS&CO Way," which has been distributed to all employees and was included in the company's 2001 annual report (figure 9.1).

Values have traditionally played a central role at LS&CO. In fact, the company has long been considered to operate according to a multi-stakeholder approach.[66] Through its four core values—Empathy, Originality, Integrity, and Courage—LS&CO has consistently endeavored to balance stakeholders' concerns with profit generation in furtherance of its vision:

People love our clothes and trust our company.
We will market the most appealing and widely worn casual clothing in the world.
We will clothe the world.[67]

LS&CO has received criticism for paying too much attention to values.[68] Even in a financially weakened position, the company has refused to sacrifice standards, even though its reluctance to globalize aggressively has placed it at a competitive disadvantage against other MNEs whose standards have not prevented them from taking advantage of overseas opportunities. Most analysts do not attribute LS&CO's financial troubles to its value-based management. On the contrary, the "spiraling" marketshare and sales slump are more often attributed to the company's complacency.[69] What LS&CO needs is to breathe life back into its "tired" brands.[70] If product innovations had matched the creativity and determinedness of

Figure 9.1
The LS&CO Way

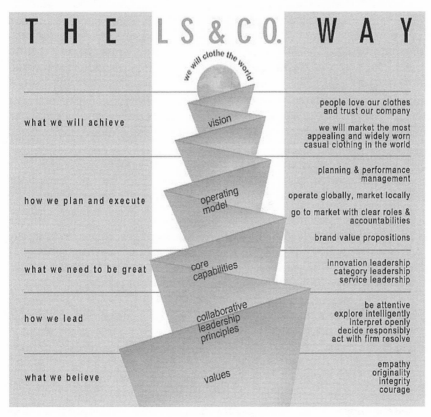

Source: Levi Strauss & Co., reprinted with permission.

efforts in the corporate responsibility arena, it is likely that sales would not have suffered.[71]

LS&CO's Global Sourcing and Operating Guidelines

Through the 1970s the majority of LS&CO facilities were owned and operated by LS&CO. During the 1980s LS&CO began to recognize the competitive necessity of contracting manufacturing overseas and gradually started releasing control over operations. Committed to maintaining its values as it transferred operations to contractors, LS&CO moved cautiously. A task force was created and charged with the responsibility of determining how LS&CO could operate via global outsourcing without jeopardizing the values on which the organization was built.[72]

Origin of the Global Sourcing and Operating Guidelines

In 1991 the task force unveiled its efforts, "The Global Sourcing and Operating Guidelines," which articulated a value-based framework to guide global sourcing relationships. The Guidelines are actually divided into two parts, in that they encompass both guidelines for sourcing relationships (the ToE) as well as criteria for identifying appropriate countries in which to do business. By publicizing those standards, the company has opened itself up to external scrutiny and a wide array of stakeholders positioned to hold the company accountable if standards are not met. LS&CO approaches sourcing relationships responsibly, and decisions to partner with contractors unfold gradually, only after careful consideration of the multiple stakeholders potentially affected.

Content of the ToE

Labeled "Terms of Engagement" (ToE), the conditions created by LS&CO's task force were designed as operative behavioral rules and encompass a set of principles to guide global sourcing decisions. They are drawn extensively from commonly held international human rights principles, such as those expressed in the United Nations' "Universal Declaration of Human Rights" and the fundamental labor rights guaranteed by the International Labour Organization.[73] Credited as the first of their kind,[74] LS&CO's ToE have served as a model for numerous subsequent efforts by other companies in the apparel and footwear industries and in other industries.[75] By 2002 virtually every apparel manufacturer in the United States had a similar code.[76]

As LS&CO has closed factories in the United States to take advantage of global sourcing opportunities, critics have responded loudly.[77] Unfortunately, they tend to focus on the decision without considering how LS&CO goes about shifting manufacturing overseas. Closer scrutiny reveals that LS&CO actually provides generous severance packages above the industry norm and invests heavily in communities when it severs relationships with them. Through a variety of financial grants, the Levi Strauss Foundation endeavors to facilitate the community's transition from its reliance on LS&CO and supports efforts such as training and outplacement and leverages personal connections to attract new business to the community and find new opportunities for former employees. Community Transition Fund grants are focused on helping communities respond to the needs of displaced workers and to bolster support services. Emphasis is on programs for job training, adult education, microenterprise, and community-wide efforts to strengthen the local economic base.[78]

The ToE are *terms* of *engagement* (see appendix 9.1); that is, for LS&CO to *engage* in a relationship with a contractor, that contractor must comply with certain *terms*. For example, ToE forbids discrimination, child labor, and abuse in the workplace. The ToE are considered a prerequisite for all contracts. If a contractor fails to abide by the ToE, that relationship can and will be terminated.

The ToE identify three types of prescriptions: zero tolerance, immediate action, and continuous improvement. Zero tolerance practices involve serious abuses, such as physical abuse, child labor, and unlawful practices. If LS&CO finds a contractor engaging in a "zero tolerance" practice, it is not tolerated.[79] LS&CO's initial procedure was to terminate the relationship with the contractor. More recently, the company has realized that pulling out is not necessarily the best way to improve working conditions in the long term. An approach has evolved through which LS&CO attempts to work with the contractor to change the situation immediately. LS&CO exits only if the contractor is uncooperative, does not appear committed to sustaining change, or is perceived as untrustworthy.[80] Another category of practices prohibited by the ToE includes "immediate action" situations. These include violations, such as wage and overtime discrepancies, that must be corrected within an agreed upon, short period of time. Other practices identified as problematic are recommended for "continuous improvement" over the long term. When LS&CO finds violations, the resulting corrective action depends on the extent and nature of those violations, in conjunction with the contractor's willingness to change its practices. LS&CO attempts to work with contractors to change their behavior. This can involve spending time with contractors to teach them how to improve their business practices.

LS&CO's goal is for the ToE to help improve working conditions around the world. According to Michael Kobori, Corporate Director of Global Code of Conduct, he wants to change "mind-sets" among contractors and other companies to encourage them to think beyond the mere "rules."[81] Terminating a relationship is a choice of last resort because, when LS&CO terminates a relationship, it loses its power to influence positive change.

LS&CO prefers to assist in raising workplace standards for as many workers as possible through regular assessments, independent regular monitoring, and training.[82] LS&CO strives to build relationships, and, through those relationships, to share the values it has adopted to create a global community of like-minded business partners.

Administrative Structure

The ToE are managed in conjunction with operating divisions. There is a regional code of conduct director or manager for each of the three global regions in which LS&CO does business: Asia, Europe/Middle East/Africa, and the Americas (Latin America, Canada, and the United States). Each manager/director is responsible for monitoring the company's relationships with sourcing partners in the region to ensure that contractors comply with the ToE. They are assisted by internal monitors who also travel through the region to oversee implementation of the ToE.[83]

"Ten years ago we primarily used quality auditors or quality people out in the field who had contact with our contractors to begin to assess them," Kobori explained.[84] The company has subsequently hired full-time employees.[85] Monitoring efforts at LS&CO are managed by 20 employees whose sole responsibility involves monitoring the company's 500 to 600 sourcing partners around the world.[86] An additional 40 employees who specialize in product and quality integrity and technical services are trained in ToE assessments and provide part-time assistance.

The monitoring process involves periodic assessments. According to Miriam Rodriguez, Code of Conduct Compliance, Regional Manager for the Americas, monitors spend more time pointing out weaknesses and suggesting areas for improvement than actually reprimanding contractors.[87] LS&CO's current approach to the ToE is primarily compliance-driven. It is about monitoring and assessing conditions. What LS&CO would like, though, according to Kobori, is to have a more partnering and consulting approach so that contractors own the process and integrate the guidelines or principles into their own management practices. LS&CO is seeing some of this, but it is not yet the norm. For this to happen, mindsets have to change so that contractors embrace the spirit as well as follow the letter of the ToE. This has already started to happen as certain contractors do not merely comply with the ToE, but have actually incorporated the underlying values in their cultures. This is reflected by a wide array of programs and initiatives that go even beyond what the ToE require.[88]

Monitoring is only one dimension of the ToE. The regional managers/directors also work with Kobori on overall improvement issues. Although Kobori does not have direct control over day-to-day operations, the three regional managers/directors work "in tandem" with him on projects to achieve global consistency, to introduce systemic improvements, and to accomplish global objectives at a regional level.[89]

As a customer, LS&CO is not involved in making the decisions to create specific programs for contractors. LS&CO nevertheless provides the impetus for many programs, as contractors attest.[90] Since the ToE are incorporated in all contracts, sourcing partners must implement programs that promote the ToE to maintain partnerships with LS&CO. In addition, the ongoing relationships with LS&CO provide contractors with ideas. ToE managers and monitors spend considerable time with contractors talking to them about ways in which they can improve their businesses. The role of monitors is to assist sourcing partners in identifying challenges and crafting possible solutions. It is not that the partners are necessarily looking for shortcuts—sometimes it just takes an outside observer to ask the right questions, and that is the role LS&CO plays.

Operation of ToE

Despite ongoing debate over codes of conduct, the experience of LS&CO has been positive.[91] Enforcing the ToE causes problems to be identified, and it brings relevant stakeholders together and involves them in the process of coming up with solutions. The first test of the enforcement of the ToE involved child labor in factories in Bangladesh. While monitoring, LS&CO discovered children working in factories. LS&CO worked with contractors to craft a successful plan that enabled children to receive salaries while attending school and to have jobs waiting for them after graduation.[92] This represented a win-win-win situation for LS&CO, the contractors, and the children.

Through the ToE, LS&CO has established cooperative relationships with sourcing partners.[93] Each sourcing partner receives an official assessment once a year. These assessments can take a couple of days depending on the size of the facility. The auditor meets with managers, views facilities, observes safety and environmental compliance, reviews personnel and payroll records, and conducts interviews with randomly selected workers. At the end of the visit the auditor presents a report to the contractor, which is kept on file and sent back to LS&CO headquarters.[94] LS&CO works with contractors to design action plans to deal with any problems identified during the assessment; and follow-up visits, which may be scheduled or unannounced, take place so that LS&CO can evaluate the changes.

The assessment serves as a mechanism through which potential problems can be identified and avoided, and through which LS&CO can provide expertise to contractors.[95] The LS&CO auditor, as an external observer, is often positioned to detect problems that the contractor, immersed in day-to-day operations, tends to overlook.[96] LS&CO provides a service to contractors and is often viewed not as an unwelcome outsider, but as a valued partner.[97]

LS&CO maintains a regular presence through local branch offices in most countries in which it does business, which are frequented by ToE managers/directors. LS&CO shares information regarding what other contractors are doing to raise the general level of awareness and productivity of contractors.[98] According to Kobori, "We're constantly working with factory management, offering suggestions, sharing some best practices with contractors from other regions, and even from other companies, in order to get them to a place where they are implementing the kinds of management practices that we like to see."[99]

Country Assessments

Broader questions emerge when LS&CO considers starting relationships in new geographical locations. LS&CO has adopted a practice of "country assessments" to address risks of LS&CO doing business in new countries and maintaining relationships in existing countries. Mo Rajan, Director, Labor and Human Rights, oversees the country assessment process. He works with outside consultants with expertise in this area to develop assessments of countries in which LS&CO is considering establishing contractor relationships. The risks of doing business in the country (i.e., political volatility, corruption, legal context, and so on) are profiled, and a numerical score from 1 to 4 is provided. This score is based on a set of categories, each ranked separately and then collapsed into a single score. The score measures the perceived risk for LS&CO to do business in the country. If a country receives a 1 or 2, then the country is deemed to exhibit acceptable risk, and particular contractors can be evaluated in terms of their adherence to LS&CO's ToE. If a country receives a 3, LS&CO carefully evaluates the types of risks present and considers particular contractors with extreme caution. If the country receives a 4, LS&CO will not do business in that country.[100]

In 2000 LS&CO was confronted with an opportunity to do business in El Salvador. The country assessment was performed, and El Salvador received a 3. El Salvador had just suffered a devastating earthquake and was barely recovering. Infrastructure throughout the country was sorely in need of repair. In addition, it is a common practice in El Salvador for pregnancy tests to be given to women prior to employment. The purpose of this testing is discriminatory—it is used to prevent hiring pregnant women because of the cost of benefits. In addition, government oversight appeared minimal and arguably corrupt. El Salvador was nevertheless anxious to attract foreign investment, and restrictions on companies willing to do business in El Salvador were minimal.

Acknowledging such risks, LS&CO also recognized the value of contributing to an economy in dire need of foreign investment coupled with the opportunity to develop a strong presence early on in a growing economy with a potentially strong apparel industry. LS&CO entertained negotiations with a potential contractor. Because of LS&CO's confidence in the contractor's ability to comply with its ToE, LS&CO decided to enter El Salvador.[101]

The country assessment serves as a guide. Unless the assessment is a 4, it is used on an ongoing basis to keep LS&CO abreast of the risks to manage so that decision makers can determine whether risks are worth bearing and monitors are in touch with indicators of which to be wary once relationships in that country are established. Country assessments are performed before LS&CO considers doing business in a country, and they are maintained on an annual or periodic basis. If the score changes, LS&CO then revisits its decision to do or not do business in that country.[102]

A contribution of the country assessment process lies in its use as a tool for identifying risks so that they can be managed. When an assessment reveals a risk, LS&CO is better prepared to assist contractors as relationships develop in that country. In El Salvador, for example, the assessment identified a common practice of pregnancy testing, which forms the basis for discrimination. LS&CO emphasized to its contractor in El Salvador that pregnancy testing is unacceptable under the ToE and would not be tolerated.

China and the Guidelines

An early application of LS&CO's "Global Sourcing and Operating Guidelines" occurred in the early 1990s with regard to doing business in China. China presented a market of more than one billion customers. In addition, labor was plentiful and cheap. The problem was that there was increasing evidence of serious human rights violations in China. LS&CO confronted a difficult decision regarding whether it should remain in China.[103]

The company considered the situation carefully.[104] In late 1992 a task force was assembled, the China Policy Group (CPG), which was charged with the responsibility of applying a "principled reasoning approach" in making a recommendation regarding sourcing and the development of potential sales and marketing business ventures in China.[105] The CPG applied the newly developed guidelines. Although some members of the group believed that LS&CO could do business in China in an ethical manner if certain conditions were met, others felt that the seriousness of the human rights concerns indicated that withdrawing from China and not pursuing new business ventures was the appropriate course of action most in keeping with the company's guidelines.

After nearly six months of deliberations, and as a result of "pervasive violations of basic human rights," LS&CO decided gradually to reduce and withdraw its contracted production work in China and chose not to pursue a direct investment in China.[106] In early May 1993, LS&CO announced its decision to be the second American company to withdraw from China.[107] The company subsequently reduced its sourcing in China by approximately 70 percent.[108]

China's constant battle with human rights led LS&CO to decide that it was inconsistent with its values to support business there.[109] This was a legendary decision for LS&CO. Although some critics deemed this a mere publicity stunt, much of the world applauded as LS&CO seemed to place values above profits in refusing to remain in a potentially lucrative marketplace for fear of jeopardizing corporate values.[110]

In April 1998 LS&CO revisited its thinking regarding doing business in China and ended its self-imposed restrictions on sourcing in China and opened the door to exploring opportunities for a sales and marketing presence.[111] This was a business decision prompted by changing circumstances, such as Hong Kong's repatriation with China. In addition, LS&CO had acquired several years of practical experience implementing the ToE worldwide, and this increased its comfort level in managing relationships in China so as to promote good workplace standards and remedy problems when they arose.[112] According to Linda Butler, "We felt we could do business in China consistent with responsible business practices and our guidelines."[113]

Human rights violations are still rampant, and the political and legal systems are still corrupt. Indeed, companies doing business in China today continue to receive abundant criticism.[114] By applying its guidelines, LS&CO nevertheless determined that it could influence change in China only by doing business there, and that, in light of changes in the apparel industry, it would be severely handicapped by staying out of China. This is a decision that LS&CO has made consistent with its principles. The company recognizes the risks of doing business in China, but is convinced that its presence will lead to positive change for workers.

PROGRAM STUDY: ENFORCING THE ToE IN MEXICO

Not all sourcing relationships run smoothly, as evidenced by LS&CO's experience with IBIS de Mexico a little more than a decade ago. LS&CO has a number of sourcing partners in Mexico, several in Aguascalientes— a state in central Mexico. In the mid-1990s, through its continuous monitoring of ToE implementation, LS&CO discovered that IBIS, a sewing factory, was not complying with the ToE. While no zero tolerance violations were detected, numerous other violations were found. Warnings were issued, but no significant changes took place.[115]

Inspiration and Vision: Idea Generation/Inception

When the ToE were introduced, LS&CO had to demonstrate its commitment to them. "As the first company to institute such guidelines, the initial challenges were convincing contractors that there was a need for such a code," recalled Joe Maccarrone, Vice President U.S./Latin American Customer Fulfillment and a member of the original working group that developed the guidelines. "But eventually contractors realized that embracing these standards would actually help them attract new customers and grow their business while simultaneously improving the lives of their employees."[116]

It is not the policy of LS&CO to terminate contracts immediately upon a finding of violations. This would, according to LS&CO, create more harm than good. The underlying goal is to affect change and protect worker rights, and LS&CO believes that this happens by working with contractors, not by abandoning them. It was LS&CO's assumption that, by identifying the problems and working with the contractor in Aguascalientes, the contractor would arrive at possible solutions and the relationship could be maintained.[117]

Establishment and Implementation

IBIS did not heed LS&CO's admonitions. Nominal changes took place, if any. After several months, LS&CO decided it had no choice but to terminate the relationship. At that time LS&CO accounted for 70 percent of the factory's capacity. Since the ToE are incorporated in all sourcing arrangements, and since those terms had been violated, the relationship was terminated.[118] Rodriguez reflects on this with sadness. Although it was IBIS who violated the terms, she considers it a disappointment shared by LS&CO, in that LS&CO was not able to influence positive change.[119]

An interesting series of events occurred following LS&CO's decision to terminate the contract. IBIS quickly realized how seriously LS&CO took the ToE; it also learned how much it could cost to lose LS&CO as a customer. Not only did LS&CO constitute a significant portion of the contractor's business, but other customers tended to rely on LS&CO's assessment of a contractor as a barometer. Regardless, the issues LS&CO had identified were serious and would result in financial losses in the long term if not the short term if they were not addressed.[120]

At this juncture, IBIS traveled through a range of responses. First came anger: "Who does LS&CO think they are?" Then IBIS started realizing that it did not matter; they had failed 600 people—their workers. They saw the workers they had to terminate, and they felt responsible. Somewhat overwhelmed, they starting thinking, "How can we change this, or should we even try?" IBIS then quickly started trying to make changes to improve the issues that LS&CO had identified. While the contractor wanted desperately to regain LS&CO as a customer, it realized that it was going to have to change to stay in business, even without LS&CO as a customer.[121]

One of the first things IBIS did was to create a human resources department. While commonplace in most MNEs, it is frequently nonexistent in companies in developing and emerging countries or exists only with limited functions such as payroll and record keeping. To have a human resources department requires that managers view workers as assets, and many companies, particularly in developing and emerging countries, are still built on the assumption that workers are expendable. The creation of a human resources department and the hiring of a human resources director constituted a major improvement, which paved the way for multiple subsequent additional improvements.[122] Eduardo Franco Padilla was hired as the first Director of Human Resources for IBIS one month after LS&CO terminated its relationship. He was hired to help the company evaluate and correct its approach to understanding and meeting compliance issues.[123]

During the following months, IBIS continued to make improvements. Padilla speedily created new systems, hired new people, and created middle management teams to streamline operations.[124] According to Padilla, the owners of the factory "behaved like children"—they did not believe that LS&CO would carry out its threats.[125] He accepted the challenge of reinventing the company. This was a learning process for Padilla and the company. He was initially frustrated by reading other companies' codes of conduct because he did not find what he was looking for. He started talking to workers in the factory and asked them what life was like for them. When he did that, he knew what he had to do. According to Padilla if you want to find out what workers need and what sort of benefits to provide, you need to ask them.[126]

Padilla urged LS&CO to give IBIS a second chance, and LS&CO eventually agreed to renew the relationship.[127] During the 18-month hiatus, IBIS had changed its mind-set and had acquired values consistent with LS&CO's ToE.[128]

Continued Program Assessment

The relationship with IBIS continues to grow. IBIS has done an about-face: not only have the changes served to provide for a renewed partnership with LS&CO, but the contractor has also discovered that respecting the values embodied by LS&CO's ToE can serve to attract additional customers and can lead to a more efficient and productive workplace. The relationship between LS&CO and IBIS has become even stronger.[129]

As a result of the changes prompted by LS&CO's audit, IBIS now enjoys greater efficiency, better margins, and lower costs. The company's image has improved within the community and with regard to attracting customers. Employees are more involved in social activities, show less aggression, and are more receptive to teamwork. Complying with the ToE breathed life into IBIS. It is no longer just a place to work; people identify with the company and smile.[130] IBIS and LS&CO have now been working together for approximately 15 years.

This course of action, having to terminate a relationship with a sourcing partner, is generally not LS&CO's preference. This situation nevertheless illustrates the tremendous influence that LS&CO can exercise. Compliance with the ToE is nonnegotiable.[131]

PROGRAM STUDY: ToE FROM THE GROUND UP IN EL SALVADOR

Like other countries in Central America, El Salvador has recently emerged from bloody internal strife. As the country began to recover from the effects of a 12-year civil war ending in 1992 that claimed 75,000 lives, it suffered another significant blow in 2000 when an earthquake razed the country and increased the death toll by an additional 10,000.[132] These events have created a risky social, political, and economic environment that initially prevented LS&CO from engaging in sourcing relationships in the country.

LS&CO was recently approached by a potential sourcing partner in El Salvador who actually represents a joint venture between a Colombian laundry facility, Allwash (owned by Inversions S&F, S.A., in Colombia) and IBIS de El Salvador (owned by IBIS, the same Mexican sewing factory with which LS&CO previously terminated its relationship). Part of the reason that LS&CO agreed to contract with a nascent operation in El Salvador was that it had a history with the companies involved in the joint venture. LS&CO had a strong positive history with the Colombian laundry and an increasing respect for IBIS since the relationship had been repaired. LS&CO was confident that these two companies understood the objectives of LS&CO's ToE and would institute policies and procedures consistent with them, and that the three of them together could navigate successfully through the risks of doing business in El Salvador.[133]

The IBIS/Allwash joint venture has now been operating in El Salvador for approximately 16 months in the private free zone of El Pedregal in the community of Rosario La Paz, which is located on the outskirts of the capital city. This joint venture illustrates how the ToE can be incorporated from the ground up.

Inspiration and Vision: Idea Generation/Inception

Through their relationships with LS&CO, the companies involved in the joint venture had both developed an understanding of the importance of the ToE and acquired an appreciation for similar values apart from what was required to satisfy LS&CO. They found that they had undergone a transition from viewing LS&CO as the feared watchdog to relying on the company as a monitor that could assist them in identifying potential issues before situations escalated. They found that LS&CO was not looking for perfection, but for continuous improvement. By working with LS&CO, they were therefore, together, able to address potential issues and make the operation stronger in the process.[134]

Establishment and Implementation: IBIS de El Salvador

IBIS took the first steps in El Salvador. Padilla oversaw the move into El Salvador, which took 18 months. For six months Padilla lived in El Salvador. He met with people and companies and lived in the community. During that time, he adopted a variety of personas to learn as much as he could about the country. Once he was a journalist, another time a factory worker. He attended union meetings, socialized, and immersed himself in the culture. He became acquainted with the geography, politics, logistics, and people.[135]

Construction of the factory began in February 2001; hiring began in April. Within two days Padilla had hired 72 workers for the sewing factory. When asked his criteria, he said, simply, "Values." During the interviews, Padilla veered away from traditional questions and attempted to carry on conversations with applicants so that he could endeavor to discern their values. He said that he could train people with regard to skills, but he did not want to have to fight value conflicts.[136] In addition, Padilla noted that he did not mention that LS&CO was connected with the factory, because "it would attract too many people" and the company was only hiring a small number at that time.[137] Padilla did not want to alienate people by turning them away, particularly since he expected to be hiring again as the company grew. LS&CO has a reputation throughout Latin America. Even though LS&CO is the customer, its influence has been widespread.

Once the decision was made to enter El Salvador, Padilla noted the risks. The textile industry in El Salvador was easily corrupted and already evidenced a number of bad habits and a relatively strong Korean presence. Padilla decided to build on values from the ground up through extensive orientation. The learning from the experience of IBIS in Mexico was that values relate to both morality and the bottom line, that is, how a business behaves in terms of moral decision making affects its bottom line. The objective was for ethics "to become so natural, having it within us to be ethical, that it can't be reversed. In Mexico, it was hard to understand that, if you do it right in the first place, everything else will fall into place."[138] Padilla was determined to learn from past experience about doing things right, from the start.

Since workers were hired while the factory was still being built, they spent the next month in training at various locations: on site at the factory, on the beach, and so on. IBIS paid the workers as if they were working in the factory, but, in reality, for the first month, workers were being paid to be trained. Seminars were conducted, presentations were made, and skits took place—all to teach company values to the workers. In June the factory opened its doors.[139] A year later the workforce had grown significantly in size, with 180 workers at IBIS and 850 at Allwash.

Continued Program Assessment

Values (such as trust, quality, reliability, and so on) can be incorporated from the beginning. Through its ongoing influence over sourcing partners, LS&CO is changing behavior, as is evidenced by this new venture, which is creating an organization consistent with LS&CO's ToE from the ground up. Although the joint venture, still a nascent operation, does not operate without complication, LS&CO has found that having the ToE at its core helps in resolving the difficulties that arise.[140]

Padilla emphasized the role of LS&CO as a partner in the company's successes. According to Padilla, it is a "mutual relationship. . . . If she doesn't look for me, I'll look for her."[141] In other words, companies actually appreciate LS&CO's assistance. According to Padilla, LS&CO serves three purposes: (1) as a consultant, LS&CO keeps companies moving toward continuous improvement by identifying areas in which they can become stronger; (2) as a moral authority, LS&CO helps companies determine the appropriate courses of action; and (3) as a barometer, LS&CO aids companies in evaluating the potential impact of different choices. Padilla likens the relationship to a marriage: "Sometimes we don't like what we hear, but they are clear."[142]

Ongoing challenges exist for this joint venture. While both partners have demonstrated considerable understanding of and support for the ToE, they have found different methods of manifesting their respect for the underlying principles. As the companies endeavor to work together, they are finding it difficult to blend the disparate cultures. There are actually three cultures interacting—the cultures of the Mexican sewing factory, the Colombian laundry, and the El Salvadoran workers and the environment.

The resounding message derived from the experience of these companies in El Salvador is that there is no single formula or right answer regarding how to comply with the ToE. Both have a noble vision—they are just different visions. For IBIS and Allwash, the challenge lies not in figuring out how to comply with the ToE, but in determining how to reconcile two different management styles of incorporating the ToE.

PROGRAM STUDY: RESPECTING EMPLOYEES— LAUNDRY IN AGUASCALIENTES[143]

Few contractors have the opportunity to build ToE from the ground up, because most of LS&CO's sourcing relationships begin with existing contractors. For example, LS&CO also has a long-standing relationship with a laundry in Aguascalientes, where IBIS is also located, that has made major strides with regard to respecting worker rights.

The Mexican-based company is located in an industrial park, not a free trade zone. The laundry began in 1987 and started working with LS&CO in 1990. At that time the factory had 6 washers, 5 dryers, and 100 employees. Today the factory has 31 washers, 14 dryers, 3 extractors, 31 pressers, 5 boilers, and 1 water treatment plant. The company now manages 246 different washes for LS&CO. Total capacity is 350,000 units/week, 60 percent of which is for LS&CO. The laundry employs 1,782 workers. Since its inception, the human resources department, started after 1993, has taken on an active role. In fact, it can be said that human resources has been "operationalized," for human resources is responsible for the programs that have been introduced.[144]

Inspiration and Vision: Idea Generation/Inception

The laundry facility in Aguascalientes clearly reflects both the influence of LS&CO and the company's commitment to the ToE. According to the Human Resources Director, the *inspiration* for the laundry's worker programs resulted largely from the company's relationship with LS&CO. Her personal vision is to "marry human resources and production."[145] Her goal is to ensure that workers are respected and not treated as "two sets of hands and legs."[146] LS&CO has helped to show her how that can be possible.

While LS&CO rarely makes specific recommendations to contractors, through ongoing conversation, insinuation, and identification of troublesome areas, LS&CO has served as a catalyst for change.[147] The vision, though, for the specific programs implemented by the contractor has emanated from the Human Resources Director, according to Rodriguez.[148] Rodriguez indicates that this laundry has created initiatives that rival best practices in the region.[149]

Establishment and Implementation

The Human Resources Director has created a workplace that endeavors to recognize the multifaceted needs of workers. She provides a menu of benefits available to employees. The nexus of her programs comes from the premise that employees have needs. Her goal is to identify their needs and maximize the ability of their income to cover those needs.[150]

Professional Services

The Human Resources Director endeavors to provide services that enhance the ability of workers to be productive. Workers who are weakened by treatable medical conditions or distracted by outside influences are not as productive as they could be.

Medical assistance is a primary benefit offered by the company. Medical services are provided to employees, their families, and members of the surrounding communities. The company currently offers medical, dental, and optometry clinics. Beginning in 1999, the Human Resources Director worked with the community to sponsor vaccination, nutrition, and mental health campaigns. She is currently exploring opportunities for further outreach. Since public health care in Mexico is generally poor, particularly in smaller cities and remote rural areas, companies play a vital role in providing additional assistance. This is not the only company to provide a medical clinic, but one of the few to reach out to the community.

Not only has the Human Resources Director organized medical and dental clinics, but she has also established clinics through which employees can receive confidential, free legal and social work and psychological services. These programs are unique, according to Rodriguez.[151] Through her human resources representatives on the floor, the Human Resources Director identifies workers who might be in need of assistance and directs them to the appropriate counselors. In addition, she provides referrals for workers who approach her. She initially provided on-site office space for the clinics, but found that it compromised confidentiality, because other workers could see co-workers seeking assistance. To avoid that sort of deterrence, she changed the policy to protect workers' privacy.[152]

Value-Added Services

The Human Resources Director has created several programs that help to provide value added services to workers' income. For example, she has worked with local vendors to provide groceries and related products to workers at a lower cost. Every Friday there is an on-site open air market accessible to all workers. Goods are offered at a significantly reduced price (sometimes less than 30 percent). This benefits both workers and local vendors. A payment plan option has also been established for larger items such as bikes. Workers can pay for the items on time and then get them after they have been paid for. In addition, she has expanded the products offered at the market to include toys, computers, shoes, and other miscellaneous items.[153]

The company also creates value by offering free transportation to work. A goal with such a program is employee retention. Roads in Mexico are poor, public transportation is unreliable, and cars are expensive. Transportation helps get employees to work on time and it gets them there so that they are able to start the day more comfortably. In addition, there are some workers who live in remote communities and would not be able to hold jobs at the laundry if they were not provided transportation. The transportation program thus provides outreach to wider communities and enables them to gain employment to improve their quality of life. Beginning with 4 routes in 1994, the laundry now handles 20 routes.

In addressing employee needs, the Human Resources Director has also attended to payment of wages. Although workers are accustomed to cash payments, the laundry recognized this as disadvantageous. Cash is easier to spend and lose, and workers carrying cash on paydays are targets for robbers. The Human Resources Director had an ATM machine installed at the laundry and created a direct deposit payment plan. In this way workers have constant access to their money, but they are encouraged to save it and spend it only as needed. In addition, they are able to check their payments regularly to ensure that they are accurate. This is of particular importance where trust is often absent.

The installation of the ATM took a day, but training the workers to use and trust the ATM took 45 days. The company had to teach workers that they were still being paid even though they were not receiving anything tangible. In addition, they had to be taught how to do the math—many workers lack education.

The laundry has also initiated an internal savings bank. The idea of a savings bank is not unique among LS&CO contractors, but it is not common in Aguascalientes. Through participation in the bank, employees are able to obtain low-interest loans and make purchases that might otherwise be impossible. Through this program the company both teaches workers the value of saving money and enables them to increase their buying power. By 1999 the bank had more than 1,000 members enlisted.

Another popular program involves housing assistance. The company works with the government to have houses distributed through the INFONAVIT program assigned to laundry workers. In addition, representatives from the company assist workers in preparing the tedious paperwork and going through the laborious process of buying a house. In 1999 the company was able to help 100 workers buy houses.

Employee Recognition

According to the Human Resources Director, peer recognition is important to workers. Programs have therefore been introduced to promote loyalty and productivity by recognizing certain categories of employees at an annual ceremony. The worker with the highest performance and the workers in the most productive area in the plant receive financial awards as well as recognition, and employees who have worked at the plant for certain numbers of years receive gold, silver, or copper medals. A program for "Employee of the Month" has also been introduced. This employee receives a prize that includes a bonus for food.

To stimulate worker creativity, the Human Resources Director initiated the IDEAS program in 1997 to reward workers for ideas. In that year alone 215 ideas were proposed. Workers who came up with particularly insightful ideas about how processes could be improved were rewarded. One worker, for example, addressed the problem of jeans that were stained during the wash process. The worker figured out that stains occurred when jeans were put in the machine during the cycle when Clorox was being inserted. He suggested that a light go on when Clorox was inserted to warn workers not to put jeans in the machine. As a result of this idea, the quantity of stained jeans dropped from 2 percent to 0 percent.[154]

Environmental Initiatives

Workers also benefit from the health, safety, and environmental issues covered by the ToE compliance. For example, water treatment standards have resulted in health and cost savings for the entire community in which the laundry operates. Water is a scarce resource in central Mexico. In 1995 the ToE required that water treatment be enhanced. While that represented a significant financial investment, results have been overwhelmingly positive. In fact, since the industrial park was required to comply with similar standards in order for the factory to comply with the ToE, all of the businesses in the park have shared in the benefits. In addition, the laundry has been asked to train others, including the industrial park, to comply with the standards.[155]

Continued Program Assessment

Although the Human Resources Director is directly responsible for these programs, the influence of LS&CO has prompted the company to support them. It is through the ongoing relationship with and guidance offered by LS&CO that such programs and others continue. According to the new general manager, "We recognize the contribution that LS&CO has given to our growth. They have worked much to guide us and help us to put into operation everything that makes a laundry to be considered in fulfillment with TOE requirements. This has brought us a subsequent benefit to our employees, to our way of working and to our own lives."[156]

The Human Resources Director indicated that the programs currently offered are merely a beginning—she is continuing to create and implement new initiatives, consistent with LS&CO's goal of continuous improvement and reflective of a culture focused on workers and the environment "inside the company as well as outside."[157]

PROGRAM STUDY: CONTINUING CHALLENGES OF A LARGE-SCALE OPERATION—KORAMSA IN GUATEMALA

Guatemala is a country that suffers from severe disparities. The wealthiest 10 percent of the population receives nearly half of all income; the top 20 percent receives two-thirds of all income. Guatemala's economy, the largest in Central America, remains primarily agricultural, though industry is growing. Guatemala has experienced numerous problems regarding free association, particularly in recent years. In July 2001 a mob assaulted union supporters in an attack that lasted for hours, and many of the workers were injured.[158] Union leaders are deterred from organizing through a number of means, including threats of plant closings. Considering the 27 apparel plants closed in the first six months of 2001, union leaders recognize that the threats are real.[159] The Korean presence in Guatemala is strong, and rumors abound regarding human rights violations in Korean factories.[160] Since rights in Guatemala are deteriorating, the presence of companies who promote workers' rights like LS&CO's contractor, Koramsa, is important.[161]

Koramsa is a garment manufacturer located in Zone 7 (a municipal designation, not a free trade zone or industrial park) of the capital city. Koramsa is one of 227 apparel factories in the country, which together employ approximately 91,300 full-time workers. Koramsa represents 12 percent of the workforce in the apparel industry in Guatemala. Koramsa currently has about 10,400 employees. The workforce is young, with 89 percent between 18 and 25 years old. Most of the workforce is single.[162]

Owned and operated by a Guatemalan family who founded the company in 1988, Koramsa has been involved with LS&CO for more than 10 years, but also works with customers such as Osh Kosh B'Gosh, Dillard's, and Kohl's. LS&CO accounts for 65 percent of the company's capacity. A natural connection exists between the vision of the company founders and the values of LS&CO. The founders wanted to contribute to the development of their country and its people through the creation of a maquiladora that respects workers.[163] Having made a strong contribution in this area, Koramsa is now looking toward the future, and the company's new goal is to compete globally. To compete effectively, Koramsa believes that it needs to become full-service—a "customer-driven organization with an integrated supply chain."[164]

Koramsa has found that its primary challenge relates to the size of the organization. Its size coupled with the country's poor infrastructure makes it incumbent upon the company to offer services, such as health care, that governments in developed countries ordinarily provide. The diversity of the worker population (in terms of culture, religion, geography, and so on) makes it somewhat difficult to determine what the workers' needs and interests are. Koramsa has thus chosen to satisfy basic needs through a variety of initiatives.

Inspiration and Vision: Idea Generation/Inception

The vision that guides Koramsa originates from both the influence of LS&CO and the responsible leadership of the company's senior managers. Among the senior managers are people who create programs and people who are adept at identifying others who can create and promote successful initiatives.

Establishment and Implementation

The size of Koramsa cannot be overstated. In some areas 10,000 people constitute a small town. Viewed in this light, Koramsa has found it necessary to provide a combination of need-based services and programs that assist in connecting people with one another and with Koramsa.

Housing

Koramsa recently confronted difficulties associated with identifying and providing appropriate benefits when attempting to provide subsidized housing for employees. The company publicized the initiative and even involved employees in the planning and construction. Of the 1,000 houses planned, less than 5 were actually sold. Koramsa learned that it had to do a better job of taking cultural differences into account. It is likely that more houses did not sell because people were more comfortable living where they were with their families. Questions have been raised regarding how the plan could have been implemented more effectively. The location of the houses could have been more carefully considered, or Koramsa could have opted simply to assist in the funding process.[165]

Diversity

The housing disappointment reflects the diversity of both the workforce and the country. Guatemala has numerous indigenous cultures with distinct dialects. Language creates barriers, as does dress, culture, and habits.

Koramsa respects the diversity of the country and the company and supports measures that help diversity thrive. Koramsa encourages people to dress according to local customs, and numerous workers, particularly women, work in their colorful tribal attire.

Koramsa has attempted to create subgroups with which workers can identify, for the company has found that people learn best from one another—about skills and norms. Koramsa has allowed subcultures to emerge within each of the nine factories that comprise the company. In fact, each has its own radio announcer, who helps to contribute to the individual factory's personality. In each factory, supervisors organize workers into teams, so that workers are able to identify with a small group of people from whom they can learn and whom they can use as behavioral guides.

That is essential. For many workers, this is their first job. A large number come from the outskirts of town, and they are not familiar with modern conveniences. Communication and training are about more than on-the-job skills and can involve teaching basic information: how to use a toilet, how to use a knife and fork; that workers are expected to arrive at the same time every day; and that workers are expected to work every day. Through the teams, workers teach one another. In this way, diversity is both managed and promoted.[166]

Education

Koramsa values education because, through education, workers can better themselves and become stronger contributors to the organization. In 2002 the company initiated the Koramsa School of Systematic Studies project, with 425 students participating in primary, secondary, and high school education. Koramsa both organized the program and partially subsidized it. The philosophy of the company is "Help us by helping yourself."[167]

Financial Benefits

Although the legal minimum wage is about $145.00 per month, the average salary for Koramsa employees is close to $215.00 per month. Koramsa also provides scholarships for employees' children. These scholarships are granted without restriction on receipt of a copy of the children's grades. Through the posthumous program fund, Koramsa provides financial support for families of employees who die while working at Koramsa, even if their deaths are unrelated to work. A modest sum, it provides at least for the burial. Workers who get married also receive a wedding bonus.[168]

The solidarism program also translates into financial benefits for employees. Employees can put 5 percent of their salary into a special fund for savings. The fund is used throughout the year to supply shops on-site where groceries are sold at a discounted cost. Workers can apply for loans when special situations arise. At the end of the year 60 percent of what workers invested is returned. The program is entirely voluntary, but workers must participate in the program to take advantage of services such as the loan program and shops.[169]

Banking

A consequence of diversity and operating in an underdeveloped country involves challenges linked to payment. Workers in Latin America expect cash. This can present a number of associated problems, particularly with a company Koramsa's size.[170]

Until recently 10,400 people were paid in cash twice a month. It is the usual practice—bank accounts are not common.[171] Then Koramsa was attacked. The intended robbers had watched how the company operated, realized how much cash changed hands on those two days each month, and created a plan to steal the money. The contractor was fortunate, in that the intended theft was thwarted and no one was harmed, but it prompted the company to reconsider payment options.[172]

After the incident, things had to change—for the safety of workers and the factory. In two weeks the system was changed completely. The Human Resources Director arranged for employees to be paid by check, and payments were staggered over different days each month.[173]

While this might not seem significant for a company in a developed country, it constituted a major challenge in Guatemala. The company had to teach workers that they were still being paid, even though they were not receiving cash. We tend to take checks for granted—workers in Guatemala thought they were being cheated.[174]

A significant amount of training took place, in both large and small groups. Small groups proved an effective tool. Once the company was able to get one worker to understand, he or she was then used to help communicate more effectively with co-workers.[175] This transition to a new payment process has prompted Koramsa to think about additional changes. The company is starting to train workers about the benefits of bank accounts.[176]

Health Services

Koramsa has excelled with regard to health services. Under the guidance and leadership of a medical doctor, Koramsa has introduced multiple initiatives that contribute to the health and wellness of employees and their families. In this area Koramsa is truly a model for other MNEs.[177]

Because medical care provided by the government is so poor, Koramsa developed a medical clinic on-site. Complete confidentiality is maintained, so that workers are not inhibited from seeking the proper treatment. The view is that healthy employees are productive employees. Koramsa's approach to health is holistic. With that in mind, eye clinics and dental clinics have also been established (see photo 9.1). In addition, a subsidized pharmacy is located next to the clinics.[178] While other companies provide medical clinics, Koramsa is unique in regard to the other services and the extent of the health care coverage.

According to Koramsa's doctor, the clinic provides both preventive and curative medicine: 60 percent preventive, 40 percent curative. This includes flu shots and vaccinations against hepatitis, diphtheria, and tetanus, as well as periodic examinations. Workers are also given Gatorade periodically throughout the day for rehydration, and fluoride is provided weekly. This is important because many workers have never received dental care.[179]

Koramsa conducts an annual health fair attended by employees and families. More than 20,000 people attended last year's event. The fair combines typical carnival rides and games with booths on health-related topics. Each year the fair has a theme, and teams from each factory create booths and present shows. In this way Koramsa associates health with entertainment and involves employees in the event.[180]

Meals

Koramsa decided not to provide meals to employees. While the company acknowledges the need for healthy and clean meals, Koramsa was reluctant to become involved in a business—the cafeteria business—in which it lacks expertise. The company arrived at a creative alternative. Koramsa has designated meal locations but, instead of handling food, the company allows local vendors to provide meals. The company supports the local community by providing work, and still stays out of an area in which it lacks expertise. Koramsa carefully screens and monitors food providers to ensure quality and safety.

Continued Program Assessment

Challenges for Koramsa are ongoing. Guatemalan law requires that factories have nursery provisions for working parents (particularly mothers). While the law is not generally enforced, Koramsa is concerned about meeting the needs of its workers, even without motivation from a legal mandate. In this case, an on-site nursery would not be practicable. Through interviews and surveys, Koramsa has found that workers would prefer other benefits. In the Guatemalan culture families take care of their own, and they would not welcome having strangers take care of children. Regardless, Koramsa is exploring ways of providing assistance to working

Photo 9.1 Dental clinic in Koramsa. *Source:* **Tara Radin**

parents. The company approached several local nurseries, but they were not willing to serve such a large working population.[181]

Koramsa now tackles the challenge of communicating benefits effectively and efficiently to employees. The company has redesigned its orientation program to ensure that workers are informed about benefits. In addition, periodic newsletters are distributed. Human resources is now making use of the teams in which the factories are divided to communicate via the small groups.

While the company continues to serve an increasing population, it must deal with the same sorts of issues that competitors confront, such as high turnover and low worker loyalty. While this is always a concern, Koramsa has adopted a novel philosophy. Even if workers leave, they are made better off by having been at Koramsa, and they will carry with them the tools and standards they have learned.

The experience of Koramsa is that, even though people leave, they come back. Koramsa notes that the textile industry in Guatemala suffers from high turnover. According to the President of Koramsa, the level of turnover at Koramsa is probably somewhat lower than in competitors' factories. At Koramsa about 40 percent of the workforce is stable, while the remaining 60 percent is constantly turning over. Many people in the industry come to Koramsa for their first job, and many leave because they do not know what it is like to work and they think that it will be different elsewhere. Koramsa has learned to welcome people back, because they do come back.[182]

LS&CO'S ONGOING EFFORTS

LS&CO's articulated goal is to change behavior.[183] It wants companies to adopt codes and promote better working conditions and is happy to provide its ToE as a model.

Testing ToE

LS&CO's commitment to the ToE extends beyond paper. During the late 1990s the company partnered with contractors, NGOs, and academicians in order to assess operation of its ToE. First in the Dominican Republic, subsequently in the Philippines, LS&CO conducted pilot studies. The view was, as expressed by Rodriguez, "We believed that if you could bring everyone to the table, we could achieve a better solution than any one party could do alone."[184]

LS&CO organized a team incorporating representatives from multiple stakeholder groups—LS&CO, contractors, NGOs, and academicians. Together, for six months, they were charged with measuring the effectiveness of the implementation of the ToE. As a team, they designed their procedure and process.[185]

The project was initially greeted by a degree of skepticism, particularly with regard to NGOs. NGOs have traditionally been critical of MNEs. Once the project started, people pulled together. The results have been overwhelmingly positive. People actually listened to one another, and the resulting recommendations for improvements continue to be implemented worldwide. One of the learning points was that LS&CO needs better training of internal monitors.[186] The organization is currently developing enhanced training procedures.

Government Advocacy

One of the more distinctive ways in which LS&CO is affecting change is through government advocacy. LS&CO has adopted a proactive, visible, and vocal role in approaching political officials. The view is that the government should play a role in improving global labor practices, such as by conditioning favorable trade status with the United States on having standards in place that protect workers. In this way LS&CO is endeavoring to improve the plight of workers worldwide.[187]

LS&CO addressed written testimony to the Senate Finance Committee with regard to Trade Promotion Authority (TPA) legislation, which allows the President to negotiate international trade agreements. LS&CO urged the Committee to condition the President's TPA on the requirement that the connection between trade policy and international labor issues be taken into account. LS&CO is urging the United States government to require countries to protect worker rights in order to be eligible to benefit from beneficial trade policies. Although LS&CO is not alone in advocating the connection between labor practices and trade benefits, it is the only company to have spoken out publicly.[188]

LS&CO also confronts representatives of foreign governments. In 2001 representatives of the company met with the Minister of Labor in Guatemala to seek legislative reform.[189] LS&CO responded with a letter of appreciation when the Minister assisted in bringing the law in compliance with the ILO conventions.[190]

Sourcing Grants

Sourcing grants represent another vehicle through which LS&CO endeavors to improve the condition of workers around the world. Although the grants are administered by the Levi Strauss Foundation, LS&CO's commitment to the ToE leads the Foundation and company to provide grants to community organizations located in LS&CO sourcing communities. LS&CO's overall philanthropic program focuses on grant making in communities in which employees and contractors' employees live and work. This covers both domestic communities and global communities in which LS&CO has sourcing partners.[191]

In China the Foundation has partnered with the Asia Foundation in an attempt to improve worker rights in the country. As part of the decision to reengage in China, LS&CO committed to elevating the condition of workers, not just in its contractors' factories. The Asia Foundation has begun a number of initiatives aimed at workers. An open meeting was conducted in which worker issues were discussed, and a newspaper column was created through which workers could ask questions and have them answered. In addition, the Asia Foundation has worked with local companies to circumvent the absence of local government support and create a nongovernmental arbitration committee through which workers could have grievances addressed.[192]

Sourcing grants complement LS&CO's contractor-specific relationships in countries in which it does business. To reiterate, LS&CO's goal is to improve labor practices in general, and this is accomplished not only by working with sourcing partners but also by investing directly in their communities.[193]

CONCLUSION

LS&CO serves as a model among MNEs. Through its creation and ongoing implementation of the ToE, LS&CO has demonstrated that a company can achieve profits with principles.

A decade of working with the ToE has afforded LS&CO a breadth of experience. Indeed, LS&CO has arguably "changed the landscape of the apparel industry."[194] "We are in one of the most competitive industries in the world," commented CFO Bill Chiasson, "and in the middle of a very significant business turnaround. However, this does not give us license to abandon or compromise our standards and values. As reinforcement, recently our chairman, CEO, and the leader of our worldwide supply chain reminded our employees that our terms of engagement are a nonnegotiable aspect of our business. Fundamentally, it is a question of how you choose to run your business."[195]

According to Kobori, the ToE have resulted in numerous improvements. They have ensured consistency, prompted worker-focused programs, led to supply chain integration of principles, and affected industry practices.[196] The question for LS&CO now remains, "Where do we go next with ToE and corporate social responsibility?"[197]

NOTES

1. David Drickhamer, "Consumer Cries for Sweatshop-Free Products Drive Big-Name Brands to Extraordinary Lengths to Monitor Working Conditions at Contractor Plants," *Industry Week*, June 2002, p. 31.

2. Section written with Adam Birnbaum.

3. Henry Welt and Deborah Sorell, "Keeping Off the Hot Seat," *Apparel Industry* Magazine, September 1996.

4. Levi Strauss & Co., "Levi Strauss & Co. Names Six U.S. Plants To Close," LS&CO, Media Center (8 April 2002), http://www.levistrauss.com/news/press release.asp?r=1&c=0&cat=0&pr=530&area=Americas (accessed 30 August 2002); John Nidecker, "Consolidation in the Apparel Industry," *Weekly Corporate Growth Report* (7 January 2002).

5. Graham Howarth, Tania Martino, Samantha Melton, Alan Miegel, Jonathan Morley, and Matthew Weissman, "LEVI'S: A Company as Durable as Its Jeans" (2001), http://shakti.trincoll.edu/~ghowarth/levi.html (accessed 30 August 2002).

6. Dina ElBoghdady, "Stitching Together a Strategy: Levi Strauss to Move Manufacturing Overseas," *Washington Post*, 9 April 2002, p. E1.

7. Interview by Tara Radin with Miriam Rodriguez, Code of Conduct Compliance, Regional Director for the Americas, Latin America, 15–19 July 2002.

8. Gary Gereffi, Ronie Garcia-Johnson, and Erika Sasser, "The NGO-Industrial Complex," *Foreign Policy* (July/August), http://www.foreignpolicy.com/issue_julyaug_2001/gereffi.html (accessed 30 August 2002).

9. Hector Figueroa, "In the Name of Fashion: Exploitation in the Garment Industry," *NACLA Report on the Americas* 29, no. 4 (1 January 1998): pp. 34–40; Maureen C. Carini, "Apparel & Footwear," Standard & Poors: Industry Surveys (30 May 2002), www.netadvantage.standardandpoors.com/netahtml/IndSur/ (accessed 30 August 2002).

10. Figueroa, "In the Name of Fashion."

11. Jenny Strasburg, "Appalachian Travails: A Tiny Georgia Town Faces Life

Without Its Levi Plant, Its Economic Lifeblood," *San Francisco Chronicle,* 16 June 2002.

12. Drickhamer, "Consumer Cries for Sweatshop-Free Products," p. 31.

13. Levi Strauss & Co., "Levi Strauss & Co. Names Six U.S. Plants To Close."

14. David L. Wilson, "Do Maquiladoras Matter?" *Monthly Review* 49, no. 5 (1997), pp. 28–34 .

15. Geri Smith, "The Decline of the Maquiladora," *Business Week,* 29 April 2002.

16. Smith, "Decline of the Maquiladora."

17. Smith, "Decline of the Maquiladora."

18. Smith, "Decline of the Maquiladora."

19. Smith, "Decline of the Maquiladora"; John Nidecker, "Consolidation in the Apparel Industry," *Weekly Corporate Growth Report,* 7 January 2002.

20. Smith, "Decline of the Maquiladora."

21. Smith, "Decline of the Maquiladora."

22. Alisa Solomon, "The Global Economy, as Told Through a Tee: Shirts Off Their Backs," *Village Voice,* 5–11 December 2001.

23. Wilson, "Do Maquiladoras Matter?"

24. US/LEAP, "Maquila Worker Campaigns" (2002), http://www.usleap.org/Banana/bananatemp.html (accessed 30 August 2002).

25. Diane Lindquist, "Rules Change for Maquiladoras," *Industry Week* 250, no. 1 (2001): 23–26.

26. Susan Tiano, *Patriarchy on the Line: Labor, Gender, and Ideology in the Mexican Maquila Industry* (Philadelphia, Pa.: Temple University Press 1994); Christine E. Bose and Edna Acosta-Belen, *Women in the Latin American Development Process* (Philadelphia, Pa.: Temple University Press, 1995).

27. Interview by Tara Radin with Koramsa Human Resources Director, José Antonio Mayorga, Guatemala, 17 July 2002.

28. Yongsun Paik, "Confucius in Mexico: Korean MNCs and the Maquiladoras," *Business Horizons* 41, no. 6 (1998): 25–33.

29. Paik, "Confucius in Mexico."

30. Paik, "Confucius in Mexico."

31. Interview by Tara Radin with representatives of LS&CO sourcing grant recipients, Guatemala, 18 July 2002.

32. Tula Connell, "Maquila Melée," *In These Times: Independent News and Views* (2001), http://www.inthesetimes.com/issue/26/03/news2.shtml (accessed 30 August 2002).

33. Garment & Leather Workers' Federation International Textile, "EC Adopts Resolution on Korean Companies Operating Overseas" (October 2001), http://www.itglwf.org/displaydocument.asp?DocType = Background&Language = & Index = 208 (accessed 30 August 2002).

34. Thomas Donaldson, "The Promise of Corporate Codes of Conduct," *Human Rights Dialogue/Carnegie Council on Ethics and International Affairs* 2, no. 4 (2000): 16–18.

35. Greenhouse, "UNITE, Retail, Wholesale and Department Store Union, AFL-CIO, Interfaith Center on Corporate Responsibility," *New York Times,* 6 November 1998.

36. Greenhouse, "UNITE, Retail, Wholesale and Department Store Union."

37. Alan Howard, "Will the Fair Labor Association Be Fair?" (2002) http://

www.amrc.org.hk/Arch/3703.html; Fair Labor Association, "Fair Labor Association Awarded $750,000 Grant as Part of the Department of State Anti-Sweatshop Initiative" (16 January 2001), http://www.fairlabor.org/html/press.html (accessed 30 August 2002).

38. LS&CO joined FLA in 1999. Robert Collier, "Levi's Joins War Against Sweatshops," *San Francisco Chronicle*, 21 July 1999.

39. Fair Labor Association, "Participating Companies" (2002), http://www.fairlabor.org/html/affiliates/corporate.html.

40. Fair Labor Association, "FLA Makes Major Strides" (24 October 2001), http://www.fairlabor.org/html/press.html.

41. Fair Labor Association, "Fair Labor Board Approves Seven Companies for Participation in FLA's Monitoring Program: Accredits First Independent External Monitor" (24 January 2001), http://www.fairlabor.org/html/press.html (accessed 30 August 2002); Fair Labor Association, "FLA Makes Major Strides."

42. Fair Labor Association, "Fair Labor Association Awarded $750,000 Grant as Part of the Department of State Anti-Sweatshop Initiative," (16 January 2001), http://www.fairlabor.org/html/press.html (accessed 30 August 2002).

43. Fair Labor Association, "Fair Labor Association Awarded $750,000."

44. Fair Labor Association, "Fair Labor Association" (2002), http://www.fairlabor.org (accessed 30 August 2002).

45. Fair Labor Association, "Fair Labor Association Awarded $750,000."

46. Fair Labor Association, "Fair Labor Association Awarded $750,000."

47. Joseph Pereira, "Apparel Makers Back New Labor Inspection Group," *Wall Street Journal*, 10 April 2001).

48. Howard, "Will the Fair Labor Association Be Fair?"

49. Fair Labor Association, "FLA Makes Major Strides."

50. Fair Labor Association, "For Immediate Release: New Changes to Increase the Transparency, Independence, and Scope of the FLA" (2002), http://www.fairlabor.org/html/FLA_PR_April_2002.html (accessed 30 August 2002).

51. Fair Labor Association, "For Immediate Release." For more information, see Fair Labor Association, "Changes to the FLA: A Comparison of the Old and New System" (2002), http://www.fairlabor.org/html/new_fla_comparison.html (accessed 30 August 2002).

52. Worker Rights Consortium, "Workers Rights Consortium Mission Statement," http://www.workersrights.org/about.asp.

53. Worker Rights Consortium, "Mission Statement."

54. Shahien Nasiripour, "USC Apparel Makers Under Fire," *USC Daily Trojan*, 28 March 2002.

55. "New Era Cap, CWA Contract Ratified," *Business Wire*, 27 June 2002.

56. LS&CO, "About LS&CO/Invention of Levi's® 501® Jeans," http://www.levistrauss.com/about/history/jeans.htm (accessed 30 August 2002).

57. For a detailed description of the history of LS&CO, see Graham Howarth, Tania Martino, Samantha Melton, Alan Miegel, Jonathan Morley, and Matthew Weissman, "LEVI'S: A Company as Durable as Its Jeans" (2001), http://shakti.trincoll.edu/~ghowarth/levi.html (accessed 30 August 2002).

58. LS&CO, 2001, "Levi Strauss & Co. Annual Financial Report 2001," Producer.

59. ElBoghdady, "Stitching Together a Strategy."

60. LS&CO, "About LS&CO/Worldwide," http://www.levistrauss.com/about/ (accessed 30 August 2002).

61. LS&CO, "About LS&CO/Americas," http://www.levistrauss.com/about/ lsa/index.htm (accessed 30 August 2002).

62. LS&CO, "About LS&CO/Worldwide."

63. Value Line Investment Survey, "Guess, Inc." (2002), http:// www.valueline.com/secure/vlispdf/stk1700/vlispdf/F10898.pdf (accessed 30 August 2002); Louis Lee, "Why Levi's Still Looks Faded," *Business Week,* 22 July 2002, p. 54.

64. Business & Company Resource Center, "Rankings: SIC = 2325," galenet. galegroup.com/servlet/BCRC (accessed 30 August 2002).

65. LS&CO, "Levi Strauss & Co: Annual Financial Report 2001" (Levi Strauss & Co., 2001).

66. Corporate Social Responsibility Forum, "Business and Human Rights," http://www.pwblf.org/csr/csrwebassist.nsf/content/a1a2a3e4.html#levi (accessed 30 August 2002).

67. LS&CO, "About LS&CO/Values and Vision" (2002), http://www. levistrauss.com/about/vision/ (accessed 30 August 2002).

68. Karl Schoenberger, *Levi's Children: Coming to Terms with Human Rights in the Global Marketplace* (New York: Atlantic Monthly Press, 2001).

69. Lee, "Why Levi's Still Looks Faded," p. 54; Kelly Barron, "Getting a Rise Out of Levi's," *Forbes,* 26 November 2001, p. 156.

70. Lee, "Why Levi's Still Looks Faded"; ElBoghdady, "Stitching Together a Strategy."

71. "Levi-Strauss—Can Levi's Engineer a Reversal of Fortunes," *Marketing,* 18 April 2002.

72. Interview by Tara Radin with Director Mo Rajan, Labor and Human Rights, San Francisco, 20–21 June 2002.

73. LS&CO, "Social Responsiblity/Gobal Sourcing and Operating Guidelines," http://www.levistrauss.com/responsibility/conduct/guidelines.htm (accessed 30 August 2002).

74. Drickhamer, "Consumer Cries for Sweatshop-Free Products."

75. Interview by Tara Radin with Director Michael Kobori, Global Code of Conduct, San Francisco, Calif., 20–21 June 2002.

76. Kobori, interview.

77. LS&CO, "Levi Strauss & Co. Names Six U.S. Plants To Close," LS&CO Media Center (8 April 2002), http://www.levistrauss.com/news/pressrelease.asp?r = 1&c = 0&cat = 0&pr = 530&area = Americas (accessed 30 August 2002); Michael Liedtke, "Levi Strauss Not Alone in Shifting Clothing Production Overseas," *Associated Press State and Local WireQ,* 9 April 2002.

78. Interview by Tara Radin with Theresa Fay-Bustillos, Executive Director, Levi Strauss Foundation, and Vice President, Worldwide Community Affairs, San Francisco, Calif., 20 June 2002.

79. Kobori, interview.

80. Kobori, interview.

81. Kobori, interview.

82. Kobori, interview.

83. Kobori, interview.

84. Drickhamer, "Consumer Cries for Sweatshop-Free Products."

85. Drickhamer, "Consumer Cries for Sweatshop-Free Products."

86. Drickhamer, "Consumer Cries for Sweatshop-Free Products."

87. Kobori, interview.

88. Kobori, interview.

89. Kobori, interview.

90. Kobori, interview.

91. "Who Can Protect Workers' Rights? The Workplace Codes of Conduct Debate," *Human Rights Dialogue/Carnegie Council on Ethics and International Affairs* 2, no. 4 (2000): 3–4; Stephen Frost, "Factory Rules Versus Codes of Conduct: Which Option Makes Sense for Business," *Human Rights Dialogue/Carnegie Council on Ethics and International Affairs* 2, no. 4 (2000): 3–4.

92. LS&CO, "ToE Anniversary Story for Eureka" (12 November 2001).

93. Kobori, interview.

94. Kobori, interview.

95. Kobori, interview.

96. Rajan, interview.

97. Rajan, interview; Kobori, interview.

98. Mo Rajan, interview.

99. Drickhamer, "Consumer Cries for Sweatshop-Free Products."

100. Rajan, interview.

101. Rajan, interview.

102. Rajan, interview.

103. Timothy P. Perkins, Colleen O'Connell, Orosco Carin, Mark Richey, and Matthew Scoble, "Levi's in China?" School of Economics and Business Administration, Saint Mary's College of California (2002), http://homepages.bw.edu/~dkrueger/BUS329/readings/28levi.html (accessed 30 August 2002).

104. William Beaver, "Levi's Is Leaving China," *Business Horizons* 38, no. 2 (March 1995): 35.

105. Lynn Sharp Paine and Jane Palley Katz, "Levi Strauss & Co.: Global Sourcing (A)," *Harvard Business School Case No. 9–395–127* (Cambridge, Mass.: Harvard Business School Publishing 1994, revised 27 February 1997). See also Beaver, "Levi's Is Leaving China."

106. Lynn Sharp Paine and Jane Palley Katz, "Levi Strauss & Co.: Global Sourcing (B)," *Harvard Business School Case No. 9–395–128* (Cambridge, Mass.: Harvard Business School Publishing, 1994, revised 10 March 1995).

107. "Levi Strauss to Cut China Production Due to Human Rights Fears," *Bloomberg News*, 2 May 1993. Timberland was the first American company to pull out. Donna K. Walters, "Firms Unshaken by U.S. Terms for China Trade: Country's Most Favored Nation Status Is Now Linked to Human Rights, but Companies Say Their Role Is Not that of Lobbyist," *Los Angeles Times*, 7 June 1993, p. D3.

108. Interview by Tara Radin with Linda Butler, Senior Manager, LS&CO Worldwide Communications, San Francisco (30 August 2002).

109. Perkins, O'Connell, Carin, Richey, and Scoble, "Levi's in China?"

110. Beaver, "Levi's Is Leaving China." See also "Levi's Followed Its Conscience out of China, Executive Says," *Bloomberg News*, 12 May 1993; Pam Solo, "Trade as Aid: Socially Responsible Foreign Business Investment," *Bulletin of the Atomic Scientists* 51, no. 4 (July 1995): 54.

111. Meryl Davids, "Global Standards, Local Problems," *Journal of Business Strategy* (January/February 1999).

112. Joanna Ramey, "Levi's Will Resume Production in China after 5-Year Absence," *WWD* 71, no. 175 (9 April 1998): 1.

113. Butler, interview.

114. Ramey, "Levi's Will Resume Production."

115. Interview by Tara Radin with Miriam Rodriguez, Code of Conduct Compliance, Regional Director for the Americas, Latin America (15–19 July 2002).

116. LS&CO, "ToE Anniversary Story for Eureka."

117. Rodriguez, interview.

118. Rodriguez, interview.

119. Rodriguez, interview.

120. Interview by Tara Radin with Eduardo Franco Padillo, Director of Human Resources, IBIS de Mexico, El Salvador (18 July 2002).

121. Padillo, interview.

122. Padillo, interview.

123. Rodriguez, interview.

124. Padillo, interview.

125. Padillo, interview.

126. Padillo, interview.

127. Padillo, interview.

128. Padillo, interview.

129. Padillo, interview; Rodriguez, interview.

130. Padillo, interview.

131. LS&CO, 2001, "ToE Anniversary Story for Eureka."

132. U.S. Department of State, "Background Note: El Salvador" (2002), http://www.state.gov/r/pa/ei/bgn/2033.htm (accessed August 30, 2002).

133. Rodriguez, interview.

134. Padillo, interview.

135. Padillo, interview.

136. Padillo, interview.

137. Padillo, interview.

138. Padillo, interview.

139. Padillo, interview.

140. Padillo, interview.

141. Padillo, interview.

142. The owners of this laundry have requested that it and its managers remain unnamed.

143. Padillo, interview.

144. Interview by Tara Radin with Human Resources Director, Aguascalientes laundry (15 July 2002).

145. Human Resources Director, Aguascalientes laundry, interview.

146. Human Resources Director, Aguascalientes laundry, interview.

147. Human Resources Director, Aguascalientes laundry, interview.

148. Rodriguez, interview.

149. Rodriguez, interview.

150. Human Resources Director, Aguascalientes laundry, interview.

151. Rodriguez, interview.

152. Human Resources Director, Aguascalientes laundry, interview.

153. Human Resources Director, Aguascalientes laundry, interview.

154. Human Resources Director, Aguascalientes laundry, interview.

155. Human Resources Director, Aguascalientes laundry, interview.

156. Human Resources Director, Aguascalientes laundry, interview.

157. Human Resources Director, Aguascalientes laundry, interview.

158. Connell, "Maquila Melée."

159. Connell, "Maquila Melée."

160. Interview by Tara Radin with sourcing grant recipients, Guatemala (16 July 2002).

161. CountryWatch, "U.N. Official Concerned About Rights in Guatemala" (22 August 2002), www.countrywatch.com/cw_wire.asp?vCOUNTRY = 69&UID (accessed 30 August 2002).

162. Interview by Tara Radin with Koramsa Human Resources Director, José Antonio Mayorga, Guatemala (17 July 2002).

163. Interview by Tara Radin with Koramsa Product Management Director, Juan Fernando Lara, Guatemala (17 July 2002).

164. Lara, interview; interview by Tara Radin with Koramsa General Manager, Carlos Arias, Guatemala (17 July 2002); interview by Tara Radin with Koramsa Managers, Guatemala (17 July 2002).

165. Interview by Tara Radin with Koramsa President, Alvaro Ruiz, Guatemala (17 July 2002).

166. Lara, interview.

167. Lara, interview; Koramsa managers, interview.

168. Interview by Tara Radin with Koramsa President, Alvaro Ruiz and Managers, Guatemala (17 July 2002).

169. Ruiz, interview; Koramsa Managers, interview.

170. Interview by Tara Radin with Koramsa Human Resources Director, José Antonio Mayorga, Guatemala (17 July 2002); Koramsa Managers, interview.

171. Mayorga, interview; Koramsa Managers, interview.

172. Mayorga, interview; Koramsa Managers, interview.

173. Mayorga, interview; Koramsa Managers, interview.

174. Mayorga, interview; Koramsa Managers, interview.

175. Lara, interview; Koramsa Managers, interview.

176. Mayorga, interview; Koramsa Managers, interview.

177. Lara, interview; Koramsa Managers, interview.

178. Lara, interview; Koramsa Managers, interview.

179. Lara, interview; Koramsa Managers, interview.

180. Lara, interview; Koramsa Managers, interview.

181. Ruiz, interview; Koramsa Managers, interview.

182. Ruiz, interview.

183. Interview by Tara Radin with Director Michael Kobori, Global Code of Conduct, San Francisco, Calif. (20–21 June 2002).

184. Corporate Social Responsibility Forum, "Business and Human Rights," http://www.pwblf.org/csr/csrwebassist.nsf/content/a1a2a3e4.html#levi (accessed 30 August 2002).

185. Kobori, interview.

186. Kobori, interview.

187. Rajan, interview.

188. For additional support, see Connell, "Maquila Melée."

189. Rajan, interview.

190. Mo Rajan, "Letter to Juan Francisco Alfaro Mijangos, Minister of Labor" (2001).

191. Rajan, interview.

192. Interview by Tara Radin with Theresa Fay-Bustillos, Executive Director, Levi Strauss Foundation, and Vice President, Worldwide Community Affairs, San Francisco, Calif. (20 June 2002).

193. Fay-Bustillos, interview.

194. LS&CO, "ToE Anniversary Story for Eureka."

195. Fay Hansen, "The Globalization Backlash," *Business Finance*, February 2001, p. 44.

196. Kobori, interview. LS&CO, "ToE Anniversary Story for Eureka."

197. LS&CO, "ToE Anniversary Story for Eureka"; Kobori, interview.

APPENDIX 9.1

Levi Strauss & Co.
Terms of Engagement

- **Ethical Standards**

We will seek to identify and utilize business partners who aspire as individuals and in the conduct of all their businesses to a set of ethical standards not incompatible with our own.

- **Legal Requirements**

We expect our business partners to be law abiding as individuals and to comply with legal requirements relevant to the conduct of all their businesses.

- **Environmental Requirements**

We will only do business with partners who share our commitment to the environment and who conduct their business in a way that is consistent with Levi Strauss & Co.'s Environmental Philosophy and Guiding Principles.

- **Community Involvement**

We will favor business partners who share our commitment to improving community conditions.

- **Employment Standards**

We will only do business with partners who adhere to the following guidelines:

Child Labor: Use of child labor is not permissible. Workers can be no less than 15 years of age and not younger than the compulsory age to be in school. We will not utilize partners who use child labor in any of their facilities. We support the development of legitimate workplace apprenticeship programs for the educational benefit of younger people.

Prison Labor/Forced Labor: We will not utilize prison or forced labor in contracting relationships in the manufacture and finishing of our products. We will not utilize or purchase materials from a business partner utilizing prison or forced labor.

Disciplinary Practices: We will not utilize business partners who use corporal punishment or other forms of mental or physical coercion.

Working Hours: While permitting flexibility in scheduling, we will identify local legal limits on work hours and seek business partners who do not exceed them except for appropriately compensated overtime. While we favor partners who utilize less than sixty-hour workweeks, we will not use contractors who, on a regular basis, require in excess of a sixty-hour week. Employees should be allowed at least one day off in seven.

Wages and Benefits: We will only do business with partners who provide wages and benefits that comply with any applicable law and match the prevailing local manufacturing or finishing industry practices.

Freedom of Association: We respect workers' rights to form and join organizations of their choice and to bargain collectively. We expect our suppliers to respect the right to free association and the right to organize and bargain collectively without unlawful interference. Business partners should ensure that workers who make such decisions or participate in such organizations are not the object of discrimination or punitive disciplinary actions and that the representatives of such organizations have access to their members under conditions established either by local laws or mutual agreement between the employer and the worker organizations.

Discrimination: While we recognize and respect cultural differences, we believe that workers should be employed on the basis of their ability to do the job, rather than on the basis of personal characteristics or beliefs. We will favor business partners who share this value.

Health & Safety: We will only utilize business partners who provide workers with a safe and healthy work environment. Business partners who provide residential facilities for their workers must provide safe and healthy facilities.

Source: Levi Strauss & Co., reprinted with permission.

## CHAPTER 10

Dow Chemical Company: Responsible Care Program in Thailand

Richard E. Wokutch[1]

Firms in the chemical industry face common challenges regarding the safe handling and disposal of the hazardous substances they use. These substances, though important for many products we use on a daily basis, can pose serious threats to chemical industry workers and communities surrounding their plants. This chapter deals with a voluntary international chemical industry initiative, Responsible Care,[2] which promotes the responsible development, use, and disposal of chemicals and chemical by-products. Underlying this effort is a recognition that firms in the industry, workers, and society at large share common interests in the responsible care of these substances and that collaborative efforts to respond to environmental challenges can be more effective than any firm could achieve individually.

This chapter looks in particular at the implementation of Dow Chemical Company's Responsible Care program in its operations in Thailand by its Dow in Thailand and Dow Chemical Pacific Limited units. The chapter shows that multinational corporations and their industry associations can be important sources of technological expertise for developing countries in environmental, health, and safety issues. Also provided is a model for the ways in which firms might collaborate in addressing other issues of mutual concern.

A reasonable question might be why would a case concerning an environmental program be included in a book about labor-oriented programs operated by global companies in developing countries. Certainly in terms of popular perceptions, corporate environmental impacts and programs are more closely associated with the welfare of the community in general rather than with employee concerns. But safety and health specialists have long known that environmental issues are a crucial component of the overall occupational safety and health conditions of a workplace or firm. And nowhere is the connection more obvious than in the chemical industry, in which inappropriate handling of chemicals could have disastrous results both for workers and the local community. The connection between environmental activities and worker welfare is further highlighted by the current trend in industry to combine environmental, health, and safety (EH&S) functions in the same corporate department, as is the practice at Dow.

Dow Chemical Company, ranked by *Fortune* magazine[3] as the world's largest chemical company, was initially incorporated in 1897. In 1900, shortly after incorporation, Dow merged with the Midland Chemical Company to form the basis of the modern company. The firm grew domestically during the early decades of the twentieth century, and then during the 1940s Dow expanded internationally with the organization of Dow Chemical of Canada. During World War II Dow Chemical and Corning Glass formed Dow Corning to produce silicones for the military. Dow Chemical Pacific Limited was formed in 1957, and it includes Dow's operations in Thailand as well as operations in the rest of the Asia-Pacific region.[4]

In its early days of operation Dow concentrated on the production of bleach, but over the years the company has developed a wide range of new products and applications for consumer and commercial use. Products are now manufactured for a number of markets including food, transportation, health and medicine, personal and home care, and building and construction. Dow is headquartered in Midland, Michigan, and has operations in close to 170 countries around the world. Dow's 1999 merger with Union Carbide substantially increased the size of the firm but at the same time has posed a number of challenges, including those related to merging of organizational structures and corporate cultures as well as Dow's inheriting of problems left over from Union Carbide's Bhopal disaster.[5] In 2001 Dow's revenues of $27.8 billion ranked it number 60 on the *Fortune* 500 listing of U.S. companies, and it ranked number 152 on *Fortune's* Global 500 for 2000, with employees totaling approximately 42,000.[6] Dow ranked second in the chemical industry on *Fortune's* 2002 list of most admired companies, trailing just behind DuPont.[7]

Inspiration, Idea Generation, and Inception: Dow Chemical and Responsible Care

Responsible Care is a voluntary chemical industry action program established for the purpose of ensuring the safe handling of chemicals throughout the life of a product. One key feature of Responsible Care is that it provides chemical firms with an industry forum in which to share best practice information regarding the safe handling of chemicals. It also provides an institutional vehicle for other forms of cooperation among member firms that may be attempting to address common environmental challenges.

During the 1960s the environmental movement pushed its way onto the center stage of public consciousness and debate and garnered broad public support in the United States and Western Europe. This movement posed numerous challenges for firms in the chemical industry. These firms were targeted for special criticism by environmental activists who were concerned about the environmental effects of the companies' products and production processes. In response to this criticism and the enactment of numerous environmental regulations, chemical companies became much more serious about controlling the environmental effects of their products. When they did, the early thinking by the chemical manufacturers as well as environmentalists was that the firms needed to be responsible for the chemicals they produced "from cradle to grave." However, according to Judy Castledine, EH&S director for Dow Chemical Pacific Limited, it became apparent over time that that view was too limited. According to her, a more appropriate metaphor for how Dow and other Responsible Care participants needed to view their responsibilities for these products is "from lust to dust."[8] This suggests that the companies are responsible for the product and its effects from the initial idea leading to the creation of the product until its disintegration into a benign part of the environment.

Responsible Care has its origins in a 1977 initiative of the Canadian Chemical Producers Association (CCPA) to develop guidelines on the safe handling of hazardous chemicals. Bob Boldt, a retired Dow Canada Vice President, was heavily involved in the initial development of the guiding principles for Responsible Care through his work on a CCPA subcommittee attempting to draft environmental principles and complementary work he was doing with Dow trying to operationalize them. Dow Chemical Company has been an active participant in Responsible Care since its inception.

Union Carbide's 1984 Bhopal disaster, although not directly precipitating the Responsible Care program that had already been in development for several years, did provide the impetus for chemical industry firms in Canada and the United States to formalize Responsible Care activities and membership requirements. Subsequently, this program quickly spread to other industrialized countries.[9] As a novel example of voluntary industry cooperation to address a social problem related to industry activities, Responsible Care can provide a model for cooperative efforts to address common industry problems. As such, the lessons we can learn from studying it have implications beyond the chemical industry.

Responsible Care programs now operate in 45 countries and are coordinated at the national level by national chemical industry associations. Adoption of a Responsible Care program is a requirement for membership in these associations. There are differences in the way the programs are structured owing to different national conditions, but all contain eight essential common features:

- A formal commitment on behalf of each company to a set of guiding principles signed, in the majority of cases, by the chief executive officer
- A series of codes, guidance notes, and checklists to assist companies in implementing the commitment
- The progressive development of indicators against which improvements in performance can be measured
- An ongoing process of communication on health, safety, and environment matters with interested parties inside and outside the industry
- Provision of forums in which companies can share views and exchange experiences on implementation of the commitment
- Adoption of a title and a logo that clearly identify national programs as being consistent with and part of the concept of Responsible Care (the Responsible Care logo for Thailand is shown in figure 10.1)
- Consideration of how best to encourage all member companies to commit and participate in Responsible Care
- Systematic procedures to verify the implementation of the measurable (or practical) elements of Responsible Care by the member companies[10]

Through Responsible Care, "member companies are committed to support a continuing effort to improve the industry's responsible management of chemicals."[11] Beyond these eight common features every participating

Figure 10.1
Thai Responsible Care Logo

Source: Reprinted with permission from Dow in Thailand

country has its own version of the program specifically tailored to its needs. Thus to provide an example, the following is a brief summary of the key elements of the American Chemistry Council's Responsible Care program.

Guiding Principles

The American Chemistry Council explains the industry's reasoning for undertaking the Responsible Care initiative, its environmental intentions, and the program's guiding principles as follows:

Our industry creates products and services that make life better for people around the world—both today and tomorrow. The benefits of our industry are accompanied by enduring commitments to Responsible Care in the management of chemicals worldwide. We will make continuous progress toward the vision of no accidents, injuries, or harm to the environment and will publicly report our global health, safety, and environmental performance. We will lead our companies in ethical ways that increasingly benefit society, the economy, and the environment while adhering to the following principles:

- To seek and incorporate public input regarding our products and operations
- To provide chemicals that can be manufactured, transported, used, and disposed of safely
- To make health, safety, the environment, and resource conservation critical considerations for all new and existing products and processes
- To provide information on health or environmental risks and pursue protective measures for employees, the public, and other key stakeholders
- To work with customers, carriers, suppliers, distributors, and contractors to foster the safe use, transport, and disposal of chemicals
- To operate our facilities in a manner that protects the environment and the health and safety of our employees and the public
- To support education and research on the health, safety, and environmental effects of our products and processes
- To work with others to resolve problems associated with past handling and disposal practices
- To lead in the development of responsible laws, regulations, and standards that safeguard the community, workplace, and environment
- To practice Responsible Care by encouraging and assisting others to adhere to these principles and practices[12]

Codes of Management Practices

Responsible Care uses six codes of management practices.[13] They are described in brief below.

1. Community Awareness and Emergency Response Code—This code focuses on communication of relevant safety, health, and environmental information to the

local community, including being responsive to questions regarding these matters from members of the community. A second focus is the development of emergency response procedures to quickly and competently handle emergencies.

2. Pollution Prevention Code—This code provides guidelines to achieve continuous reductions of all forms of pollutants released into the air, water, and land. It also recommends a number of management approaches for achieving this, including inventorying and evaluating wastes generated and released at production sites, establishing priorities for waste reduction, concentrating first on source reduction, second on recycling/reusing, and third on treatment. Other prescribed activities include encouraging and supporting waste reduction efforts by others (e.g., contractors and customers), assisting local government in waste and pollution reduction efforts, and providing relevant education and training.

3. Process Safety Code—This code focuses on the prevention of fires, explosions, and chemical releases and is complementary to activities discussed in the pollution prevention code and the employee health and safety code. The focus is on activities related to production processes from the initial design stage through manufacturing, handling, and on-site storage. Management practices are prescribed in four interrelated domains: management leadership, technology, facilities, and personnel.

4. Distribution Code—This code specifies procedures for the reduction of risks associated with the transportation, storage, and other handling of chemicals.

5. Employee Health and Safety Code—This code provides guidelines for promoting the safety and health of workers and others influenced by company operations, such as contractors, visitors, and the general public. Guidelines for environmental protection are also provided. Guidelines provided include prescribed safety and health program management approaches, measures for the identification and evaluation of safety and health hazards, and methods for preventing and controlling hazards beginning first with attempting to achieve inherently safe design then progressively relying on material substitution, engineering controls, administrative controls, and finally personal protective equipment.

6. Product Stewardship Code—The purpose of this code is to encourage integration of safety, health, and environmental considerations into the design, production, distribution, and disposal of products.

Contained in each of these codes are provisions for establishing a dialogue with the public, instituting self-evaluations, establishing performance measures, and establishing performance goals. Following are brief explanations of these provisions.

Dialogue with the Public

Members of Responsible Care attempt to solicit public input regarding matters of concern through advisory panels. These panels seek to elicit participation and advice from environmentalists, educators, and health and safety specialists.[14]

Self-Evaluations

Responsible Care member firms conduct annual evaluations of company progress toward compliance with each of the codes described above. These evaluations serve as a measure of the success of company environmental efforts and as a management tool.[15]

Measures of Performance

In addition to self-evaluations, each code has performance measures that aid in giving the public a better understanding of the Responsible Care program and its progress.[16]

Goals and Performance:

To measure performance, Responsible Care participants establish company-specific goals reflecting their stakeholder concerns and expectations, and publicly report on their progress each year.[17] Guidelines are also provided to help ensure the comparability of reporting on goal performance. Reports are regularly provided showing yearly progress with respect to implementation of practices specified by all six of these codes.

Integration: Organizational Structure for Responsible Care at Dow

The principles and activities of Responsible Care at Dow are carried out through the EH&S organizational structures. The top Safety and Health Officer at Dow is Larry Washington, Corporate Vice President, Environment, Health and Safety, Human Resources, and Public Affairs. Along with vice presidents in other functional areas such as operations, legal, finance, and research and development and with business group presidents, Washington reports directly to Dow's President and CEO, Mike Parker. An environmental, health, and safety subcommittee of the board of directors is also involved with setting policy for Dow in this domain. Area directors such as Judy Castledine in the Asia-Pacific region coordinate EH&S activities in their geographic areas of responsibility. EH&S staff at Dow facilities in the Asia-Pacific region report to her functionally as well as to their site leader or site director. As noted below, corporate staff like Castledine will periodically visit plant sites to conduct inspections. They will also work with plant-level personnel on matters pertaining to record keeping and training. Castledine in turn reports to Sam Smolik, global vice president for EH&S, who in turn reports to Larry Washington at Dow headquarters in Midland, Michigan.

As noted above, companies implementing Responsible Care programs are directed to solicit input on their operations from the general public.

Dow does this at the corporate level through its Corporate Environmental Advisory Council. It was first formed in 1991 and was the first such external advisory group in the worldwide chemical industry. The council comprises environmental experts who meet two or three times yearly to provide advice on environmental matters. In addition, Dow has 30 community advisory panels at Dow plant locations.[18]

Implementation: EH&S Operations

Because of the nature of the industry in which it operates, Dow's most important occupational safety and health challenges are interrelated with environmental issues, so these matters are considered together. Dow Chemical Company in recent years has implemented a behaviorally based occupational safety and health approach. The fundamental thesis of this approach is that engineering improvements to equipment and processes can enhance safety and health only so far, and that further improvements beyond that require the elimination of human errors. Behaviorally based approaches reinforce and reward desired safety and health procedures by, for example, tying bonuses to the achievement of injury and illness reduction goals. This approach also entails acknowledging people for doing things the right way rather than just criticizing those who do things incorrectly. Nevertheless, activities detrimental to safety and health are discouraged through a variety of means. Behaviorally based safety and health practices are not meant to replace traditional safety and health measures to reduce or eliminate hazards but rather to supplement them.

Behavioral approaches to occupational safety and health were pioneered by DuPont Corporation, and its widely publicized success with them has led a great many other companies to adopt similar approaches in recent years. This trend has, in turn, generated a considerable amount of criticism from opponents of those approaches, who criticize the techniques and philosophy behind these methods for dealing with occupational safety and health issues. Critics contend that behaviorally based approaches to safety and health essentially blame the victim when accidents happen. Moreover, because of the rewards and penalties built into the approaches critics are concerned that supervisors and accident victims will be tempted to hide injuries that do occur, thereby compounding the problems.[19]

Dow's behavioral approach to EH&S takes into account the ABCs (antecedents, behaviors, and consequences) of safety, health, and environment activities and attempts to modify the antecedents and behaviors to achieve the desired consequences, that is, operations that are safe, healthy, and environmentally sound. Dow's approach to safety and health is also considered to be consistent with employee empowerment programs being used at Dow in which workers take accountability and responsibility and manage themselves as a team, rather than relying on top-down hierarchical management.

When asked what things, in her view, Dow does particularly well in the environmental, health, and safety domain, Castledine noted four areas:

- Integrating EH&S concerns into everyone's work processes. There is a saying among safety and health professionals that "safety is everyone's business." Unfortunately, all too often EH&S issues become secondary priorities for other workers and managers. EH&S specialists end up being the only ones paying careful attention to these matters. According to Castledine, Dow has been able to avoid this problem.

- Reducing waste. Dow executives profess to believe that environmental activities will save money in the long run, and they prefer to reduce waste at the source rather than focusing on waste treatment or disposal. The acronym WRAP (waste reduction always pays) is frequently referred to in order to promote this philosophy. While conceding that DuPont has long been known as a leader in worker safety throughout industry, Dow representatives believe that they are particularly strong in the environmental area.

- Implementing hazard management. According to Castledine, Dow has a very active toxicology group that makes hazard management an area of strength.

- Implementing globalization processes. Dow attempts to make sure that the good things done at Dow in the EH&S arena are done globally. The company attempts to ensure that wherever production facilities are located their operations meet or exceed applicable local government standards or Dow corporate standards, whichever are higher. The implementation in Thailand of this globalization process through the Responsible Care program is, of course, the focus of this case.

Dow also publishes a corporate environmental, health, and safety report on an annual basis.[20] Publication of this report is consistent with the value of transparency articulated by Responsible Care.

Dow's performance in the environmental, health, and safety areas has received some favorable external recognition. The company was ranked number one in the chemical industry in 2000 on the Dow Jones Sustainability Group Index. In addition, it was ranked first among energy and chemical companies on a *Financial Times* survey of the world's most respected companies in 2000, and it was rated the best chemical company in the United States by *Forbes* in the same year.[21] Dow was also rated number one on the Dow Jones Sustainability Index in 2001.[22] In 2000 Dow, along with 31 other companies, received an Energy Star Partner of the Year Award from EPA administrator Carol Browner. These companies were cited for their use of energy efficient technologies and their communications about the benefits of these technologies to consumers and other businesses.[23]

Despite these favorable external reviews, Dow has received much criticism from environmentalists and other social activists over the years. Major controversies have pertained to specific products such as dioxin, Agent Orange, and Dursban and have resulted in extensive litigation and considerable bad publicity. Dow has also been accused of exercising excessive political influence in pursuit of more lax environmental standards in U.S. regulatory and legislative arenas. Other criticisms include Dow's involvement with the Dow-Corning silicone gel breast implants and health concerns related to them; its manufacture of napalm for military use during the Vietnam War; and the acquisition of Union Carbide, which still bears the stigma of involvement in the Bhopal disaster in which thousands of people died from a chemical explosion at one of its plants.[24] To put these criticisms in perspective, though, it is worth noting that the chemical industry has served as somewhat of a lightning rod for criticisms from environmentalists, and other firms in the industry have had similar problems.

The scope of this case does not allow us to explore the merits of the criticisms about Dow's activities in these areas. As noted in the introduction to this volume, these cases are not intended to be an overall evaluation of the labor practices (or in this case, EH&S practices) of focal companies, but rather descriptions of particular labor-oriented programs that merit attention as potential models for other firms operating in developing countries. Thus we will proceed to discuss Dow's participation in the Responsible Care program in Thailand. First, however, we will review the overall operations of Dow in Thailand.

DOW IN THAILAND[25]

Dow Chemical first established a sales office in Thailand in 1967. With the encouragement of the government, Dow in Thailand, as the operations there are formally known, began production at a polystyrene plant in 1978 in Phrapadaeng, an industrial area about 25 kilometers south of the Bangkok metropolitan area. At that time the Thai government, through the board of investment, was actively promoting foreign investments and offered Dow in Thailand a 10-year exclusive tax incentive on polystyrene if it would begin production there and provided that the plant satisfied domestic demand. After those 10 years, Dow in Thailand was required as part of the promotion condition to pick a local partner with which to operate the plant. The Phrapadaeng plant closed in 1996. A new facility that Dow in Thailand built in 1975 in an industrial region near the city of Map Ta Phut was the most significant investment in Thailand's petrochemical industry at the time. With subsequent investments at this site, it became the largest Dow production facility in the entire Pacific region, although it has recently relinquished that distinction with the start-up of a large Dow joint venture in Malaysia.

Dow in Thailand currently comprises three businesses—Dow Chemical Thailand, Dow AgroSciences (Thailand), and the SCC-Dow Group. These first two businesses handle imports of Dow products to Thailand. They include agricultural products sold to farmers for use in growing crops, and raw materials sold to Thai manufacturers for use in the production of a wide range of items from paint to personal care items. These operations account for about 20 percent of Dow in Thailand's business.

The SCC-Dow Group accounts for the remaining 80 percent of Dow in Thailand's business. This is composed of a set of joint ventures between Dow in Thailand and elements of the Siam Cement Group, a large Thai company that has been in operation almost as long as Dow Chemical Company itself. Formal collaboration between Dow in Thailand and the Siam Cement Group began in 1987 and now consists of five operating companies: Pacific Plastics (Thailand), Siam Synthetic Latex Co., Siam Polystyrene Co., Siam Styrene Monomer Co., and Siam Polyethylene Co. These companies produce a number of basic chemicals and plastics that go into other products in industries such as furniture and bedding, automotive, electrical appliances, construction, and paint. Some of the more easily recognizable items produced by these businesses include coatings for high-quality paper (such as that used in glossy magazines), carpet backing, plastic cases for television and computer monitors, and disposable plastic for packaging.

Collaborative ventures such as these are actively encouraged by the Thai government. The ventures provide a vehicle to attract foreign capital, technology, and technical personnel while keeping Thai businesses involved with development. Multinational companies are very closely scrutinized in Thailand and are expected to perform to a higher standard than domestic companies. No doubt, this phenomenon occurs in other countries, even the United States, but it seems to be particularly pronounced in Thailand, where foreigners are required to pay more for all sorts of things because it is assumed that they can afford it. Thus even parks and museums have different admission rates for foreigners than for Thais.

The researcher had the opportunity to visit Dow in Thailand operations at the Map Ta Phut site located about 100 miles southeast of Bangkok on the coast of the Gulf of Thailand in Rayong Province. Industrial development has been encouraged in this region by the government to reduce the problems associated with excessive concentration of population and industry in Bangkok and also to take advantage of natural gas reserves located in the Gulf of Thailand, which are piped ashore at Rayong. Interviews were conducted with a number of individuals, including the site director for the entire Map Ta Phut operations, Richard Smith; the human resources manager, Sawang Luechapatanaporn; the environmental, health and safety leader, Watanapahu Thanissorn; and others concerned with various aspects of occupational health and safety, environmental issues, medicine, and personnel and production issues. The researcher also had the opportunity to talk informally with several technicians during a one-and-a-half-hour plant tour. Although these conversations usually took place in the presence of the tour guide, who was a midlevel manager, the candor of the conversations did not seem to be affected. Managers at the head office in Bangkok were also interviewed, including Jim Fitterling, the country manager and managing director for Dow in Thailand. Also interviewed was a key individual in the implementation of Responsible Care in the region, Judy Castledine, who as previously mentioned is the Asia-Pacific area EH&S director and is located in Hong Kong. She and her colleagues audit environmental regulations at Dow in Thailand operations on an annual basis and provide advice and support services throughout the year.

Establishment and Integration at Dow in Thailand: Environmental, Safety, and Health Organizational Structure

The top Dow in Thailand officer is Jim Fitterling. Because of the variety of businesses with which Dow in Thailand is involved, his reporting relationships are somewhat complicated. With respect to the 100 percent Dow in Thailand businesses, Fitterling reports to Patrick Ho in Hong Kong. For joint venture business, he reports to Apiporn Pasawat, the President of Siam Cement Company Petrochemical Business, and Romeo Kreinburg, a corporate operating board member at headquarters in Midland, Michigan. Although Fitterling's main office is located in Bangkok, he visits the Map Ta Phut operations about once per month.

According to Thai law any work site with more than 50 employees must have a safety officer with at least 180 hours of safety training. Such sites are also required to have a safety committee (referred to as a Safety and Working Environment Committee) that meets at least once per month. Both the Map Ta Phut plant and the Bangkok office exceed this minimum employment criterion, so there are parallel safety structures in these two Dow operating locations. In this case we focus on the operations at Map Ta Phut. The organization of the EH&S Department at Map Ta Phut is provided in figure 10.2. The EH&S leader also chairs the Safety and Working Environment Committee, which is composed of managers, employee representatives, and the site safety officer. A diagram of the organization of this department/committee is provided in figure 10.2. The committee's activities in recent years include running safety promotion programs, developing safety-training packages, and conducting safety inspections.

In addition to the staff described above, the Map Ta Phut plant has a medical department that can provide emergency medical care as well as conduct preventive medical screening. The medical department consists of a full-time nurse and a part-time contract doctor. Reportedly, hyperten-

Figure 10.2
Structure of EH&S Department

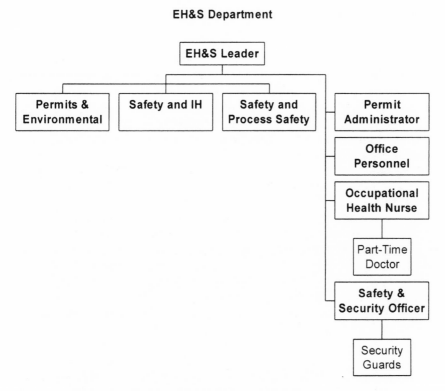

Source: Reprinted with permission from Dow in Thailand.

sion and elevated cholesterol levels are the most common medical problems encountered in workers at the Map Ta Phut plant.

Integration at Dow in Thailand: Operations and Philosophy

Like the rest of Dow, Dow in Thailand follows a triple bottom line operating philosophy, seeking to achieve financial, environmental, and social objectives in its business operations. Dow in Thailand adopted the Responsible Care program in 1993, and this initiative is viewed as a key component of its efforts to operationalize the triple bottom line philosophy.

In 2000 Dow in Thailand had over 22 billion baht (approximately $500 million) in sales, and Dow's total investments exceeded 15 billion baht (about $450 million).[26] A total of 419 people are directly employed in its operations, and an additional 200 contractors regularly work with the company. Contractor employment fluctuates markedly at Dow in Thailand; substantially more contractors work on-site when new machinery is being installed or existing machinery is being overhauled for a change in production.

The workforce at Dow in Thailand facilities is, by and large, well educated and, by Thai standards, quite well paid. All of the engineers and supervisors employed at Dow in Thailand operations are graduates of universities, technical colleges, or trade schools, and most of the technicians in operations have a diploma-level education. According to Jim Fitterling the company has no problem recruiting the very best graduates of Thai institutions. They are attracted by the generous pay and benefits and the prestige of working with a global company. Moreover, engineering school graduates who are recruited find the possibility of overseas work very appealing. In addition to the glamour of living abroad, an overseas assignment, because of the differences in pay scales, could provide engineers or managers with a substantial financial windfall that would ensure their financial security for life. Some of the technicians have also had the experience of working overseas on new plant start-ups and other temporary assignments.

The base pay for entry-level technicians is approximately 10,000 baht per month assuming 13 months base pay plus a variable pay target of 2 months bonus (based on performance), a 4,500 baht per month special allowance,[27] and an estimated 25 percent extra for overtime. This works out to about $3,250 per year, not including bonus, special allowance, and overtime. Total compensation of about $6,000 per year is approximately equivalent to five times what a worker would make earning the minimum wage in Bangkok and surrounding areas, 165 baht per day or about $1,280 per year.[28] (See Thailand country narrative at Web site: http://pres.depaul.edu/hartman/BeyondSweatShops/CountryReports for a further discussion of wage and other labor issues in Thailand.) Experienced technicians at Dow can make even more. The proportion of total compensation tied to bonuses is significant, and it is felt to be a strong motivator of performance. These bonuses are based 37.5 percent on financial performance; 37.5 percent on environmental, safety, and health performance; and 25 percent on personal performance (achievement vs. goals). Notably, bonuses of top managers are also tied to safety and health and financial performance.

At the Map Ta Phut site there are approximately 210 workers. They are mostly male (82 percent male and 18 percent female), and they are predominantly young (58 percent are under 30 years of age). The workforce is described as being very enthusiastic and extremely competent even though, because of their relatively young age, they do not have a great deal of experience. Much of the production at Map Ta Phut is automated, and a visitor is struck by the fact that there are very few workers in production areas. A factory area half the size of a football field may have just a couple of workers, mainly checking controls and the machinery and making adjustments when necessary. Under normal operating conditions, more of the technicians are working in the control room, where they supervise production by monitoring gauges showing pressures, temperatures, and flows of contained substances as well as other controls.

Because production of chemicals and by-products is an around-the-clock operation, there are three shifts at Map Ta Phut: 8:00 A.M. to 4:00 P.M., 4:00 P.M. to 12:00 midnight, and 12:00 midnight to 8:00 A.M. The normal schedule is to work six days and then have a two-day break. Workers alternate shifts and this is, of course, physically difficult because of the disruption of sleep patterns. Several technicians and managers were asked about this schedule, and opinions varied. One common theme heard was that this was a fair way to share the inconvenience of night work. But one technician specifically cited shift work when asked what he liked *best* about his job. He said that he and at least some of his fellow technicians welcomed the opportunity to have their days free for shopping, banking, and other activities that are more difficult to do at night. He did, however, note that this work schedule does bother his supervisor.

A few years ago the Thai government passed a law designed to protect women from shift work and chemical exposure. The law, which would have effectively precluded women from working at Map Ta Phut and at other chemical production facilities, was protested by the petrochemical industry and was eventually rescinded. This reopened the door for female engineers and technicians to pursue careers at Map Ta Phut. Currently, about 40 percent of the exempt workforce of Dow in Thailand is female.

Integration at Dow in Thailand: EH&S Operations

Dow in Thailand's approach to environmental, health, and safety matters is highly consistent with the Dow Chemical Company corporate approach described above. As such it has a behavioral orientation, with an emphasis on antecedents, behaviors, and consequences pertaining to EH&S. In line with this, signage plays a role in encouraging desired behaviors and discouraging undesired behaviors (see photo 10.1).

As noted previously, one of the concerns of critics of behaviorally based occupational safety and health approaches is that incentives and disincentives built into the system may encourage a worker who experiences an injury to hide the fact and not report the incident. This could of course cause problems for the injured worker and lead to more serious subsequent incidents if the causal factors are not addressed. According to Fitterling there has not been evidence of any covering up of accidents, and he notes that workers understand that hiding a significant injury would be a serious infraction that could lead to termination. Still, he concedes

Photo 10.1 Signage at Dow Thai operation encouraging desired behaviors and discouraging undesired behaviors. *Source:* **V. Vorapong, Dow Thailand**

that workers might not report each and every minor injury. This is not necessarily due to the behaviorally based occupational safety and health (OSH) approach, however; reticence to report bad news is consistent with Thai culture[29] and, in some sense, it can be ascribed to human nature.

According to Fitterling eliminating human error and ensuring that workers follow appropriate operating procedures are the greatest challenges with respect to safety, health, and environment Dow in Thailand faces. Technological problems tend to be more straightforward. Where technical solutions to problems do exist, eliminating these problems is mainly a matter of applying the right technology and making the necessary investments. These investments may not be trivial, and installing the new technology may require shutting down operations, the cost of which can be substantial, but such technological solutions are more predictable than remedies that rely on eliminating human error. In contrast, the behaviorally based safety and health approach is well suited for dealing with hazards posed by human error. According to Fitterling Dow in Thailand's greatest safety, health, and environmental concerns center on "loss of primary containment" (i.e., leaks, breaks, and spills) and transportation safety. Release of products or in-process materials into the environment by virtue of a leak, break, or spill or a transportation accident could pose serious threats both for workers and for members of the broader community.

Contractors often pose a special problem for the achievement of company EH&S goals. Frequently contract employees are not as well trained, as tuned in to the corporate culture, or as committed to corporate goals as regular employees. Dow in Thailand tries to address that problem by treating contractors the same as regular employees. It puts contract workers through the same sorts of training programs as regular employees (or requires the contractor to do so). EH&S inspections of contractor work areas are conducted on a regular basis (every 1–2 days for "intense" projects and once per week on other projects) by Dow in Thailand's EH&S staff as well as by managers in whose areas contractors are working. Dow in Thailand also provides rewards to contractors for achieving certain EH&S goals (e.g., so many days without a reportable injury).

During the visit to the Map Ta Phut site the researcher had the opportunity to meet with a worker who had suffered a broken leg in the last significant workplace accident at that site. The worker said that the break occurred when a broken pipe swung and hit him, and it was not clear who was responsible for the pipe having been broken. A report about the incident was written up and distributed throughout Dow in Thailand, but the worker did not feel he was punished in any sort of way. In fact, he reported being well taken care of by the company.

Implementation at Dow in Thailand: Responsible Care

The Responsible Care program is Dow in Thailand's major response to the environmental, health, and safety challenges posed by its operations, as is the case with its corporate parent. As noted above, Responsible Care programs are cooperative industry-wide endeavors that operate and are organized in each country. Dow in Thailand has taken a strong leadership role in the implementation of Responsible Care in Thailand. This has reportedly been motivated by the company's desire to be a good corporate citizen as well as a concern for the environment. Its leadership in this has been made possible by its greater technical expertise relative to that of local companies and its access to other relevant resources and expertise at the Dow corporate level. One example of Dow in Thailand's leadership in this area is in the development of an emergency response plan for the Map Ta Phut area. The need for this was driven home by several environmental incidents in Thailand in recent years, including a major fire at a Thai Oil refinery in Map Ta Phut. These incidents have highlighted the weaknesses of the existing governmental and industry emergency response capabilities and plans. Dow worked with the local authorities in Map Ta Phut (Industrial Estate Authority of Thailand) and other employers in the Map Ta Phut industrial site to develop an emergency response plan, which was approved in 2001. This plan catalogs which parties in the area have which types of emergency response capabilities and what roles they will play in the event of an emergency.

An important mechanism for working with the other employers in Map Ta Phut is a group called the Map Ta Phut Plant Managers' Committee, an organization that Dow's Map Ta Phut site director Richard Smith has chaired for a number of years. This organization also coordinates with government in other locations on technical matters such as emergency response because of its expertise in this area and the government's lack of equipment and/or technical expertise. The need for this coordination was highlighted by a 2001 incident in which a truck carrying toxic chemicals crashed on a Bangkok expressway. As a result of the accident, chemicals spilled out of the truck and were washed into the sewer system, posing a serious environmental hazard. In addition to this hazard, fumes from the accident threatened a nearby school. Safety information needed to be sent from the Map Ta Phut site, resulting in a dangerously long delay of 3 to 4 hours in addressing the problems. As a result of this incident the government passed a number of environmental regulations, but many are skeptical about how rigidly these will be enforced. Therefore, industry leaders including Dow in Thailand representatives working through the Chemical Industry Club and the Petroleum Institute of Thailand (PTIT) have been discussing improving their own emergency response procedures and capabilities to compensate for the perceived government weaknesses.

The Chemical Industry Club is the organizational vehicle for coordinating the Responsible Care program in Thailand. Like many other industry associations, the Chemical Industry Club is more or less autonomous but is operated under the auspices of the Federation of Thai Industries, which is a part of the Thai Ministry of Industry. The Chemical Industry Club has been the driving force behind efforts to raise the standards for Responsible Care in Thailand, and Dow in Thailand has actively participated in this.

Like the Chemical Industry Club, PTIT provides a vehicle for industry cooperation with government to address local needs. This is an association of firms in the petroleum industry that is funded and supported by member contributions. PTIT collects and disseminates various statistics on the industry, and it provides a forum for firms to work together on environmental, health, and safety issues. Jim Fitterling represents the company in the Petrochemical Processing Committee, which has formal meetings quarterly and working sessions monthly.

That committee is exploring various waste treatment options. Previously, there had been only one licensed hazardous waste treatment company in all of Thailand. It was granted a monopoly by the Thai government, but it could not possibly handle all the waste generated. In fact, Fitterling cited estimates that it could handle only about one-fifth of the hazardous waste generated in Thailand. In addition, wastes are disposed of in landfills, which is not an environmentally sound long-term solution. Thus, the activities of this committee are likely to produce environmental benefits in Thailand, but there was also a certain degree of self-interest involved here for Dow in Thailand. Because this waste treatment company was a monopoly, it was able to charge high fees. The government has recently issued permits to firms to incinerate their hazardous wastes and now is working to define how to transport the waste to these incinerators. This issue has also been considered by the Chemical Industry Club, and its position on this is similar to that of PTIT.

Another example of leadership in collaborative efforts to deal with environmental issues is Dow in Thailand's coordination of a visit by the head of the Polystyrene Packaging Council of North America. That organization deals with a range of environmental issues related to expanded polystyrene packaging, including conducting long-term epidemiological studies of health effects on workers. The head of this council was visiting Thailand at the invitation of polystyrene producers in Thailand, including Dow in Thailand, to discuss matters of local concern and explore how the producers in Thailand might receive help from the North America group.

The 2000 edition of the *Dow in Thailand Public Report* provides data with respect to progress on implementation of different aspects of Responsible Care in Thailand. According to one diagram titled "Progress Toward Implementation of Responsible Care in Thailand,"[30] 97 percent of the designated management practices for implementing Responsible Care have been put into place in Dow in Thailand's operations. This compares with 100 percent of the Responsible Care practices that have been implemented in Dow's operations in North America, 99 percent in Europe, 97 percent in the Pacific region, and 96 percent in Latin America.

Continued Program Assessment and Improvement: EH&S Performance

Dow in Thailand has received recognition for its efforts in the safety, health, and environment areas in the company and in Thailand. The Map Ta Phut operations received a Dow Environmental Care award in 1993–1994, which is awarded to no more than 10 percent of all Dow plants worldwide. In 1996 the SCC-Dow Group was awarded the Ministry of Industry's Outstanding Environmental Award, and in June 2001 it received ISO 14001 certification. Dow in Thailand also recently passed the milestone of 15 million contractor employee-hours worked without an injury, and the SCC-Dow operations at Phrapadaeng were retired in 1996 without ever recording a days-away-from-work case.[31]

The researcher had the opportunity to interview several labor activists and government labor officials and to inquire whether they know about any problems at Dow in Thailand's operations.[32] No substantive criticisms of Dow in Thailand's operations were elicited in response to these queries. Labor activists in Thailand are generally more concerned with organizing workers in multinationals and their subcontractors that employ larger numbers of lower-paid workers, such as in the apparel industry. Also at the time of the interview labor activists were engaged in a campaign against the U.S. jewelry company Almond. (See Thailand Country Narrative, at Web site: http://pres.depaul.edu/hartman/BeyondSweatShops/CountryReports.) Government officials noted that in general multinationals did a good job of abiding by government regulations, and there were no major problems at Dow in Thailand of which they were aware. Of course, given the nature of Dow in Thailand's business, criticism of the company would be both quick in coming and severe should a major accident occur in its operations.

Dow in Thailand issued a public report for 2000 that includes performance measures on a number of dimensions of safety, health, and environment.[33] We discuss these reported results in this section. The organization and content of the report closely parallels that of its corporate parent's[34] and, like that report, is designed to provide transparency regarding its operations and to satisfy public interest and curiosity. Performance results reported in this document are related to Dow's corporate goals set in 1995 extending out to the year 2005 for areas such as distribution safety; progress toward implementation of Responsible Care activities; and reduction in the rate of injury and illness, motor vehicle accidents, and chemical spills and releases. Financial and production performance information are also provided in the report.

Transportation Incidents

Data on transportation incidents for Dow in Thailand are contained in figure 10.3. Transportation incidents include all moderate to serious events that occur during shipment of products from Dow's facilities to its customers. Dow in Thailand has been substantially above the Dow Global's goal line and Dow Global's actual experience for several years recently. Dow in Thailand's rate of 0.93 incidents per 10,000 shipments in 2000 is approximately 3 to 4 times higher than Dow Global's rate in the same year. To put this in context though it is noteworthy that traffic conditions in Thailand, especially in Bangkok, are widely believed to be among the worst in the world.

In considering Dow in Thailand's EH&S performance, it should be noted that it takes place in a social, cultural, and economic context in

Figure 10.3
Transportation Incidents

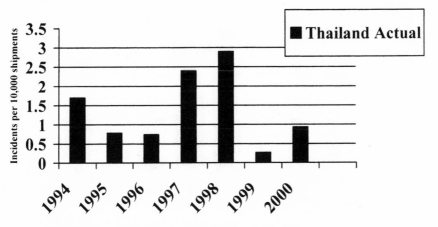

Source: Dow in Thailand Public Report—2000 Results, reprinted with permission of
Dow Chemical Corp.

which there is less emphasis placed on safety and health than there is here
in the United States. In some sense, less obvious or immediate safety,
health, and environmental benefits could, in economic terms, be considered "luxury goods," that is, goods that are in greater demand at higher
income levels. Many people in Thailand are focused on other, apparently
more pressing economic needs. Certain activities we would consider unacceptable are common practice in Thailand. Thus, for example, it is not
uncommon to see pick-up trucks loaded with 10 to 15 workers standing
in the bed of the truck driving down the highway at very high rates of
speed. This context makes the implementation of Responsible Care both
more challenging and more important.

Motor Vehicle Accidents

In addition to keeping track of incidents pertaining to the transportation
of its products to its customers, Dow Chemical Company monitors the
overall motor vehicle accident rate (see figure 10.4). In recent years Dow
in Thailand has emphasized safe driving training and has been able to
reduce the overall motor vehicle accident rate from over twice the Dow
Global rate (10.9 vs. 5.1 accidents per million miles) in 1994 to just under
the rate in 2000 (3.1 vs. 3.7).[35] However, in 2000 Dow in Thailand suffered
the loss of one worker in a motor vehicle accident fatality.

Figure 10.4
Motor Vehicle Accident Rate

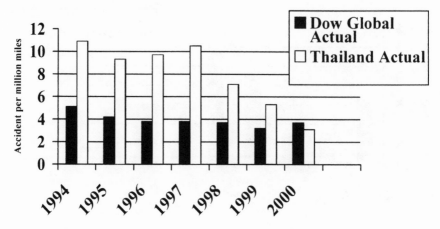

Source: Dow in Thailand, *Dow in Thailand Public Report—2000 Results,* reprinted
with permission of Dow Chemical Corp.

Loss of Primary Containment Incidents

Dow in Thailand's (Map Ta Phut operations) experience with loss of
primary containment (leaks, breaks, and spills) for the years 1994 to 2000
is provided in figure 10.5. Dow Chemical Company defines an *incident* to
be a leak, break, or spill of 50 kilograms or more. These incidents are not
necessarily cases in which the wider community is exposed to a hazard;
secondary containment procedures are likely to prevent wider exposure.
As the graph indicates, the worst year was 1999 in which there were seven
incidents of loss of primary containment. There were no incidents in
1995—the best of recent years; and as of early November 2001, there were
two such incidents. The jump in containment incidents from 1995 through
1999 is attributed to the start-up of two new operations in Map Ta Phut.
These two are the largest Dow in Thailand operations at that site.

Occupational Injury and Illness Experience

Dow in Thailand has done consistently well in recent years in terms of
its overall injury and illness rate relative to Dow Chemical Company as
a whole. In 2000 Dow in Thailand recorded 0.38 injuries and illnesses per

Figure 10.5
Leaks, Breaks, and Spills—Map Ta Phut Operations

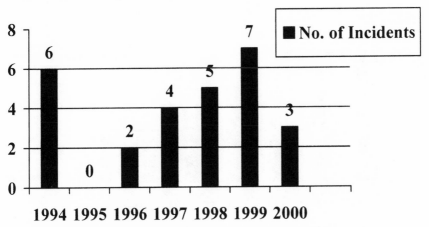

Source: Dow in Thailand, *Dow in Thailand Public Report—2000 Results,* reprinted with permission of Dow Chemical Corp.

200,000 hours worked compared with 0.98 for Dow Global, and during the 1994–2000 period it averaged 0.41 compared with 1.70 for Dow Global (see figure 10.6). These statistics cover both Dow employees and contractors working at Dow facilities, and they use OSHA injury and illness definitions.

Before the time period covered by these most recent statistics, the SCC-Dow Group recorded a period of 4 million employee-hours without a day-away-from-work case (DAWC) injury. And between 1992 and 1999 the Map Ta Phut operations recorded 14.5 million employee-hours worked without any contractor DAWCs.

Jim Fitterling notes that accurate measurement and control of airborne emissions are more of a challenge at the Map Ta Phut plant than is controlling water emissions. The plant is not a big producer of wastewater. In fact, the latex plant, which is the largest user of water among Dow in Thailand's operations, recycles 100 percent of its water. Graphs of chemical emissions and wastewater visually display the opposite trends in the amounts of these two forms of pollution at the plant in recent years. Chemical emissions include carbon dioxide, nitrogen, hydrogen, and oxygen and are normally created during production or as by-products of the production process. The increase in chemical emissions is attributed

Figure 10.6
Injury and Illness Rate, Dow Employees and Contractors

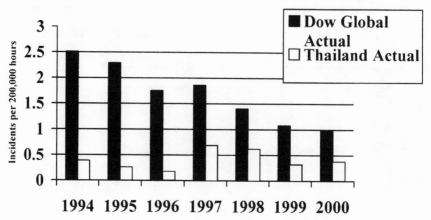

Source: Dow in Thailand, *Dow in Thailand Public Report—2000 Results,* reprinted with permission of Dow Chemical Corp.

to an increase in production due to the opening of polystyrene, styrene, and polyethylene plants. Process wastewater is water that may have come into contact with chemicals and is therefore treated to remove the chemicals before discharge. Total wastewater generated at the Map Ta Phut operations saw a large temporary increase in 1977 because of the start-up of a styrene monomer plant that required a large amount of water for cleaning and commissioning the equipment. Overall though the trend in wastewater discharge during the 1994–2000 period is downward (see figure 10.7).

CONCLUSIONS/IMPLICATIONS

Firms in the chemical industry face common environmental threats, and it could be reasonably argued that environmental problems, whether of the scale of a Bhopal disaster or of a more routine level, hurt all of the firms. As a result, a common response to environmental threats such as that provided by Responsible Care makes a great deal of sense. Responsible Care appears to be a novel and apparently effective way for chemical industry firms to address common problems in a collaborative way. It thus provides a potential model for firms to work cooperatively in addressing

Figure 10.7
Wastewater and Chemical Emissions—Map Ta Phut Operations

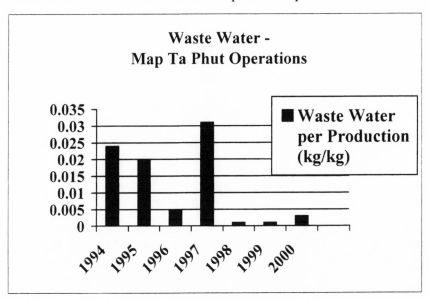

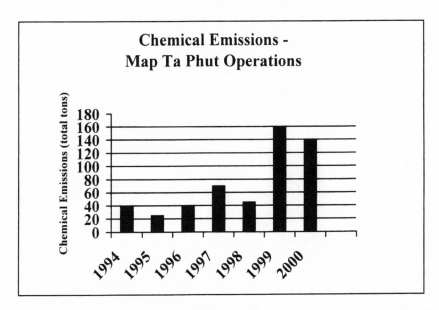

Source: Dow in Thailand. *Dow in Thailand Public Report—2000 Results,* reprinted with permission of Dow Chemical Corp.

other problems. Furthermore, industry associations that have been set up to coordinate Responsible Care programs can serve as conduits for important technical assistance to government agencies in the implementation of environmental, health, and safety policy in developing countries. In many cases the multinational firms in these associations have valuable technical knowledge and equipment that may not be otherwise available to these agencies in pursuing environmental, health, and safety goals.

NOTES

1. The author gratefully acknowledges the research assistance of Valerie Janosky in the preparation of this chapter.

2. "Responsible Care" is a registered trademark.

3. "The 2002 *Fortune* 500 Industry Rankings," *Fortune Magazine*, http://www.fortune.com/lists/F500/indsnap_8.html (accessed 3 July 2002).

4. Historical information on Dow Chemical Corporation and its Pacific region operations and information on its current operations come from Dow Chemical Corporation, *Dow: Public Report 1999* (Midland, Mich.: Dow Chemical Corporation, 2000); Dow Chemical Pacific, *Dow Pacific: Public Report 1999* (Hong Kong: Dow Chemical Pacific, 2000); and the Dow Chemical Corporation Web site, http://www.dow.com/Homepage/index.html (accessed 2 August 2002).

5. Dow Chemical Corporation.

6. "The 2002 *Fortune* 500 Industry Rankings."

7. "America's Most Admired Companies," *Fortune Magazine*, http://www.fortune.com/lists/mostadmired/index_alpha_d.html (accessed 6 August 2002).

8. Interview by author with Judy Castledine, 4 December 2001, Hong Kong.

9. Canadian Chemical Producers' Association, "Responsible Care," http://www.ccpa.ca/english/sitemap/index.html (accessed 11 February 2002).

10. European Chemical Industry Council, "Responsible Care," http://www.cefic.be/activities/hse/rc/ (accessed 11 February 2002).

11. European Chemical Industry Council, "Responsible Care."

12. American Chemical Industry Council, "Responsible Care," http://www.americanchemistry.com/ (accessed 19 March 2002).

13. American Chemical Industry Council, "Codes of Management Practices," http://www.americanchemistry.com/rc.nsf/unid/lsgs-4eesac?opendocument (Accessed 19 March 2002).

14. American Chemical Industry Council.

15. American Chemical Industry Council.

16. American Chemical Industry Council.

17. American Chemical Industry Council.

18. "Beyond Responsible Care: Ethical Corporation Interviews Scott Noesen, Director of Sustainable Development, The Dow Chemical Company," *Ethical Corporation* (January 2002), pp. 7–10; and Dow Chemical Corporation, *Dow: Public Report 1999* (Midland, Mich.: Dow Chemical Corporation, 2000), p. 48.

19. For a description of behaviorally based occupational safety and health approaches and a further discussion of the arguments about their desirability, see:

Richard E. Wokutch and Craig VanSandt, "The Role of Occupational Health and Safety Management in the United States and Japan: The duPont Model and the Toyota Model," in *Systematic Occupational Health and Safety Management: Perspectives on an International Development,* ed., Kaj Frick, Per Langaa Jensen, Michael Quinlan, and Ton Witlhagen (Oxford, U.K.: Elsevier Science, 2000), pp. 367–89.

20. See, for example, Dow Chemical Company, "A Global Work Process for a Better Future: Environment, Health & Safety 2000 Update."

21. Dow Chemical Corporation, *Dow Public Report—2000 Results* (Midland, Mich.: Dow Chemical Corporation, 2001).

22. Dow Jones, "Dow Jones Sustainability Index," http://www.sustainability-index.com (accessed 2 August 2002).

23. Alex J. Sagady & Associates, "Michigan's Dow Chemical and Whirlpool Honored by Carol Browner" (22 March 2000), http://www.glin.net/lists/enviro-mich/2000–03/msg00154.html (accessed 2 August 2002).

24. See, for example, the Greenpeace critique of Dow and dioxin, http://www.greenpeace.org/~usa/reports/dow2.html (accessed 6 August 2002). See also Jason Ku, "The Dow Nightmare: 10 Reasons Why President Shapiro Should Resign from the Dow Board of Directors," http://www.princeton.edu/~progrev/98–99/n6_jk.html (accessed 6 August 2002); Infact, "Hall of Shame Campaign," http://www.infact.org/ (accessed 6 August 2002); CorpWatch, "Relay Hunger Strike for Justice in Bhopal," http://www.corpwatch.org (accessed 6 August 2002); and Public Citizen, "The National Association of Manufacturers: A Study in Hypocrisy," http://www.citizen.org (accessed 7 August 2002).

25. Material for this section comes from Dow Chemical Corporation, "Dow in Thailand," *Dow in Thailand Public Report—2000 Results* (Bangkok, Thailand: Dow Chemical Corporation); Dow Chemical Corporation, *SCC-Dow Group* [brochure] (Bangkok, Thailand: Dow Chemical Corporation); interviews conducted by the author with Dow personnel in Thailand 27 and 28 November 2001, in Map Ta Phut and Bangkok, Thailand, respectively, and with Judy Castledine at Dow Chemical Company's Asia-Pacific headquarters in Hong Kong on 4 December 2001. In addition, subsequent electronic and other communications with these parties provided further clarification of many points.

26. Dow Chemical Corporation, "Dow in Thailand," p. 6.

27. This allowance is for housing, commuting, and other extra costs associated with working away from Bangkok, from which many of Dow's Map Ta Phut employees come.

28. Thai Labour Campaign, http://www.thailabour.org (accessed 29 January 2002), contains a discussion of recent changes in the minimum wage in Thailand.

29. Henry Holmes and Sucada Tangtongtavy (with Roy Tomizawa), *Working with the Thais: A Guide to Managing in Thailand* (Bangkok, Thailand: White Lotus Company, 1997).

30. Dow Chemical Corporation, "Dow in Thailand," p. 8.

31. Dow Chemical Corporation, *SCC-Dow Group,* p. 11.

32. Interview by author with Phil Robertson, AFL-CIO, 29 November 2001, in Bangkok, Thailand; interview by author with Junya Yimprasert, coordinator, Thai Labour Campaign, 29 November 2001, in Bangkok, Thailand; interview by the author with Jiratorn Poonyarith, deputy director general, Department of Labour Protection and Welfare, Ministry of Labour and Social Welfare, 29 November 2001,

in Bangkok, Thailand. Several assistants of the deputy director general also participated in this latter interview.

33. Dow Chemical Corporation, "Dow in Thailand," *Dow in Thailand Public Report—2000 Results*.

34. Historical information on Dow Chemical Corporation.

35. Figures do not include commuting accidents in personal vehicles.

CHAPTER 11

Pro-Child Institute: Combating Child Labor through Collaborative Partnerships in the Brazilian Shoe Industry

J. Lawrence French and Richard E. Wokutch[1]

CHILD LABOR: A BACKGROUND

In recent years, one of the matters of greatest concern with respect to international labor practices has been the exploitation of child labor. Accurate estimates of the extent of child labor are difficult to come by, in large part because many types of child labor are illegal. The most frequently cited estimates come from the International Labour Organization (ILO), and these put the number of child workers in the 100 to 200 million range.[2] More recently the ILO has suggested that the number of child workers is probably even higher.[3]

When discussing child labor it is useful to begin by trying to explain precisely (or as precisely as possible) what is meant by the term. Two factors—the age of the worker and the nature of the activity—are usually delineated in definitions. According to the ILO, child labor is generally taken to mean work performed by children under the age of 15 (14 in developing countries).[4] In addition, in defining the term, a distinction is often made between certain work activities or household chores that are considered harmless and those that are considered harmful and injurious. Senator Tom Harkin makes this distinction in arguments he presented in Congress in support of legislation he has been championing to curb child labor abuses:

Keep in mind the distinction between child work and exploitive child labor. The legislation does not bar children from selling newspapers, shining shoes, or working on the family farm, but, rather, prohibits work in the hazardous jobs of mining and industry under abusive conditions.[5]

This distinction is useful, but it still leaves open the question of what constitutes exploitation or abuse of children in work situations. The ILO points out that answering that question can, in many cases, be exceedingly difficult:

But by what criteria is it possible to set priorities according to risk? It is certainly helpful to start with a list of industries, occupations and working conditions know (sic) to place children in jeopardy, but generic information of this sort does not automatically address the most vexing questions. How does one decide whether one kind of work is more detrimental to children than another? How can one rank injurious effects of different types? Is vision loss worse than lung disease? How much physical risk equates with how much psychosocial jeopardy? How should short- and long-term effects be compared? In setting priorities, such questions are inescapable, but there are no easy or universal answers to them, and the process of deciding who to consider most at risk necessarily involves an element of subjective reasoning.[6]

Because of the difficulties of providing fine-tuned assessments of risks, the United Nations with the support of the United States has focused international attention on combating "the worst forms of child labor." The ILO Convention 182, established in 1999 and already ratified by 117 countries, specifically targets for elimination such unambiguously immoral forms of child labor as child slave labor, drug trafficking, prostitution, pornography, and participation in armed conflicts.[7]

As the controversy about child labor intensified in the past 10 to 15 years, it has become clear that the general public seems to have a special interest in the welfare of child workers that in some sense exceeds their interest in worker welfare issues in general. As a result, companies and industries that have come under criticism have quickly responded to address the charges. This case deals with one such industry initiative, the Instituto Pró Criança, or Pro-Child Institute (PCI for short), which is an effort of the shoe industry of Franca, Brazil, seeking to address charges of child labor abuses. We begin first by delineating the reasons children work—both the supply and the demand factors. We then explore the extent of the phenomenon and attitudes about it on a national basis in Brazil and then in the municipality of Franca, Brazil. Following this overview, we focus on PCI, considering first inspiration and vision-setting issues, and then PCI's establishment, integration, and implementation (including aims, goals, and the overall operation of the program). We will concentrate in particular on PCI's primary program, its inspection and labeling program. We then outline the ancillary programs that support the inspection program. Finally we consider efforts to improve the program, efforts to assess its impact, likely future developments pertaining to the program, and implications of this case.

Why Do Children Work?

In seeking to understand the operations and the impact of PCI it is useful to consider the issue of why children work. Discussions of why child labor occurs typically differentiate between demand-side factors and supply-side factors.

Demand Factors

The most frequently cited demand factor is the lower cost of child workers. As noted by the U.S. Department of Labor,[8] child workers are willing to accept lower wages than those paid to adult workers, and employers do not have to make contributions to any social security system for them.

But the low cost of child labor is not the only factor that leads employers to want to hire child workers. A study commissioned by the ILO cites a number of nonpecuniary advantages for hiring child laborers.[9] These are grouped in three categories: awareness and innocence, tradition, and physical characteristics:

Awareness and innocence

1. More docile and less troublesome.
2. Greater willingness to do repetitive, monotonous work.
3. More trustworthy and innocent, so less likely to steal.
4. Less absenteeism (none if bonded).
5. Do not form trade unions.

Tradition

6. Tradition of hiring child labor by employers.
7. Traditional occupations with children working alongside parent(s).
8. Social role of employer to provide jobs to families in the community.
9. Employers' need for laborers. Children are available and ask for jobs, so why not hire child labor?

Physical characteristics

10. Better health (young, health not yet spoiled by work).
11. Irreplaceable skills (note not true in fact).[10]

The U.S. Department of Labor[11] also notes that some employers claim that they hire child workers out of a feeling of sympathy for them. According to this line of argument, the employer, feeling sorry for impoverished children, gives them the opportunity to elevate their economic circumstances through work.

Supply Factors

Poverty is the most commonly cited reason for children's desire to work. It is argued that children are forced to work because of the need to supplement a low household income. Anker and Melkas[12] note that in some of the poorest countries of the world family survival necessitates children working. However, Anker and Melkas, the U.S. Department of Labor, UNICEF,[13] and our own observations in Franca suggest that poverty is not always the primary factor in child work. Children sometimes work for a sense of independence. Often this drive for independence grows out of conflicts with parents regarding their children's needs and wants pertaining to a vast array of consumer items (e.g., branded clothing, makeup, cigarettes, music, and alcohol.)[14] Children often work to be able to purchase prestige consumer items that otherwise would be out of their reach. Moreover, parents often encourage children to work to equip them with marketable skills, teach them important workplace values, and foster their personal development. Many children share the belief that the workplace constitutes a school of sorts. Finally, often children work because they have nothing better to do and parents need for them to be occupied and supervised. Both parties often believe the old adage that idle hands do the devil's work.[15]

A number of factors related to educational systems are also relevant to the supply of children seeking work. The availability, quality, cost, and perceived relevance of school are important. To the extent that schooling is not available, is of low quality, is expensive, or is perceived to be irrelevant to the child's present and future welfare, children and their parents are more likely to favor work for the child over schooling.

Child Labor in Brazil

According to a recent report on social labeling in Brazil[16] the Brazilian National Census Bureau estimated in 1995 that there were over 4.1 million children between the ages of 5 and 14 working in Brazil and over 520,000 children between the ages of 5 and 9 working. Over 3 percent of all children in the 5–9 age range were found to be working, and over 20 percent of children in the 10–14 age range, with much higher percentages found in rural areas. Agricultural work is the most common occupation of boys, and domestic work is most common for girls.

It should be noted that the majority of child laborers in Brazil also attend school. Attendance is mandatory from years 7 to 14 to ensure that all complete at least eight grades. However, large numbers of school-age children and inadequate investments in primary and secondary education limit the daily hours in class to 4 to 5, with schools offering morning, afternoon, and evening sessions. As a consequence, they find many hours outside the classroom available for work.

Of course not everyone thinks that the incidence of child labor in Brazil is a problem. Many Brazilians feel that early work experiences help young people develop skills and work habits that will prove valuable later in life. And many successful Brazilians cite their own work as children as having been instrumental in their later success in life. (It is worth noting that many U.S. citizens feel the same way about their own early work experiences.) In addition, many Brazilians would agree with the neoclassical economic argument that the use of child labor, although in certain respects undesirable, is in fact necessary for economic development in developing countries.[17]

Despite these arguments defending the practice of child labor, there is a strong ethical case against many forms of the practice. It has been argued that those forms of child labor that threaten the physical or psychological welfare of children are unethical.[18] This is based on the contention that children have a basic right to develop to their potential as human beings. Of course determining which forms of work pose a serious threat to a child's development can be difficult itself as the ILO quote at the beginning of this chapter clearly illustrates.

Franca

Franca is a medium-sized city of about 285,000 located about 240 miles northwest of the city of São Paulo in the southern Brazilian state of São Paulo. With the expansion of the shoe industry in the 1970s, Franca has become a leading center for the production and export of men's leather shoes. By the mid-1980s the industry had grown to employ about 36,000 workers, but intensifying international competition in the 1990s halved direct employment and substantially reduced production. Nonetheless, roughly 400 shoe manufacturers continue to produce about 20 million pairs annually and export 25 percent of them to the United States. Supporting the manufacture of shoes are numerous suppliers. About 25 tanneries operate on the periphery of town, providing diverse forms and qualities of leather. Somewhere on the order of 2,200 to 2,400 *bancas,* or sewing shops, serve as labor subcontractors to the manufacturers. Numerous small manufacturers and distributors of shoe components and inputs to the manufacturing processes (e.g., machinery and chemicals) are found there as well. Complementing these suppliers are a host of small firms on the distribution side, including local marketing firms, export agents, trucking operations, and financial services specialists.

The problems of Franca's shoe district in the 1990s have been felt throughout the city. The contraction of this industry has increased the unemployment rate and pushed growing numbers into the informal sector of cash payments for off-the-books work. Oftentimes, this occurs in the shops of labor subcontractors. Although some subcontracting of labor-intensive activities has always characterized Brazil's shoe industry, the practice has increased with heightened pressures to reduce costs. The vast majority operate small, family-run shops, often in rooms of their houses, and frequently employ family members. Among the latter have been growing numbers of children, who typically work part-time; receive very, very low wages, if anything; and remain in school.

The rising incidence of unemployment and child labor in the 1990s has exacerbated conflicts between the shoe employers and shoe workers. The latter, represented in the early 1990s by the Shoemakers Union of Franca, launched a broadside attack, with published accusations and evidence of extensive child labor that had international repercussions and eventually led to the founding of PCI. In the latter half of that decade, the workers' party succeeded in translating widespread concerns over unemployment into an electoral victory in local government elections. To date, it has maintained its hold despite continuing economic problems in this municipality, which were quite evident in early 2002 when the local government had to delay issuing paychecks to government workers because of a lack of funds.

Child Labor in Franca

In the context of increasing global concern about the problems of sweatshop labor and child labor occurring in the late 1980s and early 1990s, the Shoemakers Union of Franca raised allegations of abusive working conditions in the shoe industry of Franca, including the exploitation of child labor. A 1994 study conducted by this union, in conjunction with UNICEF,[19] surveyed 1,561 elementary school children (ages 7–13) in 16 of Franca's 45 public schools who worked as well as studied. They appear to comprise about 15 percent of the students in these schools. They worked, on average, 4 to 5 hours per day, with 73 percent working in the shoe industry. Although most of the shoe workers were employed in their parents' shops, they were often exposed to toxic chemicals. The results of this study, which proved to be quite controversial, received extensive publicity in the Brazilian news media.

These stories were in turn picked up by the international press; one *Orlando Sentinel* article titled "Latin Town's Child Labor Tarnishing Its Image"[20] labeled Franca the "capital of child labor" in Brazil. The growing notoriety of Franca led to its inclusion in the 1994 U.S. Department of Labor report[21] on industries exporting to the United States that relied on child labor to lower their costs and ease their entrance into foreign markets. With that kind of negative publicity there was concern that exports to the United States, Brazil's most important customer for shoes, might be harmed by U.S. consumer boycotts or governmental efforts to limit market access. According to the Brazilian Shoe Manufacturers Association

(Abicalçados), the United States accounts for nearly 70 percent of Brazil's leather shoe exports, Argentina is second with 8.5 percent, and the U.K. third with 5.5 percent.[22]

It is worth noting that many, if not most people in Franca felt that these stories were exaggerated. In addition, many questioned the motivations of the union in publicizing these charges, suggesting that it was an attempt to gain negotiating leverage and to eliminate job competition that child workers posed to union members. Nevertheless, there was strong support for the notion that something needed to be done. That something, it turned out, was the establishment of the Pro-Child Institute.

PRO-CHILD INSTITUTE[23]

Inspiration and Vision Setting: Idea Generation/Inception

In the wake of the controversy about child labor abuses in Franca, the local shoe employers' association was inspired in November 1995 to create a nonprofit organization, called the Pro-Child Institute, for the stated purpose of eliminating child labor in the footwear industry and, more generally, improving the welfare of children through educational activities. The full name is Instituto Empresarial de Apoio à Formação da Criança e do Adolescente or the Employers' Institute in Support to the Development of Children and Adolescents, but it is usually referred to as Instituto Pró-Criança or PCI. Joining the shoe employers as sponsors have been two other entities: the local commercial employers association of Franca and the regional organ of the state commercial and industrial employers. This buy-in from various stakeholders was critical to the integration of a single perspective on these issues and the design of PCI's vision.

Partnerships such as this can be extremely effective in serving the needs of multiple stakeholders. Research conducted by Business Partners for Development (BPD), a consortium of private-sector firms, found that partnerships present a number of opportunities, including the following:

- Win new contracts based on past performance.
- Improve existing performance.
- Gain know-how and experience with working in poor communities.
- Improve public image by contributing to social and economic development.
- Lower risks and improve financial performance through partnerships.

BPD also identified several risks, including the following:

- Financial weakness of the project may lead to unsustainability.
- Co-funding may be pulled out or cut.

- Unrealistic expectations may be raised among other partners.
- Short-term pressures may threaten partnerships.
- The company's own power may be imposed on other partners.[24]

Establishment, Integration, and Implementation

At the time the controversy about child labor in Franca began, the Abrinq Foundation (Fundação Abrinq) located in nearby São Paulo already had in operation a social labeling program, Programa Empresa Amiga da Criança—the child-friendly company program, or PEAC, established in 1990. PEAC staff members were reportedly quite helpful in starting PCI, and they continue to provide assistance. This relationship led PCI to focus its initial energies in 1996 on developing a similar labeling program to encourage local firms to affiliate. Those promising to avoid the use of child labor received the right to affix a stamp, designed by PCI, on the shoe boxes sent to retailers (see figure 11.1.). Later, a monitoring program was developed to periodically check on PCI-affiliated firms. Although the orientation of PEAC is different (it designates companies in a variety of industries as being "child friendly," whereas PCI labels shoes as having been made without the use of child labor), PEAC served as a

Figure 11.1
Pro-Child Institute Logo

Source: Reprinted with permission of Instituto Pró-Criança, Franca.

model for the development of PCI,[25] and it is not uncommon for firms in the shoe industry to belong to both organizations. According to reported survey results close to 1,350 firms belong to PEAC, with shoe firms making up the largest industrial grouping. The connection between PEAC and PCI has been characterized as a type of mentoring relationship.[26]

Because of existing social and environmental factors, PCI had to continually reassess its vision and the integration of that vision into practice. For instance, as PCI developed its labeling program, skeptics in and outside Franca as well as officials in the shoe industry argued for the need for expanding their activities in two ways. The first of these involved more direct engagement with the bancas, or labor subcontractors, who employed the vast majority of child laborers to encourage them to affiliate with PCI and forswear these employment practices. By the end of 1997 virtually all subcontractors of the PCI-affiliated manufacturers had been persuaded to join PCI because of the threat of losing their contracts. To facilitate the withdrawal of young family members from work, PCI worked with many businesses and public agencies to expand the after-school educational and recreational opportunities for these children. While the direct subcontractors have been brought into the PCI program, many second-tier subcontractors continue to remain outside.

In 1998 PCI began to address a second issue—how to determine the veracity of claims by manufacturers and subcontractors that they didn't use child labor. For that purpose a local university was contracted to develop an auditing program. The first inspections were carried out in the fall of 1998. No child laborers were found in any of the 30 manufacturers or 103 subcontractors audited. The auditors noted that although all the subcontractors' children were in school, most were not involved in any organized educational or recreational activities in non-school hours.

All the PCI-affiliated manufacturers (currently about 45) and 10 percent to 20 percent of the approximately 1,200 suppliers are visited on a biannual basis. In exchange for agreeing to submit to these inspections and successfully passing them, the manufacturers may use the PCI label reading "No Child Labor Was Used in the Manufacture of This Product" and place it in the shoeboxes of the shoes they produce (see figure 11.2). Member firms support the operation of PCI through contributions of from R$50 to R$400 (U.S.$17–U.S.$133) per month, depending on size. Bancas pay R$10 (about U.S.$3.33).[27]

Inspections are carried out by faculty members of the local university (faculty of economics, business administration, and accounting of Franca or FACEF), who are paid a stipend of R$35 (about U.S.$12) for each inspection. According to inspectors a first offense (i.e., evidence that a child is working in a PCI factory) will result in a warning. A second offense will result in a firm being expelled from the PCI program. PCI uses the

Figure 11.2
"No Child Labor" Stamp

Source: Reprinted with permission from Instituto Pró-Criança, Franca. Translation:
No child labor was used in the manufacture of this product.

criterion of under 16 years of age recently adopted nationally in Brazil for
defining child labor (see discussion below).

There are currently two FACEF members who serve as inspectors. To
date there has been no formal training program for them, because it was
not believed to be necessary. Both reportedly had a great deal of experience in the shoe industry before becoming inspectors. One previously
owned his own shoe firm, and the other worked for a number of years in
the industry. It is likely, however, that some training will probably be
required if inspections broaden in scope as is now expected (see discussion
below).

Aims and Goals of PCI

Although PCI was developed to combat child labor and therefore defend the interests of the shoe industry, especially its export sector, its aims are broader than that. Its supporters have long understood the need to replace work activities with educational and recreational programs that would both occupy children's out-of-school hours and promote their development. The aims of PCI are twofold: (1) to mobilize, join, articulate, organize, make feasible, and support actions that have the objective of promoting education, leading toward the full development of children and teenagers, preparing them as good citizens demanding their rights and being duly qualified for work and (2) to combat child labor with the municipality of Franca.[28]

PCI operates several programs to meet these aims, but the most important is the labeling program. To accomplish the overall aims of PCI, the general thrust of the labeling program is that those firms choosing to affiliate with PCI promise not to use child labor or allow their principal suppliers, bancas, to use child labor in the production of shoes. And as noted above, they also agree to submit to periodic surprise inspections to ensure that they are abiding by the agreement. Significantly, many in the shoe industry deny that child labor was a problem in Franca when this controversy began in 1995. They see this program primarily as a means of certifying that child labor is not being used, rather than as a program to eliminate child labor.

At present, manufacturers are obliged to adopt the following procedures to participate in the labeling program.

Program for the Prevention and Eradication of Child Labor in the Footwear Sector—"Pro-Child" Stamp

Procedures that a firm is obliged to follow

1. Do not employ ... those who are less than 16 years of age, obeying the law which prohibits this—Article 7, XXXIII in the Federal Constitution.

2. Not to contract services of third parties who employ those who are less than 16 years of age.

3. Motivate one's chain of production to not employ those who are less than 16 years of age.

4. Be a contributing member of the Pro-Child Institute.

5. Use only subcontractors who have the Pro-Child Institute's card.

6. Respect the rules concerning the use of the Pro-Child stamp.

7. Accept a biannual inspection within the industry to check the correct application of the procedures necessary for keeping its obligations.

8. Perform a biannual inspection on at least 10 percent of the companies that

serve the industry, to prove that it is keeping its commitment in not employing those who are less than 16 years of age.

9. Keep the Pro-Child cards of its subcontractors handy to show during biannual inspections.

10. Hand over to the inspector during the biannual inspections the names and addresses of the companies serving the industry.

11. Pay special attention to the visits from companies serving the industry, keeping in mind the problems of employing those who are less than 16 years of age, and reporting any indication of child labor to the Pro-Child Institute.

12. Include the theme, the prevention and eradication of child labor, on the agendas of meetings held with employees and with companies working for the industry.[29]

Ancillary Programs

In addition to the labeling program PCI operates a number of ancillary programs designed to provide constructive activities for children for whom work is no longer a legally viable option. These are designed both to keep the children occupied so that they don't get into trouble and to teach useful skills. PCI (and its primary sponsor, the shoe industry) sees its role not as a direct provider of services or programs, but rather primarily as a catalyst or intermediary between the displaced child laborers and institutions in the larger society with capabilities for providing developmental opportunities.

Ancillary programs include classes on topics such as auto mechanics, typing, computers, English, Portuguese, arts, music, and various sports. PCI literature lists 33 different programs providing 576 scholarships for student participants:

1. SESI—swimming—20 scholarships

2. SENAI and PRO-CHILD— auto mechanics —52 scholarships

3. FACEF and Regional São Paulo State Government Association—80 scholarships

4. FACEF—computers—100 scholarships

5. Pro-Child—typing—120 scholarships

6. Know How—English—39 scholarships

7. CCAA—English—6 scholarships

8. CCBEU—English—6 scholarships

9. Cultura Inglesa—English—2 scholarships

10. Talento—arts—2 scholarships

11. Franca Informática—computers—3 scholarships

12. Infosystem—computers—6 scholarships

13. Datadados—computers—8 scholarships

14. Mrs. Byte—computers—2 scholarships

15. Centro Violonistico Villa Lobos—guitar—1 scholarship

16. Núcleo Musical Lúcia Garcetti—music—1 scholarship

17. Gisella Studio de Dança—ballet—16 scholarships

18. Raquel e Camilla—ballet—10 scholarships

19. Clinica Francana de Basketball—basketball—15 scholarships

20. Bit Company—computers—3 scholarships

21. C&N—computers—11 scholarships

22. Datacenter—computers—4 scholarships

23. Sistec—computers—2 scholarships

24. Bate-Bola—soccer—3 scholarships

25. Exercícius Academia—gymnastics—1 scholarship

26. Claudia Garcia Ballet—ballet—10 scholarships

27. Si Toque—music—3 scholarships

28. Universidade de Franca—computers—15 scholarships

29. Easy Way—English—3 scholarships

30. Mergulho—swimming—14 scholarships

31. Escrivever—Portuguese—5 scholarships

32. Wizard—English—1 scholarship

33. Calçados Sandalo—shoe worker—12 scholarships[30]

The need for such alternative activities grew dramatically in December 1998 when the federal government raised the criterion age for determining child labor from under 14 to under 16. One reason was to combat increasing adult unemployment. A second reason was to help the solvency of the social security system, which was being drained by people who were able to retire at a very young age after 30 years of work because they had started working as adolescents. Because the ages for compulsory education are from 7 to 14 in Brazil, the extent to which PCI reduces child labor in Franca will result in adolescents with time on their hands. This was of course already a problem, as most students go to school only half a day because of limited funds for education. (In Franca, there are three school "shifts," from 7 A.M. to 12 noon, from 1 P.M. to 6 P.M., and from 7 P.M. to 10:45 P.M.) But the change in the minimum working age, of course, aggravates the problem. And because parents are likely to be working, the prospect of unsupervised teenagers and younger children with large blocks of unstructured free time getting into trouble is very real. This is one of the reasons the establishment of the supplementary activities noted above was considered an important component of PCI activities. There is a recognition of the importance of after-school activities throughout Brazil, and an effort is being made to ensure that such activities are provided by the schools. According to the ILO officials children enrolled in federal programs designed to ensure that they stay in school and out of the labor force are required to participate in educational and recreational activities during non-school hours. However, a scarcity of funds to finance these activities is clearly a problem.[31] This is one reason for the rise of the other programs alluded to above.

In 2001, in response to the change in minimum working age from 14 to 16, PCI launched an apprenticeship program that would enable a limited number of 14- to 15-year-olds to become apprentices in the shoe industry and develop their vocational skills in a number of areas while receiving a salary. Titled "I Can Get Ahead," the two-year program is, at present, limited to relatively needy adolescents in at least the fifth grade, with preference given to children of present employees of sponsoring manufacturing firms. Participants spend their mornings learning on the job and two hours in the afternoon in classroom study. They are required to attend their regular schools during the evening shift (7 P.M.–10:45 P.M.).

In Franca a number of other organizations have instituted a variety of activities for adolescents. To understand how the overall goal of providing opportunities for the development of children is being addressed on a community-wide basis, we hope to explore these activities in future research. These other programs include (1) a joint union/local government program involving three components: paying children to stay in school and not to work, providing child care and recreational opportunities for children, and providing children with vocational training and (2) a Rotary Club apprenticeship program, Guarda Mirim, to provide apprentice jobs and vocational training. The existence of these programs reflects the belief that there are many underlying reasons for child labor and problems associated with the practice that will not be resolved simply by preventing children from working.

The joint union/local government program targets low-income families that may attempt to supplement their family income through the work of their children. Parents are paid modest sums to keep their children out of the labor force and in school. Enrolled children are also provided with recreational opportunities and some vocational training outside of school hours. Conceivably some of the income lost by child laborers displaced from shoe firms could be offset by participation in this program if the parents' income was low enough to qualify. However, poor relationships between PCI and local government officials have limited contacts between the parties and efforts to coordinate their programs. Some PCI officials remember with bitterness the role that some local government officials played in bringing the problem of child labor to light in the first place. The latter, in turn, have been inclined to dismiss at least the initial PCI efforts as mere public relations programs designed to advance the interests of the shoe industry.

The Guarda Mirim program provides ample evidence of the difficulty of distinguishing between healthy and unhealthy—in the broad sense of the terms—work experiences for adolescents. Founded about 35 years ago, this program is targeted toward 14- and 15-year-olds and is designed to give them work experiences that will help them develop good work habits and may even lead to a permanent job at their internship site—either a local firm or government agency. The 400 or so children who are in this program work 35 to 40 hours per week and earn R$160 per month (about U.S.$53). In addition, to remain in good standing, all must continue to attend school (in the evening), maintain good grades, and present no comportment problems. Moreover, they are required to work toward the development of vocational skills through attendance at two-hour workshops on weekends. For that purpose, they choose from a variety of offerings ranging from computers to auto repair to cooking. All of the interns eventually work in offices doing mainly clerical work, but many of the boys start out in a type of job akin to a male "meter maid." They sell daily parking permits and give tickets to cars parked on the streets that don't have permits displayed. After completion of their periods of "apprenticeship," many remain with their employer on a permanent basis.

Critics note the dangers of working on the streets near traffic and carrying money. And some suggest that the program is simply a cover for the local government and industry to legally exploit cheap child labor. It's noteworthy that the participation of the local government in this program by way of providing internships is harshly criticized even by some in the government. Nevertheless, program participants who were interviewed were enthusiastic about their participation in the Guarda Mirim. There are approximately five times as many applicants as apprenticeship openings each year, suggesting that these are considered attractive positions in the local community.

Improvement and Continued Program Assessment

As of the end of 2001 a total of approximately 45 shoe manufacturers had joined the PCI program. Suppliers and subcontractors of these manufacturers accounted for an estimated 1,200 bancas and according to the employer association about 60 percent to 70 percent of total production. By all accounts child labor has been virtually eliminated in these PCI principal manufacturing plants. There were no children found in these major manufacturing plants in the approximately 90 (2 x 45) inspections conducted in 2001. In addition, PCI has received significant external validation of its efforts. A brochure of PCI prominently cites a declaration from the U.S. State Department that "The shoe manufacturers in the city of Franca with the help of Abrinq, virtually eliminated child labor there and enhanced the educational opportunities of children whom they formerly employed."[32] Moreover, researchers have found no evidence of child workers in such factories during several visits to Franca, and numerous discussions of child labor with residents of the town representing a variety of socioeconomic circumstances and political orientations are consistent with these impressions.

The impact of PCI on child labor in bancas working for PCI manufacturers is harder to ascertain. This is because many of these are home-based operations, and detecting child labor violations in the home is very difficult. Moreover, because the penalty for using child labor is severe, there is a strong motivation to hide this activity. To give an example of the difficulty of detecting child labor in bancas, a child might be helping his or her parents with sewing operations in the family home. When the inspector announces his presence at the front door (by clapping, as is the custom in Brazil), the child could very easily put down the shoe he or she is working on and sit down to watch television, read, or pretend to be engaged in any of a number of activities. Thus the likelihood that an inspector would actually catch a child working in a PCI member banca is very slim. There was only one such case in 2001, and the child worker was found in a workshop separate from the home, so hiding the fact of work was not possible in this case.

Even if it is assumed that PCI efforts have pushed all child labor off the factory floors and out of the subcontractors' workshops, it is likely that an undetermined number of them have found other work. Many may have been displaced into other segments of the shoe industry that do not fall under the watch of PCI. There are large numbers of smaller manufacturers, estimated at about 300 to 350, and labor subcontractors, estimated at 1,000 to 1,200, that participate neither in PCI nor, in some cases, the employers association.[33] These entities account for roughly 30 percent to 40 percent of production, often operate informally, and have not been subjected to PCI auditing. Others may have moved on to take advantage of many opportunities for child labor in commerce and services. In some instances their new work may be even more dangerous than their shoe work, especially when it involves evening jobs, working alone, or illegal activities such as prostitution, the drug trade, or theft.

This likelihood of displacement of child laborers from one sector to another might be lessened if there were more resources made available by the shoe industry to establish out-of-school programs. Although PCI has undoubtedly made progress in increasing the opportunities for young people in this regard, the available funds appear insufficient to provide alternative activities for all children who are no longer working or who might be tempted to work.[34] Although, in theory at least, more funds could be generated by raising membership fees for firms to participate in

PCI, the concern is that any attempt to raise fees might lead some PCI member firms to drop out of the program. This would, of course, be counterproductive.

The displacement of child laborers to other sectors could also be reduced by better coordination between PCI and other institutions in the community providing activities for adolescents. With appropriate coordination it is possible that child workers displaced from PCI-affiliated firms might be absorbed into either the income-replacement program run by the union/local government or the apprenticeship program run by the Rotary Club.

Despite the Rotary Club program's potential for absorbing displaced shoe workers, PCI and industry officials have not sought to coordinate with it. Indeed, they have sometimes joined with others in questioning whether the rudimentary job skills learned qualify it as a genuine apprenticeship program despite Ministry of Labor approval. It would seem obvious that better relationships between PCI and Rotary Club officials might lead to efforts to explore possible synergies between their programs. If child laborers displaced from PCI-affiliated shoe firms are intent on working, it would seem useful to explore the possibilities of finding places for them in the Rotary Club program, perhaps modified in ways desired by PCI. That would certainly be more desirable than having the displaced child workers resort to illegal activities such as prostitution, the drug trade, or theft.

As a consequence of the problems noted above, child labor remains a serious issue in Franca. Research by French[35] allows us to assess the overall extent of child labor participation in the workforce. A survey instrument was administered to 454 12- to 17-year-olds in two Franca schools in mid-1998, before the start of the PCI auditing program and before the change in the minimum working age to 16 years. It contained a number of questions pertaining to workforce participation and work experiences of the surveyed students. The surveys were followed up with interviews with 73 children. The results, based on the subset of observations gathered randomly, are shown in figure 11.3. The first two columns contain data for 12- to 14-year-olds with the other two for 15- to 17-year-olds. The results reveal a high level of labor force participation for the younger children, with 22.4 percent working 20 or more hours a week. Nearly 60 percent of the 15- to 17-year-olds reported 20 or more hours of work per week.

Similar surveys were undertaken in mid-1999 at the same two schools. In the interim the rate of labor force participation for the 12- to 14-year-olds declined markedly to 14.6 percent (the sum total of those working 20 or more hours per week) (see figure 11.4). The decline can be attributed in part to the passage of a federal law in late 1998 raising the minimum working age from 14 to 16 years. Part of the reduction may also be due

Figure 11.3
Workforce Participation by Adolescents in Franca: 1998

1998	12-14 years		15-17 years	
	Number	Percent of Total	Number	Percent of Total
Not working by choice	91	55.7	28	14.2
Looking for work	25	15.2	47	23.9
Working 8-19 hours per week	11	6.7	5	2.5
Working 20 or more hours in shoe industry	13	7.9	70	35.5
Working 20 or more hours in commerce or services	19	11.5	34	17.3
Working 20 or more hours in other sectors	5	3.0	13	6.6
Totals	165	100	197	100

to the efforts of PCI and others in the community to eliminate child labor. Finally, it should also be noted that unemployment was rising during this period, and some of the decline may be a function of that. However pronounced the decline may be, it is clear that the incidence of child labor was still quite high in Franca. We suspect that this is most likely due to the limited coverage of PCI in terms of manufacturers and bancas (leading some children to simply change jobs) as well as the difficulty of effectively monitoring child labor in household bancas.

FUTURE DEVELOPMENTS

A strong movement is under way in Franca to streamline and modernize subcontracted work in the shoe industry, a process referred to as "regularizing production." The pressure for this is coming from several directions. The major brands that source production from Franca have gotten pressure from consumers, stockholders, labor groups, and others about the whole sweatshop labor controversy. Many have adopted codes of conduct like adidas-Salomon (see chap. 8) pertaining to working con-

Figure 11.4
Workforce Participation by Adolescents in Franca: 1999

1999	12-14 years		15-17 years	
	Number	Percent of Total	Number	Percent of Total
Not working by choice	107	68.2	80	22.4
Looking for work	22	14.0	75	21.0
Working 8-19 hours per week	5	3.2	14	3.9
Working 20 or more hours in shoe industry	9	5.7	78	21.8
Working 20 or more in commerce or services	10	6.4	83	23.3
Working 20 or more hours in other sectors	4	2.5	27	7.6
Totals	157	100	357	100

ditions for supplier firms. These major brands, however, find it difficult to enforce the codes when production takes place in bancas, for the same reasons that PCI has difficulty preventing child labor from being used in these workplaces. Thus the major brands have a strong interest in seeing production move out of the bancas and into regular workshops. At the same time a legal challenge to the practice of subcontracting work to bancas has been slowly making its way through the courts in Franca. A recent ruling affirming the illegality of subcontracting to unregistered subcontractors is adding further impetus to the move to centralize production into regular workplaces. Moreover, observers note that the economic interests of the local government, employers association, and union all coincide in the direction of moving production out of unregistered bancas into official workplaces. The government will derive more tax revenues, the employers association will have more dues-paying members, and so will the union.

The new code of conduct proposed by the shoe manufacturers to regulate subcontracting requires that the subcontractors first register their enterprise with the appropriate authorities, hire only registered workers, and pay all employment taxes and fees. Additionally, workshop areas must be separated from any household activities. Finally, children between 7 and 15 must remain outside the work areas, attend school, and participate in other programs funded by PCI affiliates either before or after their half-day school session. This move toward more regularized subcontracting will require PCI to begin monitoring a broad array of work environment issues in addition to the presence of child workers. This will present the organization with a whole new set of challenges, and the sophistication and thoroughness of inspections will need to be increased dramatically. Inspectors, who in the past just needed to check whether a child was in a workplace, will need to become experts on a wide array of workplace issues. It will be interesting to follow how PCI responds to this challenge.

Another promising development is taking place outside the shoe industry. The municipal government has begun to participate in a national program designed to help communities better coordinate the activities and programs of local firms, governmental organs, and nonprofit agencies that deal with children and adolescents. This mechanism for program coordination will presumably work in tandem with other community bodies, most notably the elected council in the city designed to safeguard children's constitutional rights, and would appear to mark an important step forward in efforts to combat child labor and enhance the welfare of children.[36]

The experiences of PCI suggest that industry collaboration can be effective in combating child labor in developing countries when this practice takes place in regular work establishments. However, child labor in the informal economy is much more difficult to monitor and control. Moreover, controlling child labor in the formal sector may actually lead to increases of the practice in the informal sector, as children seek work elsewhere. This is one reason why, in addition to monitoring workplaces, providing children with opportunities for apprenticeships, education, and recreation is so important. This case further demonstrates (through their relative absence in Franca) the value of cooperation with other programs and key actors in the community in providing a coordinated and integrated approach to the problem of child labor.

NOTES

1. Elements of this case have been drawn from several papers previously published by the authors. Richard E. Wokutch, "Child Labor: A Continuing Ethical Challenge of Globalization," presented at the International Society of Business, Economics, and Ethics meetings, São Paulo, Brazil, July 2000, published in electronic proceedings at http://www.synethos.org/isbee/C2K/Contributed%20Papers/list_view.htm; J. Lawrence French, "Adolescent Workers in Third World Export

Industries: Attitudes of Young Brazilian Shoemakers," *Industrial and Labor Relations Review* 5, no. 2 (January 2002): 308–23.

2. See for example, C. S. Clark, "Child Labor and Sweatshops: An Overview," in *Child Labor and Sweatshops*, ed. Mary E. Williams (San Diego, Calif.: Green Haven Press, 1999), pp. 10–20; U.S. Department of Labor, Bureau of International Affairs, *By The Sweat & Toil of Children*, vol. 1, *The Use of Child Labor in U.S. Manufactured and Mined Imports* (Washington, D.C: Department of Justice, 1994).

3. U.S. *Department of Labor, By The Sweat and Toil of Children*,vol. 1; International Labour Organization, *Child Labour in the World* (Geneva: International Labour Organization, 1998), http://www.dol.gov/dol/ilab/public/media/reports/iclp/sweat5/chap2ft.htm (accessed 24 January 2000).

4. International Labour Organization, "Every Child Counts: New Global Estimates of Child Labour" (April 2002), http://www.ilo.org/public/english/standards/ipec/simpoc/index.htm (accessed 26 July 2002).

5. T. Harkin, "The United States Should Ban Imports of Products Made by Children in Child Labor and Sweatshops," ed. Mary E. Williams (San Diego, CA: Greeshanen Press, 1999) pp. 38–47.

6. International Labour Organization, *Child Labour: What's To Be Done?* document for discussion at the Informal Tripartite Meeting at the Ministerial Level, Geneva (1999), http://www.ilo.org/public/english/comp/child/papers/what/what1/htm (accessed 11 January 2000).

7. International Labour Organization, "Worst Forms of Child Labour Convention 1999," http://ilolex.ilo.ch:1567/english/convdisp2 (accessed 28 July 2002).

8. U.S. Department of Labor, *By the Sweat and Toil of Children*, vol. 1.

9. Rosa M. Fischer, "Social Labeling Against Child Labor: Brazilian Experience," Centro de Estudos em Administração do Terceiro Setor, FIA, Universidade de São Paulo, Research Report (March 2000).

10. Parenthetical comment in original. Richard Anker and Sandhya Barge, eds., *Economics of the Demand for Child Labour* (New Delhi: ILO, forthcoming). Cited in Richard Anker and Helinä Amelkas, *Economic Incentives for Children and Families to Eliminate or Reduce Child Labour* (Geneva, Switzerland: International Labour Organization, May 1996), http://www.ilo.org/public/english/comp/child/papers/economic/index.htm.

11. U.S. Department of Labor, *By the Sweat and Toil of Children*, vol. 1, p. 21.

12. Anker and Amelkas, *Economic Incentives for Children and Families*.

13. Anker and Amelkas, *Economic Incentives for Children and Families*; UNICEF, *The State of the World's Children* (New York: Oxford University Press, 1997); U.S. Department of Labor, *By the Sweat and Toil of Children*, vol. 1.

14. The role of global companies in stimulating demand by children for such products and how this plays into the whole child labor phenomenon are issues worthy of consideration but beyond the scope of this case.

15. P. Horn, *Children's Work and Welfare, 1780–1890* (Cambridge, U.K.: Cambridge University Press, 1994); B. White, "Children, Work and Child Labor: Changing Responses to the Employment of Children," *Development and Change* 25 (1994): 849–78.

16. Fischer, "Social Labeling Against Child Labor."

17. See arguments, for example, in S. Alam, "Efforts to Ban Goods Made by Children Are Counterproductive," in *Child Labor and Sweatshops*, ed. Mary E. Wil-

liams, pp. 43–47; J. V. Iovine, "Product Labeling Programs May Not Reduce Child Labor," in *Child Labor and Sweatshops*, ed. Mary E. Williams, pp. 82–85; A. R. Myerson, "Sweatshops Often Benefit the Economies of Developing Nations," in *Child Labor and Sweatshops*, ed. Mary E. Williams, pp. 32–35; I. M. Stelzer, "Efforts to Reduce the Use of Sweatshops Are Misguided," in *Child Labor and Sweatshops*, ed. Mary E. Williams, pp. 58–62; "Banning Imports Made by Child Labor Won't Help Kids," *USA Today* (13 June 1996), p. A7; M. Weidenbaum, "A Defense of Sweatshops," in *Child Labor and Sweatshops*, ed. Mary E. Williams, pp. 26–28.

18. Wokutch, "Child Labor."

19. Raquel Luicursi, *Trabalho Infantil em Franca* (São Paulo, Brazil: Editora Linhasgerais, 1995).

20. *Orlando Sentinel*, 10 September 1995, p. A9.

21. U.S. Department of Labor, *By the Sweat and Toil of Children*, vol. 1.

22. Abicalçados, ABInforma, *Novo Hamburgo* (São Paulo, Brazil: Abicalçados, 2001).

23. Information for this section comes from interviews with PCI staff and participating manufacturers and a PCI brochure, "The Business Community's Strength in Favour of the Child and the Teenager" (Franca, Brazil: Instituto Pro Crianca). Further information comes from U.S. Department of Labor, Bureau of International Labor Affairs, *By the Sweat and Toil of Children*, vol. 4, *Consumer Labels and Child Labor* (Washington, D.C.: Bureau of International Labor Affairs, 1997) and Fischer, "Social Labeling Against Child Labor."

24. Business Partners for Development, "Results and Recommendations for Businesses" (2002), http://www.bpdweb.org/docs/biz4of5.pdf (accessed 1 August 2002).

25. See Fischer, "Social Labeling Against Child Labor," for a fuller description of the similarities, differences, and relationship between PCI and PEAC.

26. Fischer, "Social Labeling Against Child Labor."

27. Fischer, "Social Labeling Against Child Labor."

28. Instituto Pro Crianca, Franca: "Business Community's Strength," p. 2.

29. Instituto Pro Crianca, Franca: "Business Community's Strength," p. 2.

30. Instituto Pro Crianca, Franca: "Business Community's Strength," p. 5.

31. Fischer, "Social Labeling Against Child Labor."

32. Instituto Pro Crianca, Franca: "Business Community's Strength," p. 6.

33. Maurilo Casemiro, "Ações de Combate ao Trabalho Infantil das Indústrias Calçadistas da Cidade de Franca, SP," (Franca, Brazil: PCI, 1997).

34. Fischer, "Social Labeling Against Child Labor."

35. French, "Adolescent Workers in Third World Export Industries."

36. "Franca hosts the first meeting of the Program to Integrate Services to Children / Adolescents," *Diário da Franca* (24 May 2002), p. 4.

CHAPTER 12

International Labour Organization: Factory Improvement Programme

Ivanka Mamic and Charles Bodwell[1]

The ILO Management and Corporate Citizenship Programme has established a multisupplier training program for the development of local managers' capacity in the areas covered by the ILO Declaration on Fundamental Principles and Rights at Work as well as quality and productivity—supporting the business case for good labor practices at the factory level. The program involves 10 to 12 factories participating during a six-month period in a training and factory-level consulting/improvement program. The training takes place in a conference room setting, followed by factory visits and consulting in the specific needs of individual factories.

> What is needed is training of the national managers, to help them move up the chain. With expat managers, they are often locked in their ways. The goal is really to move up local managers.
> —MNE regional manager, Vietnam

> What you could do at the ILO is something to build up the local managers, road show training or something like that, one week a quarter over a year.
> —MNE manager, China

OVERVIEW

During the past two decades the phenomenon of globalization and the resultant increase in global economic integration have led to an unparalleled scrutiny of the ability of firms to meet their corporate social responsibility objectives. Questions have focused particularly on codes of conduct and attempts to self-regulate corporate behavior. Research by the International Labour Organization (ILO) has revealed that notwithstanding the introduction of codes of conduct, in many instances firms continue to struggle to meet their corporate social responsibility objectives. This can be attributed to a number of factors including the following:

- Poor management systems and skills in supplier factories
- Poor communication
- Language barriers
- Low literacy rates

The ILO has found that in some instances multinational enterprises (MNEs) charge their subcontractors with responsibility for the details of building and running factories, managing workplaces and workers, and dealing with local governments. It is often the case that managers in these supplier factories are faced with competing objectives but receive little direction on how to balance their core business objectives while ensuring that their corporate social responsibilities are met.

In light of the challenges outlined above, a recent initiative by the Management and Corporate Citizenship (MCC) program of the ILO has been the establishment of a multisupplier training and factory improvement program (FIP). The aim of the program is to help develop the capacity of local managers in the areas covered by the ILO Declaration on Fundamental Principles and Rights at Work, which forms the backbone of many MNE initiatives, as well as in productivity, safety and health, and human resource (HR) management. Participants in this training program will include suppliers across a variety of industries. As mentioned, codes of conduct adopted by MNEs often expressly refer to United Nations (UN) and the ILO conventions and aim to adopt best practices based on these conventions. However, in many instances management encounters significant hurdles in meeting the requirements of these codes of conduct and international conventions. Participation in the training program should increase the capacity of managers to respond to the competing demands being placed on them, facilitate the sharing of best practices, and result in changes being implemented at the factory level.

INSPIRATION AND VISION SETTING: IDEA GENERATION/INCEPTION

Problem Analysis

The ILO has been conducting an extensive research program on the management of supply chains stretching to Asia and Latin America, with a focus on labor issues. As delineated in the introduction this research has highlighted the fact that MNEs and their suppliers are under pressure to meet the demands placed on them to eliminate substandard conditions in their workplaces and achieve the universal principles as espoused in UN and the ILO conventions. Some of the challenges that corporations are confronted with include the development and implementation of codes of conduct, adherence to national legislation regarding freedom of association and collective bargaining, working hours and rest time, as well as general good business practices.

Even though some MNEs have made great efforts to effect changes in practices throughout their supply chains through overtly managing their responsibilities by integrated responsibility management approaches[2] that resemble quality management systems, the struggle continues. In many instances the adoption of codes of conduct has not been sufficient to invoke the necessary changes in the organizations because of poor management systems and skills in supplier factories and other factors that limit the effectiveness of codes of conduct. The program herein proposed attempts to a limited degree to address those shortcomings. The footwear sector provides a useful example of some of the challenges that have arisen as a consequence of the increasing subcontracting of production activities to developing countries. Research by the ILO of footwear production in China found that to a large degree MNEs charge their subcontractors with responsibilities for the details of building and running factories, managing workplaces and workers, and dealing with local governments. In many instances managers are faced with competing objectives but receive little direction on how to balance their core business objectives while ensuring that their corporate social responsibilities are met. One senior manager interviewed by the ILO in China detailed the different objectives that parties to the production process have as follows: "The government goal is to get jobs for people. The factories want to take advantage of the labor pool. And the workers want to make as much money as possible, working long hours to do so." Even though companies are making greater efforts to meet their social policy objectives, specific training on how to incorporate these objectives in management systems and to build the capacity of local managers is required.

ILO Recommended Response

The ILO factory improvement program involves 10 to 12 factories participating for a six-month period in training in a conference room setting as well as factory-level training. Training takes place at the factory level so that conference room presentations can be backed up by real-world examples based on factory walkthroughs. The aim, as mentioned, is to increase cooperation and encourage the sharing of best practices between participants. The overriding objective is to devise practical and realistic solutions to the challenges MNEs and their suppliers currently face to conduct their business profitably, ethically, and with accountability.

ESTABLISHMENT, INTEGRATION, AND
IMPLEMENTATION

The FIP is funded for four countries, two in Asia and two in Central America, with pilot activities already having been commenced in Sri Lanka. In each country the training program targets considerable improvements in working conditions and labor practices in 12 supplier factories resulting in improvements in 48 factories in total, employing an estimated 30,000 to 50,000 employees. Through the program, approximately 100 managers will receive direct training while numerous other managers will have their skills upgraded by indirect participation. The indirect beneficiaries of this training program are the workers in each of the respective participating factories who will benefit from improved management systems.

Module-Based Training, Factory-Level Improvement

The training program consists of both training modules and in-factory improvement efforts, covering a range of topics targeted at achieving compliance with the ILO's core labor standards. It is hoped that this dual process will facilitate the exchange of theories, ideas, and problem solving on the one hand, while also enabling participants to engage in action and consultation.

This module-based structure (see figure 12.1) will be replicated in each of the four country-level programs, with each of the six modules commencing with a two-day seminar on the specific topic to be covered and lasting for a one-month period. As such, each country-level program will last half a year. The suggested focus of these six modules follows.

Management Systems and Achieving Quality Improvement

The focus in the first module will be on helping managers to develop an understanding of the factory improvement approach while also creating buy-in by providing the managers with benefits that affect their bottom line. The focus during this one-month module will be on using the consulting/self-improvement methodology to target quality improvement, in part through increased dialogue between workers and management.

Productivity, Overtime, and Payroll Practices

The second module will focus through increased productivity on helping suppliers better meet national labor laws with a particular emphasis on reducing overtime hours, a goal focused on by many corporate codes. Drawing on experiences in other locations and best practices, it will do this by attempting to link productivity increases to reduced work hours

Figure 12.1
Module-Based Training, Factory-Level Improvement

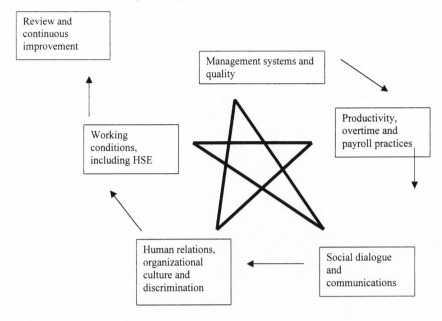

while rewarding workers for increased productivity. This module will also encompass materials to ensure fair pay practices and acceptable accounting standards.

Social Dialogue and Communications

The third module will expressly target improving communications between workers and management—an objective that is implicitly addressed throughout the FIP. The module will explore both the changes in atmosphere and management/worker relations required to increase communication and the mechanisms that can be used to improve dialogue. The module will seek both to inform and to build on efforts already begun in the earlier two modules and those that follow.

Human Relations, Organizational Culture, and Discrimination

The fourth module will seek to build on what was covered during the last module, highlighting HR practices that support code of conduct goals and core labor standards, particularly with regard to discrimination but with regard to other areas also. The focus will be on HR processes including recruitment, appraisal and promotion, training and development, and retrenchment.

Working Conditions

The fifth module will seek to use improvements achieved in the module on social dialogue and communications to identify those areas requiring improvement in working conditions. Part of the focus here would be health and safety. The module would also focus on other areas of working and work-related conditions that could improve the job satisfaction and motivation of employees. These will be specific to each factory, but might include items such as health care—for example, AIDS and HIV awareness—dining facilities, and nutritional content of meals. While for the most part housing is not provided in the garment sector in Sri Lanka, for example, factories may during this module examine ways in which they could improve living conditions for workers or address transportation concerns.

Improvement and Continued Program Assessment

The final module will target the integration of the improvement efforts into processes in the firm. Its objective will be to complete efforts already begun in other modules, to see how changes can be institutionalized, and to introduce processes for self-examination and change into the future.

Development of the modules and determination of their content will be carried out by the ILO and international experts with knowledge specific to the areas under consideration. For reasons of cost savings, it is expected that the training materials will be based where possible on already existent material adapted to the specific nature of this course, and that the managers providing training be very experienced with similar course material. As part of the UN's Global Compact and supply chains initiatives, the MCC program has begun developing training materials that address many of the points to be covered by the FIP. One example of these materials is called the total responsibility management (TRM) approach, which provides a systemic approach to thinking about how a company's multifarious responsibilities to stakeholders can be managed. This model, based on the practices of numerous companies with long supply chains, highlights the development of a responsibility vision, or inspiration, integrates that vision into practices and operations, develops indicators to measure progress, and emphasizes ongoing improvements. The TRM approach is discussed in chapter 6.

Program Structure

The FIP (see figure 12.2) will consist of a two-day seminar covering six different topics as outlined above. This seminar will be followed by factory visits by the international expert in the specific subject area together with the program coordinator. These experts will review the self-assessment

Figure 12.2
FIP Structure

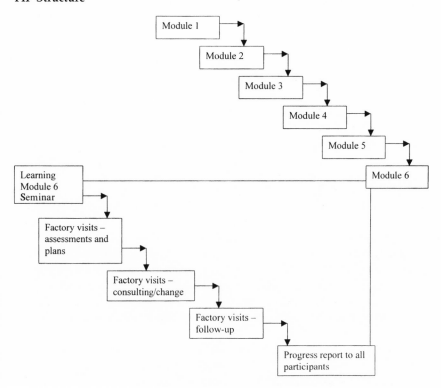

completed by the factory and develop with factory management an action plan of change to be completed both over the following month and during the course of the program. These first two steps will cover the first two weeks of each module, to be followed by rotating follow-up visits and consulting by the coordinator/expert. Finally, before the start of the next module there will be a progress report by each factory, to review improvements made and suggest plans for the future.

There will be an attempt during the two-day seminars to have considerable input on the part of factories. For this reason, one approach being considered is to have two factories present their situation in the topic area during each of the two-day seminars.

The goal of the training program is to improve a firm's ability to meet its corporate social responsibility objectives. Through the FIP, managers will focus on implementing their firm's goals and vision, key elements of the inspiration or vision-setting processes of responsibility management, and consider how to measure and integrate more responsibility practices into their operations. By focusing on the integration of responsibility management approaches particularly with respect to labor practices, firms can improve their relationships with the key stakeholder responsible for implementation—the employee.[3]

Experts

It became apparent after extensive discussions and preprogram preparations that one of the key roles in this project is that of program coordinator (an expert with considerable factory management experience) at the field level in each country in which the project takes place. This is because the coordinator will remain on the project for all six months, developing a rapport with local companies, traveling to factories with experts in each of the module areas to assess their current state, and then will be making follow-up visits during the rest of the module. There is some possibility that the person who has been appointed as program coordinator in Sri Lanka, the first country in the FIP, will continue on to the Philippines (possibly the second country in Asia) to coordinate the project there and that the coordinator hired for the Central American countries would handle both of the training programs to be carried out there.

Leading international experts in specific topic areas will be recruited in each of the areas covered by the modules, except for the final module—review and continuous improvement. This last module will be handled by the program coordinator with support from Geneva as necessary. The ILO staff may provide the expertise for modules 3 (dialogue and communications) and 4 (HR, organizational culture, and discrimination), given the ILO's considerable experience in these areas.

Rotating and Overlapping Modules

Delivery of the learning modules will occur on a rotational basis so that after a group completes training in module 1, it will automatically move to module 2, while another group commences module 1. It is expected, however, that the first training program will be conducted in its entirety before the subsequent training programs are commenced in an overlapping fashion. This will allow for feedback from the first set of training programs to be adopted into the subsequent set of training programs.

There are several benefits to the rotating nature of the modules spread over a six-month period. First, the break between modules will not be a free time, but rather will entail the completion of assignments, related both to the module just completed and the module to come in the next installment. That way, the experts' time is leveraged, and participants will be better able to take part in the training with examples taken from their own operations.

The rotating nature will also allow wider coverage by the specific topic area experts contracted by the ILO. Each expert, focused on only one module, will in addition to providing the two-day training, be able visit factories to assist with self-assessments and the development of action plans.

Participating Factory Selection and Role

It is envisaged that participating local factories will send two or three managers for each two-day seminar. These participants should be those responsible for code implementation in their factories and should be of a high enough level to champion improvement efforts. At the same time it is suggested that some number of government representatives and local NGOs also observe the seminars to improve dialogue with these important stakeholders on issues related to implementation of the corporate codes, the ILS, and national laws.

In preliminary discussions both with factory management at several locations and with apparel supplier/exporter associations, it appears that finding factories that would commit to participating in the program will not be difficult. In the words of the head of one of the associations in Sri Lanka, "It won't be hard to find 12 factories who will take part; it will be hard to choose from our 200 member factories who would like to be chosen." This appears to be the direct result of increased pressure being applied by a variety of buyer firms on the factories to comply with codes of conduct and meet labor standards, as well as a general interest by the factories in meeting these standards while maintaining competitiveness.

In terms of the factory selection process, participants will be chosen based on a variety of factors, including but not limited to the following:

a. Size—participation by medium to large factories, 500 to 2,000 employees are envisioned

b. Willingness to participate

c. Balance in the program between relatively advanced firms (in terms of labor practices and corporate social responsibility) and those firms requiring considerable improvement on labor practices

d. Location—to allow regular visits by the program coordinator and experts, factories need to be geographically concentrated

e. Possibility of expanding practices to sister factories—therefore those organizations with more than one factory will be preferred

The ILO national offices, working to identify suitable supplier participants at the national level, and the backstopping office in Geneva will share the actual task of selection. It has also been suggested that several factories that produce for the local market be included, both as comparator and as a means of demonstrating to such manufacturers that good labor practices can produce savings and higher productivity rather than just incur costs.

The role of the factories is central to the success of the program. They will be responsible for the following:

1. Sending two managers to participate in the seminars. These managers should have the power in their organizations to serve as champions of the improvement efforts.
2. Carrying out self-assessment of operations before the visit of the ILO experts.
3. Taking part in the ILO factory walkthrough and "assessment of the assessment." After this and during the same visit, the supplier would develop with the ILO experts a plan of action to be completed during the following month.
4. Carrying out the plan of action. The ILO coordinator would visit the factory during the time between seminars to consult on and assist with the improvement efforts.
5. Attending the progress report meeting to provide an update on changes that actually took place, changes that did not take place, and plans for future improvements.
6. Contributing in some way to the cost of the program, perhaps through the coverage of transportation costs for the experts during the program.

ILO Role

The ILO will be closely involved in the actual development of modules and coordination of activities. For the ILO's MCC program, this type of training program, with its inexpensive, cost-sharing approach, will be a pilot methodology to low-cost, high-impact training, in close participation with a variety of stakeholders. The ILO will also supply the experts for the program.

NOTES

1. The responsibility for opinions expressed in this chapter rests solely with the authors, and publication does not constitute an endorsement by the International Labour Office.

2. See Sandra Waddock and Charles Bodwell, "From TQM to TRM: The Emerging Evolution of Total Responsibility Management Systems," Working Paper, Boston College/ILO, 2001.

3. Waddock and Bodwell, "From TQM to TRM."

CHAPTER 13

Chiquita Brands International, Inc.: Values-Based Management and Corporate Responsibility in Latin America

Tara J. Radin

Amid financial difficulties and uncertain industry prospects, Chiquita International Brands, Inc., nevertheless embarked on an ambitious corporate responsibility (CR) program that has enhanced working conditions on its farms in Latin America. During the 1990s Chiquita spearheaded adoption of the Rainforest Alliance's Better Banana Project (BBP) as a credible industry standard by investing in significant modifications in order to achieve BBP certifications of all of its farms. This prompted Chiquita to articulate its values and revise its code of conduct to advance those values.

Companies such as Chiquita, which has taken the initiative to invest in and promote fair labor practices even without industry-wide prompting, serve as models for companies in other industries as well. Even in the wake of financial distress, Chiquita has created an ambitious corporate responsibility (CR) program that prioritizes social responsibilities and makes the company publicly accountable for both its successes and its failures.

This case illustrates how Chiquita has operationalized CR in order to promote respect for workers. Through its annual Corporate Responsibility Reports, Chiquita now publicly identifies weaknesses on its farms and commits to making improvements so as to guarantee that worker concerns are addressed and resolved. Through transparency and open communication, Chiquita has created a learning organization that serves as a model for companies in any industry.

THE BANANA INDUSTRY[1]

The banana industry has enjoyed a long and colorful history. For more than 100 years this labor-intensive industry operated primarily in remote areas of Latin America with few outside influences (see photo 13.1.). Today it employs nearly 100,000 workers, most of whom work for two companies based in the United States (Chiquita and Dole) and one in Chile (Del Monte).[2] Although the industry developed in some politically unstable environments, it nevertheless managed to function independently and has served as a major force of economic development.[3]

The banana industry has received harsh criticism for inhumane conditions imposed on laborers.[4] The industry is one of the world's most important; bananas are ranked as the fifth most important agricultural commodity in the world.[5] The industry has nevertheless become saturated and "beleaguered."[6] Although 86 million tons of bananas and plantains are produced a year,[7] less than 20 percent are actually traded on the world market.[8] To this day the banana trade remains a multimillion dollar industry in which profits garnered through a worldwide network of importers and exporters have rarely made their way down to the level of unskilled banana farmers.[9]

Socioeconomic and Political Conditions

The plight of banana farmers can be traced directly to the socioeconomic and political conditions that exist in many of the developing countries that remain leading banana producers. Various countries in Latin America and former European colonies in the Caribbean and Africa have long been the primary producers of bananas as a result of their favorable tropical climates. As a result of the political turmoil and economic instability that has marred many of these countries, there remains a lack of any real effective preventive body or measure to protect banana workers against exploitation. The absence of any sort of corporate, governmental, or industry code of ethics has left laborers struggling alone to fight for the most elementary of rights.

Common problems in the general banana industry include excessively low wages, lack of health care, inadequate benefits, child employment, exposure to aerial spraying during the picking process and chemical toxins during the packing and shipping process, and violence and intimidation against those who attempt to unionize.[10] In addition, in countries such as Ecuador, many employers have frequently practiced an informal policy through which workers who unionize are fired illegally and replaced with subcontracted "permatemp" workers.[11] Because the fine for such activity is generally less than $400, there is little deterrence.[12]

Photo 13.1 Workers on Chiquita farm in Costa Rica. *Source:* Tara Radin

Banana Trade Wars

The "Banana Trade Wars" was the name given to the battle fought over the banana industry during the 1990s between the United States and the European Union (EU) as a result of unfair trade practices.[13] The industry is clearly scarred; the battle raged from the early 1990s until April 11, 2001.[14] Among the firms hardest hit by the Wars has been Chiquita.[15]

Beginning in 1993 the EU instituted a policy of providing favored import status to former European colonies in Africa and the Caribbean, and established quotas and tariffs for banana imports from other countries.[16] This had a devastating effect on the industry, as witnessed by a downward spiral in European market share, price wars, decreased wages, plantation closings, and job cuts.[17]

Diminished returns left Chiquita on the brink of bankruptcy.[18] Chiquita convinced the government of the United States to file an international trade complaint against the EU. The World Trade Organization (WTO) arbitrated the dispute and ruled consistently in favor of the United States, and this enabled the United States to impose economic sanctions against the EU.[19]

The EU countered by proposing the controversial "first come, first served" plan, which would have effectively replaced country quotas with a regional quota.[20] Opponents feared that such a policy would result in a virtual "race to the bottom."[21] The proposal was met with equal skepticism from Chiquita and most major Latin American banana producers and countries (except Ecuador), in that it was perceived that an uninhibited marketplace would have provided an advantage to countries such as Ecuador, where the wages and general conditions imposed on workers remain the worst in the industry.[22]

Confronting growing opposition the EU finally agreed to more generalized quotas, along with the issuance of operating licenses based on loosely defined "historical trade flows" and previous import figures.[23] This system will ultimately give way in 2006, at which point all quotas are scheduled to be lifted.[24] Arguably in the right direction, this step merely constitutes temporary compliance with basic WTO requests. There now exists an even greater lack of clarity and transparency in the process by which acceptable production levels across different companies and countries are allotted. It also remains uncertain whether this policy shift will actually improve the market share of those countries and companies that initially lost out as a result of the quota system. This tumultuous time has left the industry in disarray.

Aftermath

Strategies companies adopted in anticipation of the opening up of the European marketplace have affected their current competitive positions. Chiquita and Dole, for example, adopted contrasting approaches.[25] Dole concentrated on growing its presence in Ecuador and cut back in countries with higher wages. In contrast, Chiquita largely pulled out of the Ecuadorian market and invested in countries such as Colombia and Costa Rica.[26]

Chiquita continued to support worker rights. On June 14, 2001, in an effort to aid the cause of banana workers and advocate basic rights, wages, and benefits, Chiquita went so far as to sign a joint agreement with the International Union of Foodworkers (IUF) and the Coordination of Latin American Banana Worker Unions (COLSIBA) that "commits Chiquita to respect international conventions with respect to worker rights as well as lay the basis for joint union/management efforts to address long-standing worker health and environmental concerns in the banana industry."[27]

Recent years have witnessed a number of factors that have converged and caused significant changes. The European Fyffes, based in Ireland, has become a major player, along with the Ecuadorean company, Noboa, whose bananas are labeled "Bonita" in the United States.[28] In addition, the emergence of the Internet has served to empower workers around the world, and increased environmentalism coupled with union activism have compelled change. While trends mark positive steps for the industry and the future of its workers, the process by which this change will be implemented remains largely undefined.

From an internal perspective, there are few policies or gauges intact to monitor and prevent exploitation of laborers. In Ecuador, children routinely begin working around the age of 10, their average workday is 12 hours, fewer than 40 percent of the children remain in school through the age of 14, workers continue to be exposed to toxins and unsanitary conditions on a daily basis, and reported incidents of sexual harassment continue.[29] Ecuador nevertheless remains a major producer of bananas. According to figures reported by the United Nations, Ecuador now provides 28 percent of the world's bananas.[30]

Market Conditions

While ongoing violations of worker rights continue as a result of the lack of local government action against such practices, it appears that many large exporters exacerbate the problem by receiving banana supplies from plantations in which inappropriate working conditions exist.[31] They subsequently ship the bananas off to giant supermarket chains in the United States in which there also exist virtually no checks against purchasing bananas that have been supplied by plantations in violation of human rights laws. By the time the bananas reach the supermarket shelves and enter the hands of consumers, any potential controversy that might have resulted from the exposure of inhumane labor conditions is completely erased from the picture.

As with other commodities, the consumer lacks a voice in the purchasing process as a result of layers of distributors and retailers who have direct influence on the brand of bananas that consumers ultimately have the opportunity to buy. Unlike products such as ice cream, in which end consumers can exercise their voice by choosing which brand to purchase among many, most banana retailers, such as large grocery store chains, make the choice for end consumers by buying in bulk from distributors on the basis of price. Few customers even know the brand of bananas sitting on their counter at this very minute.

The pricing of bananas remains unstable—it has fluctuated in virtually all global markets during recent years.[32] Certain countries continue to export large quantities of bananas (see figure 13.1).[33] Ecuador remains the largest exporter, and the United States, Europe, and Japan remain primary importers (see figure 13.2).

Outlook

Without support from many Latin American governments and only partial compliance from many companies, the perils of banana workers

Figure 13.1
Leading Banana Exporters—1998–2000

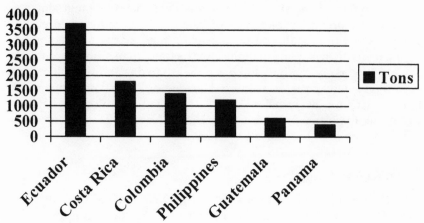

Source: The Business Roundtable, "Corporate Social Responsibility in Latin America: Practices by U.S. Companies" (2001), http://www.brtable.org/pdf/585.pdf (accessed 30 August 2002).

threaten to continue.[34] It is incumbent on individual companies to institute protections,such as through the groundbreaking alliance between Chiquita, IUF, and COLSIBA to elevate working conditions.[35] An industry-wide shift in practice will not occur until those plantations and companies that fail to adhere to the same standards stop finding willing buyers in the marketplace.

CHIQUITA BRANDS INTERNATIONAL, INC.

Although "Chiquita" has only been registered as a trademark in the United States since 1947, the company has existed for more than 100 years. It is the oldest multinational enterprise operating in Latin America.[36] The company traces its origins back to 1870, when founder Captain Lorenzo Baker purchased the first 160 bunches of bananas in Jamaica and delivered them to Jersey City after an 11-day sail.[37] During the past century Chiquita has experienced numerous changes: the United Fruit Company was created on March 30, 1899, the company issued its first annual report in 1903; "Miss Chiquita" was introduced in 1944; the Chiquita brand arrived in Europe in 1966, and the name was changed to Chiquita Brands International in 1990.[38]

Figure 13.2
Leading Banana Importers—1998–2000

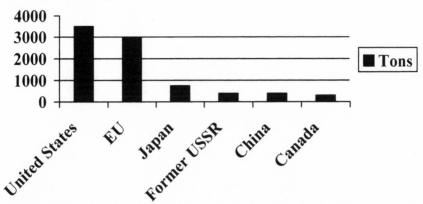

Source: The Business Roundtable, "Corporate Social Responsibility in Latin America: Practices by U.S. Companies" (2001), http://www.brtable.org/pdf/585.pdf (accessed 30 August 2002).

Based in Cincinnati, Chiquita is a leading marketer, producer, and distributor of bananas and other fresh and processed foods. While Chiquita does sell other foods and remains the leading processor of private-label canned vegetables in the United States, 55 percent of the company's total revenue comes from bananas, and the company employs 20,000 people in its Latin American banana divisions. In 2001 twelve billion bananas were sold by Chiquita around the world.[39]

Although Chiquita sells its produce in 60 countries and operates on 6 continents, the vast majority of Chiquita's banana operations are in Latin America.[40] Aside from a farm on the Ivory Coast, a joint venture in the Philippines, and a minority interest in farms in Australia, Chiquita has invested primarily in this hemisphere, in Costa Rica (where Latin American operations are headquartered), Honduras, Guatemala, Panama, and Colombia.

Costa Rica

Nestled between war-torn Nicaragua and poverty-stricken Panama, Costa Rica remains somewhat an anomaly.[41] It is a peaceful country with little turmoil and no standing army (its army was disbanded in the 1940s).

Costa Rica has a population of 3.8 million people, within approximately 19,730 square kilometers—about the size of Vermont and New Hampshire combined.[42]

Costa Rica has traditionally relied heavily on agriculture, with coffee, sugar cane, and bananas contributing significantly to the economy.[43] The economy has developed significantly during the past decade and has benefited from a rise in tourism. Costa Rica is home to rich natural attractions, such as the rain forest, the cloud forest, and the Pacuare River; tourism now accounts for a third of Costa Rica's economy.

In spite of challenges such as communication, roads, and an excessively legalistic society, Costa Rica offers a number of opportunities for foreign direct investment. In the mid-1990s, Intel set up operations in Costa Rica. This has had a dramatic impact in terms of labor shifts and economic development. In the first year that Intel arrived, its contribution to the country's economy was equal to that of bananas. Intel currently accounts for 60 percent of Costa Rica's GDP.

Although Costa Rica remains one of the more advanced countries in Latin America, it still suffers from many of the challenges associated with being an emerging country. One difficulty stems from the fact that most areas of the country do not use street names or addresses. People instead identify their homes according to proximity to other landmarks, such as large factories, pharmacies, stores, and other people's houses. Although this is more problematic for the tourist than the person living in Costa Rica, it causes subtle inconveniences. It has prompted many people in Costa Rica, particularly businesses, to use private mail couriers.[44]

Current Challenges

The past decade has been replete with challenges. Chiquita built up operations substantially in Latin America in anticipation of the opening up of the European market in the early 1990s, only to collide with restrictive quotas that resulted in the exact opposite effect.[45] The company's profits plummeted (see figure 13.3). In 1992 Chiquita suffered losses greater than $150 million. The company that had peaked with profits exceeding $100 million in 1991 was now struggling to survive. The investment in production in anticipation of the opening of the European market not only had not panned out, but actually exacerbated the problem as Chiquita had to find ways to prune operations and get rid of excess production and facilities.

Chiquita was beginning to recover when Hurricane Mitch arrived in 1999 and devastated Chiquita operations in Honduras.[46] It would have been easier for Chiquita to leave Honduras at that juncture, but the company felt responsible for rebuilding operations to contribute to the community it had served.[47] The company also believed that, with its proximity

Figure 13.3
Chiquita's Financial Performance: 1980s–1990s

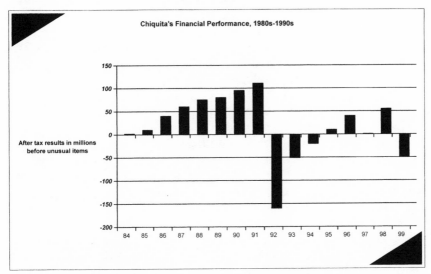

Source: Reprinted with permission of Chiquita Brands International, Inc.

to the North American market and new investments in technology and flood control, the Honduras division could provide a stable supply of high-quality, cost-competitive fruit as long as good labor relations could be maintained.

In 2002 Chiquita began to regain its financial footing. As a result of a prearranged Chapter 11 bankruptcy, the company was able to negotiate an arrangement through which Chiquita traded a 95.5 percent stake in the company for a $700 million reduction in debt and accrued interest.[48]

In the wake of great disappointment and catastrophe, and despite severe financial losses, Chiquita nevertheless shifted its focus to CR, and Chiquita continues to place CR at the forefront of its business agenda.

PROGRAM STUDY: BETTER BANANA PROJECT— CATALYST FOR CHANGE

In 1992 the Rainforest Alliance approached the banana industry and invited companies to participate in a new certification process it had created: the Better Banana Project (BBP). It was clear that it would entail an extensive review and audit process, undoubtedly coupled with required changes and a heavy investment, but the Rainforest Alliance maintained that the certification would enhance participants' reputations. The industry was unwilling to participate.

Inspiration and Vision Setting: Idea Generation/Inception

Although initially reluctant, Chiquita decided to consider cooperating with the Rainforest Alliance. Chiquita realized that the industry needed a standard and, for it to be credible, it had to be administered by a third party with no ties to the industry—it could not be merely cosmetic.[49] The Rainforest Alliance served as a viable candidate. It had origins in the non-governmental organization (NGO) community and had developed a positive presence in the public spectrum. Chiquita volunteered to test the BBP standards on two farms in Costa Rica.[50]

The BBP was an ambitious standard that covered a range of workplace issues. Components of the project addressed environmental, health and safety, and worker concerns.[51] Although the focus of the certification was environmental, as David McLaughlin, Senior Director, Environmental and Regulatory Affairs, Chiquita Brands International, Inc. based in Costa Rica, explained, the reality is that BBP touches every part of banana operations and has significantly altered the company's culture and treatment of workers. While workers at Chiquita were not historically treated unfairly, the BBP caused systems to be put in place to add consistency and elevate Chiquita's attentiveness to worker rights and working conditions.

The BBP served as the catalyst for Chiquita's movement toward formalized CR initiatives, because it caused Chiquita to see how different dimensions of business (environmentalism, health and safety, worker rights, profitability, and so on) are interconnected. Through the BBP process and the subsequent move toward CR, Chiquita has progressed beyond the mere protection of basic worker rights to the creation of an integrated workplace that values workers as individuals.

Establishment and Implementation

The initial BBP certification was a two-year procedure that encompassed the development of a learning process to be adapted organization-wide to improve production practices systems, materials management, and labor relations practices.[52] It was a procedure that focused on long-term developments and results, and that dictated cultural change throughout the organization.

BBP certification has had a far-reaching effect.[53] In terms of ecosystem conservation, enhanced processes affect workers in creating a safer, more environmentally aware work environment. In addition, since many workers live on the farms, their living conditions are improved. The certification process has triggered the institution of reforestation programs along rivers, canals, public roads, and around all public areas. Waste management has also been affected and, as part of the certification, Chiquita has been required to devise creative uses for recyclables. Chiquita has used recycled plastic in a number of ways, for example, for the creation of bricks for walkways and a pedestrian bridge between one of the farms and a local community. Chiquita recycled more than 3.1 million kilos of plastics in 2000 alone.

Worker safety has also been emphasized. Training has been enhanced and medical checkups are provided. Protective equipment has been improved and increased, and reentry periods are enforced to prevent exposure to dangerous pesticides. Facilities, such as laundries, showers, and warehouses, have also been improved. Periodic audits ensure that working conditions are at least satisfactory.

Another positive consequence of the BBP certification has been a vast improvement in facilities. Specific performance guidelines have been created for each component. Every farm is audited for compliance on an annual basis by the Sustainable Agriculture Network, a group of NGOs throughout Latin America (which includes the Rainforest Alliance).[54] In line with continuous improvement, objectives are made increasingly stringent from one year to the next.

Continued Program Assessment

All farms owned by Chiquita today in Latin America—119 farms in 5 countries—are certified through the BBP. This has constituted a major effort in terms of time, resources, and manpower. It has taken eight years and has required a capital investment of more than $20 million.[55]

During this process Chiquita has had to learn to trust external partners; continued certification demands that external auditors have complete access to all production records and facilities for the entire year. According to former President and CEO Steve Warshaw, this has been advantageous: "That work [BBP certification] helped us see the value of tough third-party standards and of opening ourselves to outside scrutiny."[56] This has helped workers because exposing business practices to external scrutiny has provided Chiquita with performance benchmarks.

BBP certification has played an instrumental role in promoting cultural change within Chiquita, particularly with regard to transparency.[57] BBP prompted Chiquita to begin a dialogue with workers and other stakeholders that had not previously taken place. Chiquita learned to ask workers about their concerns and ideas, and this has led to positive workplace improvements. Workers have been given a voice. One worker recommended that a sample tray be provided for workers in the packing plant, and that simple addition has improved quality performance in the plants.

Chiquita enjoys a more positive role in the industry as a result of BBP certification, and workers benefit from the increased attention paid to labor issues. The process has taught managers to anticipate concerns before they become problems. Following BBP certification, Chiquita experienced natural "growing pains."[58] Even though Chiquita's values were already seemingly embedded in the company culture and operations, it still took time to learn how to get systems and procedures to reflect those values consistently.[59] What began as an environmental initiative has ended up transforming the organization and has raised the standards for the entire industry.[60]

PROGRAM STUDY: CHIQUITA'S CORPORATE RESPONSIBILITY PROGRAM

As a result of BBP certification, Chiquita developed an understanding of the importance of emphasizing CR. A series of initiatives has resulted in a trickling-down sense of empowerment among workers. While Chiquita avoids using the word *empowerment* because of its various connotations, that is essentially what the company has accomplished through its CR program. The premise is that respecting workers is the morally right thing to do and that demonstrating that respect motivates workers to enhance their performance.

Inspiration and Vision Setting: Idea Generation/Inception

In October 1998 a Corporate Responsibility Steering Committee was created that brought together senior and middle managers from business units and corporate headquarters in a conversation to explore how Chiquita could operationalize CR. Committee members communicated through monthly meetings, in person and via video and telephone conference calls.

Chiquita's experience with the BBP taught the company the importance of paying attention to stakeholders—particularly workers. Chiquita has endeavored through CR to integrate respect and protection for workers by developing systems that provide for transparency and open dialogue, and make concerns visible so that they can be addressed.

Establishment and Implementation

The overall goal for the Steering Committee lay in determining how to introduce values-based management. The first question was, "What are our values?"[61] The Committee involved nearly 1,000 employees in interviews and discussions about personal values and perceptions of Chiquita values to arrive at a set of shared values, which were articulated in 1999 as Chiquita's "Living by Our Core Values" (see appendix 13.1).

In 2000 these values were translated into Chiquita's "Code of Conduct ... Living by Our Core Values," which revised the company's 1993 code and established standards for behavior consistent with principles of ethics, law, and social responsibility (see Table of Contents of Chiquita's "Code of Conduct . . . Living by our Core Values," appendix 13.2).[62] The contribution of this code is the addition of "social responsibilities" to the other ethical and legal responsibilities for which Chiquita had traditionally considered itself accountable.[63] Among the social responsibilities that Chiquita identifies are the requirements of the Social Accountability 8000 (SA8000) labor standard, including restrictions against child labor, forced labor, discrimination, and coercive disciplinary practices as well as guarantees for adequate health and safety conditions, freedom of association and collective bargaining, reasonable working hours, and fair wages.[64] Chiquita has established a public goal of achieving third-party certification of all of its owned banana operations in Latin America to the SA8000 standard, and in March 2003 Chiquita in Costa Rica earned the distinction of becoming the first agricultural enterprise in Central America to achieve SA8000 certification.[65]

Chiquita's "Code of Conduct" is noteworthy in regard to the public accountability to which it pledges. In the "Code" Chiquita commits to "publicly report on our progress as we achieve and verify our compliance with these responsibilities."[66] Chiquita has honored this commitment with the publication and distribution of its annual "Corporate Responsibility Report"[67] (see figure 13.4). Although other stakeholder concerns are addressed, these reports are directed at employees. In the reports Chiquita provides a comprehensive assessment of operations and details its performance vis-à-vis its social responsibilities. The company identifies its measures, describes its indicators, and openly discloses areas in which improvements are needed—where Chiquita has fallen short of its expectations. For example, the 2000 Report disclosed discrimination in the Honduras division: Women had not been promoted into supervisor roles, preemployment pregnancy and AIDS testing were required, and workers over 40 years old were not hired.[68]

Publication of these reports signaled a new spirit of openness at Chiquita.[69] Following the first assessment, the results of which were published in the "2000 Corporate Responsibility Report," Chiquita committed to conducting periodic assessments to be presented in annual reports. The company's "2001 Corporate Responsibility Report" was issued in November 2002 and is available at www.chiquita.com. The results of the most recent assessment will appear in Chiquita's "2002 Corporate Responsibility Report," currently awaiting publication.

Another significant step occurred with the appointment of a Corporate Responsibility Officer. Prior to 2000, CR efforts and initiatives had fallen within the province of individual operating managers. Programs were in place, but there was a glaring absence of consistency and general oversight of endeavors. Chiquita lacked a channel through which concerns could be addressed and ideas implemented. A potential solution emerged with

Figure 13.4
Summary of Compliance with the SA8000 Standard from Corporate Responsibility Report

		Santa Marta, Colombia	Turbo, Colombia	Costa Rica	Guatemala	Honduras	Armuelles, Panama	Bocas, Panama
Child Labor								
	Use of Child Labor	U	C	C	N[1]	N[2]	C	C
	Remediation Policy	U	C	C	C	C	C	C
	Limits on Young (age 15-17) worker hours	U	C	C	N[3]	C	C	C
	Hazards to young workers	U	C	C	N[4]	C	C	C
Forced Labor								
	No forced labor	U	C	C	C	C	C	C
Health and Safety								
	Accident and injury prevention	U	N[5]	N[6]	N[7]	N[8]	N[9]	N[10]
	Senior management rep. Accountable	U	A	C	A	C	A	C
	Regular and recorded training	U	N[11]	C	N[12]	N[13]	C	C
	Systems to prevent and respond to threats	U	A	C	C	A	A	A
	Clean bathrooms, potable water and food storage	U	C	C	N[14]	N[15]	N[16]	N[17]
	Housing	U	C	C	N[18]	N[19]	C	C
Freedom of Association								
	Freedom of association	U	C	C	N[20]	C	C	C
	Parallel means where law restricts	U	NA	NA	NA	NA	NA	NA
	No discrimination against union reps.	U	C	C	C	C	C	C
Discrimination								
	Non-discrimination in employment	U	C	C	N[21]	C	N[22]	N[23]
	Respect practices and needs	U	C	C	C	C	C	C
	No sexually abusive behavior	U	C	C	N[24]	C	C	C
Disciplinary Practices								
	No mental or physical abuse or punishment	U	C	C	C	C	C	C
Working Hours								
	Regular – max. 48 hours and 1 day off in 7	U	C	C	C	N[25]	C	N[26]
	Overtime – max. 12 hours, voluntary, paid extra	U	N[27]	C	N[28]	N[29]	C	N[30]
Compensation								
	Wages meet legal minimums, indus-try standards & basic needs	U	C	C	N[31]	C	N[32]	N[33]
	Convenient pay with full detail	U	N[34]	N[35]	C	C	C	C
	No use of labor contractors to avoid benefits	U	C	C	C	C	C	C
Management Systems		U	A	C	A	A	A	A

Source: Adapted from Chiquita Corporate Responsibility Report 2001, reprinted with permission of Chiquita Brands International, Inc.

the naming in 2000 of Jeff Zalla, the leader of the steering committee, as Chiquita's first Corporate Responsibility Officer.[70] That he reports directly to the CEO and Audit Committee of the Board of Directors demonstrates the support and interest of upper management and Chiquita's continued commitment to CR. Although this sort of position is not unique to Chiquita, it is not common in the banana industry.

Chiquita strives toward continuous improvement in terms of CR. The final stage of its CR implementation program began after the first report was issued. Referred to as "Corporate Responsibility for the Long Term," this program involves facilitator-led sessions delivered to senior management teams in each business unit. The purpose of these sessions is to provide guidance to help teams apply CR to their systems, structures, and management practices, "to embed Core Values and Code permanently into our daily work lives."[71] Chiquita remains committed to teaching managers how to administer CR and show respect to workers.

Continued Program Assessment

Although Chiquita considers itself a company with a history of values-based management, it has only been within the past several years that the company has taken steps to communicate its values and business practices externally.[72] A number of major steps have taken place (see figure 13.4). Chiquita has evolved from a company without any sort of formal CR program into an industry leader with values-based management and CR at the forefront as named priorities. At virtually any farm, the values are prominently displayed, and all workers are aware of the values and what they mean to Chiquita.[73]

Chiquita has determined that there are several factors critical to the success of its CR program. The commitment of senior managers coupled with the involvement of operating managers have been instrumental to the success of the company's CR efforts. In addition, careful selection of external partners to ensure credibility and integrity has remained important. Chiquita has set high performance standards against which to be measured, and has demanded rigor, honesty, and transparency.[74]

Chiquita has identified a number of challenges still to be tackled. The creation of effective and efficient management systems remains an ongoing challenge, as does communication and worker training. Chiquita recognizes potential value in determining ways to build relationships with other stakeholders, such as unions, NGOs, and suppliers, in order to collaborate on shared concerns such as goal setting and safety. In addition, Chiquita hopes to widen the debate in the food and agriculture community.[75]

Cyrus Freidheim, Jr., named Chairman and CEO of Chiquita on March 19, 2002, emphasizes the company's commitment to its values: "They are the bedrock on which we build our business. We must constantly strive to live them fully."[76] Freidheim contends that values are the staple that holds stakeholders to the organization. "[G]ood relationships help drive bottom-line performance, good relationships are built on values. For example, when we treat employees with respect, they are more loyal and productive," Freidheim pointed out. "When we act ethically, we earn the respect of our business partners and suppliers. . . . Values-based leadership is the best way to build a great company and key to delivering shareholder value."[77] (See figure 13.5.)

Case Study of Corporate Responsibility: Chiquita in Costa Rica

Chiquita has played a prominent role in the communities in which its farms are located. Not only has it made contributions through the provision of jobs, but the company has also taken a proactive role in developing new infrastructure by committing to establishing farms in previously inaccessible locations.[78]

Infrastructure poses a major obstacle in many developing and emerging countries, and it affects many of the countries in Latin America in a number of common ways. Transportation of both goods and employees can

Figure 13.5
Chiquita Corporate Timeline

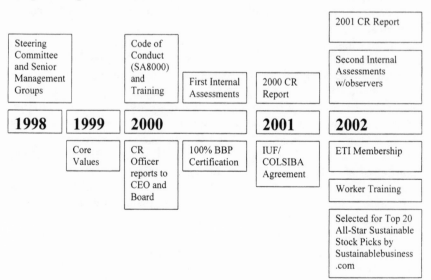

Source: Reprinted with permission from Chiquita Brands International, Inc.

Figure 13.6
Chiquita Values Flowchart

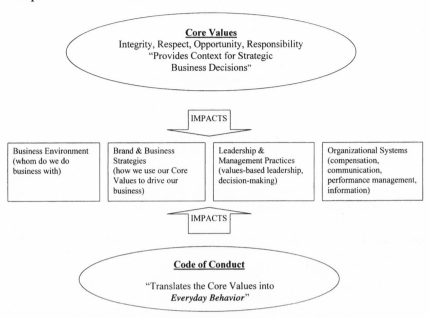

Source: Reprinted with permission from Chiquita Brands International, Inc.

pose a significant impediment. Roads are horrible—even in Costa Rica, one of the more advanced countries in Latin America. In addition, the weather serves as a double-edged sword. Chiquita operates in Latin America because of the tropical, fertile climate. That same climate causes torrential rains that result in periodic landslides that place lives, property, and transportation plans in jeopardy. In addition, the basic infrastructure—water treatment, phone lines, power plants, and so on—is often underdeveloped except in the larger cities.

As Chiquita developed farms in Costa Rica, it had to build a significant portion of the infrastructure required to operate them—Chiquita had to construct power facilities, lay phone lines, and build the roads to get to the farms. This was a service to both communities and workers, for it enabled Chiquita to provide jobs to workers who lived in the remote areas, and it made those areas more accessible.[79]

Inspiration and Vision Setting: Idea Generation/Inception

In Costa Rica the tenor of Chiquita's operations is and has been that of responsible business. While CR is a relatively new part of Chiquita's culture, systems that have been in place in Costa Rica for years are consistent with Chiquita's new CR program. Indeed, formalization of the program provides support for what Chiquita has been working to accomplish in Costa Rica and Latin America for decades.

The impetus for CR initiatives at Chiquita has been driven at least in part by McLaughlin. His official role puts him in charge of the CR program in Latin America. McLaughlin previously rotated through different positions throughout Costa Rica, including general manager, and through those roles he made decisions and created initiatives that were consistent with values-based management.[80] Observing his interaction with workers and managers in Costa Rica underscores that point. Many of his ideas have been implemented and have become part of the company's accepted practices and procedures. What is being codified today at Chiquita is by and large the method by which McLaughlin ran operations in Costa Rica a decade ago. This is not to say that all credit for the recent thrust toward CR at Chiquita goes to McLaughlin, but he certainly has played a significant role, as a strong manager, visionary leader, and vocal member of the Chiquita team.

Establishment and Implementation

While producing bananas for delivery around the world, Chiquita in Costa Rica has also found itself in the business of anticipating worker needs and offering possible solutions. The needs of workers in a developing or emerging country are different from those of workers in a developed country, and Chiquita has taken extra steps to learn about local workers to determine how the company can best assist them both in the workplace and in their personal lives. Chiquita offers a range of benefits and incentives that are valuable to workers and make the workers more valuable to Chiquita through greater productivity and satisfaction. Through an array of programs, Chiquita endeavors to contribute to the community in which it exists along with workers, managers, and the rest of Costa Rica.

Communication   Chiquita's relationship with workers begins with adequate, effective, and appropriate communication.[81] To show respect for them, Chiquita tailors messages to the language and medium with which the workers are most comfortable. Instead of attempting to address employees uniformly, the company takes into account the differences among its employees. Even though Chiquita is headquartered in the United States, where English is the primary language, Chiquita makes an effort to have all important documents translated into Spanish. The company recognized that "translation" entails more than overcoming a language barrier. The company has thus also created a special worker training pamphlet that illustrates through clear and simple graphics and text the essence of the company's Core Values and Code of Conduct, including workers' rights and responsibilities as Chiquita employees. Integrity, for example, is depicted simply in the manual as it emerges between two people who trust one another. Although Costa Rica boasts a high 95 percent literacy rate, documents are translated into Spanish and presented graphically primarily because of the high illiteracy rates in many of the other Latin American countries.[82]

Communication remains important with regard to the workers' daily work lives. Each farm has an "information center" where workers are able to obtain useful information, for example, information that enables them to track their teams' performance as compared with that of other teams and to be kept abreast of farm performance goals.

Farm Living   Chiquita has continued its relationship with workers by connecting their work and personal lives. As Chiquita has built farms throughout Latin America, it has designed these farms as communities in which workers could live and work. The company has equipped these farms with medical clinics, convenience stores, recreation facilities, and other amenities. Homes have also been built on a number of farms. Since farms are often located in remote areas where transportation is poor, Chiquita considered it necessary and advantageous to have at least some housing available to attract workers. It is worth noting that the housing was provided as an added benefit, not in lieu of any salary. A number of companies have been criticized for providing workers with low-cost housing in lieu of their wages; this practice has been widely criticized on the grounds that it translates into robbing the workers of their fair wages. Chiquita offers housing on farms purely as an added benefit,[83] and special provisions were often made for single pregnant women. Several women on different farms mentioned that Chiquita made sure that they received housing when they became pregnant.[84]

Chiquita's experience with company-owned housing has been different from what it expected. While ostensibly a benefit, the provision of free housing has translated into a potential liability, for both the company and employees. The employees appear to take the housing in stride. When asked, those who live in Chiquita-owned housing do not have major complaints, and those who live away from the farm do not feel deprived.[85]

Chiquita has begun to wonder whether providing housing really lies in its best interests and the interests of the workers. The company has found that providing free housing places it in the awkward position of doubling as both employer and landlord for many workers. This can prove problematic if a worker is dissatisfied with something having to do with his or her housing. There is a potential danger that workers' dissatisfaction with housing can lead to counterproductive behavior in the workplace.

Even in instances in which workers are satisfied, Chiquita has begun to believe that there are important lessons about ownership to be learned and that the recipients of free housing are not being given the opportunity to learn them. Many people who live on the farm seem to lack an understanding of the importance, value, and pride of ownership, and they seem disconnected from the recognition of responsibilities connected to property use and owndership. Because the workers do not own their homes and do not suffer the consequences of loss, they tend not to take care of the property.

Chiquita has also come to realize that, in serving as landlord, the company is forced to invest heavily in property maintenance as a result of both normal wear-and-tear and workers' neglect. Chiquita also recognizes a pattern of property neglect on the part of many workers, and believes that they would treat the property better if they owned it. The company is now beginning to fear that giving temporary housing to employees makes them less apt to strive to own their own homes. Further, Chiquita has confronted an additional problem when workers retired. Because they do not own their homes, when they change jobs or retire, they become homeless or dependent on other family members for housing.[86]

Chiquita still provides a lot of housing, but plans are under way to change this gradually. The company has experimented in other countries with programs that promote worker ownership of their own homes, and the results to date have been positive. In Honduras, for example, an extensive pilot project is under way through which land was bought and 600 houses are being built. Chiquita worked with the federal government of Honduras, municipalities, the union, and NGOs to arrange for opportunities for workers to buy these houses. Similarly, in Panama, Chiquita has arranged for houses near the farms to be sold at subsidized prices, and workers have valued the opportunity to explore home ownership.[87] Chiquita is committed to improving the condition of its workers in the long term, not just during the length of the worker's direct relationship with Chiquita.

Farm Work   On a banana farm there are two categories of work: line work in the packing plant and field work. Field work includes general field tasks (including drainage, weed control, pruning, fertilization, and nematode controls), harvesting, and fruit protection (bagging and guying). Field tasks and fruit protection work can be performed individually, while harvesting requires three-person teams. The farm is divided into parcels, and workers are moved from parcel to parcel from one day to the next. To protect workers, pesticides are sprayed only on parcels where field work is not being performed.[88]

Workers at Chiquita in Costa Rica are paid primarily by piece work according to their production. This enables workers to plan their own schedules and exercise control over their income. This involves minimal supervision—only one supervisor per 75 to 100 hectares (about 250 acres).[89]

In accordance with *papaya*, Chiquita posts workers earnings' on a daily basis.[90] This is a practice dictated by local cultural expectations in Costa Rica and is not unique to Chiquita. Banana workers check the postings to find out what their own earnings are and to compare them with those of their co-workers. The transparency actually helps maintain worker motivation and productivity.

Chiquita has also implemented an annual bonus scheme that is unique to the company, industry, and country. All workers are eligible for two bonuses a year, one mid-year in June, the other after December. These bonuses are earned if teams and farms meet quality and cost targets. A newsletter distributed every six months keeps workers informed about the goals and bonuses.

Monetary prizes are awarded for workers who devise ideas that assist in performance or productivity. For example, one worker was recognized for originating a plan to avoid scarring as bananas were moved from the fields to the packing plants. Workers appreciate both the monetary awards as well as the opportunity for peer and supervisory recognition.

Nonfinancial Worker Incentives　　Chiquita offers a wide range of opportunities to workers. Even in instances in which implementation of worker initiatives are not accompanied by worker prizes, workers still benefit from the pride of having made a contribution that has been recognized by the company.[91] Interestingly, of all the workers asked about their perspective on Chiquita, no one mentioned pay as a major concern. Chiquita pays comparably to, if not better than, other employers in Costa Rica. Regardless, workers seemed to respond more to other sorts of stimuli. A few workers said, "Of course, pay could always be more," but many workers found ways to supplement their pay.[92]

A female supervisor mentioned that she found Chiquita a supportive environment.[93] She has had the opportunity to be promoted within the company, and that is important to her. In addition, she wants to continue improving herself. When she decided to take a special computer course for non-work-specific reasons, she paid tuition for the course, but Chiquita agreed to give her paid leave on Saturdays so that she could attend classes.[94]

Women in general seem to feel comfortable on the farms.[95] While the proportion of female supervisors does not adequately reflect the female worker population, some of that has to do with personal desires. A couple of women admitted that they were not interested in being promoted.[96] Pregnant women are supported. Pregnant women on different farms admitted that they were afforded the opportunity to change job functions to less stressful areas during pregnancy.[97]

Chiquita looks for ways to help work seem rewarding. As workers receive training, on many farms they receive licenses to wear to show skills they have learned. Several workers spoke proudly about how they received personal congratulations and small celebrations thrown by supervisors. Personal incentives seem popular among workers at Chiquita.

In addition, Chiquita hosts "Banana Olympics." Each year, top workers in various field and packing tasks travel to one division and compete again each other in a series of competitive events. This is followed by a celebration during which their high level of expertise is recognized.

Free Association   Chiquita is the most unionized of banana companies, with about 15,000 unionized workers in Central America and Colombia.[98] Only a few of Chiquita's farms in Latin America are unionized, however. Even though unions are legal in Costa Rica, there, only about 15 percent of Chiquita's farms there are unionized, which is roughly comparable to the percentage of the general working population in Costa Rica that is unionized.[99] Most farm workers have opted instead to institute permanent committees that serve similar roles, but without what workers perceive as politics and unnecessary bureaucracy. When asked, most workers prefer not to belong to unions.[100] At Chiquita, they have found that they do not need union protection.[101] Direct lines of communication are established and maintained with supervisors, and that provides workers with their primary channel for comments and complaints.[102]

A number of workers commented that they had reported problems to supervisors, and there was no fear of retribution.[103] While problems were not always solved as quickly as workers might have liked, no one had any serious complaints.[104]

It appeared that on many farms unions did not play an important role because of the community that existed in the workplace and on the farms. Having workers live on the farms seems to have contributed toward stronger communication among workers and between workers and managers. In addition, lack of infrastructure causes workers to bond together. Workers belong to teams that take care of basic services such as fire and safety. They are trained in emergency medicine so that farms do not have to rely on outside assistance, which is often slow and inadequate. In the late 1980s Chiquita suffered a fire in one of its oil palm facilities. The emergency team was not able to put it out before damage was done, but the fire was put out before the municipal fire engine arrived.[105]

Discussions about the emergency and safety teams revealed an underlying sense of community at Chiquita.[106] While some workers were admittedly proud on an individual level about their participation on the teams, the louder message was that they felt obligated as members of a community to obtain the emergency training to take care of their friends.[107]

Continued Program Assessment

Although Chiquita has made significant efforts toward respecting workers and their rights, it is important to keep in mind that Chiquita views ethics and social responsibility as a goal that always lies outside reach. Chiquita remains on a path of continuous improvement; as standards are approached, the goals are raised.

Monitoring   As part of the Rainforest Alliance's BBP certification, the Sustainable Agriculture Network conducts regular unannounced audits of the farms through which it monitors environmental, safety, and worker conditions to ensure compliance with relevant standards. In addition, Chiquita conducts periodic social audits using teams of trained internal assessors drawn from a variety of functional areas. A single human resources manager, responsible for environmental and CR issues, handles routine monitoring. He attends weekly meetings with NGOs regarding environmental issues and spends other days visiting farms conducting audits.[108]

Although these audits are internal, they are taken seriously. A senior manager accompanies the auditor to verify findings. A positive relationship appears to exist between the auditor and farm members. During an observed audit, even when the auditor noted areas for improvement, the response was collaborative, not antagonistic.[109]

Human Resources   As Chiquita continues to look for ways to enhance its performance, the company is beginning to support development of people. A woman was recently promoted to serve as manager for training and development. She was even provided with a classroom specifically designated for training.[110]

In this role, the manager is responsible for training, but she has reconceived the notion of what training means at Chiquita. In many companies training is about providing workers with skills to perform a function. This is how training has traditionally been viewed at Chiquita. According to the manager, though, training should fall within the realm of people development.[111] The manager has recently initiated a program called "Performance Management" through which all employees—workers, supervisors, and managers—receive career counseling. Employees complete surveys that are then reviewed by the manager. She then meets with them individually to discuss career paths within Chiquita.[112]

When the manager introduced the program, she met with someone in accounting who seemed dissatisfied. He mentioned that he wanted to work as a financial analyst. After determining his qualifications, the manager leveraged her connections within the company to put him in touch with someone in finance. As it turned out, he was able to make the transition into the department he preferred but, even if the fit had not been successful, the key here was that the employee was given a voice and an opportunity.[113]

CONCLUSION

Chiquita has discovered that CR, the umbrella within which environmentalism, ethics, and worker issues fall, is of vital strategic importance.

It results in risk reduction, brand enhancement, quality, productivity, standards of excellence, and actual cost savings. Through CR, Chiquita is able to develop and promote trust among stakeholders and pride in their association with an industry leader. While transparency and open communication can prove challenging, they have led to rewards for both banana workers and Chiquita.

CR at Chiquita is a work in progress. The people at Chiquita continue to look for new ways through which they can embody the values they articulate.

NOTES

1. Section written with Adam Birnbaum.
2. US/LEAP, "Banana Worker Campaigns," http://www.usleap.org/Banana/bananatemp.html (accessed 30 August 2002).
3. Interview by Tara Radin with David McLaughlin, Guapiles, Costa Rica, 8–10 July 2002.
4. Banana Link, "The Banana Trade," http://www.bananalink.org.uk/trade/btrade.htm (accessed 30 August 2002).
5. Anne-Claire Chambron, "Straightening the Bent World of the Banana," Banana Link (February 2000), http://www.bananalink.org.uk/trade/btrade.htm (accessed 30 August 2002).
6. McLaughlin, interview. Although the banana industry is sometimes considered profitable, the reality is that bananas are a commodity product, with thin margins and historically declining prices (for the past 20 years). At the current time, there is an oversupply. The public financial records of major banana producers indicate that the industry is suffering.
7. Chambron, "Straightening the Bent World of the Banana."
8. Chambron, "Straightening the Bent World of the Banana."
9. Banana Link, "The Banana Trade."
10. With the exception of pesticide exposure, the above problems are not faced on Chiquita farms, which compose about 15 percent of the Latin American industry. They are most prevalent in Ecuador and on farms not producing for the major exporters.
11. Human Rights Watch, "Ecuador: Widespread Labor Abuse on Banana Plantations," (25 April 2002), http://www.hrw.org/press/2002/04/ecuador0425.htm (accessed 30 August 2002).
12. US/LEAP, "Banana Worker Campaigns."
13. US/LEAP, "Banana Worker Campaigns."
14. US/LEAP, "Banana Worker Campaigns."
15. Traci Carl, "Era Ends in Latin America as Banana Industry Slides: Protracted Trade War Hurt Chiquita's Ability to Compete," *Washington Post*, 2 December 2001, p. A28.
16. Anthony DePalma, "U.S. and Europeans Agree on Deal to End Banana Trade War," *New York Times*, 12 April 2001.
17. Banana Link, "The Banana Trade."

18. DePalma, "U.S. and Europeans Agree."

19. US/LEAP, "Chiquita Brands International, Inc.," http://www.usleap.org/Banana/bananatemp.html#Chiquita (accessed 30 August 2002).

20. US/LEAP, "'First Come, First Served': A Race to the Bottom for Banana Workers," background memo (13 March 2001), http://www.globalexchange.org/economy/bananas/leap031301.html (accessed 30 August 2002).

21. US/LEAP, "Chiquita Brands International."

22. Chiquita, "Chiquita, Others Firmly Oppose EU Commission's 'First-Come, First-Served' System," press release (20 December 2000), http://www.chiquita.com/announcements/releases/pr001220w.asp (accessed 30 August 2002); US/LEAP, "'First Come, First Served.'"

23. DePalma, "U.S. and Europeans Agree."

24. DePalma, "U.S. and Europeans Agree."

25. US/LEAP, "Chiquita and Dole Taking Different Paths," US/LEAP newsletter (December 2001), http://www.usleap.org/Banana/Chiquita%26DoleDiffPaths12–01.html (accessed 30 August 2002).

26. US/LEAP, "Chiquita and Dole Taking Different Paths."

27. US/LEAP, "The Banana Industry Crisis and the Trade Wars," http://www.usleap.org/Banana/bananatemp.html (accessed 30 August 2002); US/LEAP, "Chiquita Brands International"; Chiquita, "IUF, COLSIBA and Chiquita Sign Historic Agreement on Trade Union Rights for Banana Workers," press release (14 June 2001), http://www.chiquita.com/announcements/releases/pr010614a.asp (accessed 30 August 2002).

28. Hoovers Online, "Chiquita Brands International, Inc.," Company Capsule, http://www.hoovers.com/co/capsule/1/0,2163,11551,00.html (accessed 30 August 2002); Dana Frank, "Our Fruit, Their Labor and Global Reality," *Washington Post*, 2 June 2002, p. B5.

29. Human Rights Watch, "Ecuador: Widespread Labor Abuse on Banana Plantations" (25 April 2002), http://www.hrw.org/press/2002/04/ecuador0425.htm (accessed 30 August 2002); see also Juan Forero, "In Ecuador's Banana Fields, Child Labor Is Key to Profits," *New York Times*, 13 July 2002.

30. Frank, "Our Fruit, Their Labor and Global Reality."

31. McLaughlin, interview.

32. Food and Agriculture Organization of the United Nations, "Bananas: Commodity Notes" (2002), http://www.fao.org/ES/ESC/esce/cmr/cmrnotes/CMRbae.htm (accessed 30 August 2002).

33. The Business Roundtable, "Corporate Social Responsibility in Latin America: Practices by U.S. Companies" (2001), http://www.brtable.org/pdf/585.pdf (accessed 30 August 2002).

34. Banana Link, "Alternatives for the Future," http://www.bananalink.org.uk/future/alt_f.htm (accessed 30 August 2002).

35. US/LEAP, "The IUF, Chiquita and Trade Union Rights," *International Union of Foodworkers Bulletin*, editorial (September 2001), http://www.usleap.org/Banana/Chiquita/IUFArticleonGlobalAgreement9–01.html (accessed 30 August 2002).

36. US/LEAP, "Chiquita Brands International."

37. Chiquita, "Chiquita History," http://www.chiquita.com/ (accessed 30 August 2002).

38. Chiquita, "Chiquita History."

39. Chiquita, "Chiquita Brands International, Inc., 2001 Annual Report and Form 10-K" (Chiquita Brands International, Inc., 2001).

40. Hoovers Online, "Chiquita Brands International."

41. Even though Panama's per capita GDP is estimated to be twice as much as that of Ecuador, Nicaragua, or Honduras, the people still suffer from poverty, particularly as compared with Costa Rica.

42. Infoplease.com, "Costa Rica: Land and People," http://www.infoplease.com/ce6/world/A0857591.html (accessed 30 August 2002).

43. U.S. Department of State, "Background Note: Costa Rica," (April 2002), http://www.state.gov/r/pa/ei/bgn/2019.htm (accessed 30 August 2002).

44. McLaughlin, interview.

45. McLaughlin, interview.

46. Chiquita, "Chiquita Reports Damage from Hurricane Mitch," press release (2 November 1998), http://www.chiquita.com/announcements/releases/pr981102.asp (accessed 30 August 2002).

47. McLaughlin, interview; Chiquita, "Chiquita Reports Damage From Hurricane Mitch."

48. Sonja Sherwood, "Chiquita's Top Banana," *Chief Executive* (June 2002), p. 18; Chiquita, "Chiquita Emerges From Pre-Arranged Chapter 11 With Solid Financial Structure," press release (19 March 2002), http://www.chiquita.com/announcements/Restruct_Lang/PR020319english.asp (accessed 30 August 2002); Hoovers Online, "Chiquita Brands International."

49. McLaughlin, interview.

50. McLaughlin, interview.

51. McLaughlin, interview.

52. McLaughlin, interview; Chiquita, "Chiquita Achieves Major Milestone in Environmental and Social Certification of Banana Farms," press release (16 November 2000), http://www.chiquita.com/announcements/releases/pr001116a.asp (accessed 30 August 2002).

53. Rainforest Alliance, "The Rainforest Alliance Helps Chiquita Produce a 'Better Banana' and Transforms an Industry" (2000), http://www.sdearthtimes.com/et1200/et1200s10.html (accessed 30 August 2002).

54. Chiquita, "Chiquita Brands International, Inc., 2001 Annual Report."

55. McLaughlin, interview.

56. McLaughlin, interview.

57. Chiquita, "Better Banana Project," http://www.chiquita.com/ (accessed 30 August 2002); Chiquita, "EnviroChiquita: Better Banana Project," http://www.envirochiquita.com/ (accessed 30 August 2002).

58. McLaughlin, interview.

59. McLaughlin, interview.

60. Rainforest Alliance, "The Rainforest Alliance Helps Chiquita."

61. McLaughlin, interview.

62. Chiquita, "Code of Conduct," http://www.chiquita.com/ (accessed 30 August 2002).

63. Chiquita, "Code of Conduct."

64. Chiquita, "Code of Conduct."

65. McLaughlin, interview.

66. Chiquita, "Chiquita Brands International, Inc,. 2001 Annual Report," Chiquita, "Chiquita Brands International, Inc., 2000 Annual Report.

67. Other companies, such as Shell, McDonald's, and Motorola, have also published reports documenting their environmental, ethical, and social performance.

68. Chiquita, "Chiquita Brands International, Inc., 2000 Corporate Responsibility Report" (2000), http://www.chiquita.com/ (accessed 30 August 2002).

69. Chiquita, "Code of Conduct."

70. Chiquita, "Chiquita Brands International Promotes Jeffrey M. Zalla to Corporate Responsibility Officer," press release (27 November 2001), http://www.chiquita.com/announcements/releases/pr011127a.asp (accessed 30 August 2002). Zalla was given additional responsibilities one year later when he was also named vice president of corporate communications.

71. "CR Training and Implementation Status as of April 2001," *Corporate Responsibility News* 4 (2001): 4.

72. McLaughlin, interview.

73. McLaughlin, interview; interview by Tara Radin with Luis Garnier, Guapiles, Costa Rica, 8 July 2002.

74. McLaughlin, interview.

75. McLaughlin, interview.

76. "Chiquita's Core Values: Here to Stay," *Corporate Responsibility News* 9 (April 2002): p. 1. See also Sherwood, "Chiquita's Top Banana."

77. "Chiquita's Core Values: Here to Stay."

78. McLaughlin, interview.

79. McLaughlin, interview.

80. McLaughlin, interview.

81. Garnier, interview.

82. Garnier, interview.

83. McLaughlin, interview.

84. Interview by Tara Radin with farm workers, Costa Rica (9–10 July 2002).

85. Farm workers, interview.

86. McLaughlin, interview.

87. McLaughlin, interview.

88. McLaughlin, interview.

89. McLaughlin, interview.

90. Chiquita does not take credit for creating this program. It is a local custom, with which Chiquita complies.

91. Farm workers, interview.

92. Farm workers, interview.

93. Farm workers, interview.

94. Farm workers, interview.

95. Farm workers, interview.

96. Farm workers, interview.

97. McLaughlin, interview.

98. US/LEAP, "Banana Worker Campaigns."

99. McLaughlin, interview.

100. McLaughlin, interview.

101. Farm workers, interview.

102. Interview by Tara Radin with Farm Workers, Costa Rica (9–10 July 2002).

103. Farm workers, interview.

104. Farm workers, interview.

105. McLaughlin, interview.

106. Farm workers, interview.

107. Farm workers, interview.

108. Interview by Tara Radin with manager of environmental issues and CR, Guapiles, Costa Rica (9–10 July 2002).

109. Manager of environmental issues and CR, interview.

110. Manager of environmental issues and CR, interview.

111. Manager of environmental issues and CR, interview.

112. Manager of environmental issues and CR, interview.

113. Manager of environmental issues and CR, interview.

APPENDIX 13.1

Living by our Core Values

Our Core Values resulted from interviews and discussions with approximately 1,000 employees worldwide about their personal values and the values they believe Chiquita should stand for. It is clear that these same values we hold dear as employees are also critical to sustaining trusting and successful relationships with our consumers, shareholders, suppliers, host governments, and communities.

Integrity

- We live by our Core Values.
- We communicate in an open, honest and straightforward manner.
- We conduct business ethically and lawfully.

Respect

- We treat people fairly and respectfully.
- We recognize the importance of family in the lives of our employees.
- We value and benefit from individual and cultural differences.
- We foster individual expression, open dialogue and a sense of belonging.

Opportunity

- We believe the continuous growth and development of our employees is key to our success.

- We encourage teamwork.
- We recognize employees for their contributions to the company's success.

Responsibility

- We take pride in our work, in our products, and in satisfying our customers.
- We act responsibly in the communities and environments in which we live and work.
- We are accountable for the careful use of all resources entrusted to us and for providing appropriate returns to our shareholders.

APPENDIX 13.2

Table of Contents of Chiquita "Code of Conduct . . . Living by our Core Values"

Contents

Additional Readings

BOOKS

Amnesty International. *Global Trade, Labour and Human Rights.* London: Amnesty International United Kingdom, 2000.

Amsden, Alice. *Asia's Next Giant: South Korea and Late Industrialization.* New York: Oxford University Press, 1989.

Bauer, Joanne R., and Daniel A. Bell. *The East Asian Challenge for Human Rights.* Cambridge: Cambridge University Press, 1999.

Berquist, Charles. *Labor in Latin America: Comparative Essays on Chile, Argentina, Venezuela, and Colombia.* Stanford, Calif.: Stanford University Press, 1986.

Betcherman, Gordon. "An Overview of Labor Markets World-Wide: Key Trends and Major Policy Issues." In *World Bank Employment Policy Primer.* Geneva: World Bank, April 2002.

Betten, Lammy. *International Labor Law.* Deventer, Netherlands: Kruder Law International, 1993.

Bhagwati, Jagdish N., and Robert E. Hudec, eds. *Fair Trade and Harmonization: Prerequisites for Free Trade? Vol. 1, Economic Analysis.* Cambridge, Mass.: MIT Press, 1996.

——. *Fair Trade and Harmonization: Prerequisites for Free Trade? Vol. 2, Legal Analysis.* Cambridge, Mass.: MIT Press, 1996.

Bowie, Norman E. *Business Ethics: A Kantian Perspective.* Malden, Mass.: Blackwell, 1999.

Brown, Harold I. *Perception, Theory, and Commitment.* Chicago, Ill.: University of Chicago Press, 1977.

Cardoso, F. H., and Enzo Faletto. *Dependencia e Desenvolvimento (Dependency and Underdevelopment).* Santiago: ILPES, 1967.

Ching Yoon Louie, Miriam. *Sweatshop Warriors: Immigrant Women Workers Take On the Global Factor.* Cambridge, Mass.: South End Press, 2001.

Connor, Tim. *Still Waiting for Nike to Do It.* San Francisco, Calif.: Global Exchange, 2001.

Cooney, Sean, Tim Lindsay, Richard Mitchell, and Ying Zhu, eds. *Law and Labour Relations in East Asia.* Sydney: Federation Press. Forthcoming 2003.

De George, Richard. *Competing with Integrity in International Business.* New York: Oxford University Press, 1993.

De La Torre, Jose, Yves Doz, and Timothy Devinney. *Managing the Global Corporation: Case Studies in Strategy and Management.* New York: Irwin/McGraw-Hill, 2001.

Das, Dilip K. *Global Trading System at the Crossroads: A Post-Seattle Perspective.* New York and London: Routledge, 2001.

Donaldson, T. *The Ethics of International Business.* New York: Oxford University Press, 1989.

Donaldson, Thomas, and Thomas Dunfee. *The Ties That Bind.* Boston, Mass.: Harvard Business Press, 1999.

Drucker, Peter F. *Post-Capitalist Society.* New York: HarperCollins, 1993.

Elkington, John. *Cannibals with Forks: The Triple Bottom Line of 21st Century Business.* Gabriola Island, B.C.: New Society Publishers, 1998.

Enderle, Georges, ed. *International Business Ethics.* Notre Dame, Ind.: University of Notre Dame Press, 1999.

Frankfurt, Harry G. *The Importance of What We Care About.* Cambridge: Cambridge University Press, 1988.

Freeman, R. Edward. *Strategic Management: A Stakeholder Approach.* Boston: Pitman, 1984.

French, Peter. *Corporate Ethics.* Fort Worth, Tex.: Harcourt Brace, 1995.

Fung, Archon, Dara O'Rourke, Joshua Cohen, ed., and Charles Sabel. *Can We Put An End To Sweatshops?* Boston, Mass.: Beacon Press, 2001.

Gewirth, Alan. *Human Rights: Essays on Justification and Applications.* Chicago, Ill.: University of Chicago Press, 1982.

———. *Reason and Morality.* Chicago, Ill.: University of Chicago Press, 1978.

Gills, Dong-Sook S., and Nicola Piper, eds. *Women and Work in Globalising Asia.* London and New York: Routledge, 2002.

Hausman, Daniel M., and Michael S. McPherson. *Economic Analysis and Moral Philosophy.* Cambridge: Cambridge University Press, 1996.

Hepple, B. A., ed. *The Making of Labor Law in Europe.* London and New York: Mansell, 1986.

International Confederation of Free Trade Unions. *Behind the Wire: Anti-Union Repression in the Export Processing Zones.* Brussels: ICFTU, 1998.

International Labour Organization. *Decent Work, Report of the Director-General to the 87th International Labor Conference.* Geneva: ILO, June 1999.

———. *Reducing the Decent Work Deficit—A Global Challenge, Report of the Director-General to the 89th International Labor Conference.* Geneva: ILO, June 2001.

———. *World Employment Report 1998–1999.* Geneva: ILO, 1999.

Johnson, Chalmers. *MITI and the Japanese Miracle.* Berkeley, Calif.: University of California Press, 1984.

Kerr, Charles, John T. Dunlop, Frederick H. Harbison, and Charles A. Meyers. *Industrialism and Industrial Man*. Middlesex: Penguin, 1964.

Korey, William. *NGOs and the Universal Declaration of Human Rights: A Curious Grapevine*. New York: Palgrave MacMillan, 1998.

Krugman, Paul. *Pop Internationalism*. Cambridge, Mass.: MIT Press, 1998.

Lal, D. *The Poverty of Development Economics*. London: Institute of Economic Affairs, 1983.

Lécuyer, Normand, ed. *New Forms of Labour Administration: Actors in Development*. Geneva; International Labour Office, 2002.

Linnemann, Hans, ed. *Export-Oriented Industrialization in Developing Countries*. Singapore: Singapore University Press, 1987.

Logino, Helen. *Science as Social Knowledge*. Princeton, N.J.: Princeton University Press, 1990.

Longworth, Richard C. *Global Squeeze: The Coming Crisis for First-World Nations*. Chicago, Ill.: Contemporary Books, 1998.

Magdoff, F., J. Foster, F. Buttel, eds. *Hungry for Profit: The Agribusiness Threat to Farmers, Food, and the Environment*. New York: Monthly Review Press, 2000.

Marx, Karl. *Capital: Volume 1*. New York: Vintage Books, 1977.

Melden, A. I. *Rights and Persons*. Berkeley, Calif.: University of California Press, 1977.

McMurtry, John. *Unequal Freedoms: The Global Market as an Ethical System*. West Hartford, Conn.: Kumarian Press, 1998.

Mittellman, James H. *The Globalization Syndrome*. Princeton. N.J.: Princeton University Press, 2000.

Moran, Theodore H. *Foreign Direct Investment and Development: The New Policy Agenda for Developing Countries and Economies in Transition*. Washington, D.C.: Institute for International Economics, 1999.

———. *Beyond Sweatshops: Foreign Direct Investment and Globalization in Developing Countries*. Washington, D.C.: Brookings Institution Press, 2002.

Murray, Jill. *Transnational Labor Regulation: The ILO and EC Compared*. The Hague: Kluwer Law International, 2001

North, Douglas. *Institutions, Institutional Change, and Economic Performance*. New York: Cambridge University Press, 1990.

Nurkse, Ragnar. *Problems of Capital-Formation in Underdeveloped Countries*. New York: Oxford University Press, 1962 ed.

Nussbaum, Martha. *Women and Human Development*. New York: Cambridge University Press, 2001.

Organisation for Economic Cooperation and Development. *International Trade and Core Labor Standards*. Paris: OECD, 2000.

———. *Trade, Employment and Labor Standards*. Paris: OECD, 1996.

Philipson, Tomas J., and Richard A. Posner. *Private Choices and Public Health: The AIDS Epidemic in an Economic Perspective*. Cambridge, Mass.: Harvard University Press, 1993.

Prebisch, Raul. *The Economic Development of Latin America and its Principal Problems*. New York: United Nations, 1950.

Rajaee, Farhang. *Globalization on Trial*. Ottawa, ON: International Development Research Centre, 2000.

Ranis, G., and J. Fei. *Development of the Labor Surplus Economy: Theory and Policy.* Burr Ridge, Ill.: Irwin, 1964.

Raynauld, André Jean-Pierre Vidal. *Labour Standards and International Competitiveness.* Cheltenham, U.K.: Edward Elgar Publishing, 1998.

Rosenblaum, Jonathon D. *Copper Crucible,* 2nd ed. Ithaca, N.Y.: ILR Press/Cornell University Press, 1998.

Ross, Andrew, ed. *No Sweat: Fashion, Free Trade, and the Rights of Garment Workers.* New York: Verso, 1997.

Rostow, W. W. *The Stages of Economic Growth: A Non-communist Manifesto.* Cambridge: Cambridge University Press, 1960.

Santoro, Michael A. *Profits and Principles: Global Capitalism and Human Rights in China.* Ithaca, N.Y.: Cornell University Press, 2000.

Schoenberger, Karl. *Levi's Children.* New York: Atlantic Monthly Press, 2000.

Sen, A. K. *Commodities and Capabilities.* Amsterdam: Elsevier Scientific Publishing, 1982.

Sen, Amartya. *Development as Freedom.* New York: Alfred A. Knopf, Inc., 1999.

———. *On Ethics and Economics.* Oxford: Blackwell Publishers, 1987.

Shaw, Randy. *Reclaiming America: Nike, Clean Air and the New National Activism.* Berkeley, Calif.: University of California Press, 1999.

Shue, Henry. *Basic Rights.* Princeton, N.J.: Princeton University Press, 1980.

Tavis, Lee A. *Power and Responsibility.* Notre Dame, Ind.: University of Notre Dame Press, 1997.

Teubner, Gunther, ed. *Global Law Without a State.* Aldershot: Dartmouth Press, 1997.

United National Development Programme. *Human Development Report 2000.* New York: Oxford University Press, 2000

Varley, Pamela, ed. *The Sweatshop Quandary: Corporate Responsibility on the Global Frontier.* Washington, D.C.: Investor Responsibility Research Center, 1998.

Wade, Robert. W. *Governing the Market: Economic Theory and the Role of Government in Taiwan's Industrialization.* Princeton, N.J.: Princeton University Press, 1992.

Welch, Claude, ed. *International Non-governmental Human Rights Organizations: Making a Difference?* Philadelphia: University of Pennsylvania Press, 2000.

Werhane, Patricia H. *Moral Imagination and Management Decision Making.* New York: Oxford University Press, 1999.

Wick, Iengborg. *Workers' Tool or PR Ploy? A Guide to Codes of International Labour Practice.* Siegburg, Germany: SÜDWIND Institute, 2001.

Williams, Oliver, ed. *Global Codes of Conduct: An Idea Whose Time Has Come.* South Bend, Ind.: University of Notre Dame Press, 2000.

Wolf, Diane Lauren. *Factory Daughters: Gender, Household Dynamics, and Rural Industrialization in Java.* Berkeley, Calif.: University of California Press, 1992.

World Health Organization. *Children at Work: Special Health Risks, Technical Report Series No. 756.* Geneva: ILO, 1987.

Yeates, N. *Globalization and Social Policy.* London: Sage, 2001.

ESSAYS, ARTICLES, AND OTHER PUBLICATIONS

Akst, Daniel. "Nike in Indonesia, Through a Different Lens." *New York Times,* 4 March 2001, sec. 3, p. 4.

Alfaro, Afredo Hualde. "Corporatism, Nationalism, and Industrial Relations in Mexico." In *Colonialism, Nationalism, and the Institutionalization of Industrial Relations in the Third World*, edited by Sarosh Kuruvilla and Bryan Mundell. Stamford, Conn.: JAI Press, 1999.

Araghi, Farshad. "The Great Global Enclosure of Our Times: Peasants and the Agrarian Question at the End of the Twentieth Century." In *Hungry for Profit: The Agribusiness Threat to Farmers, Food and the Environment*, edited by Fred Magdoff, John Bellamy Foster, and H. M. Fredrick. New York: Monthly Review Press, 2000.

Baker, M., L. Hartman, and B. Shaw. "Global Profits, Global Headaches." South-Western Publishing CaseNet Series. Cincinnati, Ohio: ITP Publishing, 1999.

Arnold, Denis G. "Exploitation and the Sweatshop Quandary." *Business Ethics Quarterly*. Forthcoming 2003.

Arnold, Denis G., and Norman E. Bowie. "Sweatshops and Respect for Persons." *Business Ethics Quarterly*. Forthcoming 2003.

Bagwell, Kyle, and Richard W. Staiger. "The Simple Economics of Labor Standards and the GATT." *NBER Working Paper* No. w6604, 1998.

Barron, Kelly. "Gaplash." *Forbes*, 14 June 1999, p. 110.

Basu, Kaushik. "International Labor Standards and Child Labor." *Challenge* 42, no. 5 (September/October 1999): pp. 80–93.

Berle, A. A., Jr. "Corporate Powers as Powers in Trust." *Harvard Law Review* 44 (1931): p. 1049.

———. "For Whom Corporate Managers Are Trustees: A Note." *Harvard Law Review* 45 (1932): p. 1365.

Berry, Albert, and Frances Stewart. "The Evolution of Development Economics and Gustav Ranis's Role." In *Development, Duality and the International Economic Regime*. Ann Arbor, Mich.: University of Michigan Press, 1999.

Bliss, C. J., and N. H. Stern. "Productivity, Wages, and Nutrition, 1: The Theory." *Journal of Development Economics* 5 (1978): pp. 331–62.

———. "Productivity, Wages, and Nutrition, II: Some Observations." *Journal of Development Economics* 5 (1978): pp. 363–98.

Blythell, Paul. "Women in the Workforce." In *The Industrial Revolution and British Society*, edited by P. O'Brien and R. Quinault. Cambridge: Cambridge University Press, 1993.

Brown, Drusilla. "International Trade and Core Labor Standards: A Survey of the Recent Literature." In *Labor Market and Social Policy Occasional Papers*, No. 43. Paris: OECD, 2000.

Campaign for Labor Rights. "Labor Alerts." Washington, D.C.: Campaign for Labor Rights, 22 February 1999.

Castells, Manuel, and Alejandro Portes. "The World Underneath: The Origins, Dynamics, and Effects of the Informal Economy." In *The Informal Economy: Studies in Advanced and Less Developed Countries*, edited by Alejandro Portes, Manuel Castells, and Lauren Bentos. Baltimore, Md.: Johns Hopkins University Press, 1989.

Chandler, Susan. "Look Who's Sweating Now." *Business Week*, 16 October 1995, pp. 96, 98.

Chapman, Steven. "How Americans Can Stop Child Labor Abroad." *Chicago Tribune*, 4 December 1994, p. 3.

Charnovitz, Steve. "Fair Labor Standards and International Trade." *Journal of World Trade Law* 20 (1986): pp. 61, 68.

Collier, Robert. "U.S. Firms Reducing Sweatshop Abuses, But Wages Still at Poverty Levels." *San Francisco Chronicle*, 17 April 1999, A1.

Cumings, Bruce. "The Origins and Development of the Northeast Asian Political Economy: Industrial Sectors, Product Cycles, and Political Consequences." *International Organization* 38, no. 1 (winter 1984): pp. 1–40.

Deyo, Frederic C. "State and Labor: Modes of Political Exclusion in East Asian Development." In *The Political Economy of the New Asian Industrialism*, edited by Frederic C. Deyo. Ithaca, N.Y., and London: Cornell University Press, 1987.

Diller, Janelle. "A Social Conscience in the Global Marketplace? Labor Dimensions of Codes of Conduct, Social Labelling and Investor Initiatives." *International Labor Review* 138 (1999): pp. 99.

Dodd, E. Merrick, Jr. "For Whom Are Corporate Managers Trustees?" *Harvard Law Review* 45 (1932): p. 1145.

Donaldson, Thomas. "Values in Tension: Ethics Away from Home." *Harvard Business Review* (September 1996): pp. 48, 58.

Donaldson, Thomas. "Values in Tension: Ethics Away from Home." *Harvard Business Review* (September 1996): pp. 48, 58.

Donaldson, Thomas, and Thomas Dunfee. "Integrative Social Contracts Theory: A Communitarian Concept of Economic Ethics." *Economics and Philosophy* (April 1995): p. 85.

———. "Toward a Unified Conception of Business Ethics: Integrative Social Contracts Theory." *Academy of Management Review* 19 (1994): pp. 252, 264.

Donnely, Jack. "Human Rights and Asian Values: A Defense of 'Western Universalism.'" In *The East Asian Challenge for Human Rights*, edited by Joanne R. Bauer and Daniel A. Bell. Cambridge: Cambridge University Press, 1999, pp. 60–87.

Dunfee, Thomas W. "Corporate Governance in a Market With Morality." *Law & Contemporary Problems* 62 (summer 1999): p. 129.

"East and West: The Reach of Reason." *The New York Review of Books*, 20 July 2000, pp. 33–38.

"Envoy Defends Nike's Practices in Vietnam." *Financial Times*, 12 April 1999, p. 4.

Fenwick, Colin. "Slaves of the State: The Implications of Private Prisons for International Regulation of Prison Labor." Paper presented at the Cycles of Labor Regulation Conference, held by the Regulatory Institutions Network and the History Program of the Research School of Social Sciences at the Australian National University, Canberra, June 2002.

"For Citizens of Vietnam, Nike Is the Place to Work." *Oregonian*, 6 March 1999, p. C7.

Frederick, William C. "The Moral Authority of Transnational Corporate Codes." *Journal of Business Ethics* 10 (1991): p. 165.

Freeman, Bennett. "Drilling for Common Ground." *Foreign Policy* 125 (July/August 2001): p. 50.

Freeman, Bennett, et al. "A New Approach to Corporate Responsibility: The Voluntary Principles on Security and Human Rights." *Hastings International and Comparative Law Review* 24, no. 3 (spring 2001): pp. 423–49.

French, Peter. "The Corporation as a Moral Person." *American Philosophical Quarterly* 16 (1979): pp. 207–17.

Frenkel, Stephen J., and Duncan Scott. "Compliance, Collaboration, and Codes of Labor Practice: The adidas Connection," *California Management Review* 45 (1 October 2002): pp. 29–49.

Friedman, Milton. "The Social Responsibility of Business Is to Increase Its Profits." *New York Times Magazine,* 13 September 1970, p. 32.

Fung, A, D. O'Rourke, and C. Sabel. "Realizing Labor Standards." *Boston Review* 26 (2001): pp. 1–35.

Gereffi, Gary. "Global Production Systems and Third World Development." *Working Paper Series on New International Context of Development,* No. 4, UW-Madison Global Studies Research Program, 1993.

———. "The Organization of Buyer-Driven Commodity Chains: How U.S. Retailers Shape Overseas Production Networks." In *Commodity Chains and Global Capitalism,* edited by Gary Gereffi and Miguel Korzeniwicz. Westport, Conn.: Praeger, 1994.

Gereffi, Gary, Ronnie Garcia-Johnson, and Erika Sasser. "The NGO-Industrial Complex." *Foreign Policy* 125 (July/August 2001): pp. 56–66.

Gilley, Bruce. "Sweating it Out." *Far Eastern Economic Review* 164, no. 18 (10 May 2001): pp. 40–41.

"Globalization Bad for Health, Says UN Agencies." *Financial Times,* 10 June 1999.

Greenhouse, Steven. "Four Companies Gain Accord in Labor Suit." *New York Times,* 10 August 1999, late ed., p. A10.

———. "Nike Critic Praises Gains in Air Quality at Vietnam Factory." *New York Times,* 12 March 1999, p. C3.

Guvenli, Turgut, and Rajib Sanyal. "Ethical Concerns in International Business: Are Some Issues More Important Than Others?" *Business and Society Review* 107, no. 2 (summer 2002): pp. 195–206.

Halal, William, and Kenneth Taylor. "21st Century Economics: A Synthesis of Progressive Economic Thought." *Business and Society Review* 107, no. 2 (summer 2002): pp. 255–74.

Hartman, Laura P. "Tee-Shirts and Tears: Third World Suppliers to First World Markets." In *Business, Institutions and Ethics: A Text with Cases and Readings,* edited by John Dienhart. New York: Oxford University Press, Inc., 2000. Reprinted in Smith, Jeffrey. *Business Ethics: Ethical Decision Making and Cases, 5E.* Marblehead, Mass.: Houghton Mifflin, 2003.

———. "The Ethical Challenge of Global Labor Standards." *Journal of Employment Discrimination Law* (winter 1999): p. 77.

Hartman, Laura P., Bill Shaw, and Rodney Stevenson. "Exploring the Ethics and Economics of Global Labor Standards: A Challenge to Integrated Social Contract Theory." *Business Ethics Quarterly,* v. 13, no. 2 (2003): 193–220.

Hartman, Laura P., B. Shaw, and R. Stevenson. "Human Resources Opportunities to Balance Ethics and Neoclassical Economics in Global Labor Standards." *Business & Professional Ethics Journal,* v. 19, nos. 3&4 (2001): 73–116.

Hendry, John. "Universalizability and Reciprocity in International Business Ethics." *Business Ethics Quarterly* 9, no. 3 (1999): pp. 405, 413–14.

Hess, David. "Social Reporting: A Reflexive Law Approach to Corporate Social Responsiveness." *Journal of Corporation Law* 25 (1999): pp. 41–86.

Husted, Bryan W. "A Critique of the Empirical Methods of Integrative Social Contracts Theory." *Journal of Business Ethics* 20, no. 3 (1999): pp. 227–28.

"Indonesian Workers to Get Boost in Entry-Level Wages." *Wall Street Journal*, 24 March 1999, p. B2.

Josephs, Hilary K. "Labor Law in a 'Socialist Market Economy': The Case of China" *Columbia Journal of Transnational Law* 33 (1995): p. 559.

Kearney, Neil. "Corporate Codes of Conduct: The Privatised Application of Labor Standards." In *Regulating International Business*, edited by Sol Picciotto and Mayne Ruth. Houndsmill, Basingstoke: Macmillan/Oxfam, 2000.

"Knight Speaks Out on Improving Globalization." *Financial Times*, 1 August 2000, p. 15.

Koo, Hagen. "The Dilemmas of Empowered Labor in Korea: Korean Workers in the Face of Global Capitalism." *Asian Survey* 40 (March/April 2000): pp. 227–50.

Kuruvilla, Sarosh. "Economic Development Strategies, Industrial Relations Policies and Workplace IR/HR Practices in Southeast Asia." In *The Comparative Political Economy of Industrial Relations*, edited by Kirsten S. Weaver and Lowell Turner. Madison, Wis.: IRRA, 1995.

Kuruvilla, Sarosh, and Bryan Mundell. "Introduction" and "Conclusion." In *Colonialism, Nationalism, and the Institutionalization of Industrial Relations in the Third World*. Stamford, Conn.: JAI Press, 1999.

"Labor Secretary Herman Speaks Out Against Child Labor." *Apparel Industry Magazine*, November 1997, p. 12.

Lamb, David. "Economic Program Revitalizing Thailand's Countryside." *Los Angeles Times*, 27 February 2000, p. A34.

Landsburg, Steven. "The Imperialism of Compassion." *New York Times*, 23 July 2001, p. A14.

Leary, Virginia. "Lessons from the Experience of the ILO." In *The United Nations and Human Rights: A Critical Appraisal*, edited by Philip Alston. Oxford: Clarendon Press, 1992.

Lee, Ching Kwan. "Localistic Despotism" and "Familial Hegemony." In *Gender and the South China Miracle: Two Worlds of Factory Women*. Berkeley, Calif.: University of California Press, 1998.

Lewis, W. Arthur. "The Shifting Fortunes of Agriculture." In *Agriculture and its Terms of Trade*. In Proceedings of the Tenth International Conference of Agricultural Economists. Lalitha Mahal, Mysore, India. London: Oxford University Press, 1960.

Maitland, Alison. "Human Rights and Accountability." *The Financial Times*, 13 June 2002, p. 15.

Maitland, Ian. "The Great Non-Debate Over International Sweatshops." Reprinted in *Ethical Theory and Business*, 6th ed., edited by Tom L. Beauchamp and Norman E. Bowie. Englewood Cliffs: Prentice Hall, 2001. First published in *British Academy of Management Conference Proceedings* (September 1997): pp. 240–65.

Marshall, Samantha. "Executive Action: Cultural Sensitivity on the Assembly Line." *Asian Wall Street Journal*, 25 February 2000.

Mathews, Jessica T. "Power Shift." *Foreign Affairs* 77, no. 1 (January/February 1977): pp. 50–66.

Mayer, Don. "Hypernorms and Integrative Social Contracts Theory." In *Proceedings International Association for Business and Society*. Hilton Head, S.C., March 1994.

Murray, Jill. "Corporate Codes of Conduct and Labor Standards." In *Mastering the Challenge of Globalization: Towards a Trade Union Agenda*, edited by Robert Kyloh. Geneva: ILO, 1998.

———. "The European Union's External Powers and Labor Standards." Conference paper presented to the University of Oxford Institute of European and Comparative Law Colloquium on Constitutionalism and Employment Policy in European Union Law, May 2002.

———. "Labor Rights, Corporate Responsibilities: The Role of ILO Core Standards." In *Corporate Responsibility and Ethical Trade: Codes of Conduct in the Global Economy*, edited by Rhys Jenkins et al. U.K.: Earthscan. Forthcoming 2003.

———. "A New Phase in the Regulation of Multinational Enterprises." *Industrial Law Journal* 30 (2001): pp. 255–72.

———. "The Sound of One Hand Clapping? Regulation Theory and International Labor Law." *Australian Journal of Labor Law* 14 (2001): pp. 306–26.

Murray, Jill, and Anthony O'Donnell. "'Sweat or Starve': Sweated Labor and the Regulatory Imagination in Australia." Conference paper presented to the "Cycles of Labor Regulation" Conference, held by the Regulatory Institutions Network and the History Program of the Research School of Social Sciences at the Australian National University, Canberra, June 2002, on file with author.

National Labor Committee. *Zoned For Slavery*. 1999, video.

Oestreich, Joel. "What Can Businesses Do to Appease Anti-Globalization Protestors?" *Business and Society Review* 107, no. 2 (summer 2002): pp. 207–20.

O'Higgins, Paul. "'Labor Is Not a Commodity': An Irish Contribution to International Labor Law." *Industrial Law Journal* 26 (1997): pp. 225–34.

Orentlicher, Diane, and T. Gelatt. "Public Law, Private Actors: The Impact of Human Rights on Business Investment in China." *Northwestern Journal of International Law and Business* 66 (1993): p. 14.

Ramasastry, Anita. "Corporate Complicity: From Nuremberg to Rangoon: An Examination of Forced Labor Cases and Their Impact on the Liability of Multinational Corporations." *Berkeley Journal of International Law* 91 (2002): pp. 91–147.

Ranis, G. "Industrial Sector Labor Absorption." *Economic Development and Cultural Change* (April 1973).

Ratner, Steven. "Corporations and Human Rights: A Theory of Legal Responsibility." *Yale Law Journal* 111 (2001): p. 443.

Rodgers, Gerry. "Labour, Institutions and Economic Development: Issues and Methods." In *The Institutional Approach to Labour and Development*, edited by G. Rogers, K. Foti, and L. Lauridsen. London: Frank Cass, 1996.

Rosenbaum, Ruth, and David Schilling. "In Sweatshops, Wages Are the Issue." *The Corporate Examiner*, 5 May 1997.

Rosenstein-Rodan, P. "Notes on the Theory of the Big Push." In *Economic Devel-*

opment for Latin America, edited by H. Ellis. Proceedings of a conference held by the International Economic Association. London: Macmillan, 1961, 1963.

Satyanarayan, K., et al. "Effect of Early Childhood Nutrition and Child Labour on Growth and Adult Nutritional Status of Rural Indian Boys around Hyderabad." *Human Nutrition: Clinical Nutrition,* no. 40 C (1986).

Schermerhorn, John. "Terms of Global Engagement in Ethically Challenging Environments: Applications to Burma." *Business Ethics Quarterly* 9, no. 3 (1999): pp. 485, 488.

Seidman, Gay. "Social Movement Unionism in Transition: Labor and Democratization in South Africa." In *Research on Democracy and Society: Extremism, Protest, Social Movements, and Democracy,* edited by Frederick Weil. Stamford, Conn.: JAI Press, 1996.

Sen, Amartya. "Human Rights and Asian Values." In *Business Ethics in the Global Marketplace,* edited by Tibor R. Machan. Stanford, Calif.: Hoover Institution Press, 1999.

————. "Well-being, Agency and Freedom: The Dewey Lectures 1984." *Journal of Philosophy* 82 (April 1985): pp. 197–8.

Sethi, S. Prakash. "Codes of Conduct for Multinational Corporations: An Idea Whose Time Has Come." *Business and Society Review* 104, no. 3 (1999): pp. 225–41.

Shaffer, Gregory. "Globalization and Social Protection: The Impact of Foreign and International Rules in the Ratcheting Up of U.S. Privacy Standards." *Yale Journal of International Law* 25 (winter 2000).

Siddique, S. A. "Industrial Relations in a Third World Setting: A Possible Model." *The Journal of Industrial Relations* 31 (September 1989): pp. 385–401.

Singer, Hans W. "The Distribution of Gains Between Investing and Borrowing Countries." *American Economic Review* 40 (1950): pp. 473–85.

"Smelly Sneakers." *The Asian Wall Street Journal,* 2 March 2001, p. 6.

Spar, Debora L. "The Spotlight and the Bottom Line." *Foreign Affairs* 77, no. 2 (March/April 1998): pp. 7–13.

Spar, Debora, and James Dail. "Of Measurement and Mission: Accounting for Performance in Non-Governmental Organizations." *Chicago Journal of International Law* 3, no. 1 (spring 2002): pp. 171–81.

Sternin, Jerry, and Robert Choo. "The Power of Positive Deviancy." *Harvard Business Review* (January/February 2000): pp. 12–14.

Stiglitz, Joseph E. "Duality and Development: Some Reflections on Economic Policy." In *Development, Duality and the International Economic Regime,* edited by Gary Saxonhouse and T. N. Srinivasan. Ann Arbor, Mich.: University of Michigan Press, 1999.

Takea, I. "A New Direction of Integrative Social Contracts Theory." *Journal of Japan Society for Business Ethics* (1996): pp. 3–15.

Tatsuo, Inoue. "Liberal Democracy and Asian Orientalism," In *The East Asian Challenge for Human Rights,* edited by Joanne R Bauer and Daniel A. Bell. Cambridge, U.K.: Cambridge University Press, 1999, pp. 27–59.

Thomas, Henk. "The Erosion of Trade Unions." In *Globalization and Third World Trade Unions: The Challenge of Rapid Economic Change,* edited by Henk Thomas. London: Zed Books, 1995.

Thompson, Ginger. "Mexican Labor Protest Gets Result." *New York Times*, 8 October 2001, p. A3.

Tucker, Amanda. Comments transcribed by Richard Wokutch, in "Nike and Its Critics." *Organization & Environment* 14, no. 2 (June 2001): pp. 207–237.

Ubektu, A. K. "An Industrial Relations System for a Developing Country: The Case of Nigeria." Ph.D. thesis, Sussex University, 1981. In Siddique, S. A. "Industrial Relations in a Third World Setting: A Possible Model." *The Journal of Industrial Relations* 31 (September 1989): pp. 385–401.

Umezu, M. "International Communitarianism and Moral Consensus Building Procedure." *Journal of Japan Society for Business Ethics* 2 (1995): pp. 21–32.

United Nations Conference on Trade and Development. "Working for Manufacturers Without Factories." In *World Investment Report 1994: Transnational Corporations, Employment and the Workplace.* New York: United Nations, 1994.

United States Department of Labor. "Press Release USDL: 96."

Van Liemt, Gijsbert. "Minimum Labour Standards and International Trade: Would a Social Clause Work." *International Labour Review* 128, no. 4 (1989): p. 433.

Waddock, Sandra, and Charles Bodwell. "Foundation Principles for Making Corporate Citizenship Real." Working paper, Boston College and ILO, 2001.

———. "From TQM to TRM: The Emerging Evolution of Total Responsibility Management (TRM) Systems." Working paper, Boston College and ILO, 2001.

Waddock, Sandra, Samuel B. Graves, and Charles Bodwell. "Responsibility: The New Business Imperative." Working paper, Boston College and ILO, 2001.

Webster, Eddie. "Diffusion of the Molotov Cocktail in South African Industrial Relations: The Burden of the Past and the Challenge of the Future." In *Colonialism, Nationalism, and the Institutionalization of Industrial Relations in the Third World*, edited by S. Kuruvilla and B. Mundell. Stamford, Conn.: JAI Press, 1999.

Williamson, John. "What Washington Means by Policy Reform." In *Latin American Adjustment: How Much Has Happened?* edited by John Williamson. Washington, D.C.: Institute for International Economics, 1990.

Wilson, Andrew "Special Report: Business and Human Rights." *Corporate Social Responsibility Magazine, Special Report* 2, no. 1 (2001): p. 7.

Wolf, Diane. "Linking Women's Labor with the Global Economy: Factory Workers and Their Families in Rural Java." In *Women Workers and Global Restructuring*, edited by Kathryn Ward. Ithaca: ILR Press, 1990.

Zhu, Yu, and Iain Campbell. "Economic Reform and the Challenge of Transforming Labor Regulation in China." *Labor and Industry* 7 (1996): p. 42.

INTERNET RESOURCES

AccountAbility. http://www.accountability.org.uk/ (accessed 5 August 2002).

adidas-Salomon. "Our World: Social and Environmental Report 2000." http://www.wfsgi.org/SGI/Press/Press_rel_SM/adidas_clearer_social_and_environmental_report_2001.pdf (accessed 12 August 2002).

AmericasCanada.org. "Summit of the Americas: Final Declaration." 22 April 2001. http://www.americascanada.org/eventsummit/declarations/declara-e.asp (accessed 7 August 2002).

Amnesty International. http://www.amnesty.it/ailib/aipub/1998/ACT/A7000 198.htm (accessed 7 August 2002).

Annan, Kofi. "Global Compact." The Global Compact. http://65.214.34.30/un/ gc/unweb.nsf/content/thenine.htm (accessed 12 August 2002).

Ashagrie, Kebebew. "Methodical Child Labour Surveys and Statistics: ILO's Recent Work in Brief." International Labour Organization. http://www.ilo.org/ public/english/comp/child/stat/stats.htm (accessed 1 August 2002).

———. *Statistics on Working Children and Hazardous Child Labor in Brief.* Geneva: ILO, 1998. International Labour Organization. http://www.ilo.org/public/ english/standards/ipec/simpoc/stats/child/stats.htm (accessed 5 August 2002).

Ballinger, Jeff. "Once Again, Nike's Voice Looms Larger than That of Its Workers." Behindthelabel.org. http://www.behindthelabel.org (accessed 5 August 2002).

Blowfield, Mike. "Governance and Supply Chains: An Ethical Approach to Responsibility." Ethical Trading Initiative. http://www.eti.org.uk/pub/ publications/2001/12-art-govsupp/index.shtml (accessed 7 August 2002).

Browne, John. "The Role of Multinational Corporations in Economic and Social Development of Poor Countries." *Ethical Corporation.* http:// www.ethicalcorp.com/printtemplate.asp?idnum=206 (accessed 8 August, 2002).

Canadian Business for Social Responsibility. http://www.cbsr.bc.ca/ (accessed 7 August 2002).

Caux Roundtable. "Principle for Business." http://www.cauxroundtable.org/ ENGLISH.HTM (accessed 1 August 2002).

———. "Strategic Direction Statement." http://www.cauxroundtable.org/ MISSION.HTM (accessed 1 August 2002).

Clean Clothes Campaign. "Codes." http://www.cleanclothes.org/codes.htm (accessed 5 August 2002).

Codes of Conduct. http://www.codesofconduct.org/ (accessed 5 August 2002).

Connor, Tim. "We are Not Machines: Despite Some Small Steps Forward, Poverty and Fear Still Dominate the Lives of Nike and Adidas Workers in Indonesia." March 2002. Oxfam/Community Aid Abroad. http://www.caa.org.au/ campaigns/nike/reports/machines/index.html (accessed 1 July 2002).

Corporate Social Responsibility—Europe. "Business and Human Rights Programme." http://www.csreurope.org/csr_europe/activities/Programmes/ humanrights/humanrights.htm (accessed 2 August 2002).

Council for Ethics in Economics. "Keidanren Charter for Good Corporate Behavior." http://www.businessethics.org/keidan.htm#charter (accessed 5 August 2002).

Economic Research Institute. "Vietnam—Compensation & Benefit Legislation, Vietnam—Minimum Remuneration." http://www.erieri.com/freedata/ hrcodes/vietnam.htm (accessed 7 August 2002).

Ehrlich, Jennifer. "Sweatshop Swindlers." *South China Morning Post.* One World Media. http://www.1worldcommunication.org/labornews.htm—Sweat shop%20Swindlers (accessed 12 August 2002).

Elliott, Kimberly Ann. "The ILO and Enforcement of Core Labor Standards." *International Economics Policy Brief.* Washington, D.C.: Institute for International Economics, July 2000, *updated* April 2001. http://www.iie.com/policybriefs/news00–6.htm (accessed 8 August 2002).

Enderle, Georges, and Glen Peters. "A Strange Affair? The Emerging Relationship Between NGOs and Transnational Companies." PricewaterhouseCoopers. http://www.pwcglobal.com/uk/eng/ins-sol/survey-rep/ngoreview_allsalliukeng.html (accessed 12 August 2002).

Ethical Trading Initiative. http://www.ethicaltrade.org/_html/about/basecode_en_short/framesets/f_page.shtml (accessed 5 August 2002).

———. www.ethicaltrade.org (accessed 12 August 2002).

Ethics Officers Association. "Business Conduct Management Standards Project Update." http://www.eoa.org/BCMS/bcms.html (accessed 5 August 2002).

European Commission. "Corporate Social Responsibility: A Business Contribution to Sustainable Development." http://europa.eu.int/comm/employment_social/soc-dial/csr/csr_index.htm (accessed 12 August 2002).

European Union Committee on Development and Cooperation. "Report on EU Standards for European Enterprises Operating in Developing Countries: Toward a European Code of Conduct." Clean Clothes Campaign. http://www.cleanclothes.org/codes/howit.htm (accessed 12 August 2002).

European Union Online. "Democratization, the Rule of Law, Respect for Human Rights and Good Governance; the Political Issues of the Partnership between the European Union and the ACP States: March 12, 1998." http://europa.eu.int/comm/external_relations/human_rights/ip/report_98.pdf (accessed 7 August 2002).

Fabian, Teresa. "Social Accountability 8000 (SA8000)—the first Auditable, Global Standard for Ethical Sourcing Driven by CEPAA," 1998. http://www.citinv.it/associazioni/CNMS/archivio/lavoro/Presentazione_SA8000.html (accessed 5 August 2002).

Fair Labor Association. http://www.fairlabor.org/ (accessed 5 August 2002).

Fenwick, Colin. "Private Benefit from Forced Prison Labor: Case Study on the Application of ILO Convention 29." July 2001. International Confederation of Free Trade Union. http://www.icftu.org/displaydocument.asp?Index=991212919&Language=EN (accessed 1 July 2002).

Forest Stewardship Council United States. "Principles and Criteria." http://www.fscus.org/html/standards_policies/principles_criteria/index.html (accessed 5 August 2002).

G8 Labor Ministers. "Labor Policies in a Rapidly Changing Global Economy, 1999." http://www.g7.utoronto.ca/g7/labour/labourfeb24.htm (accessed 1 July 2002).

Global Alliance for Workers and Communities. http://www.theglobalalliance.org/ (accessed 7 August 2002).

Global Exchange. "The Shame of Saipan." ABC *20/20*. http://www.globalexchange.org/economy/corporations/saipan/2020expose.html (accessed 1 August 2002).

Global Reporting Initiative. http://www.globalreporting.org/index.htm (accessed 5 August 2002).

"Global Sullivan Principles of Social Responsibility." http://www.global
    sullivanprinciples.org/principles.htm (accessed 5 August 2002).
Golub, Stephen. "Are International Labor Standards Needed to Prevent Social
    Dumping." *Finance & Development* (December 1997): pp. 20, 22. Interna-
    tional Monetary Fund. http://www.imf.org/external/pubs/ft/fandd/
    1997/12/pdf/golub.pdf (accessed 31 July 2002).
Henderson, David. *Misguided Virtue: False Notions of Corporate Social Responsibility.*
    London: Institute for Economic Affairs, 2001. Institute of Economic Affairs.
    http://www.iea.org.uk/record.php?type=publication&ID=143 (accessed
    8 August 2002).
Hoovers Online. "Adidas-Salomon: (Capsule)." http://www.hoovers.com/co/
    capsule/2/0,2163,92632,00.html (accessed 5 August 2002).
International Confederation of Free Trade Unions. "A Trade Union Guide to
    Globalization." http://www.icftu.org/displaydocument.asp?Index=99120
    9485&Language=EN (accessed 7 August 2002).
International Council on Human Rights. "Beyond Voluntarism: Human Rights and
    the Developing International Legal Obligations of Companies." http://
    www.ichrp.org/cgi-bin/show?what=project&id=107 (accessed 12 Au-
    gust 2002).
International Labour Organization. *Child Labour: Targeting the Intolerable.* Geneva:
    ILO, 1998. http://www.ilo.org/public/comp/child/publ/target/index.
    htm (accessed 31 July 2002).
———. "Convention Concerning the Prohibition and Immediate Action for the
    Elimination of the Worst Forms of Child Labour." http://ilolex.ilo.ch:1567/
    scripts/convde.pl?C182 (accessed 1 August 2002).
———. "Facts and Figures on Child Labor." 1999. http://www.ilo.org/public/
    english/standards/ipec/simpoc/ (accessed 31 July 2002).
———. "Forced Labor in Myanmar (Burma), Report of the Commission of In-
    quiry." http://www.ilo.org/public/english/standards/relm/gb/docs/
    gb273/myanmar.htm (accessed 7 August 2002).
———. "Fundamental ILO Conventions." http://www.ilo.org/public/english/
    standards/norm/whatare/fundam/ (accessed 1 August 2002).
———. Press Release ILO/02/31, "ILO Annual Conference Adopts New
    Measures to Tackle the Challenges of Globalisation." http://www.ilo.org/
    public/english/bureau/inf/pr/2002/31.htm (accessed 7 August 2002).
———. "ILO Conventions." http://www.ilo.org/public/english/info/index.htm
    (accessed 7 August 2002).
———. *ILO Declaration on Fundamental Principles and Rights at Work.* Geneva, ILO
    86th Session, 1998. http://www.ilo.org/public/english/10ilc/ilc86/
    com-dtxt.htm (accessed 1 August 2002).
———. "ILO Declaration on Fundamental Principles and Rights at Work and Its
    Follow-Up, Adopted by the International Labor Conference at its 86th
    Session, Geneva, 18 June 1998." http://www.ilo.org/public/english/
    standards/decl/declaration/text/index.htm (accessed 7 August 2002).
———. "New ILO Report Warns of 'Destructive Backlash' If Societies Ignore
    Social Inequities." 2000. http://www.ilo.org/public/english/bureau/
    inf/magazine/36/wlr2000.htm (accessed 5 August 2002).

———. "A Pioneering ILO Global Report Calls for More Widespread Respect for Rights at Work." 2000. http://www.ilo.org/public/english/bureau/inf/magazine/35/voice.htm (accessed 5 August 2002).

———. "Statistics: Revealing a Hidden Tragedy." 2001. http://www.ilo.org/public/english/standards/ipec/simpoc/stats/4stt.htm (accessed 5 August 2002).

———. "Text of ILO Conventions." http://ilolex.ilo.ch:1567/public/English/docs/convdisp.htm (accessed 1 August 2002).

———. "Tripartite Declaration on Multinational Enterprises." http://ilolex.ilo.ch:1567/public/50normes/ilolex/pdconv.pl?host = status01&textbase = iloeng&document = 2&chapter = 28&query = %28%23docno%3D2819 7701%29 + %40ref&highlight = &querytype = bool (accessed 7 August 2002).

———. "Work-Related Fatalities Reach 2 Million Annually." *ILO Press Release*. 24 May 2002. http://www.ilo.org/public/english/bureau/inf/pr/2002/23.htm. (accessed 8 August 2002).

Jefferson, Lashawn R., and Phoebe McKinney. "A Job for Your Rights: Continued Sex Discrimination in Mexico's Maquiladora Sector." Human Rights Watch. http://www.hrw.org/reports98/women2/ (accessed 1 August 2002).

Jensen, Holger. "A Tale of Two Swooshes in Indonesia." *Rocky Mountain News*. http://www.rockymountainnews.com/7/2/2000 (accessed 7 August 2002).

Kearney, Neil. "Sweatshops: An Ugly Stain on American Fashion." U.S. Department of Labor. http://wwwdol.gov/opa/media/press/opa/opa96287.htm (accessed 1 August 2002).

Krugman, Paul. "In Praise of Cheap Labor." http://web.mit.edu/krugman/www/smokey.html (accessed 1 July 2001).

Marymount University Center for Ethical Concerns. "The Consumer and Sweatshops." www.marymount.edu/news/garmentstudy/findings.html (accessed 12 August 2002).

Maskus, Keith E. "Should Core Labor Standards Be Imposed Through International Trade Policy?" *World Bank Working Paper No. 1817*. August 1997. http://www.worldbank.org/research/trade/wp1817.html (accessed 8 August 2002).

Mehta, Pradeep S. "Textiles and Clothing—Who Gains, Who Loses, and Why." 1997. CUTS-India. http://www.cuts-india.org/1997–5.htm (accessed 5 August 2002).

Merriam Webster Dictionary. "Sweatshop." http://www.m-w.com (31 July 2002).

Moberg, David. "Never Let Them See You Sweat." *InTheseTimes.com*. http://www.inthesetimes.com/issue/25/23/moberg2523a.html (accessed 12 August 2002).

Mott, Elwood K. "Sweatshop for Levi Strauss, Ann Taylor, LA Gear and Gap." Sweatshop Watch. http://sweatshopwatch.org/swatch/what/mott.html (accessed 1 August 2002).

Murray, Jill. "Corporate Codes of Conduct and Labour Standards: Bureau for Workers' Activities Working Paper." International Labour Organization. http://ilo.org/public/english/dialogue/actrav/publ/codes.htm (accessed 1 August 2002).

Myerson, Alan R. "In Principle, a Case for More 'Sweatshops.'" *New York Times*, 22 June 1997, late edition, Section 4, p. 5. National Center for Policy Analysis. http://www.ncpa.org/pd/pdint152.html (accessed 1 August 2002).

New York Daily Tribune. 7 March 1845. "1845 Tribune." Smithsonian Institution. http://www.americanhistory.si.edu/sweatshops/history/2t5.htm (accessed 14 August 2002).

Nikebiz.com. www.nikebiz.com (accessed 5 August 2002).

Nike, Inc. "Corporate Responsibility Report, 2001." http://www.nike.com/nikebiz/nikebiz.jhtml?page = 29 (accessed 12 August 2002).

Nike, Inc. "Nike Statement Regarding Indonesia Report." Company press release. 7 March 2002. http://www.nike.com/nikebiz/news/pressrelease.jhtml?year = 2002&month = 03&letter = c (accessed 7 August 2002).

Oneworld.net. "Trade-US/Viet Nam: Landmark Trade Accord Signed." http://www.oneworld.net/cgi-bin/index.cgi?root = 129&url = http%3A%2F%2Fwww%2Eoneworld%2Eorg%2Fips2%2Fjuly00%2F01%5F55%5F005%2Ehtml (accessed 7 August 2002).

Organisation of American States. "Inter-American Democratic Charter, 2001, Article 10." http://www.oas.org/charter/docs/resolution1_en_p4.htm (accessed 1 July 2002).

Organisation for Economic Cooperation and Development. "OECD Guidelines for Multinational Enterprises." http://www.oecd.org/EN/document/0,,EN-document-187-5-no-27-24467-187,FF.html (accessed 1 July 1 2002).

O'Rourke, Dara. "Comments on the Vietnam Section of the Tuck School Report: Nike, Inc.: Survey of Vietnamese and Indonesian Domestic Expenditure Levels." http://web.mit.edu/dorourke/www/PDF/tuck.pdf (accessed 8 August 2002).

———. "Monitoring the Monitors: A Critique of PricewaterhouseCoopers Labor Monitoring." September 2000. http://web.mit.edu/dorourke/www/PDF/pwc.pdf (accessed 7 August 2002).

———. *Smoke from a Hired Gun: A Critique of Nike's Labor and Environmental Auditing in Vietnam as Performed by Ernst & Young.* San Francisco: Transnational Resource and Action Center, 2002. Corporate Watch. http://www.corpwatch.org/issues/PID.jsp?articleid = 2488 (accessed 8 August 2002).

Reuters, Joanne. "Report Says Nike, Adidas Factories Still Sweatshops." Global Exchange. http://www.globalexchange.org/economy/corporations/nike/reuters030702.html (accessed 12 August 2002).

Robinson, Mary. "Beyond Good Intentions: Corporate Citizenship for a New Century." World Leaders Lecture to the Royal Society for the Encouragement of Arts, Manufacturers and Commerce. London, England. 7 May 2002. http://www.bsr.org/BSRResources/Magazine/Columnists.cfm?DocumentID = 842&DocumentTypeID = 23 (accessed 12 August 2002).

Stakeholder Alliance. http://www.stakeholderalliance.org/ (accessed 5 August 2002).

Steele, David. "The 'Living Wage' Clause in the ETI Base Code: How To Implement It?" Ethical Trading Initiative. http://www.eti.org.uk/pub/publications/2000/06-livwage/index.shtml (accessed 1 July 1 2002).

Sweatshop Watch. "First Ever Lawsuits Filed Charging Sweatshop Conspiracy."

http://www.sweatshopwatch.org/swatch/marianas/lawsuit.html (accessed 1 August 2002).

———. "The Garment Industry." http://www.sweatshopwatch.org/swatch/industry (accessed 1 August 2002).

Transparency International. http://www.transparency.org/sourcebook/index.html (accessed 5 August 2002).

UNITE. "Stop Sweatshops." http://www.uniteunion.org/sweatshops/whatis/infosheet.html (accessed 1 August 2002).

UNITE v. The Gap et al. http://www.globalexchange.org/economy/corporations/saipan/complaint.html (accessed 1 August 2002).

United Nations Conference on Trade and Development. *World Investment Report 2000.* Geneva, 2000. http://www.unctad.org/wir/contents/wir00content.en.htm (accessed 12 August 2002).

United Nations. "Adopted and opened for signature, ratification and accession by General Assembly resolution 2200A (XXI) of 16 December 1966; entry force 3 January 1976, in accordance with article 27." http://www.unhchr.ch/html/menu3/b/a_cescr.htm (accessed 1 August 2002).

———. "Appendix C: Excerpts from the Convention on the Rights of the Child." Human Rights Watch. http://www.hrw.org/reports/2000/frmwrk006–09.htm (accessed 1 August 2002).

———. "Article 3(2), *Convention on the Rights of the Child,* G.A. res. 44/25, annex, 44 U.N. GAOR Supp. (No. 49) at 167, U.N. Doc. A/44/49 (1989)." United States Department of Labor. http://www.dol.gov/ilab/media/reports/iclp/sweat5/appendixf.htm (accessed 5 August 2002).

———. "The Global Compact: Executive Summary of a High Level Meeting to Launch the Global Compact." July 2000. http://www.un.org/partners/business/gcevent/press/summary.htm (accessed 5 August 2002).

———. "Human Development Reports 1996." http://hdr.undp.org/reports/global/1996/en/default.cfm (accessed 1 August 2002).

———. "United Nations: 50th Anniversary of the Universal Declaration of Human Rights." http://www.un.org/rights/50/decla.htm (accessed 1 August 2002).

———. "Universal Declaration of Human Rights, 1948, General Assembly Resolution 217 A (III), Article 23 (3)." http://www.unhchr.ch/udhr/miscinfo/carta.htm (accessed 5 August 2002).

United States Department of State. "Vietnam—World Factbook." http://www.tradeport.org/ts/countries/vietnam/wofact.html (accessed 7 August 2002).

———. "Vietnam—Background Notes." http://www.tradeport.org/ts/countries/vietnam/bnotes.html (accessed 7 August 2002).

———. "The Voluntary Principles on Security and Human Rights." http://www.state.gov/www/global/human_rights/001220_fsdrl_principles.html (accessed 12 August 2002).

University of Toronto. "Clarkson Centre." http://www.mgmt.utoronto.ca/~stake/CCBE/index.htm (accessed 5 August 2002).

University of Wisconsin. "Report on the Living Wage Symposium." http://www.lafollette.wisc.edu/livingwage/Final_Report/report.htm (accessed 12 August 2002).

Van Heerden, Auret. "Heyday for Free Zones, But Will They Last." International Labour Office. http://wwwid21.org/insights/insights28/insights-iss28-art03.html (accessed 1 August 2002).

Weissbrodt, David S. "Human Rights Principles and Responsibilities for Transnational Corporations and Other Business Enterprises." U.N. Doc. E/CN.4/Sub.2/2002/XX/Add.1, E/CN.4/Sub.2/2002/WG.2/WP.1/Add.1, 2002. http://www1.umn.edu/humanrts/introduction05–01–02final.html (accessed 12 August 2002).

White, Heather. "Educating Workers: A Response to 'Realizing Labor Standards.'" http://bostonreview.mit.edu/BR26.1/white.html (accessed 8 August 2002).

World Bank. "Core Labour Standards Took Kit." http://wbln0018.world bank.org/HDNet/hddocs.nsf/View + to + Link + WebPages/AE07D 22AF8F2088285256935005BAD6A?OpenDocument (accessed 1 July 2002).

World Health Organization. "The World Health Report 1999—Making a Difference." http://www.who.org/whr (accessed 1 August 2002).

World Federation of the Sporting Good Industry. "WFSGI Code of Conduct—Guiding Principles." http://www.wfsgi.org/SGI/activities/Code_Conduct.htm (accessed 12 August 2002).

World Monitors. "Ethics Officers Propose ISO Standard on Business Conduct." http://www.worldmonitors.com/showarticle.cfm?Key = 1493 (accessed 5 August 2002).

Index

About the Contributors

DENIS G. ARNOLD is Assistant Professor of Philosophy at the University of Tennessee, Knoxville. He received his Ph.D. in Philosophy from the University of Minnesota and is a past fellow of the National Endowment for the Humanities. His work in ethics and business ethics has appeared in *American Philosophical Quarterly, Business Ethics Quarterly, Business and Society Review, History of Philosophy Quarterly,* the *Journal of Business Ethics,* and other publications.

CHARLES BODWELL is a senior specialist in the United Nations' International Labour Office, focusing on corporate citizenship and labor practices in global supply chains. Before joining the ILO, he was a graduate researcher at Cambridge while also serving as a visiting professor at the Helsinki School of Economics and visiting scholar at Stanford University. He has worked for IBM, Agfa, and Schlumberger. After completing studies in engineering at Michigan State University, he worked as a systems engineer at Schlumberger, the French-U.S. oil services company. He then earned an MBA at McGill University in Montreal and a master's degree in international management at the Escuela Superior de Administracion y Direccion de Empresas (ESADE) in Barcelona. He held a variety of positions with the United Nations Industrial Development Organization from 1991 to 1998. His research interests center on the linkages at the factory level between productivity, quality, and labor practices.

J. LAWRENCE FRENCH is Associate Professor of Management in the Pamplin School of Business at Virginia Tech and teaches organizational behavior, international management, and business ethics. He has conducted sociological research on workplace issues, including participation, employee ownership, union democracy, telecommuting, and child labor. Since his service as a Peace Corps volunteer, he has been interested in problems faced by workers in Brazil. His recent research focuses on child labor in Brazil's shoe industry and involves extensive interviewing and surveys of working children. A recent publication on this issue appears in *Industrial and Labor Relations Review* (January 2002).

LAURA P. HARTMAN is Associate Vice President for Academic Affairs at DePaul University, where she is responsible for coordinating the development of new academic programs. She is also Professor of Business Ethics and Legal Studies in the Management Department in DePaul's College of Commerce. Hartman's scholarship focuses on the ethics of the employment relationship, with a primary emphasis in the areas of global labor conditions and standards, and the impact of technology on the employment relationship. She has written numerous textbooks, including *Employment Law for Business* and *Perspectives in Business Ethics*. Previously, Hartman held the Grainger Chair of Business Ethics at the University of Wisconsin–Madison School of Business. She has also served as an adjunct professor of business law and ethics at Northwestern's Kellogg Graduate School of Management. Hartman serves on the board of directors of DePaul's Institute for Business and Professional Ethics, previously held DePaul's Wicklander Chair in Professional Ethics, and served as chair of the University's Public Service Council. She is past president of the Society for Business Ethics and is co-founder and past co-chair of the Employment and Labor Law Section of the Academy of Legal Studies in Business. In addition, she was co-editor of the section's *Employment and Labor Law Quarterly* and served as president of the Midwest Academy of Legal Studies in Business for the 1994–1995 term. Hartman graduated magna cum laude from Tufts University and received her law degree from the University of Chicago Law School.

JONATHAN D. LONDON is a Ph.D. candidate in the Department of Sociology at the University of Wisconsin–Madison. He has lectured on industrial relations in developing countries at Wisconsin's Industrial Relations Research Institute. London is completing a dissertation on social provision in Vietnam, based on nearly three years of research in Vietnam. The dissertation examines changes in the conduct and outcomes of Vietnam's mass education and health policies in relation to the country's changing political and economic institutions. An article based on the dissertation has recently been published in *American Asian Review*.

IVANKA MAMIC is a specialist with the Management and Corporate

Citizenship Programme of the International Labour Office. She has recently completed indepth research on the implementation of codes of conduct across supply chains in the footwear, apparel, and retail sectors—Business and Code of Conduct Implementation: How Firms Use Management Systems for Social Performance, 2003, Geneva, International Labour Office. She has a master's of philosophy in development studies from the University of Cambridge, UK as well as a bachelor of law and a bachelor of economics from the University of Queensland, Australia. Before joining the ILO she worked as an associate to a Senior Member of the Australian Administrative Appeals Tribunal focusing on labor related issues such as unfair dismissal. She has also worked as a project manager for the Department of Defence in Australia and as a case examiner for insolvency proceedings for the Department of Trade and Industry in the UK.

JILL MURRAY is a Lecturer in the School of Law and Legal Studies, La Trobe University, Australia. She has published works on the ILO, the European Community and the OECD in relation to labor regulation. In 2001, she published *Transnational Labour Standards: The ILO and EC Compared.* Current projects include continuing work on corporate codes of conduct, the history of Australian labour law, and the future options for regulatory change in the labor field under conditions of globalization.

TARA J. RADIN is Assistant Professor of Management and General Business at the Frank G. Zarb School of Business, Hofstra University, where she teaches business ethics, business and society, international management, and strategy. She is an active member of the Society for Business Ethics, the Academy of Management/Social Issues Division, and the International Association of Business and Society. Her research encompasses topics such as employment, international labor practices, technology, privacy, corporate governance, and stakeholder theory, and includes publications in journals such as *Business Ethics Quarterly, Journal of Business Ethics,* and *American Business Law Journal.*

MICHAEL A. SANTORO is a Associate Professor in the International Business and Business Environment Department at the Rutgers Graduate School of Management, where he teaches courses in the ethical and legal aspects of the pharmaceutical business; business ethics; business law; human rights; and business, government, and society. Santoro is a Fellow at the Prudential Business Ethics Center at Rutgers and has been an adjunct lecturer in ethics at Harvard's John F. Kennedy School of Government. As a research associate at Harvard Business School, he wrote or co-authored nearly 30 case studies and teaching notes on ethical and legal topics such as global protection of intellectual property, insider trading, the federal sentencing guidelines, and the Fair Credit Reporting Act. His book *Profits and Principles: Global Capitalism and Human Rights in China* (2000) has been favorably reviewed in *The New York Times Book Review* and *Foreign Affairs*. His writings have appeared in *The Wall Street Journal, Foreign Policy*, the *International Herald Tribune, The Asian Wall Street Journal*, the *South China Morning Post, Business & the Contemporary World, Current History*, and the *Harvard Journal of World Affairs*. In the summer of 2000 he traveled in the Yangtze Basin area of China, where he investigated working conditions in factories that manufactured products with the Rutgers logo.

SANDRA WADDOCK is Professor of Management at Boston College's Carroll School of Management and senior research fellow at BC's Center for Corporate Citizenship. She has published extensively on corporate responsibility, corporate citizenship, and multi-sector collaboration in journals such as *The Academy of Management Journal, Strategic Management Journal, The Journal of Corporate Citizenship, Human Relations*, and *Business & Society*. Author of *Leading Corporate Citizens: Vision, Values, Value Added* (2002), she co-edited the two-volume series, *Unfolding Stakeholder Thinking* and is editor of *The Journal of Corporate Citizenship*. She a founding faculty member of the Leadership for Change Program at Boston College.

RICHARD E. WOKUTCH is Pamplin Professor of Management at Virginia Tech. He has also held positions as visiting assistant research professor at the Center for the Study of Values, University of Delaware, visiting Fulbright research professor at the Science Center Berlin, West Germany, and visiting Fulbright/Mazda research professor at Hiroshima Institute of Technology, Hiroshima, Japan. He teaches in the social issues in management, leadership, and business ethics areas and leads student study abroad programs to Asia examining these issues from an international perspective. His research interests focus on international aspects of child labor/sweatshop labor, business ethics, and corporate social performance. His publications include two books—*Worker Protection, Japanese Style* and *Cooperation and Conflict in Occupational Safety and Health*—and articles in outlets such as *Business Ethics Quarterly, The California Management Review, Business and Society Organization and Environment*, the *Academy of Management Executive*, and *Research in Corporate Social Performance and Policy*. He has served as program chair and division chair of the Social Issues in Management Division of the Academy of Management.